THE SAUDI FILE

People, Power, Politics

THE SAUDI FILE
People, Power, Politics

Anders Jerichow

St. Martin's Press
New York

St. Martin's Press, Scholarly and Reference Division, 175 Fifth Avenue, New York, N.Y. 10010

First published in the United States of America in 1998
Printed in Great Britain

ISBN 0–312–21520–7

Library of Congress Cataloging in Publication Data

Jerichow, Anders.
The Saudi file: people, power, politics/Anders Jerichow.
p. cm.
Includes bibliographical references (p.   ) and index.
ISBN 0–312–21520–7 (cloth)
1. Human rights–Saudi Arabia. 2. Human rights–Religious aspects–Islam. 3. Islam and politics–Saudi Arabia. 4. Islamic law–Saudi Arabia. I. Title.
JC599.S33J47 1998
323'.09538–dc21   98-15224
CIP

CONTENTS

ACKNOWLEDGEMENTS

Amnesty International, Human Rights Watch/Middle East, Article 19, along with a number of dedicated people, have contributed to this book. I am highly indebted to Keith Carmichael of Redress, Lamri Shirouf of Amnesty International, Said Essoulami of Article 19, Professor Mohammed Massari of the Committee for The Defence of Legitimate Rights (CDLR) and John Franklin-Webb, all in London, as well as Joe Stork of Human Rights Watch in New York. Other people will prefer to remain anonymous; some of them Saudis abroad, others international scholars with a need to apply for visas to Saudi Arabia; and two people in Saudi Arabia with a need to apply for exit visas from the kingdom. They have contributed with ideas, inspiration and material – in spite of a considerable risk to their own future in Saudi Arabia.

In Copenhagen, Susanne Holst of Politiken has been a most helpful assistant throughout the preparation of this book. Christa Leve Poulsen and Anita Jerichow have assisted in typing the manuscript. Maps and graphics were provided by Rie Jerichow.

The publication of this book was made possible by the assistance of Politiken Foundation, Copenhagen.

INTRODUCTION

Saudi Arabia remains a closed society with a unique interpretation of Islamic law, an insistence on royal privilege and a disputed record on human rights.

While most of the world has recognized international standards of governmental duties and popular rights, the Saudi Kingdom is facing a sensitive and volatile struggle on issues such as power distribution, accountability, democratization, freedom of speech, the role of the state and the citizen, legal standards and gender. Any development is shrouded by a veil of government control.

None the less, Saudi Arabia has proven its importance to regional, indeed global security, being able to attract the forces of some thirty countries to its defence in 1990/91.

Though the vast resources of oil may be the prime reason for the international concern, the plight of its citizens may be of even greater importance. Keeping in mind the notion of the universal rights of people rather than governments, this volume illuminates the condition of the citizen of Saudi Arabia.

Acknowledging that the development of any country rests with its citizens, not with its censors, no answers are offered by the book, leaving open a large number of questions and concerns, raised by Saudi Arabians, both religious and secular, as well as by international voices, and local, regional and international organizations.

Translations from Arabic have been edited only to maintain consistency of spellings and punctuation within each piece, and to correct grammatical errors.

Anders Jerichow
Copenhagen

Chapter One

PEOPLE AND LAND

1A
Map and people

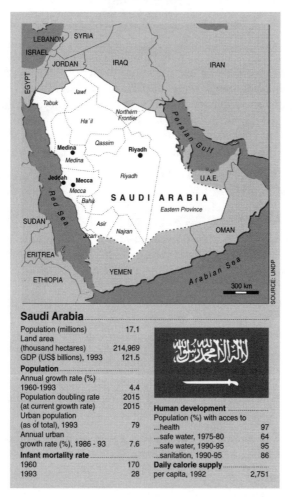

Saudi Arabia

Population (millions)	17.1
Land area (thousand hectares)	214,969
GDP (US$ billions), 1993	121.5

Population

Annual growth rate (%) 1960-1993	4.4
Population doubling rate (at current growth rate)	2015
	2015
Urban population (as of total), 1993	79
Annual urban growth rate (%), 1986 - 93	7.6

Infant mortality rate

1960	170
1993	28

Human development

Population (%) with acces to	
...health	97
...safe water, 1975-80	64
...safe water, 1990-95	95
...sanitation, 1990-95	86

Daily calorie supply

per capita, 1992	2,751

1B
Saudi Arabia in brief

Some background details on Saudi Arabia.

Location: Middle East, bordering the Persian Gulf and the Red Sea, north of Yemen. *Total area*: 1,960,582 sq km. *Land area*: 1,960,582 sq km. *Land boundaries*: total 4,415 km, Iraq 814 km, Jordan 728 km, Kuwait 222 km, Oman 676 km, Qatar 60 km, UAE 457 km, Yemen 1,458 km. *Coastline*: 2,640 km.

International disputes: Large section of boundary with Yemen still not defined; status of boundary with UAE not final; Kuwaiti ownership of Qaruh and Umm al Maradim islands is disputed by Saudi Arabia.

Natural resources: Petroleum, natural gas, iron ore, gold, copper.

Land use: Arable land: 1 percent. Irrigated land: 4,350 sq km (1989 CIA est.).

Environmental problems: Desertification; depletion of underground water resources; lack of perennial rivers or permanent water bodies has prompted the development of extensive sea water desalination facilities; coastal pollution from oil spills. *Natural hazards*: frequent sand and dust storms. *International agreements*: party to – Climate Change, Hazardous Wastes, Ozone Layer Protection; signed, but not ratified – Law of the Sea.

Population: 18,729,576 (July 1995 est.). A 1992 census according to the CIA gives the number of Saudi citizens as 12,304,835 and the number of residents who are not citizens as 4,624,459. *Age structure*: 0–14 years: 43% (female 3,952,573; male 4,065,224); 15–64 years: 55% (female 4,078,001; male 6,219,737); 65 years and over: 2% (female 203,372; male 210,669) (July 1995 est.). *Population growth rate*: 3.68% (1995 est.) *Birth rate*: 38.78 births/1,000 population (1995 est.). *Death rate*: 5.54 deaths/1,000 population (1995 est.). *Net migration rate*: 3.56 migrant(s)/1,000 population (1995 est.). *Infant mortality rate*: 48.9 deaths/1,000 live births (1995 est.). *Life expectancy at birth*: total population: 68.5 years; male: 66.79 years; female: 70.3 years (1995 est.). *Total fertility rate*: 6.48 children born/woman (1995 est.). *Ethnic divisions*: Arab 90%, Afro-Asian 10%.

Religions: Muslim 100%.

Literacy: Age 15 and over can read and write (1990). *Total population*: 62%; male: 73%; female: 48%.

Labor force: 5–6 million by occupation: government 34%, industry and oil 28%, services 22%, agriculture 16%.

Type: monarchy.

Capital: Riyadh.

Administrative divisions: 13 provinces: Al Bahah, Al Hudud ash Shamaliyah, Al Jawf, Al Madinah, Al Qasim, Ar Riyad, Ash Sharqiyah, Asir, Hail, Jizan, Makkah, Najran, Tabuk.

Independence: 23 September 1932 (unification).

National holiday: Unification of the Kingdom, 23 September (1932).

Constitution: None; governed according to Shari'a (Islamic law).

Legal system: Based on Islamic law, several secular codes have been introduced; commercial disputes handled by special committees; has not accepted compulsory ICJ jurisdiction.

Member of: ABEDA, AfDB, AFESD, AL, AMF, CCC, ESCWA, FAO, G-19, G-77, GCC, IAEA, IBRD, ICAO, ICC, ICRM, IDA, IDB, IFAD, IFC, IFRCS, ILO, IMF, IMO, INMARSAT, INTELSAT, INTERPOL, IOC, ISO, ITU, NAM, OAPEC, OAS (observer), OIC, OPEC, UN, UNCTAD, UNESCO, UNIDO, UPU, WFTU, WHO, WIPO, WMO.

Flag: Green with large white Arabic script (that may be translated as 'There is no God but God; Muhammad is the Messenger of God') above a white horizontal sabre (the tip points to the hoist side); green is the traditional colour of Islam.

Economy according to the CIA: 'A well-to-do oil-based economy with strong government controls over major economic activities. About 46% of GDP comes from the private sector. Economic (as well as political) ties with the US are especially strong. The petroleum sector accounts for roughly 75% of budget revenues, 35% of GDP, and almost all export earnings. Saudi Arabia has the largest reserves of petroleum in the world (26% of the proved total), ranks as the largest exporter of petroleum, and plays a leading role in OPEC. For the 1990s the government intends to bring its budget, which has been in deficit since 1983, back into balance, and to encourage private economic activity. Roughly four million foreign workers play an important role in the Saudi economy, for example, in the oil and banking sectors. For about a decade, Saudi Arabia's domestic and international outlays have outstripped its income, and the government has cut its foreign assistance and is beginning to rein in domestic programs. For 1995, the country looks for improvement in oil prices and will continue its policies of restraining public spending and encouraging non-oil exports.'

Exports: $39.4 billion (f.o.b., 1993 est.). Commodities: petroleum and petroleum products 92%. Partners: US 20%, Japan 18%, Singapore 5%, France 5%, South Korea 5% (1992).

Imports: $28.9 billion (f.o.b., 1993 est.). Commodities: machinery and equipment, chemicals, foodstuffs, motor vehicles, textiles partners: US 21%, Japan 14%, UK 11%, Germany 8%, Italy 6%, France 5% (1992).

Industries: Crude oil production, petroleum refining, basic petrochemicals, cement, two small steel-rolling mills, construction, fertilizer, plastics.

Agriculture: Accounts for about 10% of GDP, 16% of labor force; subsidized by government; products – wheat, barley, tomatoes, melons, dates, citrus fruit, mutton, chickens, eggs, milk; approaching self-sufficiency in food.

Defense forces: Branches: Land Force (Army), Navy, Air Force, Air Defense Force, National Guard, Coast Guard, Frontier Forces, Special Security Force, Public Security Force. *Manpower availability*: Males age 15–49 5,303,679; males fit for military service 2,949,842; males reach military age (17) annually 164,220 (1995 est.). *Defense expenditures*: exchange rate conversion – $17.2 billion, 13.8% of GDP (1994).

CIA, *Country Handbook*, the Internet.

1C
Economic indicators

Economic indicators ....

	Saudi Arabia	Arab states	Developing countries
GDP total (US$ billions), 1993	121.5	323	3,780
GDP per capita (1987 US$), 1993		1,298	769
average annual rate of change, 1980-93	-4.5	-5,4	1.0
Foreign direct net investment US $ millions, 1993	-79	1,280	55,420
Gross domestic investment (as % of GDP), 1993	24	24	26
Gross domestic savings (as % of GDP), 1993	27	23	26
Average annual rate of inflation, 1993	-	9.2	289.3

Health

	Saudi Arabia	Arab states	Developing countries
Total fertility rate, 1992	6.4	4.9	3.5
Contraceptive prevalence rate, any method (%), 1986-93	-	34	65
Pregnant Women aged 15 - 49 with anaemia (%), 1975-91	23	-	-
Births attended by trained health personal (%), 1983-94	90	46	63
Maternal mortality rate (per 100,000 live births), 1993	130	392	384
Under five mortality rate (per 1,000 live births), 1994	36	73	97
AIDS cases (per 100,000 people), 1994	0.2	0.5	6.7

Education

	Saudi Arabia	Arab states	Developing countries
Net enrolment ratio (%)			
Primary school			
... Female	57	78	84
... Male	65	89	91
Secondary School	30	44	33
... Female	38	53	39
... Male			
Tertiary students per 100,000 people			
... Female	1,215	925	365
... Male	1,092	1,435	768

SOURCE: UNDP

1D
Expatriate population

*The population of Saudi Arabia, 25 per cent of which are expatriates,
is expected to double in 16 years, wrote Asharq al-Awsat in 1995.*

At the last census in 1992 the population in Saudi Arabia was over 16.8
million; of this total 4.3 million were foreign workers. The proportion of
expatriates to Saudis is decreasing, falling from 39 percent in 1986 to 25.6
percent in 1992 . . . The national forecast for the year 2000, based on an
annual population growth rate of 3.2 percent, is 23.1 million, of whom 6.2
million will be expatriates. Some estimates place population growth in the
Kingdom as high as 4.5. percent per annum, which would double the
population in 16 years.

Expatriates in Saudi Arabia

Country	Expatriates	Percent (%)
India	1,228,652	19.6
Egypt	1,195,189	19.1
Pakistan	778,668	12.4
Philippines	450,967	7.2
Bangladesh	446,282	7.1
Yemen	424,398	6.8
Indonesia	249,458	4.0
Sudan	242,508	3.9
Syria	168,354	2.7
Jordan	155,410	2.5
Sri Lanka	135,246	2.2
Kuwait	122,519	1.9
Palestine	110,611	1.8
Turkey	92,258	1.5
Bedouins	61,246	1.0
Lebanon	52,560	0.8
United States	32,710	0.5
United Kingdom	28,868	0.5
Ethiopia	26,667	0.4
Somalia	25,818	0.4
Thailand	24,585	0.4
Morocco	21,243	0.4
Nepal	18,570	0.3
Afghanistan	16,493	0.3
Nigeria	15,541	0.3
Tunisia	13,511	0.2
Chad	11,196	0.2
Other	10,132	0.2

*Asharq al-Awsat, 12 December, 1995, quoted on the Internet by US-Saudi Arabian Business Council,
Washington, D.C.*

1E
Human development

Human development

	Saudi Arabia	Arab states	Developing countries	Industrial countries
Life expectancy at birth (years), 1993	69.9	62.1	61.5	74.3
Adult literacy rate (%), 1993	61.3	53.0	68.8	98.3
Combined first-, second-, and third level gross enrolment ratio (%), 1993	55	56	55	82
Real GDP per capita,1993	12,600	4,513	2,696	15,136

Gender-related development

	Saudi Arabia	Arab states	Developing countries	Industrial countries
Life expectancy at birth, 1993				
... Female	71.6	64.1	62.9	71.6
... Male	68.6	61.5	60.3	68.6
Adult literacy rate (%), 1993				
... Female	47.6	40.4	59.8	47.6
... Male	70.4	65.6	77.6	70.4
Combined first-, second-, and third level gross enrolment ratio (%), 1993				
... Female	51.8	51.0	50.6	51.8
... Male	57.4	63.4	59.7	57.4
Womens share of adult labour force (age 15 and above), 1990	10	25	39	10

SOURCE: UNDP

1F
Oil statistics

Oil Statistics, 1994

	Proven reserves		Production*		Reserves/ production years
	Barrels (bn)	% World share	Barrels/day (m)	% World share	
Saudi Arabia	**261.2**	**25.9**	**8.97**	**13.3**	**83.6**
Iraq	100.0	9.9	0.50	0.8	100.0
Kuwait	96.5	9.6	2.09	3.2	100.0
Abu Dhabi	02.2	9.1	2.07	2.9	100.0
Iran	89.3	8.8	3.60	5.5	68.5
Venezuela	64.5	6.4	2.68	4.3	65.4
Mexico	50.8	5.0	3.27	5.0	45.5
Russia	49.0	4.9	6.39	9.9	21.3
USA	30.2	3.0	8.36	12.0	9.8
China	24.0	2.4	2.91	4.5	22.6
OPEC	770.3	76.3	27.30	40.9	79.5

*Includes crude oil, shale oil, oil sands and natural gas liquids

Source: British Petroleum, Statistical Review of World Energy/The Economist Intelligence Unit 1996

1G
A royal family

Maternal Linkages Among the Sons of King Abdul Aziz

D.O.B.	1	2	3	4	5	6	7	8	9	10	11	12	13	14	15	16	17
1900	*Turki*																
1902	*Saud*																
1904		*Faisal*															
1910			*Muhammad*														
1912			*Khalid*														
1920				*Nasir*													
1921					*Saad*	Fahad											
1922							*Mansur*										
1923					*Musaid*			Abdullah	Bandar								
1924						Sultan											
1925					*A. Mohsin*												
1926							Mishal										
1928							Mitab										
1931						A. Rahman				Talal							
1932											Mishari						
1933						Nayef				Nawwaf		Badr					
1934						Turki			Fawwaz								
1935												A. Illah					
1936						Salman											
1937													*Majid*	*Thamir*			
1940						Ahmad						A. Majid		Mamdouh			
1941															Hidhlul		
1942														Mashhur			
1943													Sattam			Miqrin	
1947																	Hamoud

Source: Lees, Brian. *A Handbook of the Al-Saud Ruling Family of Saudi Arabia.* (London: Royal Genealogies, 1990) 'After King Fahad', *The Washington Institute Policy Papers 1994*

Chapter Two

THE BASIC LAW

2A
Royal decree on the Basic Law of Government

King Fahad, on 1 March 1982, issued a royal decree deciding to establish a basic law of government.

In the name of God, the Compassionate, the Merciful. Decree no A/90, dated 27th Sha'ban 1412.

With God's help, we, Fahad Bin Abd al-Aziz Al Saud, Monarch of the Saudi Arabian Kingdom, having taken into consideration the public interest and in view of the development of the state in various fields and out of the desire to achieve the objectives we are seeking, have decreed the following:

1. The promulgation of the Basic Law of Government in the attached form.
2. All regulations and orders and Decrees in force shall remain valid when this Basic Law comes into force until they are amended to make them compatible with it.
3. This Decree shall be published in the Official Gazette and shall come into force on the date of it's publication.

In the name of God, the Compassionate, the Merciful.

Public document, quoted from Washburn University School af Law Library, USA.

2B
The basic law of government

King Fahad, on 1 March 1982, personally formulated the basic law of the country carrying his family's name.

Chapter One: General Principles

Article One: The Kingdom of Saudi Arabia is a sovereign Arab Islamic state with Islam as its religion; God's Book and the Sunnah of His Prophet, God's prayers and peace be upon him, are its constitution, Arabic is its language and Riyadh is its capital.

Article Two: The state's public holidays are Id al-Fitr and Id al-Adha. Its calendar is the Hegira calendar.

Article Three: The state flag shall be as follows:

(a) It shall be green.
(b) Its width shall be equal to two-thirds of it's length.
(c) The words 'There is only one God and Mohammad is His Prophet' shall be inscribed in the centre with a drawn sword under it. The statute shall define the rules pertaining to it.

Article Four: The state's emblem shall consist of two crossed swords with a palm tree in the upper space between them. The statute shall define the state's anthem and its medals.

Chapter Two: Monarchy

Article Five:

(a) The system of government in the Kingdom of Saudi Arabia is monarchy.
(b) Rule passes to the sons of the founding King, Abd al-Aziz Bin Abd al-Rahman al-Faysal Al Saud, and to their children's children. The most upright among them is to receive allegiance in accordance with the principles of the Holy Koran and the Tradition of the Venerable Prophet.
(c) The King chooses the Heir Apparent and relieves him of his duties by Royal order.
(d) The Heir Apparent is to devote his time to his duties as an Heir Apparent and to whatever missions the King entrusts him with.
(e) The Heir Apparent takes over the powers of the King on the latter's death until the act of allegiance has been carried out.

Article Six: Citizens are to pay allegiance to the King in accordance with the holy Koran and the tradition of the Prophet, in submission and obedience, in times of ease and difficulty, fortune and adversity.

Article Seven: Government in Saudi Arabia derives power from the Holy Koran and the Prophet's tradition.

Article Eight: Government in the Kingdom of Saudi Arabia is based on the premise of justice, consultation (Arabic: shura) and equality in accordance with the Islamic Shari'ah.

Chapter Three: Features of the Saudi Family

Article Nine: The family is the kernel of Saudi society, and its members shall be brought up on the basis of the Islamic faith, and loyalty and obedience to God, His Messenger, and to guardians; respect for and implementation of the law, and love of and pride in the homeland and its glorious history as the Islamic faith stipulates.

Article Ten: The state will aspire to strengthen family ties, maintain its Arab and Islamic values and care for all its members, and to provide the right conditions for the growth of their resources and capabilities.

Article Eleven: Saudi society will be based on the principle of adherence to God's command, on mutual co-operation in good deeds and piety and mutual support and inseparability.

Article Twelve: The consolidation of national unity is a duty, and the state will prevent anything that may lead to disunity, sedition and separation.

Article Thirteen: education will aim at instilling the Islamic faith in the younger generation, providing its members with knowledge and skills and preparing them to become useful members in the building of their society, members who love their homeland and are proud of its history.

Chapter Four: Economic Principles

Article Fourteen: All God's bestowed wealth, be it under the ground, on the surface or in national territorial waters, in the land or maritime domains under the state's control, are the property of the state as defined by law.

The law defines means of exploiting, protecting and developing such wealth in the interests of the state, its security and economy.

Article Fifteen: No privilege is to be granted and no public resource is to be exploited without a law.

Article Sixteen: Public money is sacrosanct. The state has an obligation to protect it and both citizens and residents are to safeguard it.

Article Seventeen: Property, capital and labour are essential elements in the Kingdom's economic and social being. They are personal rights which perform a social function in accordance with Islamic Shari'ah.

Article Eighteen: The state protects freedom of private property and its sanctity. No one is to be stripped of his property except when it serves the public interest, in which case fair compensation is due.

Article Nineteen: Public confiscation of money is prohibited and the penalty of private confiscation is to be imposed only by a legal order.

Article Twenty: Taxes and fees are to be imposed on a basis of justice and only when the need for them arises. Imposition, amendment, revocation and exemption is only permitted by law.

Article Twenty-one: Alms tax is to be levied and paid to legitimate recipients.

Article Twenty-two: Economic and social development is to be achieved according to a just and scientific plan.

Chapter Five: Rights and Duties

Article Twenty-three: The state protects Islam; it implements its Shari'ah; it orders people to do right and shun evil; it fulfils the duty regarding God's call.

Article Twenty-four: The state works to construct and serve the Holy Places; it provides security and care for those who come to perform the pilgrimage and minor pilgrimage in them through the provision of facilities and peace.

Article Twenty-five: The state strives for the achievement of the hopes of the Arab and Islamic nation for solidarity and unity of word, and to consolidate its relations with friendly states.

Article Twenty-six: The state protects human rights in accordance with the Islamic Shari'ah.

Article Twenty-seven: The state guarantees the rights of the citizen and his family in cases of emergency, illness and disability, and in old age; it supports the system of social security and encourages institutions and individuals to contribute in acts of charity.

Article Twenty-eight: The state provides job opportunities for whoever is capable of working; it enacts laws that protect the employee and employer.

Article Twenty-nine: The state safeguards science, literature and culture; it encourages scientific research; it protects the Islamic and Arab heritage and contributes toward the Arab, Islamic and human civilisation.

Article Thirty: The state provides public education and pledges to combat illiteracy.

Article Thirty-one: The state takes care of health issues and provides health care for each citizen.

Article Thirty-two: The state works for the preservation, protection and improvement of the environment, and for the prevention of pollution.

Article Thirty-three: The state establishes and equips the armed forces for the defence of the Islamic religion, the Two Holy Places, society and the citizen.

Article Thirty-four: The defence of the Islamic religion, society and the country is a duty for each citizen. The regime establishes the provisions of military service.

Article Thirty-five: The statutes define the regulations governing Saudi Arabian nationality.

Article Thirty-six: The state provides security for all its citizens and all residents within its territory and no one shall be arrested, imprisoned or have their actions restricted except in cases specified by statutes.

Article Thirty-seven: The home is sacrosanct and shall not be entered without the permission of the owner or be searched except in cases specified by statutes.

Article Thirty-eight: Penalties shall be personal and there shall be no crime or penalty except in accordance with the Shari'ah or organisational law. There shall be no punishment except for acts committed subsequent to the coming into force of the organisational law.

Article Thirty-nine: Information, publication and all other media shall employ courteous language and the state's regulations, and they shall contribute to the education of the nation and the bolstering of its unity. All acts that foster sedition or division or harm the state's security and its public relations or detract from man's dignity and rights shall be prohibited. The statutes shall define all that.

Article Forty: Telegraphic, postal, telephone and other means of communications shall be safeguarded. They cannot be confiscated, delayed, read or listened to except in cases defined by statutes.

Article Forty-one: Residents of the Kingdom of Saudi Arabia shall abide by its laws and shall observe the values of Saudi society and respect its traditions and feelings.

Article Forty-two: The state shall grant the right to political asylum when the public interest demands this. Statutes and international agreements shall define the rules and procedures governing the extradition of common criminals.

Article Forty-three: The King's court and that of the Crown Prince shall be open to all citizens and to anyone who has a complaint or a plea against an injustice. Every individual shall have a right to address the public authorities in all matters affecting him.

Chapter Six: The Authorities of the State

Article Forty-four: The authorities of the state consist of the following: the judicial authority; the executive authority; the regulatory authority. These authorities co-operate with each other in the performance of their duties, in accordance with this and other laws. The King shall be the point of reference for all these authorities.

Article Forty-five: The source of the deliverance of *fatwa* in the Kingdom of Saudi Arabia are God's Book and the Sunnah of His Messenger. The law will define the composition of the senior *ulema* body, the administration of scientific research, deliverance of *fatwa* and its functions.

Article Forty-six: The judiciary is an independent authority. There is no control over judges in the dispensation of their judgements except in the case of the Islamic Shari'ah.

Article Forty-seven: The right to litigation is guaranteed to citizens and residents of the Kingdom on an equal basis. The law defines the required procedures for this.

Article Forty-eight: The courts will apply the rules of the Islamic Shari'ah in the cases that are brought before them, in accordance with what is indicated in the Book and the Sunnah, and statutes decreed by the Ruler which do not contradict the Book or the Sunnah.

Article Forty-nine: Observing what is stated in Article Fifty-three of this law, the courts shall arbitrate in all disputes and crimes.

Article Fifty: The King, or whoever deputises for him, is responsible for the implementation of judicial rulings.

Article Fifty-one: The authorities establish the formation of the Higher Council of Justice and its prerogatives; they also establish the seniority of the courts and their prerogatives.

Article Fifty-two: The appointment of judges and the termination of their duties is carried out by Royal decree by a proposal from the Higher Council of Justice in accordance with the provisions of the law.

Article Fifty-three: The law establishes the seniority of the tribunal of complaints and its prerogatives.

Article Fifty-four: The law establishes the relationship between the investigative body and the Prosecutor-general, and their organisation and prerogatives.

Article Fifty-five: The King carries out the policy of the nation, a legitimate policy in accordance with the provisions of Islam; the King oversees the implementation of the Islamic Shari'ah, the system of government, the state's general policies; and the protection and defence of the country.

Article Fifty-six: The King is the head of the Council of Ministers; he is assisted in carrying out his duties by members of the Council of Ministers, in accordance with the provisions of this and other laws. The Council of Ministers establishes the prerogatives of the Council regarding internal and external affairs, the organisation of and co-ordination between government bodies. It also establishes requirements to be fulfilled by ministers, their prerogatives, the manner of their questioning and all issues concerning them. The law on the Council of Ministers and its prerogatives is to be amended in accordance with this law.

Article Fifty-seven:

(a) The King appoints and relieves deputies of the prime minister and ministers and members of the Council of Ministers by Royal decree.
(b) The deputies of the prime minister and ministers of the Council of Ministers are responsible, by expressing solidarity before the King, for implementing the Islamic Shari'ah and the state's general policy.
(c) The King has the right to dissolve and reorganise the Council of Ministers.

Article Fifty-eight: The King appoints those who enjoy the rank of ministers, deputy ministers and those of higher rank, and relieves them of their posts by Royal decree in accordance with the explanations included in the law. Ministers and heads of independent departments are responsible before the prime minister for the ministries and departments which they supervise.

Article Fifty-nine: The law defines the rules of the civil service, including salaries, awards, compensations, favours and pensions.

Article Sixty: The King is the commander-in-chief of all the armed forces. He appoints officers and puts an end to their duties in accordance with the law.

Article Sixty-one: The King declares a state of emergency, general mobilisation and war, and the law defines the rules for this.

Article Sixty-two: If there is a danger threatening the safety of the Kingdom or its territorial integrity, or the security of its people and its interests, or which impedes the functioning of the state institutions, the King may take urgent measures in order to deal with this danger. And if the King considers that these measures should continue, he may then implement the necessary regulations to this end.

Article Sixty-three: The King receives Kings and Heads of State. He appoints his representatives to states, and he receives the credentials of state representatives accredited to him.

Article Sixty-four: The King awards medals, as defined by regulations.

Article Sixty-five: The King may delegate prerogatives to the Crown Prince by Royal decree.

Article Sixty-six: In the event of his travelling abroad, the King issues a Royal decree delegating to the Crown Prince the management of the affairs of state and looking after the interests of the people, as defined by the Royal decree.

Article Sixty-seven: The regulatory authority lays down regulations and motions to meet the interests of the state or remove what is bad in its affairs, in accordance with the Islamic Shari'ah. This authority exercises its functions in accordance with this law and the laws pertaining to the Council of Ministers and the Consultative Council.

Article Sixty-eight: A Consultative Council is to be created. Its statute will specify how it is formed, how it exercises its powers and how its members are selected.

Article Sixty-nine: The King has the right to convene the Consultative Council and the Council of Ministers for a joint meeting and to invite whoever he wishes to attend that meeting to discuss whatever matters he wishes.

Article Seventy: International treaties, agreements, regulations and concessions are approved and amended by Royal decree.

Article Seventy-one: Statutes are to be published in the Official Gazette and take effect from the date of publication unless another date is specified.

Chapter Seven: Financial Affairs

Article Seventy-two:

(a) The statute explains the provisions concerning the state's revenue and its entry in the state's general budget.
(b) revenue is entered and spent in accordance with the rules specified in the statute.

Article Seventy-three: Any undertaking to pay a sum of money from the general budget must be made in accordance with the provisions of the budget. If it is not possible to do so in accordance with the provisions of the budget, then it must be done in accordance with Royal decree.

Article Seventy-four: The sale, renting or use of state assets is not permitted except in accordance with the statute.

Article Seventy-five: The statutes will define the monetary and banking provisions, the standards, weights and measures.

Article Seventy-six: The law will fix the state's financial year and will announce the budget by way of a Royal decree. It will also assess the revenues and expenditure of that year at least one month before the start of the financial year. If, for essential reasons, the budget is not announced and the new financial year starts, the budget of the previous year will remain in force until the new budget is announced.

Article Seventy-seven: The competent body will prepare the state's final statement of account for the passing year and will submit it to the head of the council of ministers.

Article Seventy-eight: The same provisions will apply both to the budgets of the corporate bodies and their final statements of account and to the state's budget and its final statement of account.

Chapter Eight: Control Bodies

Article Seventy-nine: All the state's revenues and expenditures will come under subsequent control and all the state's movable and immovable funds will be controlled in order to confirm the good use of these funds and their preservation. An annual report will be submitted on this matter to the head of the Council of Ministers. The law will define the competent control body and its obligations and prerogatives.

Article Eighty: Government bodies will come under control in order to confirm the good performance of the administration and the implementation of the statutes. Financial and administrative offences will be investigated and an annual report will be submitted on this matter to the head of the Council of Ministers. The law will define the competent body in charge of this and it's obligations and prerogatives.

Chapter Nine: General Provisions

Article Eighty-one: The implementation of this law will not prejudice the treaties and agreements signed by the Kingdom of Saudi Arabia with international bodies and organisations.

Article Eighty-two: Without violating the content of Article Seven of this law, no provision of this law whatsoever may be suspended unless it is temporary, such as in a time of war or during the declaration of a state of emergency. This temporary suspension will be in accordance with the terms of the law.

Article Eighty-three: This law may only be amended in the same way as it was promulgated.

For an interpretation of the new law and Saudi political reform – see John Bulloch, *Reforms of the Saudi Arabian Constitution*, Gulf Centre For Strategic Studies, 5 Charterhouse Buildings, Goswell Road, London EC1M 7AN.

Other Constitutional background: see Washburn University School of Zaw Library.
Website: http://zawlib.wuacc.edu/forint/asia/saudi.html

Chapter Three

GOVERNMENT AND SHOURA COUNCIL

3A
King Fahad: Reform speech

King Fahad, in his speech on 1 March 1982, announced a set of reforms, covering a new basic statute of government and statutes for a Consultative Council as well as for regions of Saudi Arabia.

In the name of God, the Merciful, the Compassionate: Thanks be to God the Lord of all the universe and prayers and peace be upon the most noble of the Prophets, our Lord Mohammad, and upon all his family and companions.

Brother citizens: If God intends good to come to a people, he will guide them to what is better for them. God has bestowed on us countless bounties and the greatest of all of them is that of Islam, because it is the religion to which we have adhered and from which we shall not stray. We will be guided and happy through it because Almighty God has said this and has said so to His Prophet. The facts of history and reality are the best witness to this. Muslims have been happy with the Shari'ah of Islam when it became the arbiter in their life and all their affairs. In modern history, the first Saudi state was established on the basis of Islam more than two and a half centuries ago, when two pious reformists – Imam Muhammad Bin Saud and Shaykh Muhammad Bin Abd al-Wahhab, may God have mercy on their souls – agreed on that. This state was established on a clear programme of politics, rule, call for Islam, and sociology; this programme is Islam – belief and Shari'ah . . .

The application of this programme continued in all subsequent stages as succeeding rulers continued to abide by the Islamic Shari'ah. This was by the grace of God, who grants such graces to whom He wishes. This continuous upholding of the programme of Islam is based on three facts:

> The fact that the basis of the programme of Islam is fixed and is not subject to change or alteration. . . . The fact that the upholding of the programme should be continuous . . .; the fact that the rulers of this state should be faithful to Islam in all circumstances and conditions. . .

This programme could be summed up in establishing the Kingdom of Saudi Arabia on the following foundations:

1. The unification of faith which makes the people devote worship to God only without a partner, and live strongly and honourably.
2. The code of Islam which preserves rights and life, organises the relationship between the governor and the governed, controls transactions between the members of the community and safeguards general security.
3. Adopting the Islamic call and spreading it, because calling to God is among the Islamic state's greatest and most important responsibilities.
4. The founding of a suitable 'general environment', free of objectionable actions and deviations, which helps people to be honest and righteous, and this mission is the responsibility of those who support right and shun evil.
5. Achieving the 'unity' of faith which is the basis of political, social and geographical unity.
6. Adopting the means of progress and achieving an 'overall awakening' which directs the peoples' life and their livelihood, and looks after their interests in the light of Islam's guidance and its standards.
7. Achieving 'shura' which Islam has ordered, and praised whoever takes it up, as it ranked it among the qualities of the believers.
8. The Two Holy Places shall remain chaste for visitors and worshippers, as they were intended to by God, far away from all that hinders the performance of the minor and major pilgrimage and worship in the best way, and the Kingdom shall carry out this duty in fulfilment of God's right and serving the Islamic nation.
9. To defend the faith and the Holy Shrines, the homeland, the citizens and the state. These are the great bases on which the Saudi Arabian Kingdom has been established. The development of modern life necessitated the emergence from this trend of major rules during the era of King Abd al-Aziz. In view of the evolution of the state and the increase in its duties, King Abd al-Aziz – may God rest his soul – in the year 1373 AH (1953–4 AD) issued his Decree for the formation of a Council of Ministers, which is in operation to this day in accordance with its Statute issued in the year 1373 AH and the amendments that followed.

This programme is still enforced to this day, with God's grace and guidance.

Therefore, the Saudi Arabian Kingdom has never known what is called a 'constitutional vacuum'. The concept of 'constitutional vacuum' from the standpoint of text is that the state has no guiding principles or binding bases or reference sources in the field of legislation and regulating relations.

The Kingdom of Saudi Arabia has never witnessed such a phenomenon in its entire history because throughout its march it has been ruled according to guiding principles and bases and clear fundamentals to which judges, ulema and all those employed by the state refer. All the apparatus of the state currently functions according to statutes which stem from the Islamic Shari'ah and are regulated by it. Thus the fact that we are today enacting the following statutes – the basic statute of government; the statute of the Consultative Council and the statute for the regions – in new forms does not come from a vacuum. These three statutes are to strengthen something that exists and to formulate something which is already in operation. These statutes will be subject to rectification and development according to the requirements of the Kingdom's circumstances and interests. . .

The pillar and source of the basic statute of government is the Islamic Shari'ah, as this statute has been guided by the Islamic Shari'ah in defining the nature, the objectives and the responsibilities of the state, and in defining the relationship between the ruler and the ruled, which is founded on brotherhood, exchanging advice, friendship and co-operation. The relationship between citizens and those who are in charge of their affairs in this country was founded on firm bases and deep-rooted traditions of love, compassion, justice, mutual respect and loyalty stemming from free and deep-rooted convictions in the hearts of the sons of this country through successive generations. There is no difference between the ruler and the ruled; they are all equal before the law of God, and they are all equal in the love of this homeland and the eagerness to preserve its safety, unity, pride and progress. The one in charge has rights as well as duties, and the relationship between the ruler and the ruled is first and foremost and in the final analysis governed by the law of God and the tradition of His Prophet, may the prayers and blessings of God be upon him.

The basic statute of government has been inspired by these principles, and it has sought to deepen them in the relationship between the ruler and the ruled, with commitment to all that has been brought by our true religion in this respect.

As to the Consultative Council statute, it is based on Islam both in name and content, in response to the saying of God Almighty: 'And those who responded to God and performed prayers and held consultations amongst themselves and spend of what we have made available to them. . .'

The new statute of the Consultative Council provides for modernisation and development of the existing system through the bolstering of the council's framework, means and methods with more efficiency, organisation and vitality in order to achieve the desired objectives. The capabilities which will be embodied in this council will be carefully chosen so as to be able to contribute to the development of the Saudi Arabian Kingdom and its progress, taking into consideration the public interest of the homeland and the citizens.

While the Consultative Council undertakes, God willing, general consultation at the level of the state, we ought not to ignore the consultations currently practised within the state's organs through the specialised councils and committees. These structures ought to be active so that their work will complement that of the general Consultative Council.

The country has recently witnessed tremendous developments in various fields. These developments have called for a renewal of the general administrative system in the country. To meet this need and interest, the statute of regions has come to allow more organised action through an appropriate administrative leap, and to elevate the level of administrative rule in the regions of the Kingdom.

O compatriots: These statutes have been laid down after a meticulous and patient study carried out by an elite group of learned men of patience and experience, taking into consideration the distinguished position of the Kingdom on the Islamic scene, its traditions, customs, its social and cultural conditions. Therefore, these statutes have sprung from our reality, taking into consideration our traditions and customs, and adhering to our true religion. We are confident that these statutes will, with God's help, assist the state in realising all the Saudi citizen's aspirations to good and progress for his homeland and his Arab and Islamic nation. The Saudi citizen is the basic pivot for the advancement and development of his homeland and we shall not spare any effort in doing all that will ensure his happiness and reassurance.

The world, which is following the development and progress of this country, greatly admires its internal policy, which safeguards the citizen's security and stability, as well as its rational foreign policy, which is keen on establishing relations with other countries and contributing to all that bolsters the pillars of peace in this world. . . The Kingdom of Saudi Arabia has adhered constantly to the Islamic line as a system [of government], judiciary, mission, education, calling for the support of right and shunning of evil, and performing God's rites. The governors have adhered to it, and the people have adhered to it in their transactions and life.

Islam is a way of life, and there is no forfeiting what has come in God's Book, what has been confirmed by his Prophet, or what Muslims have unanimously agreed on. Our constitution in the Kingdom is the book of Gracious God, which is immune from any futility, and the tradition [sunnah] of His messenger, who does not speak irresponsibly. Whatever we disagree on we refer back to them and they are the arbiters on all statutes issued by the state. . .

In its present, as in its past, the Kingdom has been committed to the law of God. It is implementing it with all eagerness and firmness in all its domestic and foreign affairs, and, with the help of God, it will remain committed to this and very keen on it. . .

Citizens: With the help of God, we will continue with our Islamic line, co-operating with those who want good for Islam and Muslims, keen to strengthen the religion of God and the call to it, eager to ensure progress for this country and happiness for its people. We beg Almighty God to bestow on our people and our Arab and Islamic nation all good, righteousness, progress, prosperity and happiness. Thanks be to God, who bestows everything righteous.

For an interpretation of the speech and the reforms, see *Reforms of the Saudi Arabian Constitutions* by John Bulloch, the Gulf Centre for Strategic Studies, 5 Charterhouse Buildings, Goswell Road, London EC1M 7AN.

3B
Power distribution

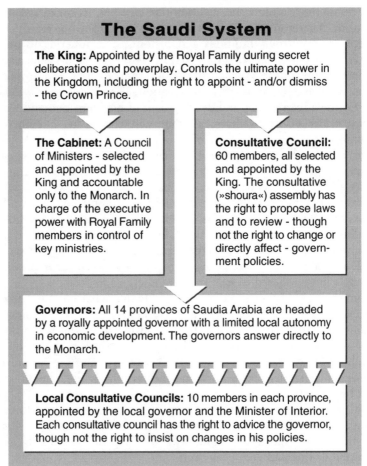

The Saudi System

The King: Appointed by the Royal Family during secret deliberations and powerplay. Controls the ultimate power in the Kingdom, including the right to appoint - and/or dismiss - the Crown Prince.

The Cabinet: A Council of Ministers - selected and appointed by the King and accountable only to the Monarch. In charge of the executive power with Royal Family members in control of key ministries.

Consultative Council: 60 members, all selected and appointed by the King. The consultative (»shoura«) assembly has the right to propose laws and to review - though not the right to change or directly affect - government policies.

Governors: All 14 provinces of Saudia Arabia are headed by a royally appointed governor with a limited local autonomy in economic development. The governors answer directly to the Monarch.

Local Consultative Councils: 10 members in each province, appointed by the local governor and the Minister of Interior. Each consultative council has the right to advice the governor, though not the right to insist on changes in his policies.

3C
Consultative Council law

Following years of debate and public speculation, King Fahad ordered the establishment of a selected council in Saudi Arabia.

In the name of God: the Merciful; the Compassionate: No. A/19 Date: 27 Shaabân 1412 AH. With the help of God Almighty: We, Fahad bin Abdul Aziz: Monarch of the Kingdom of Saudi Arabia; In line with the word of God Almighty: 'Consult them on matter'; and 'Their affairs will be decided through consultations among themselves'; and being guided by the action of the Apostle (God's prayer and peace be upon Him) in consulting with his companions; and due to the exigencies of the public interest; After having noted the Consultative Council Law, which had been enacted by Royal Order in the Hejira year 1347;

We have ordered the following:

1. Enactment of the Consultative Council Law according to the form attached hereto.
2. This Law shall replace the Consultative Council Law, enacted 1347 AH; the affairs of this Council shall be arranged by a Royal Order.
3. All the laws, orders and regulations that are in force for the time being at the date of operation of this Law shall remain operative until they have been amended so as to conform to its provisions.
4. This Law shall come into force within a maximum time limit of six months, to run from the date of promulgation.
5. This Law shall be promulgated in the Official Gazette.

The Consultative Council Law

Article One: In application of the word of God Almighty: Whereas you have been sent by God as mercy unto them; had you been rude and cruel, they would have dispersed from around you, pardon and ask forgiveness for them and consult with them on matters; if you are determined trust in God as He loves those who trust in Him. Those who have responded to their God and prayed and practised mutual consultancy and from what we gave them they spend.

Following the suit of the Apostle (God's prayer and peace upon Him) where he consulted with his companions and urged the nation to practice mutual consultation.

Therefore: A Consultative Council (CC) is hereby established, which will exercise the duties assigned to it in accordance with the provisions of this Law and of the Basic Law of Rule (Constitution); and in so doing it shall observe the precepts of the Book of God and the Sunna of His Apostle and preserve the ties of brotherhood and co-operate to do charity and observe piety.

Article Two: The Consultative Council is based on clinging to the commandments of God, venerating Him and observing piety and on an obligation to observe the sources of Islamic legislation; the members of the CC shall ensure that the public interest is being served and that the unity of the persons pursuing the same objective (the jammaa), the established system of the State and interests of the nation are being maintained.

Article Three: The CC shall be constituted of a President and sixty (60) members, who will be selected by the King from a number of scientists, experts and specialists; the rights, duties and all the affairs of the members shall be set down in a Royal Order.

Article Four: A member of the CC shall satisfy the following conditions:

(a) he must be a Saudi national, by birth and upbringing.
(b) he must be noted (well-known) for his piety and proficiency.
(c) his age must not be less than 30 years.

Article Five: A member of the CC may apply to be relieved of his post by tendering his resignation to the President of the CC who in turn will pass it to the King.

Article Six: Where a member of the CC has violated the duties of his functions, an investigation shall be carried out and his trial shall be conducted in accordance with the rules and proceedings that will be enacted by a Royal Order.

Article Seven: If, for any reason, the post of member of the CC becomes vacant, the King shall select a replacement to fill the vacancy which shall be enacted by a Royal Order.

Article Eight: A member of the CC may not take advantage of his post to draw personal benefit.

Article Nine: A member of the CC may not simultaneously occupy [combine] his post as such and any Government office or a director of any company except where the King considers that there is a necessity for so doing.

Article Ten: The President, Deputy President and Secretary General of the CC shall be appointed and dismissed by Royal Orders; their grades, rights, duties and all their affairs shall be determined by a Royal Order.

Article Eleven: Prior to commencing their duties, the President, members and the Secretary General of the CC shall take the following oath before the King:

'I swear by God Almighty that I shall be faithful to my religion, and then to my King and country; that I shall not divulge the secrets, but uphold [maintain] the interests and laws, of the State; that I shall discharge my duties truthfully, faithfully, loyally and impartially.'

Article Twelve: The seat of the CC is in Riyadh city; it may convene elsewhere within the Kingdom if the King deems the same to be appropriate.

Article Thirteen: The term of the CC is four years, according to the Hijra calendar, which begins to run from the date stated in the Royal Order which enacted the constitution thereof. The new CC shall be constituted at least two months before the date of expiration of the term of its predecessor; when the term of the CC has expired prior to the formation of a new CC, the then existing CC shall continue in office until a new CC has been formed. When a new CC is being formed at least one half of the number thereof must be new members (who have not served in the outgoing CC).

Article Fourteen: The King shall himself, or someone delegated by him each year, deliver the speech of the throne, which will comprise the internal and external policies of the State.

Article Fifteen: The CC shall give an opinion on the State's general policies, which are passed to it by the Chairman of the Council of Ministers, especially the following:

(a) discuss and express an opinion regarding the economic and social development general plan;
(b) study the laws, implementing regulations, treaties and international agreements and concessions and make suggestions with regard thereto as are deemed appropriate.
(c) interpretation of the laws;
(d) consider the annual reports submitted by the ministries and the other Government authorities, and make suggestions with regard thereto as are deemed appropriate.

Article Sixteen: The meeting of the CC shall not be valid for transaction of business unless at least two-thirds of the number of members – including the President or any one acting for him – are in attendance; resolutions of the CC shall not be valid except when they have been approved by the majority of the CC.

Article Seventeen: The resolutions passed by the CC shall be forwarded to the Chairman of the Council of Ministers, who in turn shall pass them to the Council of Ministers for consideration; when the points of view of both Councils are concordant, they shall, after being approved by the King, be enacted; but in case of dissent, the King shall approve what he considers appropriate.

Article Eighteen: The laws, treaties and international agreements and concessions shall be enacted and amended (where necessary) by Royal Decrees, and having been considered by the CC.

Article Nineteen: The CC may form select committees from among its members,as may be needed for exercising its functions; it may form special committees from amongst its members to consider any matters placed on its agenda.

Article Twenty: The select committees may seek help other than from the members of the CC as it deems fit, subject to the approval of the President of the CC.

Article Twenty-one: The CC shall have a general body to be formed of the President of the CC, his Deputy and the Chairman of the Select Committees.

Article Twenty-two: The President of the CC may file an application with the Chairman of the Council of Ministers proposing the attendance of any responsible Government officer at the meetings of the CC where the latter is deliberating on matters falling within the jurisdiction of such officer, who may take part in the deliberations without having a right to vote on the issue.

Article Twenty-three: Every ten members of the CC may introduce a bill of a new law or an amendment to any law in force (for the time being) and pass it to the President of the CC, who in turn shall pass the motion to the King.

Article Twenty-four: The President of the CC may file an application with the Chairman of the Council of Ministers requiring such documents and information as are available at the Government departments, which he deems necessary for the smooth running of the CC's business.

Article Twenty-five: An annual report shall be submitted by the President of the CC to the King concerning the activities carried out by the CC in accordance with the provisions of the bylaws of the CC.

Article Twenty-six: Except where provided otherwise in the bylaws of the CC, the Civil Service Laws shall apply to the employees of the CC.

Article Twenty-seven: A special [separate] budget shall be earmarked for the CC which must be approved by the King and the expenditure therefrom shall be in accordance with such rules as are enacted by a Royal Order.

Article Twenty-eight: The financial affairs and control, as well as the final accounts, shall be prepared [regulated] in accordance with the specific rules which will be enacted by a Royal Order.

Article Twenty-nine: The bylaws of the CC shall set down the powers of the President, his Deputy, the Secretary General, as well as the CC's machinery and the method of steering the meetings, the progress of the work of the CC and of its committees, as well as the method of voting; it will also regulate the rules of deliberations and the procedure of response and such other matters which tend to secure discipline on the floor of the CC, in such manner which enables it to carry out its functions as deemed beneficial to the Kingdom, and to the good of its people; these bylaws shall be enacted by a Royal Order.

Article Thirty: This Law shall not be amended except in the manner that has been adopted in enacting it.

Official Gazette, Issue No. 3397, 2 Ramadan, 1412 AH (6 March 1992).

3D
Duties of the Chairman of the Consultative Council

As decided by the king on the 20 August 1993.

Chapter 1: Competence of the Chairman, His Deputy and the General Secretary

Article One: The Chairman of the Council shall supervise all the work of the Council and represent it in its relations with the other quarters and bodies and speak for it.

Article Two: The Chairman of the Council shall chair the sessions of the council and the meetings of the general body, as well as chairing the meetings of the committees which he attends.

Article Three: The Chairman of the Council opens the sessions and declares there ending, announces the start of discussions during them [the sessions], takes part in these discussions, gives permission to speak and decides on the subject of the discussion, draws the attention of the speaker to the need to keep to the subject and to observe the time, ends the discussion and submits issues for votes, he also has the right to take whatever measures he sees fit and sufficient to maintain order during the session.

Article Four: The Chairman can call on the Council or the general body or any committee to hold an emergency session to discuss a certain issue.

Article Five: The Deputy Chairman of the Consultative Council shall assist the Chairman of the Council when he is present and assume his powers when he is absent.

Article Six: The Deputy Chairman shall chair the sessions of the Council and the meetings of the general body in the absence of the Chairman. In the event of their absence, the Council shall be chaired by the person chosen by the King. In chairing those sessions, he shall have the competence of the chairman of the Council.

Article Seven: The General Secretary or whoever deputizes for him shall attend the sessions of the Council and the meeting of the general body and supervise the writing of the minutes and convey to the members the dates for the sessions and the agenda, in addition to any work handed to him by the Council, the general body, or the chairman of the Council, and he shall be responsible to the Chairman for the financial and administrative affairs of the Council.

3E
Consultative Council Membership

As decided on 20 August 1993.

Article One: Membership comes into effect as of the beginning of the Council mandate, which is fixed in the rule on the foundation of the Consultative Council according to Article 13 of the Consultative Council Establishment Act. New membership shall begin on the date fixed in the Royal order appointing the new member and shall end with the termination of the Council mandate. In case the mandate expires before a new Council has been formed, membership shall continue until a new Council has been formed, as long as the member concerned has not been stripped of his membership.

Article Two: A member of the Consultative Council shall receive a monthly reward of 20,000 rials and where allowances, bonuses, compensations, privileges and holidays are concerned, shall be treated as an employee of grade 15 without prejudice to his pension payments.

Article Three: A full-time member who was in public employment before his appointment as a Council member, shall retain his grade. Time spent in public duty shall count towards seasonal salary increases, promotion and retirement. During his membership a member shall pay pension contributions according to his original employment. Combining the rewards and privileges of Council membership and job salary and privileges is not permitted. If the job salary exceeds membership rewards, the Council shall make up the difference. Where there are more privileges attached to the job than to Council membership, the member shall continue to receive them.

Article Four: In exception of Article 2, a member of the Council shall be granted a 45-day annual leave. The Chairman of the Council shall determine when a member is granted this leave. When granting leaves or leave of absence, it should be taken into account that this does not affect the quorum required for the convening of the Council session.

Article Five: A member of the Council should be totally neutral and objective in all the functions he carries out inside the Council, and should refrain from raising before the Council any subject relating to a private interest or that contravenes the public interest.

Article Six: A member of the Council should attend the sessions of the Council and its committees regularly. When an emergency prevents a member from attending a session, he should inform the Chairman of the Council or committee in writing. A member should not leave a session of the Council or a meeting of a committee before its end except with the permission of the Chairman of the Council or the Chairman of the committee as appropriate.

3F
Consultative Council duties

As decided by 20 August 1993.

Article One: If a member of the Consultative Council violates any of the duties of his function he shall be punished by the following means:

(a) He shall be censured in writing
(b) One month's allowance will be deducted
(c) He shall be stripped of his membership.

Article Two: A committee consisting of three members of the Council to be chosen by the Chairman shall investigate a member of the Consultative Council.

Article Three: The committee shall inform a member of the offence he is supposed to have committed. The committee shall hear what he has to say and take down his defence in the minutes of the investigation. The committee shall submit the result of the investigation to the general authority of the Council.

Article Four: The general authority can set up a committee consisting of three of its members, on condition that they do not include the Council's chairman or vice-chairman, to try the member who is accused of the offence. The committee can issue the punishment of censuring or deduction of the allowance. If the committee decides that membership should be taken away, it should submit the matter to the Chairman of the Council, so he can submit it to the King.

Article Five: The imposition of any of the aforementioned punishments shall not prevent any public or private lawsuit filed against the member.

3G
Consultative Council finances

As decided 20 August 1993.

Article One: The financial year of the Consultative Council shall be the financial year of the state.

Article Two: The Chairman of the Council shall prepare the draft annual budget of the Council and submit it to the King for adoption.

Article Three: After its adoption the amount of the budget shall be deposited with the Saudi Arabian Monetary Agency; drawing from it shall be against the signature of the Chairman of the Council or his Vice-Chairman.

Article Four: If the amounts listed in the budget are not sufficient to meet the Councils expenditure, or if there is an expenditure which was not foreseen when the budget was made, the Council's chairman shall prepare a statement regarding the required additional amount and submit it to the King for adoption.

Article Five: The titles and salaries of the posts of the Council shall be defined in the budget. Titles of posts shall be changed and their salaries reduced during a financial year upon the decision of the Council's Chairman.

Article Six: Occupation of posts of the 14th and 15th levels shall be made with the approval of the King. Occupation of the other posts of the Council shall be in accordance with the Civil Service Law and its documents, with the exception of any competition provisions.

Article Seven: The general authority of the Council shall lay down the principles of dealing with any persons – not members of the Council – Government officials and others, whose help is sought and the awards they are given. These principles shall be issued as per a decision by the Council's Chairman.

Article Eight: The Consultative Council shall not be subjected to the supervision of any other body. There shall be among the Council's administrative departments a management department for pre-expenditure financial supervision. The general authority of the council shall assume the supervision of such expenditure. The chairman of the Consultative Council can request a financial or administrative expert to produce a report on any financial or administrative affair for the council.

Article Nine: At the end of the financial year, the general secretariat of the Council shall prepare the final accounts. These shall be submitted by the Council chairman to the King for adoption.

Article Ten: Without prejudice to the provisions of this decree, the organization of the Council's financial affairs and accounts shall be done in accordance with the principles followed when the accounts of ministries and governmental departments are organized.

3H
Council of Ministers law

*The Saudi Cabinet, headed by the king, as decided by the king,
20 August 1992.*

Article One: The Council of ministers is an organizational body headed by the King.

Article Two: The headquarters of the Council of Ministers will be in the city of Riyadh. It would be possible for its sessions to be held in other parts of the country.

Article Three: Membership of the Council of Ministers will have to meet the following conditions:

(a) Must be of Saudi nationality by origin and upbringing.
(b) Must be known to be of propriety and competence.
(c) Must not be convicted of a crime in violation of religion and honor.

Article Four: Members of the Council of Ministers will not assume their posts until they have made the following oath: I swear by Almighty God that I will be loyal to my religion and then to my King and country, and that I will not divulge any secrets of state and that I will safeguard its interests and rules and carry out my duties sincerely, honestly and loyally.

Article Five: Membership of the Council of Ministers must not be combined with any other governmental post unless the Chairman of the Council of Ministers deems it necessary.

Article Six: While in office, a member of the Council of Minister's will not be allowed to buy or rent any state property directly, through a third party or in a state auction. He will also not be allowed to sell or rent out any of his properties to the government. He must not undertake any commercial of financial work, nor must he accept membership of the board of directors of any company.

Article Seven: The sessions of the Council of Ministers are held under the chairmanship of the chairman of the Council of Minister – the King or any of the deputies of the chairman. Its decisions are final after the King approves them.

Article Eight: The appointment of the members of the Council of Ministers or to relieve them of their posts or to accept their resignations will be by royal order. Their responsibilities will be defined in accordance with Article 57 and 58 of the Basic Law of Government. The internal statute of the Council of Ministers defines their rights.

Article Nine: The term of the Council of Ministers will not exceed four years during which it can be reformed by a royal order. In the event of the period expiring before it is reformed, it will continue to perform its work until it is reformed.

Article Ten: The minister is regarded as the direct head and the final point of reference of the affairs of his ministry. He exercises his duties in accordance with the provision of this statue and other rules and regulations.

Article Eleven:

(a) Only another minister can deputize for a minister at the Council of Ministers and (it has to be) in accordance with an order which is issued by the chairman of the Council.

(b) The deputy minister takes over the exercise of the powers of the minister during his absence.

Article Twelve: The Council of Ministers is composed of:

(a) Chairman of the Council
(b) Deputy Chairman of the Council
(c) Ministers
(d) Ministers of State who are appointed as members of the Council of Ministers by Royal order.
(e) Advisers to the King who are appointed as members of the Council of Ministers by Royal order.

Article Thirteen: Attending the meeting of the Council of Ministers is a right that belongs to its members only and to the Secretary-General of the Council. At the request of the Chairman or a member of the Council of Ministers and after the approval of the Chairman of the Council an official or expert may be permitted to attend sessions of the Council of Ministers and to present information, and explanations he may have. However, the voting shall remain exclusive to members only.

Article Fourteen: The session of the Council of Ministers will not be considered proper except when two thirds of its members attend the session. Its decisions will not be effective unless they are adopted by the majority of those attending the meeting. In the event of a tie, the Chairman will have the casting vote. In extraordinary cases the convening of the Council of Ministers will be proper when half its members attend. Its decisions will not be legal in this case accept with the agreement of two thirds of the members who are present and the Chairman has the right to evaluate the extraordinary cases.

Article Fifteen: The Council of Ministers shall not take a decisions on a matter that concerns the work of one of the ministries except in the presence of the minister in charge of that ministry or any one else that acts for him if necessary.

Article Sixteen: The deliberations of the Council of Ministers take place behind closed doors. As for its decisions they are basically public except for those which are considered to be secret by the Council.

Article Seventeen: Members of the Council of Ministers will be put on trial for offenses they may commit in their official duties, in accordance with a special statute that contains the statement of the offices and defines the procedures of the charges, the trial and the manner in which the body of the court is formed.

Article Eighteen: The Council of Ministers can form committees that include its members or others to discuss a matter that is included on the agenda so that they [the committees] submit a special report on it. The internal statute of the Council of Ministers will decide size and composition of the committee and the work procedure.

3I
Regional Authorities Establishment Law

Decided on 1 March 1992.

Article One: This Statute is aimed at improving the level of administrative work and development in the regions of the Kingdom. It is also aimed at maintaining security and order, and at guaranteeing the rights and liberties of citizens in the framework of the Islamic Shari'ah.

Article Two: The regions of the Kingdom and the headquarters of the Emirate of each region are organized by a Royal Decree upon the recommendation of the interior minister.

Article Three: Administratively, each region consists of a number of governorates, districts and centers created after taking account of demographic, geographical, and security considerations, environmental conditions and communications. The governorates are organized by a Royal Decree upon the recommendation of the Emir of the region.

Article Four: For every region there is an Emir with the rank of minister, with a deputy of distinguished grade to assist him in his work and to deputize for him in his absence. The Emir and his deputy are appointed to and relieved of their posts by a Royal Decree upon the recommendation of the Interior Minister.

Article Five: The Emir of the region is accountable to the interior minister.

Article Six: The Emir and his deputy, before they take up their responsibilities, take the following oath before the King: 'I swear by Almighty God to be loyal to my religion and then to my King and country, and not to disclose any of the State's secrets, and to protect its interests and laws and to discharge my duties with honesty, trust, loyalty and justice.'

Article Seven: Every Emir will assume the administration of the region in accordance with the general policy of the State, and in accordance with the rules of this Statute and other Statutes and motions. In particular he must:

(a) Maintain security, order and stability, and take the necessary measures to this end, in accordance with regulations and motions.
(b) Carry out judicial judgements after they become final.
(c) Guarantee the rights and liberties of individuals, and take no measure that will harm these rights and liberties, except within the limits decided by the judiciary and the law.
(d) Work for the social, economic and urban development of the region.
(e) Work for the development of public services in the region, and promote them.
(f) Administer governorates, districts and localities, and control the work of governors, district directors and heads of locality, and ensure that they discharge their duties in an adequate manner.
(g) Protect the assets and property of the state, and prevent any transgression upon them.
(h) Supervise the organs of the state and their employees in the region in order to ensure that they perform their duties well and with all trust and loyalty, taking into account the ties of the employees of ministries and various services in the region with their competent authorities.
(i) Have direct contact with ministers and heads of service, and discuss the affairs of the region with them in order to improve the performance of the bodies under his authority, and inform the interior minister about this.
(j) Present annual reports to the interior minister on the performance of public services in the region, and other affairs of the region as defined by the executory motion of this Statute.

Article Eight: An annual meeting of the Emirs of regions is to take place under the chairmanship of the interior minister to discuss issues related to regions; the interior minister submits a report on this matter to the chairman of the Council of Ministers.

Article Nine: A meeting of the governors of governorates and directors of districts is to take place at least twice a year under the chairmanship of the Emir of the region to discuss matters of the region; the Emir submits a report on this issue to the minister for the interior.

Article Ten:

(a) For each region, one under-secretary or more may be appointed with a rank no less than grade 14, in accordance with a decision by the Council of Ministers upon the recommendation of the interior minister.

(b) Each Governorate has a governor with a rank no less than grade 14; he is appointed by a decision of the chairman of the Council of Ministers upon the recommendation of the interior minister; the Governorate has an under-secretary whose rank is no less than grade 12 and who is appointed by a decision of the interior minister upon the recommendation of the region's governor.

(c) Each group B governorate will have a Governor of not less than 12th grade by a decision of the interior minister based on recommendation of the region's governor.

(d) Each group A center will have a chairman of not less than eighth grade. He will be appointed by a decision of the interior minister based on a recommendation of the region's governor.

(e) Each group B center will have a chairman of not less than fifth grade. He will be appointed by a decision of the region's governor.

Article Eleven: Governors of the regions, governors of the Governorates and chairmen of the centers should have their residences at the venues of their work and should not leave their place of work without permission from their direct superiors.

Article Twelve: Governors of Governorates and chairmen of centers will assume their duties in the concerned administrative zones within the authority delegated to them.

Article Thirteen: Governors of Governorates should administer their areas according to specifications mentioned in Article 7, except what is contained in columns 'waw', 'Ta' and 'Ya' of the article. They should supervise the works of the chairmen of centers and their staff. They should ascertain their efficiency in performing their duties and submit periodic reports to the governor of the region on the efficiency of their public service performance and other matters related to affairs of the governorates in line with the executive regulations for this system.

Article Fourteen: Each ministry or government department has services in the region. It appoints a head over its bodies in the region whose grade is not less than the twelfth grade. This head is directly related to the central body and his duty is to coordinate with the Emir of the region in the field of his work.

Article Fifteen: A council is created in each region and is called the region's council. The headquarters of this council are situated in the town where the Emir of the region has his headquarters.

Article Sixteen: The region's council consists of:

(a) The region's Emir as chairman
(b) The deputy Emir of the region as the deputy chairman
(c) The Emir's assistant
(d) The heads of the government's bodies in the region are appointed in accordance with a decision by the Prime Minister on the recommendation of the Interior Minister
(e) A number of residents whose number is not less than ten. These should be men of science, experience and specialization. They are appointed by the Prime Minister on the recommendation of the region's Emir, and on the approval of the interior ministry. Their membership lasts four years, which can be renewed.

Article Seventeen: A council member must be:

(a) Of Saudi nationality by birth and upbringing.
(b) Of recognized rectitude and competence.
(c) No younger than 30.
(d) A resident of his region.

Article Eighteen: Each member is to submit proposals in writing to the chairman of the Regional Council on matters within the Council's jurisdiction. The chairman is to include every proposal on the Council agenda with a view to putting it forward for examination.

Article Nineteen: A member of a Regional Council cannot attend the deliberations of the Council or of its committees if the topic raised relates to a personal matter, to a matter pertaining to another person whose testimony is not accepted or to a person for whom the member is acting as guardian, proxy or representative.

Article Twenty: Should the appointed member wish to resign, he is to submit a request to that effect to the interior minister through the Emir of the region concerned. The resignation will not be considered effective until the prime minister has approved it on the recommendation of the interior minister.

Article Twenty-one: Apart from the cases mentioned in this Statute, an appointed member cannot be dismissed during his membership period except by an order of the prime minister, acting on a proposal of the interior minister.

Article Twenty-two: Should a vacancy arise for any specific reason, a replacement is to be designated within three months of the date at which the vacancy arose. The new member will then fill the vacancy for the remainder of his predecessor's period, in accordance with Article 16 (e) of this law.

Article Twenty-three: The Council of the Region is responsible for studying any aspect that could improve the standard of services in the region; its particular prerogatives are as follows:

(a) To define the needs of the region and propose their inclusion in the state's plan of development.
(b) To specify useful projects in accordance with a scale of priorities and propose their endorsement in the state's annual budget.
(c) To study plans for the organization of cities and towns of the region and follow-up their implementation once they are endorsed.
(d) To follow-up aspects related to the region *vis-à-vis* the plan of development while observing a balance and co-ordination in this matter.

Article Twenty-four: The Regional Council tables any proposal involving generally useful work for the citizens of the region and encourages citizens to contribute in this respect, the proposal should be submitted to the interior minister.

Article Twenty-five: The Regional Council is prohibited from looking into any subject that is outside the scope of its prerogatives as stipulated for it by this law; its decisions will be null and void if it exceeds this scope; the interior minister issues a decision in this matter.

Article Twenty-six: The Regional Council will hold an ordinary session every three months at the invitation of its chairman, and the chairman may call for an extraordinary meeting if he deems fit. The session will include the meeting or meetings held following one invitation, and the session may be closed only after all the points on the agenda have been examined and discussed.

Article Twenty-seven: The presence at the meetings of the Regional Council is considered as a duty related to the function of members mentioned in Article 16 (c) and (d) of this Statute. They must attend in person or a person must attend in lieu of them in the event of their being away from work. As for the members mentioned in Article 16 (e), the absence of a member at two successive sessions without an acceptable excuse is grounds for dismissal from the Council. In this case, this member must not be appointed again to membership of the Council before two years have passed since the date of the decision of his dismissal.

Article Twenty-eight: The meetings of the Council are in order only if at least two-thirds of members attend them. It adopts its decisions by an absolute majority of votes of Council members. If votes are equal, then the chairman has the casting vote.

Article Twenty-nine: The regional Council must, if necessary, form special committees to examine any decree falling within the scope of its prerogatives. It can enlist the help of experienced people and specialists. It can also invite anyone it likes to attend Council meetings and to take part in the discussion without having the right to vote.

Article Thirty: The interior minister can summon the Council to convene under his chairmanship at any venue he chooses. The minister also chairs any meeting he attends.

Article Thirty-one: The Regional Council can convene only at the request of its chairman or his deputy or by order of the interior minister.

Article Thirty-two: The chairman of the Council has to submit a copy of the reports to the interior minister.

Article Thirty-three: The chairman of the Regional Council has to inform the ministries and government departments about the resolutions concerning them which are passed by the Council.

Article Thirty-four: Ministries and government departments have to comply with the resolutions passed by the Regional Council in accordance with the contents of Article 23 (a) and (b). If a ministry or government department sees fit not to agree with a resolution passed by the Regional Council on what has been mentioned it has to clarify the reasons for this to the Regional Council. If the Regional Council is not convinced that the reasons given by the ministry or government department are suitable it will refer the case to the interior minister, who will then refer it to the chairman of the Council of Ministers.

Article Thirty-five: Every ministry or department with services in the region will notify the Regional Council about the projects decided for the region in the budget as soon as it is issued. It will also notify the Council about the development plan decided for the region.

Article Thirty-six: Any minister or head of service can seek the views of the regional Council about any subject connected with his jurisdiction in the region. The council has to offer its view in this regard.

Article Thirty-seven: Upon the recommendation of the interior minister, the Council of Ministers decides on the remuneration of the chairman of the regional Council and its members, taking account of the costs of transport and residence.

Article Thirty-eight: The Regional Council can only be dissolved by a decision of the chairman of the Council of Ministers upon the recommendation of the interior minister. If that happens, new members should be appointed within three months of the date of dissolution. During the period when the Council is dissolved, the members mentioned in Article 16 (c) and (d) under the chairmanship of the emir of the region will exercise the powers of the Council.

Article Thirty-nine: The Regional Council has a secretariat residing in the region's Emirate, which will undertake the preparation of its agenda, extending timely invitations to meetings, recording the discussions that take place during the meetings, counting votes, preparing the minutes of the meetings, drafting the decisions, carrying out the necessary work to organize the Council's meetings and recording its decisions.

Article Forty: The interior minister will issue the necessary bills to implement this Statute.

3J
An Exile's Comment

By Saudi Arabian exiled writer, Muhammad H. Siddiq

The democracies of the West have followed in the footsteps of the imperialist countries of the 19th and 20th centuries in finding no need for speed in ensuring democracy in countries of the Third World, or at least in those countries which are currently congruent with Western foreign policies. The United States, while giving lip-service to the spread of democracy throughout the world, seems satisfied with the pace of change in Saudi Arabia, heralding every step of an oppressive monarchy as a meaningful gesture toward an open society. Apologists in the West, including contingents from the liberal and radical spheres, use the old argument that the culture is not oriented toward democracy, thus the country, and its people, are not yet 'ready'. I say that Saudi Arabia is ready for representative institutions with free local and national elections and an independent judiciary. How ready were the colonists before the Revolutionary War? Representative democracy in the Western form had not yet truly been created until they created it.

While I do not say that the people of Saudi Arabia are at that same flashpoint, I do contend that they, as all people, long for the opportunity to determine the course of their own lives and that of their country. The people of Saudi Arabia deserve the opportunity to create their own path, make some mistakes, and move toward a fuller representation of their culture in the global community.

The West must recognize that change is in its long-term interest. Furthermore, I believe that it is in the clear long-term interest of the West to support the democratic urge of the Saudi people, rather than work with the House of Saudi to suppress that urge.

King Fahad has not yet lost all power, but has lost a great deal, and is continuing to slip. The gap between the House of Saud and the people widens with each economic downturn, and every instance of repression. The House of Fahad is increasingly isolated from the rest of society, and the people no longer believe what the King says. It is a classic crisis of confidence in which the governed have no faith in those who govern them, and rightly so. At this juncture, I wish to ask: why would the West choose to support a government that is not only losing ground, but a government which does not share its most basic principles and values? And I wish to inform the West that the people of Saudi Arabia have had enough monopolization, centralization and depersonalization from the House of Saud. It is time for the West to hear the people of Saudi Arabia and respond.

The Saudi people must speak more clearly and loudly. In order to be heard, the Saudi people must raise their voices even louder. There has not yet been enough protest, enough voices loud enough to be heard from behind the closed doors that represent Saudi Society.

My people are afraid, and this is understandable. It is always frightening to challenge those who are willing to go to any length to suppress disagreement, including imprisonment and torture. The men and women who have spoken up have been immediately threatened by the government. There is no free speech in Saudi Arabia, none at all.

Those of you who read this book in the West must listen very closely to hear the voices of dissent, ignoring the public relations machine of the House of Saud, which is always ready to praise every act of the government and decry every act of protest.

Those of you in Saudi Arabia, and those of you living temporarily in the West, must also do your part by speaking more clearly and boldly about the reality of Saudi Arabian life. Although you may suffer for it in the short-term, in the years to come you will have the satisfaction of knowing that you have contributed to a freer Saudi Arabia. And, along with your country, you will have your integrity back. The ruling amirs must be directly confronted.

Finally, before I end this book, I would like to address the members of the ruling amirs directly. There are those among you who believe that you can buy off the entire country with oil wealth, and that material prosperity is all that the citizens want. You seem to think that is only the economy is improved, and conditions return to a more prosperous state, all the complaints will disappear.

The economy is important. It is not, however, the only thing that concerns us, your people. We want to gain economically from the oil resource that belongs to the country, not just to you. We want to have our money used wisely and effectively to establish a just and equitable community. We want to have the opportunity to benefit from the gifts we have been granted as a nation to develop fully as a people, and to assist our brothers and sisters in other countries to develop themselves.

There is more than the economy at stake here, however. Our integrity is violated every time you represent yourselves as paragons of Islamic virtue, while behaving more like exemplars of immorality and selfishness. Our humanity is violated every time we are suppressed by your authoritarian police from expressing our differing political, or religious, views. Our morality is violated when we are forced to stand by and watch as you use the wealth of the nation to violate the values and principles which we, an Islamic people, hold at the center of our being. We appeal to you to be changed in your hearts and minds, to recognize the harm you are doing to us and to yourselves. There is a place in Saudi Arabia for you, and for the contributions of each of us. We ask you to remember that you are our brothers, under Allah, not gods on earth. If you take your place within the community and work to build up the community of Islam, rather than intimidate it, you will be a blessing to us, rather than a curse.

From *Why the Boom Went Bust, an Analysis of the Saudi Government*,
Lincoln Nebraska, USA, 1995.

3K
Institutional analysis

Saudi Society seen by United States Information Service.

Although the Kingdom of Saudi Arabia is a relatively new state founded only as recently as the 1920s, it traces its roots to the eighteenth century when a tribal leader, Al-Imam Muhammad bin Saud, joined forces with puritanical religious reformer, Muhammad ibn Abdul Wahhab. The alliance of these two men and their tribes changed the political landscape of the Arabian Peninsula, even though the first state they founded was short-lived. The fundamental political question posed by this alliance between the al-Saud and the al-Wahhabi has not changed much in two centuries: How can a society and a government that do not accept the separation of religion and state adapt to the modern world?

Saudi Arabia is a monarchy without elected representative institutions or political parties. There is no written constitution. Since the death of King Abdul Aziz, who unified the Kingdom in the 1920s, based upon the regime's interpretation of Shari'a, or Islamic law. The key institutions of the Kingdom are generally headed by members of the Royal Family, the al-Saud, including the Ministries of Defense, Interior, and Foreign Affairs, as well as the Saudi Arabian National Guard and most provincial governorships. The Saudi government has tended to appoint technocrats to run ministries unrelated to national security, although members of the Royal Family occasionally serve in these positions as well.

Oil has transformed the country's economy. Millions of foreign workers have been brought in not only to work in the oil industry but also to work on large scale infrastructure projects or in private homes as domestic servants. Oil wealth has made possible the rapid urbanization of what had been an essentially pastoral society and has underwritten the elaboration of a welfare state. Critics charge that oil revenues have enriched members of the royal family and their associates shamelessly, but the middle class has grown quickly. Although just one-third of the gross domestic product (GDP), oil revenues account for three-fourths of government income.

The Saudi Royal Family numbers as many as 7,000 princes. These princes live throughout the Kingdom and are active in both the government and the private sector. Within the Royal Family, there is some given-and-take among senior princes on policy questions, although few of any generation but that of the sons of King Abdul Aziz have any voice. In theory, the Royal Family can act as the King's eyes and ears helping him to become aware of, and responsive to, the issues and concerns of ordinary people. In practice, the Royal Family does not appear to be developing as an institution that might offer the country a viable alternative to the modern bureaucratic state. Even trivial decisions are often referred to the King for lack of anyone at a lower level who both has authority and is willing to accept responsibility. No new, independent, dynamic institutions such as labor unions or political parties are allowed to develop. To the extent possible, individuals are atomized or isolated from one another by the all-powerful state.

In principle, virtually every Saudi citizen has access to a prince in the Royal Family through a system of open audiences, the so-called majlis system. The majlis allows members of the Royal Family to engage in 'constituent service' and to distribute political patronage, but it is only marginally useful as a vehicle for the expression of popular opinion on policy questions. There is no mechanism for citizens to charge their government. Since the government actively suppresses opposition views and rejects internationally accepted definitions of human rights, individuals have no safe means of expressing their opinions directly, and the government lacks any effective method for learning the wishes of the public at large.

At times the Saudi Royal Family has acted as cautious political modernizers in developing state institutions and implementing social reform, as, for example, in the 1960s when the Government insisted on opening a television station despite the opposition of religious conservatives. However, the Royal Family has opposed social and political reform when that reform has been deemed un-Islamic or has seemed to threaten the basic terms of the alliance between the al-Saud and the religious establishment.

The Royal Family spends considerable amounts of time, money, and energy burnishing its own Islamic credentials so as to ensure that no serious attack on its legitimacy to rule can be posed by Islamic religious scholars (ulema) specifically, and religious conservatives more generally. Hence King Fahad has chosen as his official title 'the Custodian of the Two Holy Mosques'.

Many of Saudi Arabia's institutions are, historically speaking, quite new. Following the political unification of the Kingdom in 1932 and the discovery of oil in 1933, the development of a modern infrastructure was achieved rather quickly. Political and administrative modernization, on the other hand, has happened at a much slower pace. Until the 1960s, affairs of state were conducted very informally, with only a handful of individuals involved in the decision-making process. The trappings of the modern bureaucratic state, with its well-defined organization charts and divisions of responsibility, have appeared only in the last thirty years. Today comparatively well-trained technocrats are beginning to assume control over the day-to-day business of governance, although most questions that touch on national security and foreign affairs are still dealt with primarily by senior members of the Royal Family or the King himself.

Institutions

The structure of government in Saudi Arabia is that of a theocratic monarchy that is markedly authoritarian in character, if arguably benevolent in its attempt to spread the benefits of a modern welfare state. The final decision-maker, arbiter, administrator, and court of last resort is the King himself. Power flows outward and downward from the throne but is not widely distributed. The King is not an absolute monarch, but the government claims that its legal system is divinely inspired, that Islamic law is the sole and sufficient guide to governing. In practical terms, therefore, the King often appears absolute in his power, even if he may be constrained by strictures of Islamic law, the necessity to maintain consensus within the Royal Family, and tradition.

The institutional structure of the government is simple in outline: the King, the Crown Prince, and other senior members of the al-Saud family control decision-making at the top of the pyramid. Beneath them comes the Council Ministers. For the purposes of USIS [United States Information Service], the most important ministries are Finance, Health, and Petroleum and Natural Resources. It is extremely difficult to predict the level at which decisions are made on any particular issue, for even apparently trivial issues may be referred to the King himself for resolution.

Other ministries of note include Industry and Electricity, Commerce, Interior, and the Saudi Arabian Monetary Agency. Another government organization that may play an important role as a means of reaching the younger generation is the General Presidency of Youth Welfare, which, among other things, has primary responsibility for the organization of cultural and sporting events, youth activities, public performances, and exhibits.

Non-royal technocrats and experts, many of whom are US-educated and who presently occupy ministerial and deputy ministerial posts, are increasingly participating in the decision-making process, primarily through framing debate, delimiting issues and providing advice. However, final decisions on all subjects of importance to the Kingdom are still the sole province of the Royal Family.

In 1993 the King appointed 60 members to a Consultative Council, or Majlis Ash-Shura. The Consultative Council began holding sessions in 1994 but has not to date publicized its work in any detail. Despite the fact that the King has recently made a point of stating that the Consultative Council will only function in an advisory capacity and that Western-style parliamentary democracy is un-Islamic, the possibility remains that the Council may develop as an institution that provides greater popular participation in the government. Forty percent of those appointed to the Council by the King have studied at American universities and have therefore experienced life in a democratic society. In short, the Consultative Council, especially the Council's more reachable staffers, is a natural focus for USIS programming.

United States Information Service, Riyadh, 1996.

3L
Sheik Muhammed Jubeir: the role of Shoura

The role of the Consultative Council according to a press release from the Embassy of Saudi Arabia.

Chairman of the Consultative Council [Majlis Al-Shura], Shaikh Muhammad Bin Jubeir, today stated that there is no way to compare the consultative system in Islam with any of the so-called democratic systems prevailing in other countries.

Chairman Bin Jubeir stated that the Consultative Council is not a legislative organ because Islamic Shariah is the sole authority to show people what is right and what is wrong, and noted that Shariah clarifies for Muslims the major principles which require to be formulated into regulations and statutes in order to be implemented. Referring to the role of the Consultative Council, he said: 'Unlike western democracies, we never legislate, we merely organize initially existing principles.' The Consultative

Council, differing from parliaments in other countries in that each member represents, not a particular area, but the entire country, plays an effective role in accelerating the wheel of social and economic development in the Kingdom. It has established a proposals committee that receives ideas from citizens and studies them before referring them to one of the eight specialized committees. In this way citizens can positively contribute to enriching the activities of the Consultative Council . . .

Press release, Embassy of Saudi Arabia, Washington, DC, 24 January 1997.

3M
King Fahad: Four years of Shoura

In augurated the fourth year of shoura council on 23 January 1997, as stated in a press release by the Embassy of Saudi Arabia in Washington, DC.

Custodian of the Two Holy Mosques King Fahd Bin Abdul Aziz inaugurated last night the first session of the fourth year of the Consultative Council (Majlis Al-Shura). On his arrival he was greeted by Crown Prince Abdullah Bin Abdul Aziz, Deputy Prime Minister and Commander of the National Guard; Prince Sultan Bin Abdul Aziz, Second Deputy Prime Minister, Minister of Defense and Aviation, and Inspector-General; a number of other royal princes; Chairman of the Shura Council Sheikh Muhammad Bin Ibrahim Bin Jubair; members of the Shura Council; and other senior officials. Addressing the meeting, King Fahd expressed his pleasure on the occasion, which 'is set to renew our valued aspirations and goals for serving our dear nation and strengthening our blessed march, and effect the continuation of our great development in the light of our Islamic faith and the noble values originating from it in terms of its text and its spirit'. Remarking that 'the Kingdom is a great entity based on the guidance and practice of Islam, which makes it a real model for any nation that applies the shari'ah of Allah to all its dealings', he referred to how [the Kingdom's founder] King Abdul Aziz established, in managing the nation's affairs, 'the principle of Shura (consultation) as enshrined in the Holy Qur'an and the Sunnah (traditions) of the Prophet'.

King Fahd went on to say: 'Our country is now at the peak of its strength because it is rich in terms of its faith, its people, and its plentiful natural resources. In addition, the grand expansion projects of the Two Holy Mosques and the Holy Sites have been completed, and all the facilities are in place to ease the mission of our brothers, the pilgrims.' He then referred to the great events that the region has witnessed in the past years, events that weakened the development of the Kingdom, and stated that in spite of these: 'Our economy is stronger than anyone could have imagined.'

Industrial development, he said, is progressing day by day. Many items which in the past were imported, are now manufactured in thousands of factories. The state gives assistance, and provides a suitable atmosphere that ensures protection, encouragement and substantial financial support as well as other benefits. The Saudi Industrial Development Fund, for example, has offered facilities and easy loans amounting to SR31 billion (US $8.3 billion) for industrial projects.

Progress in the field of education has surpassed all expectations, with a total of 23,752 schools at all levels with almost 5 million pupils, while in the sphere of higher education there are seven universities, incorporating 68 colleges with an enrolment of 155,182 students, both male and female, and another 61 women-only colleges with 100,000 female students. In addition, there are 56 specialized colleges for technology, health, and teachers' training, and 70 technical centers and institutes in the fields of industry, agriculture and commerce, catering to thousands of trainees.

As for health, the state has established integrated and specialized hospitals as well as different kinds of clinics and health centers in towns and villages throughout the Kingdom. King Fahd gave assurances that this policy will continue. Turning to the agricultural sector, he stated that Saudi Arabia is currently producing all its needs for various kinds of grains, vegetables, and fruits, adding that the development of a variety of agricultural crops would continue to be a major concern in line with the policy to realize food security. Concerning water, Kind Fahd said: 'The Kingdom is a pioneer in the field of water desalination and is the largest producer of desalinated water in spite of the high financial cost. On this occasion, I would like to say that it is the duty of all of us to rationalize water use and to conserve it in order to protect this precious wealth.'

King Fahd went on to discuss the construction sector and housing for citizens, remarking that the Real Estate Development Fund has offered SR 108 billion (US $28.8 billion) in this area. Dealing with the economic infrastructure, King Fahd said that the state has built roads, ports, and electricity facilities in record time, stating: 'All of us are working with full determination to realize the happiness and well-being of each citizen as well as to ensure security for him and his family.' The state budget, he said, reflects this every year, with the current 1997 budget including allocations for new development projects involving the establishment of mosques, schools, health facilities, water projects, dams, roads, basic infrastructure, and increased assistance for new social insurance cases, all in addition to what has already been allocated for projects in the past which are still financed by the state. Turning to the international scene, King Fahd declared: 'Our country is distinguished in its foreign relations by preserving its existing brotherly ties with the Arab and Islamic worlds and paying all its attention to Arab and Islamic causes', and made special reference to the cause of the Palestinian people and that of Al-Quds Al-Shareef [Jerusalem], reiterating support for the peace process in the Middle East. The Kingdom's relations with friends throughout the world, he said, are 'noted for their clarity, consistency, and solidarity, enlightened by the exchange of respect and mutual interest as well as cooperation for the realization of justice and the strengthening of the bases of security and stability in the interests of all humankind.'

King Fahd thanked the chairman and deputy chairman of the council, and all its members, as well as all employees, for their good efforts, wishing the council and its session well in its proceedings and hoping it will succeed in realizing the goals on which it was formed. Chairman of the Shura Council Shaikh Bin Jubair then addressed the meeting, prior to handing over to King Fahd the council's annual report. He reviewed the past three years as a period of formulating the bases for progress such as the reformation and completion of internal regulations for the new system, and the commencement of operations after preparation of the personnel. The council also strengthened its relations with other authorities inside the Kingdom, as well as building ties with similar bodies overseas. Its contacts with the latter, whether visiting them or welcoming them to Saudi Arabia, have allowed a unique opportunity to brief others on the principles of Shura as contained in Islam, spread its ideas and clarify its application in the Kingdom. This year coincides with the 70th anniversary of the establishment of the first Shura council system by King Abdul Aziz.

Sheikh Bin Jubair reported that since the first session of the current Shura Council three years ago, there have been 103 general meetings, plus 588 meetings of its eight specialized committees, which have issued 130 resolutions, 102 of them endorsed in plenary sessions. The important thing, he stated, is not the number of resolutions, but the fact that the committees have worked with foresight and deep thought, taking their time to reach decisions which will have a lasting impact on the interests of the nation and its people, are suited to the faith and the shariah, and conform to society and its circumstances.

Embassy of Saudi Arabia, Washington, DC, 23 January 1997.

Chapter Four

POLITICAL REFORM

4A
Petition for change

A petition for political reform was drafted in the fall of 1990 and signed in December by forty-three public figures from religious and secular trends, among them former cabinet ministers, prominent businessmen, writers and university professors. The petition according to Middle East Watch is believed to have been drafted by Abdalla Manna, a doctor and a journalist known for voicing critical views of the government that led to his arrest a number of times. Seeking no doubt to disassociate themselves from any radical political group and attempting to avert retribution, the petitioners went to great lengths to demonstrate their loyalty. In a long preamble, they asserted their devotion to the King and their allegiance to 'the present system of government, and to preserving the cherished royal family'. The signatories proposed the following ten reforms:

1. A systematic framework for *fatwa*. It must take into consideration the Shari's, which is infallible and unchangeable, as represented in the unequivocal texts of the Qur'an and the Hadith. But jurisprudence commentaries, Qur'an interpreters' views and the opinions of Shari'a experts that are derived from divergent scholarly doctrines are all human attempts to comprehend the Shari'a texts. These views are affected by their authors' ability to understand, given their level of knowledge and skill. Shaped by the circumstances of time and place, these views are liable to being wrong as well as right, and should be subject to debate. Indeed, there has been a consensus among scholars that no one may ever claim the sole right to determine the meaning of the Qur'an or the Hadith or monopolize the right to decide Shari'a rules. It is therefore essential that we clearly and forcefully make a distinction between what is divine and what is human. The revealed and unambiguous texts must be accepted and obeyed. But scholarly opinions may be freely examined and questioned without any limits.

2. Consider issuing a basic law of government in light of the statements and declarations made by the rulers of the country at various times.

3. Formation of a consultative council comprising the elite from among the qualified and knowledgeable opinion makers known for their honesty, forthrightness, impartiality, morality and public service, representing all regions of the Kingdom. The council must have among its responsibilities the study, development and adoption of laws and rules related to all economic, political, educational and other issues and should exercise effective scrutiny of all executive agencies.

4. The revival of municipal councils; the implementation of the Law of Provinces; and the generalization of the chamber of commerce experience as a model for all other trades.

5. The investigation of all aspects of the judicial system, in all its degrees, types and areas of competence, for the purpose of modernizing its laws and evaluating the process of preparing judges and their assistants. Every step necessary must be taken to guarantee independence of the judiciary, to assure its effectiveness and fairness, spread its authority and strengthen its foundations. Schools that train for this important field must be open to all citizens, not reserved to one group over the others in violation of the Shari's-based principle of equality of opportunity.

6. Commitment to total equality among all citizens in all aspects of their life, without distinction based on ethnic, tribal, sectarian or social origins. The principle of protecting citizens against interference in their lives except by a court order must be firmly established.

7. Media policy must be reviewed and set according to a comprehensive and precise law reflecting the most advanced legislation in other countries. This law must enable all Saudi media to exercise their freedom in preaching good over evil, calling for virtue and shunning vice, and enriching dialogue in an open Muslim society.

8. Comprehensive reform of the Associations for the Propagation of Virtue and the Deterrence of Vice (Hai'at al-Amr bi al-Ma'rouf wa al-Nahi 'an al-Munkar). A precise law must be adopted specifying their functions and the method they must follow, and setting strict rules for hiring chiefs and members of precincts, to ensure judicious and tactful preaching.

9. Although we believe that nurturing the new generation is the highest duty of Muslim women, we nevertheless believe that there are numerous fields of public life where women can be allowed to participate – within the scope of the Shari'a – thus honoring them and acknowledging their role in building society.

10. God revealed His holy books, and sent His prophets, to educate and nurture humanity, proving that education is the foremost important basis for the renaissance and progress of nations. We believe that our

country's educational system is in need of comprehensive and fundamental reform to enable it to graduate faithful generations that are qualified to contribute positively and effectively in building the present and the future of the country, and to face the challenges of the age, enabling us to catch up with the caravan of nations that have vastly surpassed us in every field.

Translated by *Middle East Watch* with the following footnotes:

Paragraph 4: 'Elections for municipal councils were common in Saudi cities until 1963 when the last elections were annulled. The 1963 Law of Provinces, allowing for a limited degree of decentralization, has never been implemented. The vague reference to the chambers of commerce points to the unequal treatment of professional groups. While the chambers are allowed to operate in relative freedom, labor unions are banned and most other trade and professional organizations are restricted. For more details on these points, see the relevant sections in this report on elections, the Law of Provinces, and freedom of association.' Paragraph 5: 'Shi'a are excluded from Shari'a colleges. A degree from a recognized Shari'a college is required to serve as a judge or as an assistant.'

Paragraph 8: 'The reference is to the controversial religious police popularly known as 'the Zealots' (al-Mataw'a or Mutawwa'in). Their tactics are sometimes arbitrary and violent. Most of them are salaried civil servants who have the right to arrest, interrogate and detain those suspected of religious infractions.'

Published in *Saudi Arabia's New Basic Laws*, Middle East Watch, New York, 1992.

4B
A Religious Petition

Following the drafting of the so-called 'secular petition', scores of top religious leaders in Saudi Arabia signed the following document in February 1991, among them Sheikh Abdel-Aziz ibn Baz, the most eminent religious figure in the country and head of the government-appointed Council of Senior Scholars and the Institution of Ifta and Scholarly Research, the government agency in charge of all religious matters. The petition was also signed by other members of the council as well as several judges, university professors and preachers.

'In this critical period, everybody has recognized the need for change. We therefore find that the most requisite duty is to reform our present conditions that have caused us to suffer these tribulations. Consequently, we ask that the ruler of the nation check the deterioration of these conditions, which need reform in the following areas:

1. The formation of a consultative council to decide internal and external issues on the basis of the of the Shari'a. Its members must be honest, straightforward and representing all fields of expertise. They must be totally independent and not be subject to any pressure that may affect the authority of the council.
2. All laws and regulations of political, economic, administrative or other nature must be reconciled with the principles of the Shari'a. Trusted committees with expertise in Shari'a should be authorized to repeal legislation not conforming to Shari'a principles.
3. In addition to possessing specialized expertise, dedication and honesty, government officials and their overseas representatives must be unswervingly moral. Failing any one of the requirements for any reason is an abuse of public trust and a fundamental cause of injury to the national interest and reputation.
4. Justice must be applied, rights granted and duties assigned in full equality among all citizens, not favoring the nobles or begrudging the weak. Abuse of authority by anyone whether by shirking obligations or denying people what is their right is a cause for the break-up and annihilation of society.
5. All government officials, especially those occupying the highest positions, must be diligently scrutinized and must all be made accountable with no exceptions. Government agencies must be cleansed of anyone whose corruption or dereliction is proven, regardless of any other consideration.
6. Public wealth must be distributed fairly among all classes and groups. Taxes must be eliminated and fees that have overburdened citizens must be reduced. Government revenues must be protected from exploitation and abuse; priority in expenditure must be given to the most urgent necessities. All forms of monopoly or illegitimate ownership must be eliminated. Restrictions imposed on Islamic banks must be lifted. Public and private banking institutions must be cleansed of usury, which is an affront to God and His Prophet, and a cause for stunting the growth of wealth.
7. A strong and fully-integrated army must be built and fully equipped with weapons of all kinds, from any source. Attention must be given to manufacturing and developing arms. The goal of the army must be to protect the country and the Holy Sites.
8. Information media must be remodeled according to the adopted media policy of the Kingdom. The goals must be to educate, serve Islam and express the morals of society. The media must be purged of anything conflicting with these objectives. Its freedom to spread awareness through truthful reporting and constructive criticism must be safe-guarded within the confines of Islam.
9. Foreign policy must be based on national interest without relying on alliances not sanctioned by the Shari'a. It must also embrace Muslim

causes. The Kingdom's embassies must be reformed to enable them to reflect the Islamic nature of the country.

10. Religious and proselytizing institutions must be developed and strengthened with financial and human resources. All obstacles preventing them from fully carrying out their objectives must be removed.

11. Judicial institutions must be unified and granted full and effective independence. Juridical authority must apply to all. It is necessary to establish an independent body whose function is to ensure carrying out judicial orders.

12. The rights of individuals and society must be guaranteed. Every restriction on people's rights and their will must be removed, to ensure the enjoyment of human dignity, within the acceptable religious safeguards.

Translated by *Middle East Watch*, according to which the petition dated February 1991, was prefaced: 'In the name of God, the Compassionate, the Merciful. Custodian of the Holy Shrines, may God guide his steps. May peace, God's mercy and His blessing be upon you. This government has been distinguished by declaring that it has adopted the Shari'a. Scholars have always performed their religious duty of providing counsel to their rulers.' According to Middle East Watch, the phrase 'on the basis of the Shari'a' in paragraph 1, was added by Shaikh Abdel Aziz Ibn Baz, confirmed in a footnote in the original.

4C
Letter to the Grand Mufti from a defected diplomat

The first Diplomat of the Saudi Arabian mission to the UN, Muhammad Abdallah Al-Khilewi, defected to the USA in May 1994. At the same time he sent this cable to the 'Religious Leader' in Saudi Arabia.

No.1a
Date: 7 Zul Hijja 1414 A.H., 17 May 1994
URGENT TELEGRAM

To: His Reverence the Grand Mufti of (K.S.A.) Sheikh Abdul Aziz Ben Baz.
Copy: Prince Abdallah Abdallah Ben Abdel Aziz, the crown prince.
Copy: Prince Talal Ben Abdel Aziz, president of BGFUND.
Copy: The president and members of the Shura council.
Copy: The Committee for the Defence of Legitimate Rights (London).

In the name of Allah, Master of the universe, and Peace be upon our Messenger, the faithful mentor, our Prophet Mohammad. Peace be upon him, his family, his companions and those who follow his guidance to the last day.

Allah (S.W.T.) says: 'Kings, when they enter a country, despoil it, and make the noblest of its people its meanest, thus do they behave.'

His Reverence Sheikh Ben Baz, thirteen years ago, to be exact on 13th of June, 1983 A.D. corresponding to 21 Shaban 1402 A.H., our people gave you the trust of 'the pledge of allegiance' after the death of the chaste king Khaled may the mercy of Allah be upon him. And because Allah has warned us that 'Tumult and oppression are worse that slaughter', every one adhered to that 'pledge' because of religious as well as rational reasons despite the fact that his brother Fahed was not up to the hopes and aspirations of many people who knew him, especially his relatives, and especially after his appointment as Interior Minister on 13 October 1962 A.D. (1382 A.H.). This tyrant king did not try to dispel the doubts about him and his brothers Nayef and Salman, especially their suspected role in the assassination of King Faisal on 13 Rabi Awal 1395 A.H. (March 1975) after he – King Faisal – put forward a serious proposal laying down conditions for the selection of rulers from the ruling family. Such a move by King Faisal did not bode well for Fahed, especially since King Faisal has previously deposed his brother Saud on 27 Jumada II 1384 A.H. So Fahed was directly involved in embroiling Faisal Ben Musaed and his American girl friend (Barbara Sherman) in a drugs addiction and dealing problem during his study in the U.S.A. He also supervised from the place of his stay in Waldorf Astoria hotel the transfer of Faisal Ben Musaed aboard his private jet from New York airport. Then he pressed for an order banning Faisal Ben Musaed from travel abroad for two years. He also helped Ben Musaed be in the presence of King Faisal while armed with a loaded pistol, despite the fact that Ben Musaed was registered as the brother of Khaled Ben Musaed who was killed during the attack on the television building. Finally, he closed the file of enquiry regarding the assassination of King Faisal in a suspiciously short time. He also caused the death of his brother Khaled who died out of distress after learning from the third Islamic summit in Makkah in 1401 A.H. that his government has supported a civil war in a muslim country.

Allah (S.W.T.) says: 'O' ye who believe! If a wicked person comes to you with any news, ascertain the truth, lest ye harm people unwittingly, and afterward become full of repentance for what ye have done.'

We the undersigned know will that you and who ever looks at this document do not accept claims without proof and can only accept facts and we share you this view. We do not have till now any documentary proof of everything that was mentioned earlier. But since the Allah has tried us with this mob – Fahed and his clan – a group of decent people from our nation have in secret and in public gathered to slow down the decline of our country both at an internal and an external level. To participate was the least we could do to help our country, we established a secret peaceful society named 'Man and Peace' on 9 Ramadan 1407 A.H. Our only legitimate aim is to affect reform by enlightened work away from ambiguity, grudges and personal interests. This is the first public statement we have made since our foundation where our efforts were concentrated for such a day.

We announce that with Allah's Grace we have managed since that day to obtain 13719 secret documents with their original stamps and signatures. Documents incoming and outgoing from the Prime Ministers office, ministries of defence, exterior, interior and the secret service (General Intelligence Dept). All documents were collected by patriot citizens of our country without the help directly or indirectly from a foreign country.

We enclose some of these documents which leave no doubt that this mob is working hard to destroy the country at two levels:

First: Stir internal differences that will result in splitting the country, God forbid. This is done by inventing enmities between the one people on sectarian grounds, sometimes between the Shia and the Sunnah, others between Hanbail, Maliki and Shafi' schools of thought, tribal feuds and regional feuds. To the extent of employing extremists from various groups to act in a way that will only take the society back to pre-Islamic feuds. Government money is being spent on such projects instead of being spent to create an atmosphere of harmony and unity.

Second: Embroiling the state at government and at people's levels in wars and enmities with Muslim countries, both Arab and non-Arab, is forcing the state to enter into nuclear agreements that are not accepted by Muslim governments or people. This is not to mention putting the whole region under the mercy of foreign nuclear fleets.

We pledge, with Allah as our witness and all the sincere people and establishments of our people that we will be fully responsible for the security and the secrecy of these documents and we will not publish anything that may endanger our security and sovereignty. We further emphasise that our group has no personal goals, political, economic or social. Therefore we will only publish from time to time things that will help achieve the demands of our preserving people, which are:

1. The implementation of clause B in article 5 of the constitution of government issued under reference number (a/90) on 27 Sha'ban 1412 A.H. under direct supervision of the Shura Council according to the \ second article of the construction of the Shura council issued on 27 Sha'ban 1412 A.H.
2. The cancellation of all that could help the disintegration of our society in any way and to clean up the government departments from all systems that will cause such tragedies especially the education and media departments.
3. Refraining from entering into any unlimited and permanent international agreements especially nuclear agreements and refusing to make our land a dumping or testing round for nuclear and other weapons.
4. Announcing that this year's Hajj is the last one where the number of pilgrims is limited, because Muslims are sick and tired of the quotas system that limits the number of pilgrims accepted every year and that decreases year after year, no matter what the excuses may be, political, security related or otherwise. Our holy places should not be used as an arena for political games with other countries.

5. The fair distribution of wealth and power by cancelling all the rules that protect monopolies and immediately stopping any special family privileges and the immediate implementation of the following:

(a) The compensation of all state employees, both civilian and military, for the unfair treatment they got since the 'pledge'. Since then they had no salary increases despite the fact that the price of commodities and services increase continuously, which means that the salaries should be increased by at least 150% to meet these price increases.

(b) Fighting the ills in our society that cause discrimination against women. Women are our mothers, sister, wives and daughters. Any woman who has two children or more, or who looks after a disabled person should be paid at least SR75000.

(c) The release of all state prisoners, political and others including foreign prisoners.

His reverence Sheik Ben Baz, we share you your prayer to Allah to save our country and the Muslim Ummah from the tortures of tumult. Our faithful people put it upon your shoulders again to work for the realisation of their legitimate demands as they have almost lost patience with this mob who understood their perseverance as cowardliness, and their silence as acceptance.

We pray Allah, then we ask you and all sincere people in our nation to work for regaining those rights before the end of this year and before those who are spiteful of our people become active. Disturbing the security inside the country does not take as much as the security agencies would like us to believe. It is no exaggeration to say that security cannot be achieved without justice. Disturbing the peace would take no more than a few matches to light up some oil or fuel installations, some burning tyres, stones and oil on the highways to cripple transport and as to the crowds of Hajj and Umrah, it would only require a few spiteful people who are sick in the spirit or after money to turn the event into a disaster.

May Allah protect us all from the tyrants and the spiteful and let us all work according to Allah's orders where He says: 'O Mankind! We created you from a single [pair] of a male and a female, and made you into nations and tribes, that ye may know each other, verily the most honoured amongst you in the sight of God is [he who is] the most righteous of you.'

We ask Allah [S.W.T.] to make our intentions sincere, our heart pure, our resolve strong and our work blessed. peace and prayers be upon our Prophets, his family and his companions.

Signed by,
Fahed Al-Kahtani Muhammad Abdalla Al-Khilewi, Founding Member Official Spokesman, Makkah New York
7 Zul Hijja 1414 A.H. 7 Zul Hijja 1414 A.H.

4D
Open letter from a citizen

Mohammad H. Siddiq, Saudi Arabian citizen, living in the USA, called on King Fahad in the newspaper 'Crescent' 1995.

King Fahd, Assalamu Alaikum: We, the people of Arabia, are outraged at how public policies are hurting our children, our families and our country. We are dismayed that after investing over $250 billion in weaponry, our country is still unable to look after its own defence. We are shocked when we learn that our national debt is $100 billion and climbing, and our budget deficit is deteriorating. We are ashamed when we see our basic human rights being violated and our freedom being depressed. We are scared at the way drugs, crime and corruption are spreading everywhere and threatening our children, our families and our homes.

We say the tragic price our children, families and country is paying demands something to be done to end what's going on. The reason for all these wrongdoings is with you. King Fahd! We see you as amoral, profoundly committed only to your own political and financial advancement, ruthless in getting your way and untrustworthy in accounting for your actions. We see you as antithetical to our values, our pocketbook and our future. We see you as disgrace to your office, worse than that, a disgrace to Islam. And we see your government as a family-based autocracy that behaves like an army of occupation, which is wasteful, out of control and prey to all sorts of special interests. We see your government as an 18th-century horse and buggy system that's trying to operate in 1995 sophisticated world of politics and economics.

Our children, families and country are being hurt too much and we believe it is unconscionable for us to remain silent. Our simple understanding of the Shura system is 'it is the right of the people to alter or abolish the government'. Therefore, we are determined to participate fully in the running of our country, to break your monopoly on power, stop the waste of country's wealth, reform the judiciary and determine foreign and other policies. We are Muslims. We do not like shallow promposity and we do not like kings or royal government. We want to change Arabia to a country in which the true belief in Allah is once again at the centre of definition of the Arabian peninsula.

We want a government in which the State is subservient to the best interests of the individuals who compose it. A government that works for us and is not captured by Fahd, Sultan, Naif, Salman or any other amir. Specifically, we want an Islamic form of government, a free enterprise economic system, a legal system which guarantees individuals equal right to jobs, education, health-care and freedom of expression, including criticism of our own government.

We want respect of human rights in a framework of Shura. We urge you to get out of the way and let the good Muslims of this nation do the necessary reform. Thank you and God bless you.

Mohammad H. Siddiq, Lincoln, Nebraska, 'The Crescent' USA, 'The Crescent'
1–15 December 1995.

Chapter Five

ISLAMIC STATE

5A
A matter of interpretation

Freedom of expression in the Muslim world is a matter of judgement by the ruling power, since Sharia does not offer a fixed position, but plenty of room for interpretation. This is stated by a Canadian writer, Marika Tamm in her 'Comparative Legal Study of Blasphemy and Subversive Speech in International Human Rights Laws and the Laws of the Muslim World':

The aim has been to take a serious look at the gulf that seems to separate the Muslim world and the Western world surrounding the prohibition of free speech in the name of 'blasphemy' or 'subversion'. It has been the premise of this study that this gulf can only begin to be bridged once those of us immersed in the Western tradition – from where international human rights law certainly had its origins – progress beyond superficial general-izations about Islam as a 'bastion of repression' and make a real effort to understand the concepts of blasphemy and subversion as they are set out in Islamic law. Certainly, not all governments that censor free speech remain faithful to the letter and spirit of the law they purport to follow – this is equally true in the West as it is in the East – but a precondition of wagging an accusative finger at 'corrupt' governments is surely an intelligent and informed basis for any such complaints.

Freedom of political expression

The study has found that under Islamic law there is generally greater scope for governments to silence political expression that offends them than there is under international human rights law. Because of the way the political organization of the Islamic state is structured, it appears to be left almost entirely up to the ruler to decide for himself how much political dissent he will tolerate. There are specific crimes in Islamic law that define 'rebellion against the government' and 'transgression against legitimate authority', but since there is so much disagreement and conflict among the various Islamic schools of law about which definitions to use, it seems that the real purpose of these crimes is effectively to enable the ruler to make his own personal judgement. Although the ruler remains bound by the 'general principles and spirit' of the Shari'a , since interpretation is never an exact science but is always the subjective construction of interested human beings, this fact actually has only limited effect in constraining and structuring the ruler's wide discretion.

There is thus a fundamental conceptual difference between the classical Islamic model of the state and the democratic constitutionalism on which international law is founded. Under the constitutional model, a government enjoys its power over the people by virtue of having received a mandate from the people to govern. It is important that individual citizens, once they accept the obligation to be bound by the authority of their rulers, retain the right to withdraw the mandate if they become dissatisfied by the government's performance. This is the rationale under which instruments such as the ICCPR (International Covenant on Civil and Political Rights, document 8B, *ed*.) have entrenched so broadly the individual right to free political criticism: it is only when such criticism is allowed that the structure of the state will continue to reflect a head of state whose authority is based not on privilege or the ability to terrorize but on the people's continued acceptance to be bound by that authority.

When we examine the clampdowns on political expression in modern Muslim states, we begin to get some idea of what sort of ramifications the Islamic political model might have. Many states have constitutional provisions or laws limiting all political expression to that which 'respects' or 'safeguards' the current governmental ideology. For instance, Iran's constitution stipulates that the mass media '*must* serve the diffusion of Islamic culture *in support of* the evolutionary cause of the Islamic Revolution' and '*must strictly refrain* from diffusion of destructive anti-Islamic practices' [emphasis added]. Egypt has penal laws banning any political expression that 'instigates hatred of the ruling system', 'humiliates government officials or the army', or 'excites public opinion'. Indonesia has an Anti-Subversion Act that defines 'subversion' as dissent from its official five-point state ideology the 'Pancasila', and not only censors such dissenting political expression but also prosecutes those responsible under its criminal laws. In Iran and Egypt the Shari'a is declared in the constitution to be a principal source of law; in Indonesia the Shari'a is not a principal source of law, but it is enshrined as the official state religion. There are grounds, then, in all these country situations for positing that the Islamic law's approach to the freedom of political expression had at least some influence in shaping these laws. Certainly, there would seem to be nothing in the Shari'a that would *prevent* a government from suppressing 'anti-Islamic', humiliating', or 'subversive' political expression once it perceives a need to protect itself from any threats to its hold on power that this free speech might constitute. International human rights law would take an entirely different view. Banning in the first instance all political expression that does not respect, does not support, humiliates, or effectively contradicts official government ideology is completely antithetical to the International Bill's stipulation that everyone must have, as a basic rule, the freedom to express their dislike of the government in power. International law does allow states to restrict these voices of dissent in certain circumstances, but it has very strict tests that a government must meet. From the international law perspective, legitimate political dissent turns into dangerous subversion only when there is force or violence used to get the message across, when the welfare of the nation as a whole is at risk, or when there is a real chance that civilized society would grind to a halt as a result of the oppositional political activities. Also, governments would be able to prohibit political 'hate propaganda' directed at them if they can establish that there is absolutely no factual foundation upon which this criticism could be based: blatant lies may be suppressed, but value judgements based on true facts, even if these hurt or offend, must be permitted.

Suppression of religious freedom

The most notable aspect of Islamic law as it affects the ability of a modern society's diversity of faiths to live together in harmony is the capital crime of apostasy. Apostasy is formally defined as 'the revocation of Islam by a Muslim'; thus at the very least it prevents any Muslims living under an Islamic state from freely changing their religion. However, in practice the law of apostasy seems to have the potential to go even further in the discouragement of religious diversity and the suppression of dissent from religious orthodoxy. For in the Sudan the apostasy law has been used to arrest, try, and execute the leader of an Islamic movement advocating reform of the Shari'a; this man was considered an apostate not because he denounced Islam – in fact, he identified himself as a devout Muslim – but because he did not accept all the doctrines and teachings exactly as set forth by the orthodoxy followed by the ruling power.

In addition to the crime of apostasy, there are two other significant areas of Islamic law that appear to allow states to curtail freedom of religious worship and expression. First, the classical Islamic concept of the 'People of the Book' appears still to be used in some states to mandate legal discrimination against all minority faiths except other orthodox Islamic schools and Christians, Jews, and Zoroastrians. Thus, for example, in Iran the followers of the Bahai faith are denied the right both to profess and practice their religion as a result of legal discrimination and routine closure and destruction by state agents of Bahai holy shrines, historical sites, and other properties.

The third main type of Islamic religious censorship appears to have its source in the Islamic ruler's discretion to create 'blasphemy'-type offenses under the *ta'azir* provisions of Shari'a criminal law. Using this power, any treatment of religious subject matter contrary to the orthodox representation may potentially be prohibited as insulting or violating the honour and reputation of Islam. Thus in Jordan, film-makers are forbidden to 'propagate atheism', and writers are prohibited from discussing Judaism or unorthodox interpretations of Islam. In Egypt, a novel with a dream sequence involving the Prophet was banned. And in Indonesia, a newspaper opinion poll ranking the popularity of the Prophet against pop stars and other secular heroes was denounced as 'blasphemous'.

While international law does allow some restrictions on offensive religious expression, these come nowhere near the wide prohibitions on anything 'unorthodox' that Islamic law has been seen to permit. The International Bill of Rights enshrines the freedom of religion for everyone; this includes the absolute right to hold any belief of one's choosing, whether it be the belief in a positive religion or the belief in no religion at all, and includes the absolute right to change one's religion at will. Thus even the narrowest interpretation of Islamic apostasy (the revocation of Islam by Muslims) is quite inimical to international human rights law.

Under international law a state may indeed prohibit the advocacy of religious hatred, a prohibition which on its face seems much like the restrictions on insult to Islam in the Islamic 'blasphemy' laws. And there does appear to exist some overlap between the two approaches, since they both agree that a subjective intention on the part of the speaker to instigate hatred is not necessary, but justify the prohibition (at least in theory) as warranted due to the harmful effect on the religious community that feels offended.

Yet there are still important differences. In Shari'a law the ruler appeals to his own judgement to decide what sort of offensive expression will harm the community's sensibilities, while in internal law the test for community agitation, hostility, or discrimination is always a local, contextual one. And under international law a state's permissible prohibition of free speech that offends public religious morality requires 'morality' to be defined not according to the government's gut feeling, as it does in Islamic law, but rather as a measure of the general consensus of the local community in contemporary times.

The central distinction between the traditional Islamic restrictions on religious expression and international law's modern, secular definitions appears thus to be that the one is concerned with 'taboo' *subject matter* while the other emphasises the *manner of expression* as the cause of the offense. For the Islamic laws of religious offense are defined with reference to certain sacred 'truths' that may not be contradicted, challenged, satirized, or ridiculed – it is the affront to the *ideas* themselves that is seen as threatening to the very fabric of Islamic society. Thus discussion of the life of the Prophet Mohammed, the teachings and beliefs of unorthodox religious sects, or generally any secular treatment of religious subject matter are all strictly forbidden. In international law, in contrast, the actual measurable *effect* that the manner of expression of the ideas in question may have on the local community is what constitutes the affront to social order. If the dissenting religious speech is expressed in such a hateful way as to incite discrimination, hostility, or violence in the community, then it may be suppressed; but there is no religious subject matter *prima facie* excluded from question, challenge, satire, or insult.

Muslim human rights charters

This outline of the basic differences between international human rights law's tests for blasphemous and subversive speech and the rules of the Shari'a considers only the orthodox, or classical, articulation of Islamic law. On the one hand, the orthodoxy is arguably the most important set of teachings for the human rights advocate to study, for the overwhelming majority of Islamic states, 'Islamization' programs, and campaigns in the name of Islamic 'fundamentalism' are indeed grounded in the orthodox tradition. When a Muslim government bans a book, closes down a play, or jails a writer, and justifies these acts by appeals to 'Islam', it is the orthodox articulation of the Shari'a that it has in mind. But on the other hand, since this tradition does appear to present such extensive barriers for international human rights campaigners to surmount, it may also be useful to examine alternative approaches to Islamic law that stake out positions close to international law's.

One such alternative approach this study has examined consists of efforts by concerned Muslim citizens living in Muslim states to draft their own 'human rights' charters, in a similar manner in which groups in Africa, the Americas, and Europe have produced parallel instruments to those proclaimed by the UN. However, while the effort has been made, the results hoped for – that the Muslim instruments would foster cooperation and consensus with the world community – seem to be a long way off from materializing. The basic problem appears to be that some of these charters model themselves almost entirely after the International Bill without making any effort to address the competing concerns of the Islamic Shari'a (e.g., the draft Charter on Human and People's Rights in the Arab World), while others set out human rights criteria on their face but then undo them all by subsuming the entire instrument to the demands of the Shari'a (e.g., the Cairo Declaration on Human Rights in Islam). Unfortunately neither of these approaches is likely to be very useful to human rights campaigners. It would certainly be welcomed by the international community if Arab governments around the world were to endorse and commit themselves to the Arab Charter, but given the extremely poor response so far this goal seems unrealistic. As for the Islamic Declaration, commitments by OIC (Organization of Islamic Conference, *ed.*) member state governments to the instrument are unlikely to help the international community, since the inherent limitations of the document take the issues back around in a circle to force a confrontation with the Shari'a one more.

Islamic law reform

The other alternative to Islamic orthodoxy that this study has touched upon is the attempt to 'reform' traditional Shari'a law to make it more in line with the social realities of the modern world. The key to the reformist position is that it contests the theory that the Shari'a law appealed to by Islamic orthodoxy today represents in its entirety a fixed, divinely inspired moral order that may no longer be improved or adapted. Instead, the reformists' examination of the history of the development of Islamic law shows that this 'divine moral order' of the Shari'a as a whole is actually a dated *human construction* of those who have traditionally held political and social power. It is true that Islamic law is ultimately based on the Holy Qur'an, which essentially consists of the divine message as transcribed by the Prophet Mohammed, but the Qur'an must necessarily be *interpreted* in order to form the body of Shari'a law that will be applied to regulate the conduct of Muslin believers. The history of Shari'a jurisprudence indeed makes no secret of the importance of interpretation: the Shari'a never consisted of the words of the Qur'an or the examples of Mohammed (Sunna) alone, but was always supplemented by the opinions and reasoning of learned Muslim men. And during the first few hundred years, ordinary, common Muslims could exercise their own powers of interpretation similarly, studying the Qur'an and Sunna and deciding for themselves how to live their lives in keeping with their faith. Later, however, the doctrine of the 'closing of the gates' of interpretation set in, and the rules of the Shari'a were deemed to be at last settled and decided and no longer negotiable by ordinary Muslim minds.

Modern Islamic law reform movements argue that interpretation or re-interpretation by everyone should continue to flourish instead of being now denied to all but the political elite. For like all texts, the Qur'an is susceptible to a multitude of potentially conflicting interpretations by interested, fallible, sometimes even ill-intentioned human beings . . .

Marika Tamm: *Freedom of Expression in the Muslim World*, prepared by International Human Rights Programme, Faculty of Law, University of Toronto, and The Canadian Center, International PEN, Toronto, Canada, 1 April, 1992.

5B
Hajj – beyond rituals

*The Muslim 'Crescent International' in April 1996 objected to the
Saudi control and use of the Hajj – the pilgrimage to Mecca.*

Not only material but even the spiritual resources of the *Ummah* have been
usurped by the declared enemies of Allah. In most Muslim countries,
mosques are 'nationalised' and *imams* are handed down *khutbahs* prepared
by the ministry of auqaf to deliver to the congregation. The *minbar* from
where the noble messenger of Allah, upon whom be peace, used to address
the believers, has today been reduced to a platform for extolling the non-
existent virtues of tyrants.

Even so sacred an institution as the Hajj has been trivialised. Few realise
today that it is the largest annual assembly of the *Ummah* where the
problems confronting Muslims worldwide should be discussed. When the
Prophets Ibrahim and Ismail, upon them both be peace, built the Ka'ba,
Allah accepted their prayer to make Makkah a city of peace and incline
people's hearts towards it (2: 125–126). Since that day, people have
performed pilgrimage to the House of Allah. The Prophet Ibrahim did not
perform simple rituals or indulge in transcendental meditation. He was the
first 'rebel' in the cause of Allah who challenged the tyrannical authority of
Nimrod. Hajj is the sunnah of such a Prophet, yet it would be difficult to
find many Muslims today who view it in this light.

There has been a deliberate attempt to divert Hajj of its true meaning
and significance as ordained by Allah in the Qur'an and exemplified by the
noble messenger of Allah. The rituals of Hajj are so ingrained that Muslims
have come to believe that that is all that is required of them. Each year,
more than two million Muslims assemble in the plains of Arafat but in this
sea of humanity everyone is only for himself/herself. There is hardly a
thought spared for the suffering Muslims. Is this what the great assembly is
all about? Are Muslims truly following the sunnah of the noble messenger
when they gather in Arafat?

The enemies of Allah can kill at will but Muslim must not defend
themselves. They must not talk about these issues even in the House of
Allah! Has not Allah commended the believers to fight if they are attacked?
. . . Tens of thousands of Muslim women have been raped in Bosnia and
Kashmir, yet Muslims must not do anything to stop these crimes. A blind,
diabetic *alim*, Shaikh Omar Abdel Rahman, is humiliated by stripping him
naked in a US prison, yet Muslims must remain silent. If Muslims cannot
talk about these issues at Hajj, where else can they do so?

When performing Hajj, Muslims are the guests of Allah because they
arrive in His House. Muslims are required to declare openly their
dissociation from all the worldly powers as commanded by Allah in the

Qur'an (9: 1–3). This awareness would lead to certain consequences. Muslims would realize that the House of Saud itself is the greatest impediment in the struggle against *kufr*. Muslims perform the Rami (symbolic stoning of the devils) but fail to make the connection that the worldly *shayateen* – the rulers of America, Britain, France, Russia, Israel, India and their agents including the House of Saud, Mubarak, Hasan, Husain *et al.* – are still safe.

Unless the Haramain are taken out of the control of the House of Saud, the sacred institution of Hajj will continue to be abused.

Editorial in the *Crescent International*, 16–30 April 1996, Toronto/Islamabad/ London.

5C
Saudi Arabia not true to Islam

Professor Muhammed Al-Mass'ari in an April 1996 interview disputed the religious legitimacy of Saudi Arabia.

Since the time of Abdel Aziz we could not declare Saudi Arabia to be a true Islamic state. It is not true to Islam and not even protecting Islam.

– *Not even protecting?*
Mass'ari: No, it has not lived up to what you would expect from the champion Islamic state in international relations. The Saudi stand in the Palestinian question? At best a neutral observer. Their stand in the Afghani affair? Miserable, doing just the job for the United States as the American cashiers. Look at Bosnia, complete misery. And this nominal title of 'Custodian of the two Holy Mosques'. It may have had a value at a time, when people could not read and write. But at a time, when 65 or 70 percent of our population read and write and hundreds of thousands graduate from high school and universities, this kind of facade will not help very much.

– *But still there is an alliance between the religious scholars, the clergy and the ruling family. You think the family has the upper hand?*
Mass'ari: Essentially since the clergy has submitted to a level of rubber stamp of our royal family . . .

– *Do they have a choice?*
Mass'ari: Oh, I think they have, but they fail to see it. We should not forget that the people issuing fatwas today are all in their sixties, seventies and eighties. So they were educated and their will and world was shaped in the fifties. At that time the power was unquestionable. But there were no Islamic forces. Now there is a very big schism with the Islamic strength posing a challenge to the rulers. It is like a root decease in a tooth, it does

not appear quickly. But when it does, you need to remove the whole thing. Now, the root of the Saud family is completely damaged – and you need to remove it just as well.

– But the family appoints the members of the ulema committee.
Mass'ari: That is one of the major arguments, common for all the present reform movements in Saudi Arabia. Actually the existing clergy are not scholars by their merits as in Islamic history. They have been made scholars by the regime. Among the thousands of students, the regime promotes those who are pro-regime and give them the role of issuing fatwas. But in Islamic history the main source of credibility has been how much the clergy has confronted the regime. The more they confronted the local regime and went to jail, the more credibility they gained. This in fact is coming back with the young generation, they are jailed in Saudi Arabian in growing numbers and their credibility and trustworthiness is increasing. Several clergy have been arrested – in the eyes of the people it will add to their credibility, since still in the people's eyes the government is not on the side of the truth. And the job of the clergy and reformers and thinkers is to make the government accountable to the people. If the clergy just goes with the government, they will be nothing but government scholars, they will never lead the masses. Remember, the scholars have no organization, and they should not have it. But they should have an accounting, controlling function.

Interview conducted in London, April 1996.

5D
The religious structure

Interpretation by the United States Information Service in Riyadh, 1996.

The 'Ulama . . .
Saudi Arabia is the birthplace of the Prophet Muhammad, the land where he first preached the creed of Islam. Islam's two holiest shrines are located in the Saudi Arabian cities of Makkah and Madina. The unification of the Kingdom and the rise of the House of Saud are inextricable bound up with the Islamic revival Wahhabism represents. The *'Ulama*, the functional equivalent of the clergy, therefore, have real power. They are probably the only group outside the Royal Family capable of having a significant impact on important decisions. They are also the only group capable of somewhat successful opposition to outlandish desires of the Royal Family.

The organizational structure of the *'ulama* in Saudi Arabia is not well understood. Technically, any man who has completed extensive religious studies can be considered an 'alim (the singular of *'ulama* – i.e., a man of religion). '*Ulama* express their influence through a higher council of '*ulama* that meets regularly with the King and senior members of the Royal Family, which seeks to use them as an important source of religious legitimacy. In addition, they act as a powerful force within the religiously based Saudi judiciary system in interpreting and applying shari'a, the Islamic legal code.

Influential 'ulama also exist outside of the formal government structures and make their views known via *khutbas* (sermons delivered in mosques on Fridays), their writings, and the production of video and audio tapes.

The King and Royal Family usually make policy changes only after consulting with this group, and the speed of socio-economic development throughout the Kingdom is a matter of constant negotiation. The King or one of his senior brothers meets weekly with the senior '*ulama*. Although the Royal Family has been able to make a considerable number of changes in Saudi society over the objections of the '*ulama* (including the introduction of the telephone, radio, television, satellite dishes, female education, de facto interest banking, and civil regulations that supplement shari'a), the '*ulama* act as powerful brake on political and social change.

Radio and television are closely controlled to insure that neither runs afoul of the '*ulama*. The charging or paying of interest by banks is prohibited as un-Islamic (although banks have exploited the device of selling 'shares' in a bank's profits as an equivalent, legal means of paying for the use of money). Religious subjects take up as much as half of the time children spend in elementary and secondary school classroom.

The '*ulama* are becoming a more heterogeneous body than they once were in Saudi society. Most of the '*ulama* (and particularly the senior ones) are old men who lack non-religious education and have never traveled outside of the Kingdom of Saudi Arabia. At one time, observers characterized the older generation as reactionary, the younger generation as more open and receptive to change. The elderly Grand Mufti of Saudi Arabia, for example, once publicly took the position that the world is flat. An emerging younger generation of '*ulama* appears to feel comfortable with Western technology even if they are as uncomfortable with Western society, whether in its secular or its Judeo-Christian manifestations, as their elders. More recently, however, such neat distinctions have clearly broken down. Some of the religious leaders who are most prominently in opposition to Westernization and even in some cases to the Saudi monarchy itself are under forty years of age. it is clear that a significant portion of the younger generation views the older religious leadership as having been 'co-opted' by the government and as having compromised 'Islamic values.' Neither 'generation' is monolithic, however, and on certain issues even leaders thought to have been co-opted by the government have shown the capacity to stake out an independent position and hold to it. The Saudi Government, for example, planned to attend the 1994 UN Conference on Population and Development in Cairo. The '*ulama*, however, on its own initiative waged a highly public campaign against the Conference, branding it an attempt to impose un-Islamic values on the Muslim world, calling for a boycott of the Conference by Muslim nations, and generating a climate of public debate so charged that the Saudi Government felt compelled to stay away from the Conference. It similarly opposed the 1995 Beijing Conference on Women. In short, the role of the *'ulama* in Saudi society is likely to be contested for years to come. Despite the fact that Saudis speak of Islam as 'a total way of life' and denounce any split between the sacred and the secular as un-Islamic, the monarchy naturally wants as a practical matter to divide the world into secular and sacred, charging the Government with the control of the secular and the *'ulama* with the carefully circumscribed sacred sphere. Tensions between the *'ulama* and the government will likely, therefore, continue to cloak itself in Islamic garb, complicating an already confusing picture.

The *'ulama* are a difficult body to contact, and even more difficult to work with on programs. Most of its members are neither interested in the bulk of USIS programming nor keen on any relationship with Westerners. Few Saudi religious leaders speak any English. Islamic universities and colleges in the cities of Makkah and Madina cannot be visited by non-Muslims. USIS does, however, maintain some contact with this group through the Imam Muhammad Bin Saud Islamic University in Riyadh, one of Saudi Arabia's premier religious colleges, and through selected contacts with other Saudi Arabian institutions and Pan-Islamic institutions.

United States Information Service (USIS), Riyadh, 1996.

5E
Ramadan message from King Fahad

King Fahad and Crown Prince Abdullah, January 1996: a Royal Embassy of Saudi Arabia press release.

On the occasion of the arrival of the Holy Month of Ramadan, Custodian of the Two Holy Mosques King Fahd Bin Abdul Aziz and Crown Prince Abdullah Bin Abdul Aziz, Deputy Prime Minister and Commander of the National Guard, today issued the following speech:
'Brother citizens:
The Holy Month of Ramadan has arrived, which Almighty God has said is the month when there was sent down the Qur'an to guide mankind and to give clear signs for judging what is right and what is wrong, and during which everyone should fast. The Prophet Muhammad declared that Ramadan is a blessed month and that fasting during it is a compulsory act, saying: 'The doors of Paradise are open and the doors of Hell are closed

during the Holy Month of Ramadan; moreover, in this month there is one night that is better than a thousand months.'

As we are receiving and welcoming this Holy Month, we would like to greet all citizens, residents, visitors and all Muslims throughout the world, praying to Almighty God to help us all fast its days and pray its nights. We also pray that all martyrs and all deceased be forgiven, whether from among our citizens or from the Muslim Nation. In this blessed month we should look at ourselves and do our best to behave in the proper and straight way to enable our fasting and our prayers to be accepted; in so doing, prosperity, security and stability will be bestowed upon us. We should continue in pious deeds in line with the verse of the Holy Qur'an that says: 'Ye who believe, bow down, prostrate yourselves, and adore your Lord, and do good, that ye may prosper.'

With the advent of this Holy Month we come to the end of a year full of developments. In spite of some relaxation in Palestine and in Bosnia-Herzegovina, there are still some painful situations such as the continuation of disputes, among the factions in Somalia, and those in Afghanistan, and in Chechnya. We have been following these events, and are aware of the ordeal of our brethren Muslims as the result of continuing war and tyranny. We are hopeful that Ramadan will bring the healing of injury and the raising of the voice of right, peace, and justice. If Muslims had meditated on the Holy Qur'an and followed its teachings and those of the Prophet and adhered to the Islamic creed in spirit as well as in letter, then the situation would not have deteriorated and Muslim ranks would not be divided. The Holy Qur'an says: 'And hold fast, all together, by the rope which God stretches out for you, and be not divided among yourselves', and again: 'Obey God and His apostle, and fall into no disputes, lest ye lose heart and your power depart; be patient and strong.' The Kingdom of Saudi Arabia, its government and its people, honored to serve the Two Holy Mosques and the pilgrims to them, and ever mindful of enabling the guests of God perform their rituals in line with the teachings of the Holy Qur'an and the Sunna, will spare no effort in the service of Islam and Muslims throughout the world.

We pray to Almighty God that all our good goals be realized and that we are all enabled to fast the days and pray the nights of this generous and blessed month.

Royal Embassy of Saudi Arabia, Washington, DC: press release via the Internet, 20 January 1996.

Chapter Six

RELIGIOUS POLICE

6A
The Muttawa

The US Army during the Gulf crises 1990/91 advised its soldiers not to argue with the religious police.

In Saudi Arabia, there exists a group known as the Organization for the Promotion of Virtue and Prevention of Vice – referred to as the Muttawa. They are the Islamic religious police. The Muttawa strictly enforce store and restaurant closings for prayer time, appropriate dress and behavior in public, and other Islamic laws and customs. They often use a switch-like stick to chastise people suspected of violations.

If you are stopped by the Muttawa be polite but firm, correct the offense, and gracefully depart the area. Do not make the situation worse by making provocative gestures or using abusive language. Do not surrender your military ID card.

If the Muttawa are accompanied by a uniformed police officer, you may have no choice but to follow his instructions, including being taken into custody. If the offense is not serious, you will be released in a relatively short time – probably with a stern lecture . . .

. . . Establishments are required to close during prayer calls. Some restaurants will request that you depart the premises during 'salla'. Others may permit you to remain but will turn out the lights or suspend serving your meal until salla ends. While shopping, you will find the souks closed for 15 to 30 minutes during salla.

If you are in a shop when the salla is called, or notice the Muttawa (religious police) signalling merchants to close by rapping their wooden sticks against the storefront, you should leave. The merchant will probably not tell you to go, but he can get into trouble which may include revocation of his license to do business. Even if you are about to strike a bargain, leave the store and return later.

Dhahran Area Guide, published by 4404th Wing (Provisional) Public Affairs Office, Eastern Province of Saudi Arabia, 1990.

6B
US Advice on the Muttawaiin

A US Embassy advisory in Riyadh described the Muttawaiin in an
'Information Guidance' publication.

Over the years, hundreds of thousands of Americans have lived in Saudi
Arabia. They and their families have enjoyed a unique cross-cultural living
experience and many have established close personal relationships with
Saudi families. In any social setting that involves a large number of
individuals from very different cultural backgrounds, however, situations
requiring judgment and discretion arise. Among these are encounters
between members of the American community and members of the
Organization for the Promotion of Virtue and Prevention of Vice – the
muttawaiin. We hope the following guidance may be helpful and contribute
to balancing relations between our two communities.

The Embassy recommends that both men and women dress conserva-
tively in public and promptly obey requests to clear shop premises at the
onset of prayer. There is no official dress code for Saudi Arabia. The
guidelines provided by Embassy are minimum requirements. They cannot
be taken as a guarantee against confrontation since many muttawaiin
would not accept as adequate the dress standards the Embassy outlines.
However, while conservative dress is obligatory, the Saudi Government
does not require Western women to wear the abaya or head scarf. An abaya
and head covering are up to the discretion and comfort of the individual
Western woman.

If, despite your best efforts, you are approached by muttawaiin, or
people who appear to be members of the organization, you should first
exercise common sense and avoid appearing either to be aggressive or
intimidated. Your primary objective should be to end the encounter as
quickly and as reasonably as possible; any objections to the encounter
itself are best channelled in writing, as soon after the incident as possible.
There is little to be gained in debating muttawaiin on the fine points of
Islam; you will not change their beliefs, but you do run the risk of being
temporarily detained at muttawaiin or police headquarters. Individuals
who have appearance of muttawaiin (beards, no iqal, shorter thobes), but
who are not accompanied by a uniformed police officer, do not have the
legal authority to detain or remove you to another premise. However,
muttawaiin who are accompanied by a uniformed police officer do have
the power to take you to police or muttawaiin or police headquarters. If a
uniformed police officer is present, you must – if requested – hand over
your iqama to the officer. You should not relinquish any documents to
muttawaiin.

Appropriate Dress for Americans in Saudi Arabia

There is no official dress code for Saudi Arabia and the guidelines below are intended to contradict specific dress codes of employers. Such regulations are often a condition of employment. What follows is a set of recommendations only. While they have been discussed with officials of the Government of Saudi Arabia, adherence to the guidelines does not guarantee freedom from difficulties as many members of the Organization for the Promotion of Virtue and Prevention of Vice – the muttawaiin – take issue with our recommendations. *Saudi customs dictate conservative dress for both men and women, particularly in public places*: The central guidance is to be sensitive to cultural mores and aware of your surroundings. If you have any questions about the appropriateness of any item of your wardrobe, make the judgment on the conservative side. You will be more comfortable in public situations if your clothing is loose fitting and inconspicuous. Women should be business-like and reserved in public, particularly in their dealings with men, e.g. male shopkeepers, since excessive familiarity or friendliness is often misconstrued in this culture.

Men: Long trousers and shirts which are not open below the collarbone are recommended. In addition, muttawaiin enforce a ban on men wearing neck jewellery when going into the souk and public areas.

Women: Clothing should be loose fitting and concealing rather than revealing. Skirts should be well below the knee. Sleeves should be at least elbow length. Pants are not recommended although Pakistani-style baggy pants covered by a long shift are often considered acceptable.

Abayas and Head Coverings: Non-Muslim Western women are not required to wear abayas or head scarves by the Saudi Government. Nevertheless, muttawaiin often challenge women who are not wearing abayas; some will also insist on head scarves, particularly in the downtown souks. An abaya worn to cover up improper or immodest dress is considered offensive by many Saudis. During certain religious proceedings, the Haj, Western women should be particularly careful in their selection of clothing, especially when travelling to or through the more traditional areas of the city.

US Embassy Advisory, Riyadh, 1996.

Chapter Seven

LAW AND ORDER

7A
Death penalty for drug offences

The Council of Senior Ulema issued a fatwa on the death penalty for drugs offences, 18 February 1987.

Due to the great assiduities of the Custodian of the Two Holy Mosques, King Fahd Bin Ahdul Al-Aziz who takes great care in protecting and securing our society from the destructive wickedness and crimes according to the fair Rules of Islam. Because of the continuance of smuggling and distribution of narcotics which harm the soul, mind and body, the Senior Ulema Council has issued a unanimous decision, No. 138, dated 20/6/1407 of Mohamedan Year, defined thus:

Firstly: With regard to the narcotic smugglers, the punishment will be the death sentence as a result of his evil work by bringing a great deal of corruption and deterioration to the country. The smuggler and the person who receives narcotics from abroad will be punished in the same way.

Secondly: With regards to the narcotics distributor, the SUC has agreed its decision No. 85, dated 11/11/1401 of Muhammaden, defined thus:
   If this is the distributor's first offence he will be severely punished either by imprisonment or by whipping or by paying a fine or all punishments depending on the ruling of the courts. If the offence is repeated the punishment will be life imprisonment in order to remove him permanently from society or the death sentence because his act, in the eyes of society and Islamic law, is an evil deed and crime is a part of him.
   Accordingly, the Custodian of the Two Holy Mosques issued a declaration to the Ministry of Justice and the Ministry of the Interior, No. 4/B/966, dated on 10/7/1407, to the effect that all courts will act according to the rulings. The Minister of the Interior is announcing it to the public and citizens. He has the Rules of Islam for a good and beneficial decision and to act as a reminder and a warning to those who are involved in these types of crimes. The ruling is to call upon all drug traffickers to stop completely.

The Minister of the Interior has given his assurance that the Ministry will carry out the decided rules immediately the Islamic Courts have decided and after the CTHM signing since a warning has been given there will be no excuse.

Recorded by Amnesty International, London.

7B
Death penalty for terrorism

The council of senior ulema in Saudi Arabia, 24 August 1988, issued an edict prescribing the death penalty for whoever has been proven – according to religious law – to have carried out an act of sabotage or misdeed which undermines security by attacking people or private or public building.

Edict No 148, dated 12/1/1409. . .
The council of senior ulema, at its 32nd session held in Ta'if from 8/1/1409 to 12/1/1409 (20-24th August 1988) noting the many incidents of sabotage – as a result of which many innocent people were killed and numerous properties, possessions and public installations destroyed – which have taken place in many Islamic and other countries, and which were carried out by people with little or no faith who are weak-willed an malicious – such as blowing up houses, setting fire to public and private properties, blowing up bridges and tunnels and blowing up or hijacking planes; in view of the noticeable rise in such crimes as these taking place in near and far countries; and because the Kingdom of Saudi Arabia, like other countries, is exposed to sabotage acts . . ., the council of senior ulema believes that there is a need to consider prescribing a deterrent punishment to whoever commits a sabotage act, whether against public installations, government interests or others with the intention of causing havoc or undermining security . . .
  The council has unanimously decided the following:

1. Whoever has been found guilty, legally, of having perpetrated an act of sabotage or corruption on earth that undermines security by aggression on life, private or public property, such as blowing up homes, mosques, schools, hospitals, plants, bridges, arms depots, water supplies and general resources of the treasury, oil pipelines, as well as the blowing up or hijacking of aeroplanes, and similar acts, will be sentenced to death . . .
2. Before the carrying out of the punishment mentioned in the previous paragraph, the judiciary courts, the appeal bodies and the higher council of justice must complete the necessary measures to ascertain facts in order to avoid guilt and protect lives, and so as to maintain the fact that this country sticks to all the necessary measures legally to ascertain that crimes have been committed and to decide their punishment . . .

3. The council sees it fit that the punishment be announced through the news media . . .

Saudi Press Agency, 29 August 1988.

7C
Commercial conduct

Human Rights Watch stated in an American court, October 1992, that the Saudi Government's 'Regular Course of Commercial Conduct' includes the use of torture and arbitrary detention in connection with commercial disputes.

According to first-hand research conducted by Middle East Watch, it is common practice for public and private enterprises to enlist the Saudi government to detain and sometimes torture adverse parties in commercial disputes. Saudi law does not require written authorization for such arrests. Disputes that can trigger detention include nonpayment of debts, employment disputes, and the failure to fulfil contractual obligations. To 'resolve' these disputes, the police detain the adverse party and use force, including slapping and beating with bamboo sticks, to secure concessions. The Division of Civil Rights *(al-Huquq al-Madaniyya)*, the division of the Ministry of Interior that is responsible for enforcement of civil claims, is particularly notorious for such abuse.

Middle East Watch knows of scores of people who are currently detained without charge or trial as a result of commercial disputes. Some of these businessmen have been kept in detention for years. After an initial period of incommunicado detention, family visits are usually authorized. The prisoner and his family are then advised to seek an accommodation with the person who initiated the complaint.

Although both Saudis and foreigners are subject to such detention and abuse, foreigners are particularly vulnerable because of the fear that they might flee, especially if their assets in the country are small in relation to the amount in dispute. Detention occurs even though foreigners may not legally leave Saudi Arabia, or the locality in which they reside, without the express permission of their *'kafil'*, or Saudi sponsor – either an employer or a senior business partner.

Police action is particularly likely if (. . .) the Saudi royal family or a prominent Saudi citizen has an interest in the case (. . .) The royal family (. . .) controls the Ministry of Interior, which oversees – either itself or through regional governors – all internal security forces in the country. The Minister of Interior is Prince Nayef ibn Abdel Aziz, and his deputy is Prince Ahmed ibn Abdel Aziz, both full brothers of King Fahd. All regional governors in Saudi Arabia are members of either the royal family or the Sudairi family, the maternal relatives of the King.

(. . .) the US government has previously acknowledged the Saudi government's use of arbitrary detention to resolve commercial disputes. In an October 8, 1986 letter to Rep. Mel Levine, then Secretary of Commerce Malcolm Baldrige wrote:

> 'The distinction between civil and criminal law remedies in Saudi Arabia is blurred, and personal detention pending the settlement of a commercial dispute can occur. . . We regularly provide businessmen with brochures and other material on Saudi Arabia containing a warning on this legal practice. We advise individuals with commercial disputes pending in Saudi Arabia not to enter the country.'

Similarly, on June 15, 1987, James B. Kelly, then a deputy assistant secretary of commerce, told the House Subcommittee on Europe and the Middle East: 'The lack of distinction between civil and criminal law in Saudi Arabia permits the detention of resident and visiting business persons for what we would consider a commercial dispute.'

Middle East Watch has investigated a substantial number of cases of businessmen and foreign workers who were detained for having run afoul of their Saudi partners or members of the royal family. Some, after their release, reported that they had been tortured during detention.

For example, in March 1991, in a villa used as a detention facility in Riyadh, Middle East Watch interviewed Abdalla Saleh al-Rajhi, a Saudi banker who had been arrested in early 1980. As of mid-August 1992, he was still in detention. Al-Rajhi was arrested after the government closed down his investment company because certain foreign investors had complained that its aggressive investment policy in precious metals had exposed them to too great a risk. After twelve years in detention, he has not been tried or allowed even to consult with legal counsel, although he is permitted family visits. A secret committee at the Ministry of Interior has reviewed his case, but its findings have not been revealed . . .

––––

(x1) At the beginning of employment and upon return from foreign travel, a foreigner must surrender his passport to the sponsor. To travel within the country, a foreigner needs his passport and a letter from his sponsor. To leave the country, a foreigner needs an exit visa, which cannot be obtained without permission of the sponsor indicated on his passport.

(x2) The US government has also described the Saudi government's related practice of denying American businessmen exit visas pending resolution of commercial disputes with their Saudi associates. In a letter to Rep. Levine dated October 21, 1986, then Assistant Secretary of State for Legislative and Intergovernmental Affairs J. Edward Fox wrote: Over the past twelve months, our Mission in Saudi Arabia has received reports of twenty-six commercial and labor disputes which have resulted in the retention of an American citizen's passport or the barring of the American's exit from the Kingdom pending resolution of the dispute.

Copies of these statements are on file in Human Rights Watch's offices.

Human Rights Watch in the Supreme Court of the United States, October Term 1992, in a motion for leave to file a brief as *amicus curiae* in support of American citizens Scott and Vivian Nelson in a case against Saudi employers.

7D
No effective remedies

Saudi Arabia provides no effective remedies for torture or arbitrary detention, said Middle East Watch 1992.

Saudi Arabia has no legal regime to protect against arbitrary arrest, lengthy pretrial detention or physical abuse. It has no bill of rights or comparable legal guarantees. It has declined to sign most international human rights agreements, including the Covenant and the Torture Convention. Indeed, Saudi Arabia was one of only a handful of countries – South Africa and former Soviet Bloc countries were the others – that did not vote for the Universal Declaration of Human Rights when it was adopted by the UN General Assembly on December 10, 1948. On March 1, 1992, amid great fanfare, King Fahd issued the Basic Law of Government – the closest that the country has ever come to adopting a constitution. The Basic Law provides in Article 26 that '(t)he state shall protect human rights according to Shari'a,' or Islamic law. This provision marks the first time in Saudi history that the government has formally acknowledged the concept of citizens' rights vis-à-vis the state.(x1) However, in the few Instances in which the new law refers to specific civil and political rights, the protection afforded is highly qualified.(x2) Moreover, the reference to the Shari'a is problematic because the Shari'a as applied in Saudi Arabia is not codified in written laws. The final nominal authority for its Interpretation is the government-appointed Council of Senior Scholars, which has traditionally deferred to the King's Interpretation in political matters, including those implicating human rights. Despite the Basic Law, the Saudi government thus retains near complete discretion to define the content and scope of the rights it will respect.

1. Saudi Law Provides No Protection Against Arbitrary Arrest and Detention.

Saudi arrest and detention procedures are governed by Imprisonment and Detention Law No. 31 of 1978, together with Bylaws issued in 1982 by the

Minister of Interior. They place few restrictions on the grounds or duration of pretrial detention. Detainees may be held indefinitely without trial or judicial review. Nor is there a requirement that family members be notified of the arrest. Although in recent years a family is often able to find out if one of its members is detained, formal notification is rare.(x3) It is equally rare for a detainee to be informed of the charges against him or her. Saudi law permits Interrogation of detainees without the benefit of counsel.

2. Saudi Law Provides No Protection Against Torture or Cruel and Inhuman Punishment.

Saudi law contains no explicit ban on torture or cruel and inhuman punishment. Indeed, the use of force to elicit confessions is common in the Saudi security system. Harsh conditions of detention are also frequently imposed to punish prisoners.

While Imprisonment and Detention Law 31 of 1978 prohibits 'any assault whatsoever on prisoners and detainees' (Article 28), the same law explicitly sanctions methods of discipline that violate international standards, such as flogging, indefinite solitary confinement, and deprivation of family visits and correspondence (Article 20). Flogging and amputations are also imposed by the courts as punishment for a variety of crimes. Saudi security officials interviewed by Middle East Watch over the past two years did not consider flogging or hitting detainees to extract confessions to be forms of torture or cruel or inhuman punishment. Although they professed a preference for the use of 'psychological methods' to obtain confessions, they believed that beating and slapping suspects is permissible and that torture consists of only severe abuse such as electric and fingernail extraction.

Despite occasional royal orders instructing detention authorities not to torture prisoners – usually issued after the death of a detainee due to torture – there have been numerous reports of torture in Saudi detention facilities. For example, in its most recent report on human rights in Saudi Arabia, the US State Department described 'credible reports of injuries and the deaths of at least two, and possibly more, persons caused by beatings or the use of excessive force while being held In official custody. In addition, there was a credible report of the torture of several foreigners in Saudi military custody' (US Department of State, *Country Reports on Human Rights Practices for 1991*, 1577, February 1992 ('Country Reports'). Middle East Watch knows of no case in which an officer accused of torture has been brought to trial in Saudi Arabia. Results of investigations into deaths in custody have never been made public. As the US State Department recently observed, 'it is general [Saudi] government policy not to respond to' reports of mistreatment of prisoners. In addition, the Saudi Government has never allowed independent observers to visit its detention facilities, with one exception, when, after months of refusal, it allowed the International Committee of the Red Cross to visit Iraqi prisoners of war following the Desert Storm military campaign on January 17, 1991.

3. There is No Independent Judiciary in Saudi Arabia to Enforce Remedies for Violations of Basic Rights.

The March 1992 Basic Law of Government formally recognizes the principle of an independent judiciary for the first time in Saudi Arabia. However, Middle East Watch has continued to receive reports from within the judiciary that judges periodically come under pressure from senior members of the royal family and other government officials, and thus still do not feel free to check official abuse of power. As the State Department noted in its most recent Country Reports, 'Jurists are . . . aware and reportedly have on occasion acceded to the power and influence of the royal family and their associates.' (. . .) Moreover, under the Saudi government's interpretation of the Shari'a, the king is the spiritual as well as temporal head of the community ('*waliyy al-amr*) and thus has broad discretion to overrule judicial decisions.

Since 1955 Saudi Arabia has had an administrative court, the Board of Grievances, which theoretically can contest government decisions. However, the Board regularity defers to the wishes of the Council of Ministers and the King. According to Article 15 of its 1982 charter, its 'judges' can be removed by the King at any time.

―――

(x1) The Saudi Government's use of the phrase 'civil rights' should not be confused with the concept of human rights, since it refers only to civil claims among private citizens. Indeed, as noted, the Saudi Ministry of Interior's Department of Civil Rights, which oversees such matters, has frequently been implicated in human rights violations in its zeal to protect property rights.

(x2) For a detailed analysis of the limits to these guarantees, see Middle East Watch, 'Empty Reforms: Saudi Arabia's New Basic Law', 1992

(x3) The US Embassy in Riyadh has complained that Saudi Authorities rarely notify it of the arrest of U.S. citizens. According to State Department officials interviewed by Middle East Watch in September 1992, Saudi Arabia has declined to sign a bilateral consular treaty to allow for immediate access.

Human Rights Watch in a court brief, 14 September 1992.

7E
Execution of perpetrators of Riyadh bombing

The Saudi Ministry of Interior according to an Internet press release 31 May 1996, announced that four men had been executed for a terrorist bomb in Riyadh in November 1995.

The Ministry of the Interior today issued a statement to the effect that Abdul Aziz Bin Fahd Bin Nasser Al-Mothem, Khalid Bin Ahmed Bin Ibrahim Al-Sa'eed, Riyadh Bin Suleiman Bin Is'haq Al-Hajeri, and Muslih Bin Ali Bin Ayedh Al-Shemrani, all four of them Saudi nationals, had been beheaded, having been found guilty of carrying out the explosion of a car bomb in the Olaya district of Riyadh last November. The statement said their crime claimed the lives of seven people, wounded more than sixty others, destroyed houses and shops in the area, wrecked several cars and caused panic in the urban district.

Their confessions were documented and submitted to three judges at the Grand Shariah Court in Jeddah, and then to three judges at the Grand Court in Riyadh, where a legal instrument was issued confirming their guilt. This document stated that the perpetrators had admitted that they had planned the crime long before carrying it out, and that they had failed in other plots involving kidnapping and assassination. The judges deemed the crime to be one most heinous and horrifying in nature because it entailed the killing of innocent people, the destruction of property, and the spread of fear and panic among citizens and residents. They stressed that Islamic Shariah (Law) had been revealed in order to safeguard the five bases of society: religion, human life, honor, reason and property, all of which were undermined and threatened by the crime perpetrated by these four saboteurs. The judges concluded that the culprits should be executed as a punishment for their heinous and most repugnant crime.

The verdict was approved by five judges at the Court of Appeals, and by the Supreme Judicial Council. Royal Decree S/628 was issued to carry out the sentence, and included the words: 'With this announcement the Ministry of the Interior affirms the concern of the government of the Custodian of the Two Holy Mosques to guarantee the security, safety and stability of this country, and emphasizes that it will spare no effort in pursuing those who let themselves be seduced into bringing harm to the security of the country or the people.'

Royal Saudi Embassy, Washington 1996

7F
US Consular Information Sheet

The US State Department Consular Office on 16 December 1996, issued an information sheet.

Country Description: The Saudi Arabian political system is a monarchy. The king is chosen from and by members of the Al-Saud family. The king rules through royal decrees issued in conjunction with the Council of Ministers, and with advice from the Consultative Council. Members of both councils are appointed by the king. Islamic law is the basis of the authority of the monarchy, and provides the foundation of the country's conservative customs and practices. Saudi Arabia has a modern and well-developed infrastructure, and facilities for travelers are widely available, although the country does not issue visas for tourism. The workweek in Saudi Arabia is Saturday through Wednesday.

Entry Requirements: Passports and visas are required. Tourist visas are not available for travel to Saudi Arabia. Frequently, only single-entry visas are issued by Saudi offices abroad. Airport visas are not available. Visas are required for persons on vessels calling at the Port of Jeddah. Visitors must have a business or personal sponsor. Women visitors and residents are required to be met upon arrival at a Saudi airport by their business or personal sponsor. Residents working in Saudi Arabia generally must surrender their passports while in the Kingdom and are required to get an exit/re-entry visa each time they leave Saudi Arabia. The sponsor (normally the employer) obtains a work and residence permit for the employee and for any family members. Family members of those working are not required by law to surrender their passports, though they often do so in practice. Those on visitor visas do not need an exit visa to leave the Kingdom. Residents carry a Saudi residence permit (Iqama) for identification in place of their passports. The US Embassy and Consulates General cannot sponsor private American citizens for Saudi visas.

Foreign residents traveling within the Kingdom, even between towns in the same province, carry travel letters issued by employers and authenticated by an immigration official or a Chamber of Commerce office. Police at all airports and dozens of roadblocks routinely arrest and imprison violators.

Visitors to Saudi Arabia generally obtain a meningitis vaccination prior to arrival. A medical report is required to obtain a work and residence permit. This includes a medical certification. For further information on entry requirements, travelers may contact the following Saudi government offices in the US:

– Royal Embassy of Saudi Arabia, 601 New Hampshire Ave., NW, Washington, DC 20037, Tel. (202) 333-2740.

- Saudi Consulate General in New York: 866 United Nations Plaza, Suite 480, New York, NY 10017, Tel.: (212) 752-2740.
- Saudi Consulate General in Houston: 5718 Westheimer, Suite 1500, Houston, TX 77057, Tel.: (713) 785-5577.
- Saudi Consulate General in Los Angeles: Sawtelle Courtyard Building, 2045 Sawtelle Blvd., Los Angeles, CA 90025, Tel.: (310) 479-6000.

Exit Permission: Residents in Saudi Arabia may not depart the country without obtaining an exit permit, which requires the approval of their Saudi sponsor. The US Embassy and Consulates General cannot apply for an exit permit for a US citizen under any circumstances.

A married woman residing in Saudi Arabia with her husband must have her husband's permission for herself and her children to depart the country, even if they are US citizens. Persons in Saudi Arabia on visitor visas do not need an exit visa to leave the country.

Security Information: The US government continues to assist Saudi authorities in their investigations of the 1995 and 1996 bombings of US military installations in Saudi Arabia. Because of continuing security concerns, official American facilities, including offices and residences of the US Embassy and various military units, have adopted a variety of measures aimed at enhancing their security. The US Embassy reminds American citizens in Saudi Arabia to exercise extreme caution and keep a low profile.

The American Embassy and consulates in Saudi Arabia inform the resident American community of security matters through a communication system known as the warden faxnet. Persons who are residing in the Kingdom should contact the US Embassy or consulates for information on their warden contacts. Americans arriving in Saudi Arabia are encouraged to register at the US Embassy or consulates and obtain the most current security information. (See section on Registration).

Saudi Customs, Religious Police, and General Standards of Conduct: Islam pervades all aspects of life in Saudi Arabia. It is the official religion of the country, and observance of any other religion is forbidden. Non-Muslim religious services are illegal and public display of non-Islamic religious articles such as crosses and bibles is not permitted. Travel to Mecca and Medina, the cities where the two holy mosques of Islam are located, is forbidden to non-Muslims.

The norms for public behavior in Saudi Arabia are extremely conservative, and religious police, known as Mutawwa'iin, are charged with enforcing these standards. Mutawwa'iin, accompanied by uniformed police, have police powers. To ensure that conservative standards of conduct are observed, the Saudi religious police have harassed, accosted or arrested foreigners, including US citizens, for improper dress or other infractions, such as consumption of alcohol or association by a female with a non-relative male. While most incidents have resulted only in inconvenience or embarrassment, the potential exists for an individual to be physically harmed or deported. US citizens who are involved in an incident with the Mutawwa'iin may report the incident to the US Embassy in Riyadh or the US Consulates General in Jeddah or Dhahran.

The Saudi Embassy in Washington advises women traveling to Saudi Arabia to dress in a conservative fashion, wearing ankle-length dresses with long sleeves, and not to wear trousers in public. In many areas of Saudi Arabia, particularly Riyadh and the central part of the Kingdom, Mutawwa'iin pressure women to wear a full-length black covering known as an abaya and to cover their heads. The result is that most women in these areas wear the abaya and carry a headscarf to avoid harassment. Women who appear to be of Arab or Asian ethnic origin, especially Muslims, face a greater risk of harassment.

Some Mutawwa'iin try to enforce the rule that men and women who are beyond childhood years may not mingle in public, unless they are family or close relatives. Mutawwa'iin may ask to see proof that a couple is married or related. Women who are arrested for socializing with a man who is not a relative may be charged with prostitution. Women who are not accompanied by a close male relative have not been served at some restaurants, particularly fast-food outlets. In addition, many restaurants no longer have a 'family section' in which women are permitted to eat. These restrictions are not always posted, and in some cases women violating this policy have been arrested.

Women are not allowed to drive vehicles or ride bicycles on public roads. In public, dancing, music, and movies are forbidden. Pornography is strictly forbidden. Homosexual activity is considered to be a criminal offense and those convicted may be sentenced to lashing and/or a prison sentence, or death.

The Hajj: American pilgrims planning to participate in the annual Hajj pilgrimage to the holy cities of Makkah (Mecca) and Medina should be aware of the following travel advice:

All travel plans should be made through a travel agent in the United States in order to book accommodations in advance. Hajj visas are required and are valid only for travel to the two holy cities. Stopovers in Jeddah or onward travel to Riyadh or other cities in Saudi Arabia are not permitted.

All foreign Muslim residents of the Kingdom may perform the Hajj once every five years. Advance approval must be obtained from an immigration office with the approval of the Saudi sponsor.

King Abdul Aziz International Airport in Jeddah is a large and modern facility, with a special terminal with facilities to accommodate hundreds of thousands of pilgrims. However, due to the extremely large number of people arriving, waiting time at the airport upon arrival during the Hajj may be as long as ten hours. Pilgrims should plan on a lengthy wait before leaving the airport on their way to Makkah or Medina. Travelers with only carry-on bags will find baggage transfer at the airport much easier than with checked baggage.

Before leaving home, travelers should make copies of their passports, including the pages stamped with Saudi visas. One copy should be left with someone at home and one taken with the traveler. Passports are turned over to Saudi officials upon arrival in the Kingdom and will be given back immediately prior to departure. Upon arrival, all pilgrims are issued an identification card or wrist-band. Travelers should carry this identification at all times. A money belt or pouch is the best way to carry valuables. Upon arrival it is possible to buy what is known as a 'Hajj belt', which is somewhat larger than American equivalents. Visitors should check with the Centers for Disease Control and Prevention, their travel agent, or a Saudi consulate or Embassy regarding recommended or required shots.

Travelers should expect extremely crowded conditions during the Hajj. Temperatures in Makkah range between 60 and 112 degrees in May. There are many facilities providing water, public accommodations, and other amenities. In case of emergency, Hajj pilgrims should contact United Agents Office (Makkah), telephone (02) 545-1444, or National Adilla Est. (Medina), telephone (04) 826-0088, and then contact the American Consulate General in Jeddah, Tel.: (02) 667-0080.

Alcohol and Drug Penalties: US citizens are subject to the laws of the country in which they are traveling or residing. In Saudi Arabia penalties for the import, manufacture, possession and consumption of alcohol or illegal drugs are severe and convicted offenders can expect sentences of jail terms, fines, public flogging, and/or deportation. The penalty for drug trafficking in Saudi Arabia is capital punishment. Saudi officials make no exceptions.

Child Custody: In Saudi Arabia, child custody decisions are based on Islamic law. It is extremely difficult for an American woman, even a Muslim, to obtain custody of her children through a Saudi court decision. Further information on this subject can be obtained in the Department of State publication 'Marriage to Saudis' which is available from the Office of Overseas Citizens Services, Department of State, Washington, DC, 20520-4818, telephone (202) 736-7000, or from the US Embassy or Consulates General in Saudi Arabia.

Traffic and Road Safety: Traffic accidents are a significant hazard in Saudi Arabia. Driving habits are generally poor, and accidents involving children drivers are not uncommon. In the event of a traffic accident resulting in personal injury, all persons involved (if not in the hospital) may be taken to the local police station. Drivers are likely to be held for several days until responsibility is determined and any reparations paid. In many cases, all drivers are held in custody regardless of fault. Those involved in an accident should immediately contact their sponsor and the US Embassy or nearest consulate.

Business Disputes: The Arabic version of a contract governs under Saudi law. Before signing a contract, American companies should obtain an independent translation to ensure a full understanding of terms, limits, and agreements. While settlement of disputes is possible, the procedures are complex and time consuming. If the Saudi party in a business dispute files a complaint with the Saudi authorities, Saudi law permits barring the exit of the foreign party from the country until the dispute is settled. US consular officers can provide lists of local attorneys to help US citizens settle business disputes, but ultimate responsibility for the resolution of disputes through the Saudi legal system lies with the parties involved.

Medical Facilities: Basic modern medical care and medicines are available in several hospitals and health centers in Saudi Arabia. Doctors and hospitals often expect immediate cash payment for health services. US medical insurance is not always valid outside the United States. Supplemental medical insurance with specific overseas coverage has proved useful. The international travelers hotline at the Centers for Disease Control and Prevention, Tel.: (404) 332-4559, has additional health information.

Information on Crime: Crime is generally not a problem for travelers in Saudi Arabia. However, private Saudi citizens who perceive that conservative standards of conduct are not being observed by a foreigner may harass, pursue, or assault the person. The loss or theft of a US passport abroad should be reported immediately to local police and the nearest US embassy or consulate. Useful information on safeguarding valuables and protecting personal security while traveling abroad is provided in the Department of State pamphlet, 'A Safe Trip Abroad'. General information about travel to Saudi Arabia can be found in the Department of State publication 'Tips for Travelers to the Middle East and North Africa'. Both pamphlets are available from the Superintendent of Documents, US Government Printing Office, Washington, DC 20402.

Registration and Embassy/Consulate Locations: US citizens who register at the US Embassy or the U.S. Consulates General may obtain updated information on travel and security within Saudi Arabia and can be included in the warden network. The US Embassy in Riyadh, Saudi Arabia, is located at Collector Road M, Riyadh Diplomatic Quarter. The mailing address is PO Box 94309, Riyadh 11693, or AmEmbassy, Unit 61307, APO AE 09803-1307. The US Embassy telephone number is (966) (1) 488-3800, fax (966) (1) 488-7275.

The Consulate General in Dhahran is located between Aramco Headquarters and Dhahran International Airport. The mailing address is PO Box

81, Dhahran Airport 31932, or Unit 66803, APO AE 09858-6803. The telephone number is (966) (3) 891-3200, fax (966) (3) 891-6816.

The Consulate General in Jeddah is located on Palestine Road, Ruwais. The mailing address is PO Box 149, Jeddah; or Unit 62112, APO AE 09811-2112. The telephone number is (966) (2) 667-0080, fax (966) (2) 669-3078.

US State Department, Washington, DC, Official Consular Information Sheet for Saudi Arabia, 16 December 1996.

7G
The Legal System

As explained by Amnesty International 1993, Saudi Arabia does not have a written penal code.

The main source of legislation is the Shari'a (Islamic law) as defined by the Wahabi interpretation of the Hanbali school of Sunni Islamic jurisprudence. The principal components of the Sharia are: the Qur'an, the holy book of Islam containing divine communications from God to Man; the Sunna (Tradition), based on the sayings and deeds of Prophet Muhammad; the Ijma (Consensus) of Senior Ulema (religious scholars) on a given issue; and the Qiyas (Analogy or Comparison) which is the use of precedent in Islamic history to pass judgement on present day events. Thus, while it is maintained that Saudi Arabia's legal system is based on God-made laws, Ijma and Qiyas are clearly Man's Interpretation of these laws.

The Shari'a is not codified in written statutes and the ultimate authority entrusted with its interpretation in Saudi Arabia is the Council of Senior Ulema, the highest religious body in the country. The Council is composed of 18 Ulema, all appointed by the King. The Head of the Council has ministerial rank, but is not a member of the Council of Ministers which effectively acts as the country's legislative and executive body. It issues Decisions (Qararat) which, once sanctioned by the King, become Royal Decrees (Maraseem Malakiyya) thus acquiring the force of law. In circumstances where it is not possible for the Council of Ministers to issue such Decisions the King promulgates Royal Ordinances (Awamir Mala-kiyya), which are also legaly binding.

The Shari'a applies to most spheres of law, including personal status and criminal law. Commercial administrative and work-related disputes are heard before specialized courts. All Shari'a courts fall under the jurisdiction of the Ministry of Justice which was established in 1970. In these courts the judge questions and cross-examines both defendant and witnesses before determining guilt or innocence. The judge has the ultimate authority to pass sentence and there are no trials by jury. However, in cases involving capital offences or amputations, the presence of three judges is required. Contrary to Saudi Arabia's own legislation (Article 33 of Nidham al-Qadha' (the Judicial System) promulgated by Royal Decree No. M/64 dated 24 July 1975), trials in political cases are held in camera and without defence counsel, most evidently in the cases of 16 Kuwaiti Shi'a pilgrims who were executed in September 1989 on charges of planting bombs in Mecca. They were tried in camera, denied access to legal counsel and convicted on the basis of 'confessions', reportedly extracted by tinder torture (see Saudi Arabia entries in Amnesty International Report 1990 and 1991).

Minor offences punishable by a short period of imprisonment or by small fines are tried before Courts of Expedient Affairs (Mahakim al-Umur al-Musta'jala), which are found in every town and most large villages or centres. The rulings of the Courts of Expedient Affairs are final unless they can be shown to be contrary to the Shari'a. Major offences are first tried in General Courts (al-Mahakim al-'Amma or al-Mahakim al-Kubra). The decisions of these courts may be appealed before the Court of Appeal (Mahkamat al-Tameez) which is based in the capital, Riyadh. The rulings of the Court of Appeal are final except in cases involving the death penalty or amputation which must be reviewed by the Supreme Judicial Council (Majlis al-Qadha' a'la). For such punishments to be carried out, they must also be ratified by the King. The Supreme Judicial Council has five permanent members appointed by the King and five non-permanent members. The Head of the Council is appointed by Royal Decree and has ministerial rank.

In addition to the court system, there is a Board of Grievances (Diwan al-Madhaiim), whose functions include receiving and investigating complaints from citizens against government officials. However, former political prisoners and prisoners of conscience have claimed that the Board has failed to investigate complaints against the security forces without the prior consent of these forces. Since its establishment in 1955, the Board of Grievances is directly accountable to the King who appoints its president by Royal Decree.

The judicial punishments embodied in the Hanbali interpretation of the Shari'a are formally enforced in Saudi Arabia. Public flogging, amputation and beheading are prescribed by the Saudi Arabian legal system as punishments for a variety of crimes. These rulings are applicable to both Muslims and non-Muslims resident in the Kingdom. For example, Muslims convicted of apostasy, i.e. those deemed to have renounced Islam, may be sentenced to death . . . Other methods used to punish religious minorities in Saudi Arabia include the arrest and detention, often without charge or trial. of prisoners of conscience; the torture or flogging of detainees and, in the case of expatriates, deportation . . .

In November 1983 a 'Statute of Principles of Arrest, Temporary Confinement and Preventive Detention' was issued by the Minister of the Interior and is believed to be still in force. It appears that this statute applies to cases involving political as well as criminal offences. Its provisions, however, are inconsistent with international standards governing pre-trial detention and fair trial . . . By failing to provide for systematic access to the outside world and for the judicial supervision of the period of detention, it creates conditions which, in Amnesty International's view, facilitate the use of torture.

On 1 March 1992, King Fahd bin 'Abdul-'Aziz issued three Royal Decrees on the Basic System of Government, the establishment of a Consultative Council and the establishment of Regional Authorities. The decrees have stressed the right to privacy and made it illegal for the security authorities to arrest, spy on, or violate basic human rights of citizens. The new Decrees do not, however, ban discrimination on the basis of religious beliefs. Restrictions on freedom of assembly, speech and thought remain intact . . .

Most of the security apparatus with responsibility for internal security and the maintenance of law and order in Saudi Arabia fall under the jurisdiction of the Ministry of the Interior. The primary police agency is the Shurta (Public Security Police) which has the authority to investigate offences, arrest suspects and refer cases to the courts. However, the grounds for arrest are generally determined by the arresting officer. . . The arresting authorities must generally obtain permission from the provincial governor before searching a private home, but warrants are not formally required. The March 1992 Royal Decrees do not address this problem sufficiently, and fall short of requiring warrants. Thus arbitrary arrests and detention are a frequent occurrence. Furthermore, there continues to be no formal or automatic procedure for contacting a detainee's family or friends. In some cases, this can mean that detainees are held for weeks before their relatives are informed of their whereabouts, thus creating the conditions for torture and ill-treatment to occur.

AI-Mabahith al-'Amma (General Investigations) is the agency which in recent years has been associated with the arrest and detention of political opponents in the Kingdom, particularly Shi'a Muslims. Its members are responsible for monitoring internal political opposition and unrest, and the administration of prisons throughout the country. They regularly hold detainees incommunicado during the initial phase of an investigation which may be of several months' duration. In addition, officers of al-Mabahith al-'Amma have frequently been involved in the systematic torture and ill-treatment of political prisoners.

The religious police, known locally as the mutawa'een, are the enforcing arm of Hay'at al-Amr bil Ma'ruf wa Nahi 'an al-Munkar, the Committee for the Propagation of Virtue and Prevention of Vice (CPVPV). The CPVPV is said to have been formed in 1927 after King Abdul-Aziz al-Saud captured the holy city of Mecca. Following the establishment of the Kingdom of Saudi Arabia in 1932, the CPVPV came under the jurisdiction of the Mufti of Saudi Possessions or Territories (Mufti al-Diyar al-Saudiyya). Since the administrative reorganization of the state apparatus during the reign of King Faisal bin 'Abdul-'Aziz (1964–1975), the CPVPV has become directly accountable to the Council of Ministers. Its members are responsible for ensuring strict adherence to established codes of conduct, and in many cases are said to have carried out their duties overzealously. In a statement at a CPVPV conference on 9 November 1992 Prince Salman bin 'Abdul-Aziz, the Governor of Riyadh and a brother of the King, was reported to have cautioned 'those responsible to be patient, wise and lenient . . . Mistakes are possible. We are all human beings who can be wrong or right and you have a big responsibility to urge good deeds and stop and confront what is forbidden and deal with it wisely.' While members of the CPVPV are required to have a good knowledge of the Shari'a, they apparently do not receive formal training as law enforcement officials. In theory, they do not have the legal authority to detain anyone beyond 24 hours, after which time they must hand him over to the public security police for questioning. In practice, however, members of the CPVPV are known to have detained suspects and to have subjected them to torture or ill-treatment during interrogation. One such case was that of Sa'id Farash, a Saudi Arabian national, who was arrested by members of the CPVPV in Mecca in November 1990. He died ten hours later, reportedly as a result of a fractured skull (see Saudi Arabia in Amnesty International Report 1992). According to information available to Amnesty International, it is members of the CPVPV who monitor non-Muslim worship in the Kingdom.

Amnesty International: 'Saudi Arabia, Religious Intolerance: The Arrest, Detention and Torture of Christian Worshippers and Shia Muslims', London, 14 September 1993.

7H
Guide to Living in Saudi Arabia

British Foreign Office advice to its citizens in the Saudi Kingdom, March 1994.

The laws of Saudi Arabia are based largely on the Koran; the system is often known as 'Shari'a'. Although punishment for some offences are harsh by British standards, the Saudis claim to have a very low crime rate. The application of the law can sometimes be the source of much misunderstanding. The Saudis understand that the ways of non-Muslims are different from their own and they will not generally interfere with what foreigners do quietly, privately and discreetly. But foreigners who take advantage of this to break the law are running serious risks. Their offences can easily become known, if only be accident, and as soon as the breach of the law comes to public attention the perpetrator will find himself in trouble, possibly quite serious trouble. The Saudis are jealous of their reputation of having a well-ordered society. They will not allow foreigners to put it at risk. . .

17. British Consular Staff in Saudi Arabia will naturally do what is in their power to assist UK nationals who are caught disobeying Saudi law. In most cases this has to be restricted to the giving of advice and to attempting to ensure that the normal correct Saudi legal processes are followed. A British Consul cannot save UK nationals from the consequences of their own actions or negligence – e.g. the implementation of customary punishment.

18. There is generally no distinction in Saudi law between Muslims and non-Muslims: expatriates in Saudi Arabia can expect to receive the full penalty for any offence which might include long prison sentences and lashes. The procedure upon arrest is usually as follows. The police will question the person arrested, carry out any relevant investigation, and require the person to make a statement. The accused may not be allowed the benefit of any outside contact (with employers, friends, consul or lawyer) as long as the investigation continues. If the police decide that there is a case to answer, the accused will be remanded in custody and probably moved from a police station to a prison until he/she can appear before a judge to confirm that the signed statement is accurate and was not made under actual physical duress. Whilst in police custody, the Consul will normally have unrestricted access to a prisoner. However, once the prisoner has been moved to prison the Consul will be granted only limited access. There will then be a further remand in custody until the trial, which the judge will conduct in accordance with Koranic law. There is no jury and, although the accused has no right to a lawyer or Embassy representative, judges can (and sometimes do) permit consular attendance. An interpreter is provided by the court. In the event of a conviction the judge will normally impose a sentence and require the person convicted to sign acceptance of the sentence (unless there is to be an appeal against conviction to a higher court). The period from arrest to sentence can be 3 months or longer in difficult cases, partly because cases involving foreigners are dealt with particularly carefully. The judge's sentence has to be confirmed (and can be increased) by a higher court, the Provincial Governor, the Ministry of Interior and in serious cases the Council of Ministers. An appeal can take up to a year to be heard. Inevitably, the movement of case files among the authorities concerned takes time, but a custodial sentence is generally reckoned to have started on the date of

arrest. Deportation procedures at the end of the custodial sentence can add to the period spent in detention. Occasionally, expatriates who offend against the law may simply be deported after a few days or weeks in police detention, but this happens rarely (despite the prospect often being confidently mooted).

19. Murder and sexual immorality such as adultery and homosexual acts carry the death penalty in Saudi Arabia. So does apostasy (renunciation of the Muslim faith). The death penalty is carried out in public, usually by decapitation. Serious and/or persistent theft is punished by cutting off the thief's right hand. This too is done in public, usually in front of the main Mosque after mid-day prayers on Friday.

20. Some cases have both criminal ('public right') and civil ('private right') aspects. For instance, after a theft or causing an accidental injury or death, the person responsible is required to make restitution or pay compensation. The question of punishment for any offence involved is usually only after private right claims have been settled. A driver who may be in no way to blame for the death or injury of another driver or pedestrian in a road accident will nonetheless have to pay 'blood money' on a varying scale to the injured party or relatives of the deceased person. The amount payable for the death of a Muslim man is now 100,000 Saudi riyals. (For Christians the amount is half this.) Motor insurance, including third party cover, is available in Saudi Arabia. It is not compulsory, however, and some Muslims assume that he is covered for third party claims even when he is driving his employee's vehicle on business: he should check positively that he is adequately covered by insurance otherwise. (Accidents can occur off the road too, and general personal liability insurance is worth considering.) The normal procedure after a road accident in which damage or injury has been caused is for the driver(s) held responsible to be imprisoned, maybe indefinitely.

21. Under Shari'a law, non-payment of debt is considered a crime, and sufficient reason for imprisonment; imprisonment does not discharge debt. It is therefore important both to avoid getting into debt personally and to keep careful accounts of any employer's funds or goods which pass through your hands. You can be held personally responsible for company debts, too, if you are considered the sole company representative in Saudi Arabia. Experience has shown that debt cases can be the most difficult to resolve, particularly if Saudi citizens are involved, as their private rights are fundamental and not subject to Royal or Government intervention. It is also necessary to take seriously any responsibility you may have for safeguarding company cash or property, whether in the safe stores overnight or in transit. If it is stolen, negligence may be alleged and a severe penalty imposed.

22. For expatriates in Saudi Arabia it is the prohibition on alcohol that causes the most difficulty. Those who indulge are punished if their activities come to police attention, especially in the event of brawling, traffic accidents, noisy parties, or simply being out in the small hours. Sentences can vary from a few weeks or months for consumption of alcohol to several years for smuggling, manufacturing or distributing. For offences strokes (lashes) are also part of the sentence; and a hefty Customs fine if smuggled liquor is involving. Stiff penalties are handed out to those found in possession of equipment for manufacturing alcohol.

Consular Department, Foreign and Commonwealth Office, London,
March 1994.

7I
US code of conduct

*The US State Department warned American citizens in Saudi Arabian
in 1994 to beware of local rules.*

Exit Permission: Residents in Saudi Arabia may not depart the country without obtaining an exit permit, which requires the approval of their Saudi sponsor. The US Embassy and Consulates General cannot apply for an exit permit for a US citizen under any circumstances. A married woman residing in Saudi Arabia with her husband must have her husband's permission for herself and her children to depart the country, even if they are US citizens. Persons in Saudi Arabia on visitor visas do not need an exit visa to leave the country.

Saudi Customs, Religious Police, and General Standards of Conduct: Islam pervades all aspects of life in Saudi Arabia. It is the official religion of the country, and observance of any other religion is forbidden. Non-Muslim religious services are illegal and public display of non-Islamic religious articles such as crosses and bibles is not permitted. Travel to Mecca and Medina, the cities where two holy mosques of Islam are located, is forbidden to non-Muslims. The norms for public behaviour in Saudi Arabia are extremely conservative, and that conservative standards of conduct are observed, the Saudi religious police have harassed, accosted or arrested foreigners, including US citizens, for improper dress or other infractions, incidents have resulted only in inconvenience or embarrassment, the potential exists for an individual to be physically harmed or deported. US citizens who are involved in an incident with the mutawwa'in may report the incident to the US Embassy in Riyadh or the US consulates General in Jeddah or Dhahran.

The Saudi Embassy in Washington advises women traveling to Saudi Arabia to dress in a conservative fashion, wearing ankle-length dresses with long sleeves, and not to wear trousers in public. In many areas of Saudi Arabia, particularly Riyadh and the central part of the Kingdom, Mutawwa'in pressure women to wear full-length black covering known as an abaya and to cover their heads. The result is that most women in these areas wear the abaya and carry a headscarf to avoid harassment. Women who appear to be of Arab or Asian ethnic origin, especially Muslims, face a greater risk of harassment.

Some Mutawwa'in try to enforce the rule that men and women who are beyond childhood years may not mingle in public, unless they are family or close relatives. Mutawwa'in may ask to see proof that a couple is married or related. Women who are arrested for socializing with a man who is not a relative may be charged with prostitution. Women who are not accompanied by a close male relative have not been served at some restaurants, particularly fast-food outlets. In addition, many restaurants no longer have a 'family section' in which women are permitted to eat. These restrictions are not always posted, and in some cases women violating this policy have been arrested.

US Department of State, Bureau of Consular Affairs, Washington, DC, USA,
22 April 1994.

7J
Danish Embassy guidelines

Guilty unless otherwise proven – the Danish Embassy in Riyadh in September 1995 issued a guideline for citizens, working in Saudi Arabia.

Foreigners Judicial Condition

Danes and other foreigners are subjected to Saudi legislation, when they reside in Saudi Arabia. The legislation and the rule of conduct in Saudi Arabia is based on the judicial philosophy of Islam and as a consequence of that the community is founded on the rule of the Koran.

A number of the crimes which are punished according to Saudi Arabian Law are in agreement with the penal code of other countries. Murder, rape and theft can be seen as examples of this. Adultery, homosexuality, possession of alcohol or consumption of it contrary to Danish Law are criminal offenses in Saudi Arabian law. Furthermore, imprisonment for debt is maintained as punishment. However, the most important differences between Saudi Arabia and Denmark are the judicial act and the way the punishment is meted out.

Unlike in Danish law the arrested is considered guilty until proved innocent, and Saudi Arabia does not have anything equivalent to our preliminary examination. They do, however, have rules about the limits of duration of punishment in connection with the preliminary investigations previous to the verdict. But these rules are interpreted differently by different courts and they will be of no use as an argument in a case. There have been examples of people who have been detained for a long period of time, because they allegedly had knowledge about a crime without any suspicion of complicity being present. The possibility of being released on bail is limited, and the rules of law are interpreted in each particular case by the local police officer.

As far as the embassy has experienced, there is no discrimination regarding the length of or the type of the punishment. This means that the crime will be judged in accordance with Saudi Arabian law regardless of the nationality of the accused. However, it is known from experience that the death penalty is only rarely imposed upon non-Muslims, and only in cases of severe crimes such as murder or smuggling of drugs. Public flogging has been enforced upon non-Muslims, including Danes.

Expulsion can be used in cases with foreigners who are not welcome in the country. That is, however, not looked upon as punishment. In cases of criminal infringements the accused will often be asked to leave the country after serving his or her sentence. In cases with Danish citizens serving their sentence the embassy will normally try to make sure the expulsion is imposed *before* the sentence is served.

Regarding the law of liability to pay damages it is important to know that as a foreigner one is likely to be held as guilty – without any unbiased assessment of the guilt – if the other side is of Saudi Arabian nationality. Furthermore, it ought to be known that due to judicial reasons it is not possible to be sentenced for interests in, for example, business negotiations.

The Forces of Law and Order – Detention – Arrest

The normal police force (al-shurta) wear gray-brown uniforms and can be contacted on number 999 all over the country. Only Saudi citizens work for the police. Few policemen in the street speak English.

The religious 'police' (al-mutaweens) is a semiprofessional organization (the Organization for the Promotion of Virtue and Prevention of Vice). Even though the members of the organization – in everyday life named mutawas – are volunteers, all 'genuine' members are paid for their work and given a certificate of identification to prove their relation to the organization.

A mutawa can be recognized by the fact that he will not be wearing the strap (aqal) around his headgear, his white coat is a bit too short and he has a long beard. The older mutawas often have henna-dyed their hair. Many mutawas have a cane, which they use to underline their instructions. A mutawa will often be accompanied by a policeman or a colleague.

Mutawas interpret the dress code in a very restricted way. Even though it is compulsory for women to cover their hair with an abbaya, violation of this law is a very common reason for being accosted in the street by a mutawa. This is most likely to happen in the areas of the traditional souqs but also in supermarkets and shopping centers, though these places in theory are considered to be 'safe'. A number of offices and places of work have al-mutaween representatives employed to make sure that their colleagues obey the rites of prayers, and they take care that employed foreigners do not demoralize the spirit of the place. The mutawas are especially active in Riyadh and the rest of the region of Najd.

If accosted by mutawas it is highly recommended to make it brief and avoid discussions which will make the situation deteriorate. The mutawas might be unreasonable, but it is better to follow their instructions than to follow them to their offices to be interrogated there.

Censorship and monitoring of telephones

It should be kept in mind when communicating in Saudi Arabia that censorship and monitoring of telephones is a normal thing. Family, friends and business liaisons should be warned in order to be careful with what they say, forward or enclose.

Advisory, Royal Danish Embassy, Riyadh, September 1995.

7K
Administration of justice

'The administration of justice in Saudi Arabia', obtained at the United States Consulate, Riyadh, 1996.

Islamic Law

It is misleading to think of Islam solely as a religion for this implies a division between religious and civil authority which does not exist. In Islam 'church' and state are in a sense one. The tenets of Islam extend well beyond matters of personal faith to govern the community's social, economic, and political life and with surprising specificity the personal life of the believer. Indeed the most distinctive feature of shari'a law is its effort to judge all human activities and relationships as either obligatory, recommended, neutral, reprehensible, or forbidden. Shari'a law thus has much wider application than western secular law. It prescribes moral, legal and religious obligations without distinguishing among them. It governs matters ranging from diet and the performance of prayers to marriage inheritance and criminal law. In a traditional Muslim society a criminal act is as an offense to both God and community. Thus heresy can be tantamount to treason and the ruler must defend the interwoven legal and religious tenets of Islam.

Shari'a law is not codified in a single work. It is derived by a judge from the Quran, the word of God revealed to the Prophet Muhammad; the sunna or deeds and sayings of Muhammad relating to matters not addressed in the Quran; ijma or the consensus of the religious scholars and ijitihad or reasoning by which jurists determine new legal principles through analogy with those established by the Quran, sunna or ijma. The Hanbili School of Shari'a Law which predominates in Saudi Arabia emphasizes literal interpretations of the Quran and sunna and minimizes the role of ijma. However, judges are free to apply precepts of any of the other three accepted schools to a case.

Many Muslim jurists believe consensus was reached on all significant issues during the first centuries of Islamic jurisprudence and there is no further need of ijtihad, by which shari'a experts apply old principles to new problems. 'The door of ijitihad is closed'. This however is not the view of Ibn Taimiyya, the 14th century jurist whose works from the Sais of Hanbili practised in Saudi Arabia. Ibn Taimiyya believed that ijtihad is necessary for the interpretation of the law. He sought to provide guidelines for the practice of ijtihad which emphasize the Quran and suanna as primary source.

King Fahd has encouraged modern Saudi jurists to use ijtihad. In a speech read on his behalf at the Muslim World League's College of Islamic Jurisprudence in January 1985, Fahd said, 'The circumstances of the age require Islamic jurists to use ijtihad as a necessary instrument for defining the correct doctrine on new issues.' Following this speech, the college adopted resolutions permitting the previously legally ambiguous practices of organ transplants, artificial insemination and burial in caskets. These resolutions will have the force of law.

Shari'a law divides crimes into three categories: hadd, ta'zir, and qisas. Hadd crimes are violations of divinely ordained commandments for which the Quran prescribes specific punishments. These crimes include highway robbery, murder, theft, adultery, apostasy, and consumption of intoxicants. Hadd cases must be initiated by the injured party. Conviction of a hadd crime requires either the confession of the accused or the testimony of at least two eye-witnesses. Penalties are severe and include execution and amputation, sometimes referred to together as qat or as cutting punishments. Ta'zir crimes are those not mentioned in the Quran which are left for the community to legislate. Ta'zir punishments include fines, imprisonment, and flogging. There can be an overlap between hadd and ta'zir crimes. In cases where the standards of evidence required for a hadd conviction cannot be met, but the judge still considers the defendant guilty, he may apply ta'zir punishment for a hadd crime. Qisas crimes include murder and cutting off part of the human body. Punishments include prelication of the injury to the defendant or the acceptance of blood money by the injured party. Blood money, known in the case of death as diya, is approximately $50.000 for a Saudi male. Blood money for injury known as arsh, is highly negotiable. Qisas crimes are also crimes against the community. The offender will probably be prosecuted under ta'zir even if the victim waves his right to retribution.

Shari'a courts

There are no juries in shari'a courts and usually no spectators or attorneys. The judge, is not simply a mediator but rather a active participant in an effort to establish the truth. He meets with the plaintiff and the defendant, questions them and their witnesses, determines guilt or innocence, and passes sentence. The judge is not bound by precedents of previous decisions and is guided only by his own judgement and widely accepted application of principles found in the Quran and sunna.

Until 1971, administration of the shari'a court system was the responsibility of the Grand Mufti of Saudi Arabia. When the last mufti, Muhammad Ibn Ibrahim Al Al-Shaykh, died in 1970, King Faisal announced his intention to create a Ministry of Justice. In July 1975, four months after Faisal's death, a royal decree placing judicial, financial, and administrative control of the shari'a courts in the hands of newly created ministry of justice was promulgated.

This decree, known as the Nitham Al-Qada, also outlined the functions of various shari'a courts and established the supreme judicial council. Summary courts (Al-Mahlamah Al-Musta'ajlah) have jurisdiction over offenses carrying less than qat penalties, assaults in which arsh is less that ten percent of diya and property disputes less than 8.000. They are presided by one relatively junior judge. More serious crimes are initially heard in the General Court (Al-Mahkamah Al-Kubra). These cases are heard by one senior judge, except in instances involving qat punishments where summary and general courts will be heard in the two appeal courts (Al-Mahkamah Al-Tammeez) in Riyadh and Makkah. Here again while most cases are heard by a panel of three judges, those involving qat punishments are heard by a panel of five.

The Supreme Judicial Council (Majlis Al-Qada Al-'Ala) is not a court as such and does not reverse appeal court decisions. It refers decisions back to lower courts for reconsideration. It is composed of twelve senior jurists, including the minister of justice, and provides overall supervision for the court system including the appointment, discipline, promotion, and transfer of judges. The supreme judicial council also analyzes legal questions referred to it by the king and crown prince and reviews all cases involving severe punishment.

The council of senior religious scholars (Lajnah Kabir Al-Ulama) is an autonomous body composed of 15 senior ulama, including the minister of justice. It is ultimately responsible for propounding the principles upon which the judges decide cases. As there is an immense body of legal opinion regarding these principles already on the books, the council meets only to consider unusual cases.

Shari'a judges are selected from those who have studied jurisprudence in one of Saudi Arabia's Islamic universities. They are initially selected by a Ministry of Justice panel and confirmed by decision of the Council of Ministers. They serve a one-year probationary period and apprenticeship under a more senior judge. Then they are sent to work in summary courts in rural districts. Promotion to higher courts in larger cities is done almost entirely according to seniority.

The Ministry of Interior

The ministry of interior also plays a role in resolving legal disputes. The provincial governor, or amir, is the senior ministry of interior official in each province. He is officially responsible for the maintenance of law and order and control of the police. In fact, his influence usually extends to all aspects of local government. Provincial amirs exercise authority both directly and through an office of civil rights (Maktab Al-Huquq Al-Madaniya) which is a bureau of the Ministry of Interior Security Forces (amin Al-Amm).

Many Saudis look to their amir for assistance in solving all their legal problems and frequently bring their disputes to the majlis or huquq, as the office of civil rights is commonly known. The amir of huquq chief first tries to resolve personal disputes in a mutually agreeable fashion. Failing this, they refer the parties to the appropriate court or ministry. In most cases the plaintiff could have gone directly to the court or ministerial tribunal if he had wanted to. Only the committees for commercial disputes require that a complaint go first to the huquq to seek settlement. The amir and huquq office do resolve minor civil matters summarily, particularly the non-payment of private debt between individuals. The solution is usually the imprisonment of the debtor until he or his family has paid.

Traffic offenses which do not involve personal injury are resolved by the Ministry of Interior traffic police (Idarat Al-Murur). Decisions concerning guilt and punishment are made either by a policeman at the scene of the incident or shortly thereafter at police headquarters. In traffic accidents the police are reluctant to assign full responsibility to one party or the other. Instead they seek compromise solutions. Appeals can be made to more senior police officers but there is no appeal to an authority beyond the traffic police.

The grievance board

Islamic jurisprudence holds the head of state responsible for arbitrating disputes between the public and the government. This can be done either personally through the majlis system, or through a designated grievance board (Diwan Al-Mathalim), such as have existed since abbasid times. In either case the ruler or his representatives must make judgements in line with the general provisions of shari'a law. They are, however, accorded considerable flexibility in resolving issues not specifically addressed in the Quran or sunna.

King Abd Al-Aziz was known for his personal handling of disputes between citizens and government. The increasing complexity of government affairs led to the creation of a formal grievance board in 1955. The board is an independent judicial body reporting directly to the king. The current president, Mohammad Ibn Ibrahim Ibn Jubair, holds cabinet rank.

In 1983 the board received a new charter which increased its independence from the executive, brought board judges up to par with those of shari'a courts in terms of salary and security of tenure, and strengthened its ombudsman role. The president of the board is appointed by the king. He in turn appoints the remaining judges, who are trained in both shari'a law and secular commercial codes. They are assisted by advisors who specialize in various branches of administrative law. They are boards in Riyadh, Jeddah, Dammam, and Abha. The administrative committee of the board comprises six judges. It sits in Riyadh and is designed as a counterpart to the Supreme Judicial Council. The administrative committee reviews cases and handles appointments, promotions, transfers, and disciplinary action. It can reverse previous decisions. The grievance board handles all suits against the government, corruption, bribery and forgery, disputes arising under the civil service or pension regulations and applications for execution of foreign court judgements. Only in the case of alleged corruption does the board review shari'a court decisions.

The labor courts

The first labor codes in Saudi Arabia were promulgated in 1947. Primarily affecting Aramco, these early regulations removed labor disputes from the jurisdiction of the shari'a courts and established special administrative tribunals known as labor offices (Maktab Al-A'ammal). These courts adjudicate matters regulated by Saudi Arabia's now extensive labor regulations, such as the dismissal of employees, working hours, vacations, rest periods, safety standards, benefits for injury on the job, and the employment of women and children.

In November 1969, King Faisal signed a royal decree approving a new labor and workmen's law establishing the present structure of the labor office. The law called for primary committees for settlement of labor disputes throughout the country and a supreme committee for settlement of labor disputes in riyadh. The primary committees consist of three judges, at least one of whom is shari'a-trained, and may issue final judgements on disputes involving sums of less than SR 3,000. More serious matters involving larger sums of money, injury or termination may be appealed to the supreme committee which consists of five judges representing the ministries of labor and social affairs, commerce, and petroleum and resources. Decisions of the supreme committee are final. In matters not specifically governed by labor regulations the committees are guided by shari'a principles.

Labor office committees are widely held to be fast, fair and easy to use. An employee can start a case simply by filing a complaint. The entire procedure, including appeal, is usually finished in three to four months. A plaintiff cannot be deported while the dispute is being resolved. Unlike shari'a courts, written evidence and contracts have predominant importance.

Commercial and financial tribunals

As Saudi Arabia's economy has grown more complex, commercial transactions have evolved new patterns not encompassed in shari'a law. In particular shari'a courts do not generally recognize the concepts of limited liability, escrow or the time value of money. Many businessmen prefer to resolve private commercial disputes either through non-binding chamber of commerce arbitration or ministry of commerce tribunals.

Commercial dispute committees exist in Riyadh, Dammam and Jeddah. They function as part of the Ministry of Commerce and use regulations issued by the ministry. Each committee consists of two shari'a court judges who are familiar with commercial regulations and a Ministry of Commerce legal advisor. A case may be brought to the committee only after attempts to resolve it by the huquq have failed. Committee decisions can be appealed to the Minister of Commerce but are seldom reversed.

The Ministry of Commerce also administers commercial paper dispute committee which deal solely with negotiable instruments such as checks and letters of credit. Like the commercial dispute committees, decisions are made by a panel of three judges, two shari'a trained and one from the Ministry of Commerce. Because the disputes are usually based on physical evidence they are resolved quickly.

Saudi firms pay zakat, the Islamic wealth tax based on profits and the value of certain fixed assets. Foreign firms pay income tax. Disputes arising over taxes are taken to Ministry of Finance tribunals which are presided over by Ministry of Finance officials and from which there is no effective appeal.

Hand-out from United States Consulate, Riyadh, December 1996; the Consulate now refers to the State Department *Yearbook on Human Rights Practices.*

7L
Nursing Wounds

The case of the two British nurses, Deborah Parry and Lucille McLauchlan, accused of murdering an Australian colleague, has brought a number of issues to the fore. The repercussions have been felt not only in terms of international relations but has also given rise to important questions in the discourse on comparative religions and laws, opening up as many suspicions and enquiries in the Muslim mind as in the average Western non-Muslim one. Of course, some of the details – of sexual lechery, lesbian jealousy and the sheer gruesome nature of the crime – propounded by the Arab media in the main – are as shocking and titillating as any mindset can be expected to be fascinated by. For Muslims especially, the interest of the international press continues to be more a question of putting Islamic Shari'a – as interpreted by Saudi Arabian judges – on trial than concentrating on the actual chain of events and legal issues. In this respect, the O J Simpson trial in the United States was an almost perfect precedent of media representation of 'celebrity trials'. Indeed, it might be far from exaggeration to suggest that the case of these two nurses is becoming just that, a celebrity trial, with increasingly less interest in the actualities of legal process and more in the symbolic representation of two young [white] women who somehow manifest the archetypal victims of Islamic justice. In sum, the symbolic relevance of this trial – and the mollycoddling approach of the media and, to a certain extent the respective British and Saudi Arabian foreign departments of state, could perhaps be viewed as indicative of the general overall relationship between the West and Islam, with the latter still very much under the critical microscope of an enlightened libertarianism.

The nurses' lawyer, Salah al-Hejailan, says the outcome lies as much in the political as the legal arena. Human rights organisations such as Fair Trials Abroad, based in London, rightly state that the issue is not one of criticism of Shari'a but the conduct of law enforcement agencies and fair trials for foreigners abroad. Trials cannot be observed, for instance. Apparently, consular officials were initially not allowed access to the women accused and the nurses were allegedly coerced into confessing. In such cases, Islamic law too would be obliged to throw the case out.

One overriding issue arising from the case is that of public executions. This year, more than eighty people have been beheaded, mainly men from developing countries (one female Nigerian was beheaded earlier in the year). There are many more on death row. Seven Pakistani children, eight women and four men all face the death penalty for allegedly concealing heroin on their bodies when stopped by police at Jeddah airport last January. Both Pakistan and Saudi Arabia have ratified the Convention on the Rights of the Child which states that children cannot be subject to capital punishment. Some people have started to ask why such people, especially Filipinos, have not been subject to similar care and attention as that of the nurses. This has led to accusations of double standards not only against the West but against the justice system in Saudi Arabia also. In Saudi Arabia, judges are by definition from the majority Hanbali school of Islamic thought and implement a particularly rigid conservative application of Shari'a rulings, often interpreted according to the Wahhabi doctrine, itself renowned throughout the Muslim world for its almost unique ultra-conservatism. The result is, of course, that if you are an indigenous Shi'a Muslim from the Eastern Province, for instance, you are still subject to the same Shari'a rulings as a follower of Hanbali doctrine.

Under Saudi law, the family of a murder victim can choose not to have the death penalty. This would also speed up the trial. Yet another angle to the case and the trial is the obstinacy of Frank Gilford, the brother of the murdered nurse, who, until recently, stated that he believed in the death penalty. The Islamic condition of taking into account the views of a victim or his/her family may be a positive component of a complicated legal system but it is open to manipulation by lawyers, especially in such high profile cases. The argument that it would be ironic for a Western family to support capital punishment makes little sense given some Western countries' own insistence on its utilisation, in addition to the intra-Western debate on this issue. Such arguments reek more of hypocrisy than irony. The bottom line is: so what if Frank Gilford believes in the death penalty? Many people in the West, as in the East, do.

In any case, it was generally assumed from the very beginning that the Saudi authorities never wanted a public beheading. The kingdom realises that if such did occur, it would sever relations – albeit temporarily since there is simply too much at stake economically – with Britain, a nation that provides some of the most sophisticated warfare technology in the world. Gilford was, in many ways, the last stumbling block, a thorn in both sides, but a man who has – and here there might be room for irony – earned a certain grudging respect for sticking to his principles.

The Saudi regime is under scrutiny not only in the West but its own Islamic credentials are under the microscope of Islamists within the kingdom. Nevertheless, the Government has bent over backwards to accommodate not only the Western sense of what is fair but the emotional views of the families of the nurses. But the notion of international standards still does not seem to be part of the Saudi equation. Saudi application of and respect for international standards goes to the heart of the nature of its own dissident community and is beyond the case of even the nurses. It tests Saudi attitudes towards its own populations (the plight of Shi'a Muslims in the Eastern Province and elsewhere), its neighbours (unpopularity among populations in other Gulf states) and its own people who are fed up with the regime's lack of responsiveness to their needs and aspirations.

No copyright or author stated. Published by 'Dialogue', the Public Affairs Committee for Shi'a Muslims, 7 October 1997.

Chapter Eight

HUMAN RIGHTS

8A
Universal Declaration of Human Rights

The General Assembly of the newly established United Nations in 1948 adopted a universal declaration of rights.

Article One: All human beings are born free and equal in dignity and rights. They are endowed with reason and conscience and should act towards one another in a spirit of brotherhood.

Article Two: Everyone is entitled to all the rights and freedoms set forth in this Declaration, without distinction of any kind, such as race, colour, sex, language, religion, political or other opinion, national or social origin, property, birth or other status.

Furthermore, no distinction shall be made on the basis of the political, jurisdictional or international status of the country or territory to which a person belongs, whether it be independent, trust, non-self-governing or under any other limitation of sovereignty.

Article Three: Everyone has the right to life, liberty and security of person.

Article Four: No one shall be held in slavery or servitude; slavery and the slave trade shall be prohibited in all their forms.

Article Five: No one shall be subjected to torture or to cruel, inhuman or degrading treatment or punishment.

Article Six: Everyone has the right to recognition everywhere as a person before the law.

Article Seven: All are equal before the law and are entitled without any discrimination to equal protection of the law. All are entitled to equal protection against any discrimination in violation of this Declaration and against any incitement to such discrimination.

Article Eight: Everyone has the right to an effective remedy by the competent national tribunals for acts violating the fundamental rights granted him by the constitution or by law.

Article Nine: No one shall be subjected to arbitrary arrest, detention or exile.

Article Ten: Everyone is entitled in full equality to a fair and public hearing by an independent and impartial tribunal, in the determination of his rights and obligations and of any criminal charge against him.

Article Eleven:

1. Everyone charged with a penal offence has the right to be presumed innocent until proved guilty according to law in a public trial at which he has had all the guarantees necessary for his defence.
2. No one shall be held guilty of any penal offence on account of any act or omission which did not constitute a penal offence, under national or international law, at the time when it was committed. Nor shall a heavier penalty be imposed than the one that was applicable at the time the penal offence was committed.

Article Twelve: No one shall be subjected to arbitrary interference with his privacy, family, home or correspondence, nor to attacks upon his honour and reputation. Everyone has the right to the protection of the law against such interference or attacks.

Article Thirteen:

1. Everyone has the right to freedom of movement and residence within the borders of each state.
2. Everyone has the right to leave any country, including his own, and to return to his country.

Article Fourteen:

1. Everyone has the right to seek and to enjoy in other countries asylum from persecution.
2. This right may not be invoked in the case of prosecutions genuinely arising from non-political crimes or from acts contrary to the purposes and principles of the United Nations.

Article Fifteen:

1. Everyone has the right to a nationality.
2. No one shall be arbitrarily deprived of his nationality nor denied the right to change his nationality.

Article Sixteen:

1. Men and women of full age, without any limitation due to race, nationality or religion, have the right to marry and to found a family. They are entitled to equal rights as to marriage, during marriage and at its dissolution.
2. Marriage shall be entered into only with the free and full consent of the intending spouses.
3. The family is the natural and fundamental group unit of society and is entitled to protection by society and the State.

Article Seventeen:

1. Everyone has the right to own property alone as well as in association with others.
2. No one shall be arbitrarily deprived of his property.

Article Eighteen: Everyone has the right to freedom of thought, conscience and religion; this right includes freedom to change his religion or belief, and freedom, either alone or in community with others and in public or private, to manifest his religion or belief in teaching, practice, worship and observance.

Article Nineteen: Everyone has the right to freedom of opinion and expression; this right includes freedom to hold opinions without interference and to seek, receive and impart information and ideas through any media and regardless of frontiers.

Article Twenty:

1. Everyone has the right to freedom of peaceful assembly and association.
2. No one may be compelled to belong to an association.

Article Twenty-one:

1. Everyone has the right to take part in the government of his country, directly or through freely chosen representatives.
2. Everyone has the right of equal access to public service in his country.
3. The will of the people shall be the basis of the authority of government; this will shall be expressed in periodic and genuine elections which shall be by universal and equal suffrage and shall be held by secret vote or by equivalent free voting procedures.

Article Twenty-two: Everyone, as a member of society, has the right to social security and is entitled to realization, through national effort and international co-operation and in accordance with the organization and resources of each State, of the economic, social and cultural rights indispensable for his dignity and the free development of his personality.

Article Twenty-three:

1. Everyone has the right to work, to free choice of employment, to just and favourable conditions of work and to protection against unemployment.
2. Everyone, without any discrimination, has the right to equal pay for equal work.
3. Everyone who works has the right to just and favourable remuneration ensuring for himself and his family an existence worthy of human dignity, and supplemented, if necessary, by other means of social protection.
4. Everyone has the right to form and to join trade unions for the protection of his interests.

Article Twenty-four: Everyone has the right to rest and leisure, including reasonable limitation of working hours and periodic holidays with pay.

Article Twenty-five:

1. Everyone has the right to a standard of living adequate for the health and wellbeing of himself and of his family, including food, clothing, housing and medical care and necessary social services, and the right to security in the event of unemployment, sickness, disability, widowhood, old age or other lack of livelihood in circumstances beyond his control.
2. Motherhood and childhood are entitled to special care and assistance. All children, whether born in or out of wedlock, shall enjoy the same social protection.

Article Twenty-six:

1. Everyone has the right to education. Education shall be free, at least in the elementary and fundamental stages. Elementary education shall be compulsory. Technical and professional education shall be made generally available and higher education shall be equally accessible to all on the basis of merit.
2. Education shall be directed to the full development of the human personality and to the strengthening of respect for human rights and fundamental freedoms. It shall promote understanding, tolerance and friendship among all nations, racial or religious groups, and shall further the activities of the United Nations for the maintenance of peace.
3. Parents have a prior right to choose the kind of education that shall be given to their children.

Article Twenty-seven:

1. Everyone has the right freely to participate in the cultural life of the community, to enjoy the arts and to share in scientific advancement and its benefits.

2. Everyone has the right to the protection of the moral and material interests resulting from any scientific, literary or artistic production of which he is the author.

Article Twenty-eight: Everyone is entitled to a social and international order in which the rights and freedoms set forth in this Declaration can be fully realized.

Article Twenty-nine:

1. Everyone has duties to the community in which alone the free and full development of his personality is possible.
2. In the exercise of his rights and freedoms, everyone shall be subject only to such limitations as are determined by law solely for the purpose of securing due recognition and respect for the rights and freedoms of others and of meeting the just requirements of morality, public order and the general welfare in a democratic society.
3. These rights and freedoms may in no case be exercised contrary to the purposes and principles of the United Nations.

Article Thirty: Nothing in this Declaration may be interpreted as implying for any State, group or person any right to engage in any activity or to perform any act aimed at the destruction of any of the rights and freedoms set forth herein.

United Nations, adopted 1948 by the General Assembly without a dissenting vote.

8B
International Covenant on Civil and Political Rights

The Universal Declaration of Human Rights, adopted by the General Assembly of the United Nations in 1948, did not have the force of law. In 1976 the Assembly adopted the International Covenant on Civil and Political Rights which transformed the original principles into treaty provisions.

PART I

Article One:

1. All peoples have the right of self-determination. By virtue of that right they freely determine their political status and freely pursue their economic, social and cultural development.
2. The States Parties to the present Covenant, including those having responsibility for the administration of Non-Self-Governing and Trust Territories, shall promote the realization of the right self-determination, and shall respect that right, in conformity with the provisions of the charter of the United Nations.

PART II

Article Two:

1. Each State Party to the present Covenant undertakes to respect and to ensure to all individuals within its territory and subject to its jurisdiction the rights recognized in the present Covenant, without distinction of any kind, such as race, colour, sex, language, religion, political or other opinion, national or social origin, property, birth or other status.
2. When not already provided for by existing legislative or other measures, each State Party to the present Covenant undertakes the necessary steps, in accordance with its constitutional processes and with the provisions of the present Covenant, to adopt such legislative or other measure as may be necessary to give effect to the rights recognized in the present Covenant.
3. Each Party to the present Covenant undertakes:
   (a) To ensure that any person whose rights or freedoms are herein recognized are violated shall have an effective remedy, notwithstanding that the violation has been committed by persons acting in an official capacity;
   (b) To ensure that any person claiming such a remedy shall have his right thereto determined by competent authority provided for by the legal system of the State, and to develop the possibilities of judicial remedy;
   (c) To ensure that the competent authorities shall enforce such remedies when granted.

Article Three: The States Parties to the present Covenant undertake to ensure that equal right of men and women to the enjoyment of all civil and political rights set forth in the present Covenant.

PART III

Article Six:

1. Every human being has the inherent right to life. This right shall be protected by law. No one shall be arbitrarily deprived of his life.
2. In countries which have not abolished the death penalty, sentence of death may be imposed only for the most serious crimes in accordance with the law in force at the time of the commission of the crime and not contrary to the provisions of the present Covenant and to the Convention on the Prevention and Punishment of the Crime of Genocide. This penalty can only be carried out pursuant to a final judgement rendered by a competent court.
3. When deprivation of life constitutes the crime of genocide, it is understood that nothing in this article shall authorize any State Party to present Covenant to derogate in any way from any obligation assumed under the provisions of the convention on the Prevention and Punishment of the Crime of Genocide.

4. Anyone sentenced to death shall have the right to seek pardon or commutation of the sentence. Amnesty, pardon or commutation of the sentence of death may be granted in all cases.
5. Sentence of death shall not be imposed for crimes committed by persons below eighteen years of age and shall not be carried out on pregnant women.
6. Nothing in this article shall be invoked to delay or to prevent the abolition of capital punishment by any State Party to the present Covenant.

Article Seven: No one shall be subjected to torture or to cruel, inhuman or degrading treatment or punishment. In particular, no one shall be subjected without his free consent to medical or scientific experimentation.

Article Eight:

1. No one shall be held in slavery; slavery and the slave-trade in all their forms shall be prohibited.
2. No one shall be held in servitude.

Article Nine:

1. Everyone has the right of liberty and security of person. No one shall be subjected to arbitrary arrest or detention. No one shall be deprived of his liberty except on such grounds and in accordance with such procedure as are established by law.
2. Anyone who is arrested shall be informed, at the time of arrest, of the reasons for his arrest and shall be promptly informed of any charges against him.
3. Anyone arrested or detained on a criminal charge shall be brought promptly before a judge or other officer authorized by law to exercise judicial power and shall be entitled to trial with a reasonable time or to release. It shall not be the general rule that persons awaiting trial shall be detained in custody, but release may be subject to guarantees to appear for trial at any other stage of the judicial proceedings, and, should occasion arise, for execution of the judgement.
4. Anyone who is deprived of his liberty by arrest or detention shall be entitled to take proceedings before a court, in order that that court may decide without delay on the lawfulness of his detention and order his release if the detention is not lawful.
5. Anyone who has been the victim of unlawful arrest or detention shall have an enforceable right to compensation.

Article Twelve:

1. Everyone lawfully within the territory of a State shall, within that territory, have the right to liberty of movement and freedom to choose his residence.

2. Everyone shall be free to leave any country, including his own.
3. The above-mentioned rights shall not be subject to any restrictions except those which are provided by law, are necessary to protect national security, public order (ordre public), public health or morals or the rights and freedoms of others, and are consistent with the other rights recognized in the present Covenant.
4. No one shall be arbitrarily deprived of the right to enter his own country.

Article Fourteen:

1. All persons shall be equal before the courts and tribunals. In the determination of any criminal charge against him, or of his rights and obligations in a suit at law, everyone shall be entitled to a fair and public hearing by competent, independent and impartial tribunal established by law. The press and the public may be excluded from all or part of a trial for reasons of morals, public order (ordre public) or national security in a democratic society, or when the interests of the private lives of the parties so requires, or to the extent strictly necessary in the opinion of the court in special circumstances where publicity would prejudice the interest of justice; but any judge rendered in a criminal case or in a suit at law shall be made public except where the interest of juvenile persons otherwise requires or the proceedings concern matrimonial disputes or the guardian of children.
2. Everyone charged with a criminal offence shall have the right to be presumed innocent until proved guilty according to law.
3. In the determination of any criminal charge against him, everyone shall be entitled to the following minimum guarantees, in full equality:
   (a) To be informed promptly and in detail in a language which he understands of the nature and cause of the charge against him;
   (b) To have adequate time and facilities for the preparation of his defence and to communicate with counsel of his choosing;
   (c) To be tried without undue delay;
   (d) To be tried in his presence, and to defend himself in person or through legal assistance, of his own choosing, to be informed, if he does not have legal assistance, of this right; and to have legal assistance assigned to him, in any case where the interests of justice so require, and without payment by him in any such case if he does not have sufficient means to pay for it;
   (e) To examine, or have examined, the witnesses against him and to obtain the attendance and examination of witnesses on his behalf under the same conditions as witnesses against him;
   (f) To have the free assistance of an interpreter if he cannot understand or speak the language used in court;
   (g) Not to be compelled to testify against himself or to confess guilt.

Article Sixteen: Everyone shall have the right to recognition everywhere as a person before the law.

Article Seventeen:

1. No one shall be subjected to arbitrary or unlawful interference with his privacy, family, home or correspondence, nor to unlawful attacks on his honour and reputation.
2. Everyone has the right to the protection of the law against such interference or attacks.

Article Eighteen:

1. Everyone shall have the right of freedom of thought, conscience and religion. This right shall include freedom to have or to adopt a religion or belief of his choice, and freedom, either individually or in community with others and in public or private, to manifest his religion or belief in worship, observance, practice and teaching.
2. No one shall be subject to coercion which would impair his freedom to have or to adopt a religion or belief of his choice.
3. Freedom to manifest one's religion or beliefs may be subjected only to such limitations as are prescribed by law and are necessary to protect public safety, order, health, or morals or the fundamental rights and freedoms of others.
4. The States Parties to the present Covenant undertake to have respect for the liberty of parents and, when applicable, legal guardians to ensure the religious and moral education of their children in conformity with their own convictions.

Article Nineteen:

1. Everyone shall have the right to hold opinions without interference.
2. Everyone shall have the right to freedom of expression; this right shall include freedom of seek, receive and impart information and ideas of all kinds, regardless of frontiers, either orally, in writing or in print, in the form of art, or through any other media of his choice.

Article Twenty:

1. Any propaganda for war shall be prohibited by law.
2. Any advocacy of national, racial or religious hatred that constitutes incitement to discrimination, hostility or violence shall be prohibited by law.

Article Twenty-one: The right of peaceful assembly shall be recognized. No restrictions may be placed on the exercise of this right other than those imposed in conformity with the law and which are necessary in a democratic society in the interests of national security or public safety, public order (ordre public), the protection of public health or morals or the protection of the rights and freedoms of others.

Article Twenty-three:

1. The family is the natural and fundamental group unit of society and is entitled to protection by society and the State.
2. The right of men and women of marriageable age to marry and to found a family shall be recognized.
3. No marriage shall be entered into without the free and full consent of the intending spouses.
4. States Parties to the present Covenant shall take appropriate steps to ensure equality of rights and responsibilities of spouses as to marriage, during marriage and at its dissolution. In the case of dissolution, provision shall be made for the necessary protection of any children.

Article Twenty-four:

1. Every child shall have, without any discrimination as to race, colour, sex, language, religion, national or social origin, property or birth, the right to such measures of protection as are required by his status as a minor, on the part of his family, society and State.
2. Every child shall be registered immediately after birth and shall have a name.
3. Every child has the right to acquire a nationality.

Article Twenty-five: Every citizen shall have the right and the opportunity, without any of the distinctions mentioned in Article 2 and without unreasonable restrictions;

(a) To take part in the conduct of public affairs, directly or through freely chosen representatives;
(b) To vote and to be elected at genuine periodic elections which shall be by universal and equal suffrage and shall be held by secret ballot, guaranteeing the free expression of the will of the electors;
(c) To have access, on general terms of equality, to public service in his country.

Article Twenty-six: All persons are equal before the law and are entitled without any discrimination to the equal protection of the law. In this respect, the law shall prohibit any discrimination and guarantee to all persons equal and effective protection against discrimination on any ground such as race, colour, sex, language, religion, political or other opinion, national or social origin, birth or other status.

Article Twenty-seven: In those States in which ethnic, religious or linguistic minorities exist, persons belonging to such minorities shall not be denied the right, in community with the other members of their group, to enjoy their own culture, to profess and practise their own religion, or to use their own language.

United Nations 1976, not signed by Saudi Arabia.

8C
The Cairo Declaration

The Member States of the Organisation of the Islamic Conference in August 1990 issued 'The Cairo Declaration on Human Rights in Islam'.

The Member States of the Organization of the Islamic Conference,

Reaffirming the civilizing and historical role of the Islamic Ummah which God made the best nation that has given mankind a universal and well-balanced civilization in which harmony is established between this life and the hereafter and knowledge is combined with faith; and the role that this Ummah should play to guide a humanity confused by competing trends and ideologies and to provide solutions to the chronic problems of this materialistic civilization.

Wishing to contribute to the efforts of mankind to assert human rights, to protect man from exploitation and persecution, and to affirm this freedom and right to a dignified life in accordance with the Islamic Shari'ah.

Convinced that mankind which has reached an advanced stage in materialistic science is still, and shall remain, in dire need of faith to support its civilization and of a self-motivation force to guard its rights.

Believing that fundamental rights and universal freedoms in Islam are an integral part of the Islamic religion and that no one as a matter of principle has the right to suspend them in whole or in part or violate or ignore them in as much as they are binding divine commandments, which are contained in the Revealed Books of God and were sent through the last of His Prophets to complete the preceding divine messages thereby making their observance an act of worship and their neglect or violation an abominable sin, and accordingly every person is individually responsible – and the Ummah collectively responsible – for their safeguard.

Proceeding from the above-mentioned principles,

Declare the following:

Article One:

(a) All human beings form one family whose members are united by submission to God and descent from Adam. All men are equal in terms of basic human dignity and basic obligations and responsibilities, without any discrimination on the grounds of race, colour, language, sex, religious belief, political affiliation, social status or other considerations. True faith is the guarantee for enhancing such dignity along the path to human perfection.

(b) All human beings are God's subjects, and the most loved by Him are those who are most useful to the rest of His subjects, and no one has superiority over another except on the basis of piety and good deeds.

Article Two:

(a) Life is a God-given gift and the right to life is guaranteed to every human being. It is the duty of individuals, societies and states to protect this right from any violation, and it is prohibited to take away life except for a Shari'a prescribed reason.

(b) It is forbidden to resort to such means as may result in the genocidal annihilation of mankind.

(c) The preservation of human life throughout the term of time willed by God is a duty prescribed by Shari'a.

(d) Safety from bodily harm is a guaranteed right. It is the duty of the state to safeguard it, and it is prohibited to breach it without a Shari'a prescribed reason.

Article Three:

(a) In the event of the use of force and in case of armed conflict, it is not permissible to kill non-belligerents such as old men, women and children. The wounded and the sick shall have the right to medical treatment; and prisoners of war shall have the right to be fed, sheltered and clothed. It is prohibited to mutilate dead bodies. It is a duty to exchange prisoners of war and to arrange visits or reunions of the families separated by the circumstances of war.

(b) It is prohibited to fell trees, to damage crops or livestock, and to destroy the enemy's civilian buildings and installations by shelling, blasting or any other means.

Article Four: Every human being is entitled to inviolability and the protection of his good name and honour during his life and after his death. The state and society shall protect his remains and burial place.

Article Five:

(a) The family is the foundation of society, and marriage is the basis of its formation. Men and women have the right to marriage, and no restrictions stemming from race, colour or nationality shall prevent them from enjoying this right.

(b) Society and the State shall remove all obstacles to marriage and shall facilitate marital procedure. They shall ensure family protection and welfare.

Article Six:

(a) Woman is equal to man in human dignity, and has rights to enjoy as well as duties to perform; she has her own civil entity and financial independence, and the right to retain her name and lineage.

(b) The husband is responsible for the support and welfare of the family.

Article Seven:

(a) As of the moment of birth, every child has rights due from the parents, society and the state to be accorded proper nursing, education an material, hygienic and moral care. Both the fetus and the mother must be protected and accorded special care.

(b) Parents and those in such like capacity have the right to choose the type of education they desire for their children, provided they take into consideration the interest and future of the children in accordance with ethical values and the principles of Shari'a.

(c) Both parents are entitled to certain rights from their children, and relatives are entitled to rights from their kin, in accordance with the tenets of the Shari'a.

Article Eight: Every human being has the right to enjoy his legal capacity in terms of both obligation and commitment, should this capacity be lost or impaired, he shall be represented by his guardian.

Article Nine:

(a) The quest for knowledge is an obligation and the provision of education is a duty for society and the State. The State shall ensure the availability of ways and means to acquire education and shall guarantee educational diversity in the interest of society so as to enable man to be acquainted with the religion of Islam and the facts of the Universe for the benefit of mankind.

(b) Every human being has the right to receive both religious and worldly education from the various institutions of, education and guidance, including the family, the school, the university, the media, etc., and in such an integrated and balanced manner as to develop his personality, strengthen his faith in God and promote his respect for and defence of both rights and obligations.

Article Ten: Islam is the religion of unspoiled nature. It is prohibited to exercise any form for compulsion on man or to exploit his poverty or ignorance in order to convert him to another religion or to atheism.

Article Eleven:

(a) Human beings are born free, and no one has the right to enslave, humiliate, oppress or exploit them, and there can be no subjugation but to God the Most-High.

(b) Colonialism of all types being one of the most evil forms of enslavement is totally prohibited. Peoples suffering from colonialism have the full right to freedom and self-determination. It is the duty of all States and peoples to support the struggle of colonized peoples for the liquidation of all forms of colonialism and occupation, and all States and peoples have the right to preserve their independent identity and exercise control over their wealth and natural resources.

Article Twelve: Every man shall have the right, within the framework of Shari'a, to free movement and to select his place of residence whether inside or outside his country and if persecuted, is entitled to seek asylum in another country. The country of refuge shall ensure his protection until he reaches safety, unless asylum is motivated by an act which Shari'a regards as a crime.

Article Thirteen: Work is a right guaranteed by the State and Society for each person able to work. Everyone shall be free to choose the work that suits him best and which serves his interests and those of society. The employee shall have the right to safety and security as well as to all other social guarantees. He may neither be assigned work beyond his capacity nor be subjected to compulsion or exploited or harmed in any way. He shall be entitled – without any discrimination between males and females – to fair wages for his work without delay, as well as to the holidays allowances and promotions which he deserves. For his part, he shall be required to be dedicated and meticulous in his work. Should workers and employers disagree on any matter, the State shall intervene to settle the dispute and have the grievances redressed, the rights confirmed and justice enforced without bias.

Article Fourteen: Everyone shall have the right to legitimate gains without monopolization, deceit or harm to oneself or to others. Usury (riba) is absolutely prohibited.

Article Fifteen:

(a) Everyone shall have the right to own property acquired in a legitimate way, and shall be entitled to the rights of ownership, without prejudice to oneself, others or to society in general. Expropriation is not permissible except for the requirements of public interest and upon payment of immediate and fair compensation.
(b) Confiscation and seizure of property is prohibited except for a necessity dictated by law.

Article Sixteen: Everyone shall have the right to enjoy the fruits of his scientific, literary, artistic or technical production and the right to protect the moral and material interests stemming therefrom, provided that such production is not contrary to the principles of Shari'a.

Article Seventeen:

(a) Everyone shall have the right to live in a clean environment, away from vice and moral corruption, an environment that would foster his self-development and it is incumbent upon the State and society in general to afford that right.
(b) Everyone shall have the right to medical and social care, and to all public amenities provided by society and the State within the limits of their available resources.
(c) The State shall ensure the right of the individual to a decent living which will enable him to meet all his requirements and those of his dependents, including food, clothing, housing, education, medical care and all other basic needs.

Article Eighteen:

(a) Everyone shall have the right to live in security for himself, his religion, his dependants, his honour and his property.
(b) Everyone shall have the right to privacy in the conduct of his private affairs, in his home, among his family, with regard to his property and his relationships. It is not permitted to spy on him, to place him under surveillance or to besmirch his good name. The State shall protect him from arbitrary interference.
(c) A private residence is inviolable in all cases. It will not be entered without permission from its inhabitants or in any unlawful manner, nor shall it be demolished or confiscated and its dwellers evicted.

Article Nineteen:

(a) All individuals are equal before the law, without distinction between the ruler and the ruled.
(b) The right to resort to justice is guaranteed to everyone.
(c) Liability is in essence personal.
(d) There shall be no crime or punishment except as provided for in the Shari'a.
(e) A defendant is innocent until his guilt is proven in a fair trial in which he shall be given all the guarantees of defence.

Article Twenty: It is not permitted without legitimate reason to arrest an individual, or restrict his freedom, to exile or to punish him. It is not permitted to subject him to physical or psychological torture or to any form of humiliation, cruelty or indignity. Nor is it permitted to subject an individual to medical or scientific experimentation without his consent or at the risk of his health or his life. Nor is it permitted to promulgate emergency laws that would provide executive authority for such actions.

Article Twenty-one: Taking hostages under any form or for any purpose is expressly forbidden.

Article Twenty-two:

(a) Everyone shall have the right to express his opinion freely in such manner as would not be contrary to the principles of the Shari'a.

(b) Everyone shall have the right to advocate what is right, and propagate what is good, and warn against what is wrong and evil according to the norms of Islamic Shari'a.

(c) Information is a vital necessity to society. It may not be exploited or misused in such a way as may violate sanctities and the dignity of Prophets, undermine moral and ethical values or disintegrate, corrupt or harm society or weaken its faith.

(d) It is not permitted to arouse nationalistic or doctrinal hated or to do anything that may be an incitement to any form of racial discrimination.

Article Twenty-three: All the rights and freedoms stipulated in this Declaration are subject to the Islamic Shari'a.

Article Twenty-four: The Islamic Shari'a is the only source of reference for the explanation or clarification of any of the articles of this Declaration.

> Cairo, 14 Muharram 1411 A.H., 5 August 1990. Minnesota Lawyers International Human Rights Committee, 'Shame in the House of Saud, Contempt for Human Rights in the Kingdom of Saudi Arabia', Minneapolis 1992.

8D
Human Rights Instruments of the Arab States and Saudi Arabia

International Human Rights Instruments signed or ratified by Arab and Islamic Countries, including all demographically Muslim countries, with the exception of Saudi Arabia.

The International Covenant on Civil and Political Rights and the International Covenant on Economic, Social and Cultural Rights have been ratified by Afghanistan, Algeria, Cameroon, Egypt, Gabon, Gambia, Iran, Iraq, Jordan, Lebanon, Libya, Mali, Morocco, Niger, Senegal, Somalia, Sudan, Syria, Tunisia and Yemen. The International Covenant on Civil and Political Rights has also been ratified by Uganda.

The International Convention on the Elimination of All Forms of Racial Discrimination has been ratified by Afghanistan, Algeria, Bangladesh, Benin (s), Burkina Faso, Cameroon, Chad, Democratic Yemen, Egypt, Gabon, Gambia, Guinea, Iran, Iraq, Kuwait, Jordan, Lebanon, Libya, Maldives, Mali, Mauritania, Morocco, Niger, Nigeria, Pakistan, Qatar, Senegal, Sierra Leone, Somalia, Sudan, Syria, Turkey (s), Uganda, the United Arab Emirates, and Yemen.

The Convention on the Elimination of All Forms of Discrimination against Women has been signed or ratified by Afghanistan (s), Bangladesh, Benin (s), Burkina Faso, Cameroon (s), Egypt, Gabon, Gambia (s), Guinea, Guinea-Bissau, Indonesia, Iraq, Jordan (s), Libya, Mali, Nigeria, Senegal, Sierra Leone, Turkey, Uganda and Yemen.

The Convention against Torture and Other Cruel, Inhuman or Degrading Treatment or Punishment has been signed or ratified by Afghanistan, Algeria, Cameroon, Egypt, Gabon (s), Gambia (s), Guinea, Indonesia (s), Libya, Morocco (s), Nigeria (s), Senegal, Sierra Leone (s), Somalia, Sudan (s), Turkey, and Uganda.

The Convention on the Political Rights of Women has been ratified by Afghanistan, Albania, Democratic Yemen, Egypt, Gabon, Guinea, Indonesia, Lebanon, Libya, Mali, Mauritania, Morocco, Niger, Nigeria, Pakistan, Senegal, Sierra Leone, and Turkey.

The Convention on the Nationality of Married Women has been ratified by Albania, Guinea (s), Libya, Malaysia, Mali, Pakistan (s), Sierra Leone, and Uganda.

The Convention on Consent to Marriage, Minimum Age for Marriage and Registration of Marriages has been ratified by Benin, Burkina Faso, Democratic Yemen, Guinea, Mali, and Niger.

The Convention for the Suppression of the Traffic in Persons and of the Exploitation of the Prostitution of Others has been ratified by Afghanistan, Albania, Algeria, Bangladesh, Burkina Faso, Democratic Yemen, Guinea, Mali, and Niger.

The Convention for the Suppression of the Traffic in Persons and of the Exploitation of the Prostitution of Others has been ratified by Afghanistan, Albania, Algeria, Bangladesh, Burkina Faso, Cameroon, Djibouti, Egypt, Guinea, Iran (s), Iraq, Jordan, Kuwait, Libya, Mali, Mauritania, Morocco, Niger, Pakistan, Senegal, Syria, and Yemen.

The Freedom of Association and Protection of the Right to Organise Convention (ILO Convention No. 87) has been ratified by Albania, Algeria, Bangladesh, Benin, Burkina Faso, Cameroon, Chad, Comoros, Egypt, Gabon, Guinea, Kuwait, Mali, Mauritania, Niger, Pakistan, Senegal, Sierra Leone, and Yemen.

The Right to Organise and Collective Bargaining Convention (ILO Convention No. 98) has been ratified by Albania, Algeria, Bangladesh, Cameroon, Comoros, Democratic Yemen, Egypt, Gabon, Guinea, Guinea-Bissau, Indonesia, Iraq, Jordan, Lebanon, Libya, Malaysia, Mali, Morocco, Niger, Nigeria, Pakistan, Senegal, Sierra Leone, Sudan, Syria, Turkey, Uganda, and Yemen.'

(s) means only signed but not ratified

Minnesota Lawyers International Human Rights Committee: 'Shame in the House of Saud, Contempt for Human Rights in the Kingdom of Saudi Arabia', Minneapolis 1992.

8E
The Case of Sheikh Muhammad al-Fassi

*Article 19, International Center Against Censorship in January 1992
made an urgent appeal on behalf of a detained sheikh.*

Muhammad al-Fassi has become the first victim of the Kingdom's post-war policy of harsh and unlawful measures to suppress political dissent.

Since October 2 1991, Sheikh Muhammad al-Fassi, a Saudi Arabian businessman, brother-in-law of Prince Turki bin Abdul Aziz who is fourth in line to the Saudi throne, and an outspoken critic of the government's Gulf war and human rights policies, has been detained at a secret location in Riyadh and reportedly has been tortured and is at risk of execution.

1. Illegal and secret extradition of Sheikh al-Fassi

Sheikh Muhammad al-Fassi arrived in Jordan with his wife and seven children on September 21 1991. He was arrested on October 2 1991 by Jordanian security forces at the Intercontinental Hotel in Amman and was subsequently handed over to the Saudi Arabian authorities, who had requested his extradition. Reportedly, his arrest was ordered by the Saudi Minister of the Interior, Prince Nayef ibn Abdul Aziz, a younger brother of King Fahd. The extradition took place, in total secrecy, at al-Hadithah crossing on the Saudi-Jordanian border. In press interviews, officials of the Saudi Arabian Embassy in Jordan denied knowledge of his enforced return.

Jordanian authorities did not reveal the reason for their compliance with the Saudi extradition request for Sheikh al-Fassi. Nor did they seek assurances that he would not be subjected to torture, *incommunicado* detention, other mistreatment or unfair trial or pre-trial procedures. The Jordanian Government violated international law by not requesting such assurances and by not respecting Sheikh al-Fassi's right to challenge, in Jordan, the decision to extradite him. The Jordanian Government, which found itself in a very difficult economic and political position at the end of the Gulf war, reportedly was pressurized by Saudi officials to hand over Sheikh al-Fassi. Many Middle-East observers believe that Sheikh al-Fassi's summary extradition was one of the many acts demanded by the Saudi Government as pre-conditions for reopening borders between the two countries, restoring diplomatic relations and resuming economic aid to Jordan.

The Saudi Arabian government sought Sheikh Muhammad al-Fassi's extradition because of his political activities. During the Gulf war Sheik al-Fassi had criticized the Saudi Arabian government. He had actively campaigned during the Gulf crisis and the war against the presence of allied armed forces in Saudi Arabia, for a peaceful solution to the crises, and for

political and democratic reforms in Saudi Arabia. Sheik al-Fassi participated in public meetings in Baghdad and elsewhere and his views were
broadcast on the radio station, Voice of the People of Najd and Hijaz,
which was transmitted from Baghdad. In the aftermath of the Gulf war, he
established a fund to send humanitarian aid to children in Iraq.

2. Incommunicado detention, torture and ill treatment

Since his illegal extradition, Sheikh al-Fassi has been held in secret
detention in a prison somewhere in Riyadh. No one has been allowed to
visit him despite appeals from his family, his lawyer and international
human rights' organizations. His *incommunicado* detention may have
facilitated conditions for the use of torture against him and he remains at
risk of continuing torture so long as he is held *incommunicado*.

Reliable sources informed Article 19 that Sheikh al-Fassi has been
shackled throughout his detention and blindfolded for long periods of time;
that he has been subjected to beatings all over his body, and to *falaqa*
(beatings on the soles of the feet); and, as a result of such beatings, that his
right hand has been fractured.

During the first week of his detention in Riyadh, sympathetic officers
allowed him to telephone his wife. He told her that he was tortured with
burning cigarettes on parts of his body and that he had suffered a heart
attack as a result of torture. He has reportedly been forced to sign
confessions extracted under torture and to read out these confessions while
being filmed by a video camera.

3. Saudi government's violation of international human rights law

Sheikh al-Fassi's arrest and *incommunicado* detention without charge is a
flagrant violation of his right to freedom of expression as guaranteed by
Article 19 of the Universal Declaration of Human Rights which states that:
'*Everyone has the right to freedom of opinion and expression; this right
includes freedom to hold opinions without interference and to seek, receive
and impart information and ideas through any media and regardless of
frontiers.*'

It is also a denial of his rights under Article 3, which states that:
'*Everyone has the right to life, liberty and security of person*'; Article 5,
which states that: '*No one shall be subjected to torture or to cruel, inhuman
or degrading treatment or punishment*'; Article 8, which states that:
'*Everyone has the right to an effective remedy by the competent national
tribunals for acts violating . . . fundamental rights*'; and Article 9, which
states that: '*No one shall be subjected to arbitrary arrest, detention or exile*'.

As of the date of this *Censorship News*, Sheikh al-Fassi has been held in *incommunicado* detention for more than three months, and the Saudi authorities have yet to acknowledge that he is held in detention or grant his family and lawyers access to him. This continuing failure violates his family's right to information, guaranteed by Article 19 of the Universal Declaration.

Quoted from *Censorship News*, Article 19, London, 16 January 1992.

8F
Minnesota Laywers Recommendation for Saudi Arabia

A draft of the Minnesota Lawyers International Human Rights Committee report, 'Shame in the House of Saud' was sent to the ambassador of Saudi Arabia in Washington for comment. The committee received no response. The committee summarized its recommendations for Saudi Arabia.

Concluding its analysis of Human Rights condition in Saudi Arabia in 1992, the Minnesota Lawyers Committee recommend that the Government of Saudi Arabia:

1. comply with the mandates of the Universal Declaration of Human Rights, and other human rights principles which it publicly has endorsed in many international fora;
2. publish and disseminate in Saudi Arabia Arabic-language versions of the Universal Declaration of Human Rights and the Cairo Declaration on Human Rights in Islam;
3. take the actions necessary to ensure that individuals are not arrested arbitrarily, imprisoned for nonviolent opposition to the government, or tortured for any reason;
4. promulgate legislation which guarantees equal rights and opportunities for women, including equal educational and vocational opportunities and freedom of movement;
5. comply with its international obligation to assure women full participation in society and full control over their personal lives;
6. respect the cultural and religious rights of the Shi'a Muslim minority, allowing the Shi'a to practice their religion and celebrate their religious holidays;
7. cease governmental discrimination against and persecution of the Shi'a minority, including discrimination in employment, education, and government service;
8. protect the rights of foreign workers and prosecute Saudi employers who abuse foreign workers;

9. issue residency permits and exit visas directly to foreign workers – not to their employers – and widely publicize where and how foreign workers may denounce and obtain redress for ill-treament, fraud, and other abuses,

10. guarantee freedom of expression in all areas of Saudi life, including artistic freedom and a truly free press,

11. guarantee freedom of movement in Saudi Arabia, including the right of all Saudi citizens freely to leave and enter the country, and permit increased access to the country by foreign journalists and human rights organizations;

12. promulgate a comprehensive penal code;

13. abolish the death penalty and other cruel and unusual punishments;

14. ratify the International Covenant on Civil and Political Rights and its First Optional Protocol, the International Covenant on Economic, Social and Cultural Rights, the International Convention on the Elimination of All Forms of Racial Discrimination, the Convention on the Elimination of All Forms of Discrimination Against Women, the Convention Against Torture and other Cruel, Inhuman or Degrading Treatment or Punishment, the Convention on the Political Rights of Women, the Concention on the nationality of Married Women, the Convention on Consent to Marriage, Minimum Age for Marriage and Registration of Marriages, the Convention for the Suppression of the Traffic in Persons and the Exploitation of the Prostitution of Others, the Freedom of (Association and protection of the Right to Organise Convention (ILO Convention No. 87), the Right to Organise and Collective Bargaining Convention (ILO Convention No. 98), the Second Additional Protocol of the Geneva Convention on the Protection of the Rights of All Migrant Workers and Members of their Families; and

15. continue to work with international organizations to dismantle the Iraqi refugee camps along the Saudi border and resettle the refugees.

> Minnesota Lawyers International Human Rights Committee: 'Shame in the House of Saud, Contempt for Human Rights in the House of Saud', Minneapolis 1992.

8G
Egyptian Organisation for Human Rights Appeal

The Egyptian Organisation for Human Rights (EOHR) in October 1994 appealed on behalf of an Egyptian doctor, sentenced to flogging in Saudi Arabia.

EOHR appeals to the international community, non-governmental organization and those concerned with human rights to strongly intervene with His Majesty King Fahd Ibn Abdul Aziz of Saudi Arabia to prevent the flogging of Egyptian physician Dr. Mohamed Kamel Mohamed Khalifa. He has been charged with telling lies and sentenced to 80 lashes in front of a school at the time when pupils are leaving, as well as to another 120 lashes – 60 after Friday prayers over a period of two weeks, in El Bakeereya – and 45 days imprisonment. He is currently held in El Brida Prison in El Qasim because he had submitted a complaint against the principal of Saoud El Kabir School in El Bekeereya, El Qasim, charging him with sexually abusing his son, a pupil at the school. He accused him of escorting the child to the school roof, injecting him with an anaesthetic and sexually abusing him.

The Egyptian doctor is further charged with letting his son and wife return to Egypt before the boy was put in a Saudi juveniles house, despite the fact that he is still suffering from depression, acute anxiety, involuntary urination and fits of crying, and fright. He is currently undergoing medical and psychiatric treatment at Ein Shams University Hospital.

EOHR has appealed to His Majesty King Fahd Ibd Abdul Aziz Al Soud, to Saudi Arabia's Ambassador to Cairo and the Egyptian Foreign Ministry to investigate the complaint by the Egyptian family, the circumstances surrounding the detention of the Egyptian physician in Saudi Arabia and the abuse of the child.

EOHR regrets that it has hardly received any response up to this point.

EOHR, Cairo, 10 October 1994.

8H
Shortcomings of the New Basic Laws

In a 1992 analysis of Saudi Arabia new basic laws, Middle East Watch
summed up improvements and shortcomings of the new texts.

The new laws codify existing legal traditions and constitutional rules in Saudi Arabia. This may make it easier for citizens to challenge their validity and appeal for their change. But the new laws do not break any new ground in providing protection for most fundamental human rights. In some key areas, such as elections and the mandate of the Consultative Council the new laws amount to backsliding from existing legislation. Such shortcomings are especially glaring in Saudi Arabia where there is no bill of citizens' rights, where the government has rejected most internationally recognized human rights agreements and where the government has historically engaged in the systematic violation of civil and political rights. The need to spell out human rights explicitly is all the more important since there is no constitutional court in the country.

1. Due Process Standards

The new laws provide no remedy to suspects, who under Saudi law are denied most due process safeguards during their arrest, detention and trial. There is no requirement in the new laws for warrants of arrest and home searches. There is no limit to, or judicial review of, pretrial detention. Nor is there an obligation to inform suspects of the charges against them or to put them on trial. There is no provision for legal counsel or legal representation of defendants who are put on trial.

2. Torture and Corporal Punishment

There is no prohibition in the new laws against torture, thus retaining existing Saudi regulations permitting the use of force during detention. Furthermore, the re-emphasis on Shari'a as the source of authority means that corporal punishment, including amputation of limbs and flogging will also continue.

3. Freedoms of Association, Assembly and Expression

The new legislation does not change the long-standing ban on free association and assembly. Under existing Saudi law, labor unions and political organizations are banned and all other forms of association are tightly controlled. Public assembly is also restricted to that approved by the government. Press laws in Saudi Arabia effectively mute free expression, a situation confirmed by the new laws.

4. Women and Minorities

The new laws do not ban discrimination based on gender or religious beliefs. By strongly restating the religious basis for Saudi law, the government appears to have foregone any attempt to provide some measure of gender equality in access to employment, education and freedom of movement. Religious minorities, both Muslims and non-Muslims, are not accorded equality with the predominant Sunni sect as interpreted by the Wahhabi school, the religious doctrine of Saudi Arabia. Religious minorities are not allowed to exercise fully their religious rites or display their symbols. Nor are they allowed to import publications necessary for their worship.

5. Foreign Residents and Refugees

Alien residents of Saudi Arabia, accounting for around one third of the population, are not afforded any protection in the new laws against arbitrary expulsion. They are still subject to summary deportation without due process. Saudi Arabia, which is not a party to any of the refugee conventions, has not changed its policy regarding refugees; the government retains full discretionary authority regardless of the interest of asylum seekers.

6. Economic and Social Rights

The bright spot in the new laws concerns the formal recognition of a number of privileges that Saudi citizens have enjoyed for some time, such as free health, education and protection for disability and in old age as being rights. In addition, the new legislation commits the state to facilitating employment to all: a significant provision if it is interpreted to include women, limited under pre-existing Saudi law to certain fields of employment.

7. Consultative Council and Elections

The proposed council is a purely advisory body. Its mandate is limited to discussing issues referred to it by the King. It will only be able to propose legislation if instructed to do so by the King. It does not have the authority to demand any government document or appearance of any government official. By September 1992, the council's members are to be appointed by the King who decides, according to the new law, their pay scale, promotions and discipline. Under the new law, every four years the King will appoint or reappoint council members. In some respects, the proposed council has more limited authority than the existing Consultative Council which was chartered in 1926 but has faded into near oblivion over the past forty years. On elections, the new laws complete the trend during the past thirty years towards the elimination of elections. They rule out elections to the Consultative Council, regional councils, and governorships.

8. The Judiciary

The new laws proclaim the independence of the judiciary, a popular demand in Saudi Arabia. Safeguarding independence, however, needs more than this proclamation.

The absence of codified laws, a provision for legal representation and a constitutional court acts against securing judicial independence. The government's tendency to bypass the judicial system altogether by deciding criminal and political cases through administrative action is a violation of equality before the law; so is interference by the ruling family in court cases.

9. US Policy

Despite a fifty-year special relationship, the US has over the years refrained from criticizing Saudi flouting of human rights principles. Once the new laws were released, the US government went out of its way to praise them, despite their obvious deficiencies. Praising them as steps towards democracy, US officials have failed to note that the new laws are only a little more than authoritarianism codified. The same administration that made holding periodic elections a test for democracy and human rights appears to accept a Saudi system which has just been formalized to rule out elections altogether, under any circumstances.

The report *Saudi Arabia's New Basic Laws* was written by Aziz Abu-Hamad, senior researcher at Middle East Watch and edited by Andrew Whitley, executive director of MEW, published in New York 1992.

8I
Saudi Student protest

The Organisation of Saudi Students in North America in September 1994 published an advertisement in the Washington Post.

Human Rights Violations in Saudi Arabia

To: President of the United States of America, Mr. Bill Clinton.

Dear Mr. President:

We are appealing to you to demand from King Fahad of Saudi Arabia, the immediate and unconditional release of Dr. Safar Al-Hawaly, 37, and Mr. Salman Al-Qudah, 39, and their supporters, all over the country. King Fahad has recently mounted *a barbaric* and *outrageous campaign of terror and Human Rights violations* against all visionaries, who are demanding reforms in an archaic and medieval police state.

On Tuesday, September 13, 1994, the Saudi authorities brought tanks, machine guns, and troops to the Qassim province to arrest Mr. Al-Qudah, a lecturer. Later that week in the western region of the country, the government arrested and jailed Dr. Al-Hawaly. These arrests were followed by the imprisonment of hundreds of supporters of change in our country.

Their crime? Speaking out critically against the regime.
The condition of the people of Saudi Arabia is deteriorating rapidly. Except for the few elite rich, the large masses of the kingdom suffer from huge political, economic, and social problems. *Serious degradation of basic Human Rights, is eroding the life of the average Saudi Citizen.* We are asking you Mr. President, the U.S. Government, and the people in the United States, to *condemn, deplore and stop the Saudi regime's campaign of terrorism that is aimed at the balanced and educated group of social reformists in Saudi Arabia.* As leaders of the 'Free World,' we implore you to support Human Rights in Saudi Arabia, just as you do in Haiti or China. Meanwhile we hold King Fahad and his regime responsible for safety of all innocent people and scholars who have been imprisoned unjustly in Saudi Arabia.

Urgently submitted by the Saudi Students in North America.

Readers: *Please call with your concerns or send your letters of support to:*

1. President Bill Clinton, White House, Phone: 202-465-1111; Fax: 202-465-2461.
2. The Saudi Embassy, USA, Phone 202-342-3800; Fax 202 944 5982.
3. Amnesty International; Phone 212-807-8400; Fax 212-627-1451.

Washington Post, 21 September 1994.

8J
Dealing with opposition

Human Rights Watch/Middle East on 17 August 1995 criticized a secret execution of a Saudi opposition Islamist and the government campaign against the opposition.

The Saudi government has carried out its first execution of an opposition activist, in a move condemned today by Human Rights Watch. On August 11, 1995, the government of Saudi Arabia beheaded Abdalla al-Hudhaif, a Saudi Islamist activist. He was convicted in a secret trial characterized by a total disregard for internationally recognized standards of due process. In the same trial, nine other Islamists were given lengthy prison sentences.

'This represents a serious escalation in the Saudi government's campaign against its Islamist opponents,' noted Chris George, executive director of Human rights Watch/Middle East. 'Over the past year, the government has arrested hundreds of Islamist activists and suppressed the opposition's criticism, but this is the first time, since the rise of Islamist opposition during the Gulf war, that an opposition activist has been executed.' Human Rights Watch also expressed its concern that the Saudi government, in announcing the recent verdicts, accused its opponents of rebellion and heresy – capital offenses in Saudi Arabia. Once branded this way, other opposition activists may also be put to death.

Al-Hudhaif, a thirty-three-year-old businessman and father of six, was accused of throwing acid on an intelligence officer possession of firearms, and 'fomenting' dissension by supporting the London-based Saudi Islamist group known as the Committee for the Defense of Legitimate Rights (CDLR) and distributing its leaflets. The acid-throwing attack is the only incident of violence that the government has attributed to the Islamist opposition since the beginning of its public activity, which has been otherwise restricted to peaceful means, including public rallies, speeches and the distribution of leaflet and audio cassettes. Although the attack on the intelligence officer was unusually cruel, disfiguring his face and other parts of his body, the resulting harsh sentence appears to be more of an attempt to stem the tide of opposition than appropriate punishment.

Human Rights Watch condemned the execution of Abdalla al-Hudhaif and deplored the secret trial during which he was denied the right to defend himself against his accusers an challenge the confessions extracted from him through the use of torture. 'We also condemn the attack on the intelligence officer,' noted Mr, George, 'but that attack does not justify the state-sanctioned execution of al-Hudhaif or his unfair trial.'

The judicial proceedings against Abdalla al-Hudhaif were marred throughout by serious violations of due process of law, including the use of coerced confessions, denial of legal counsel and blatant interference by government officials. For example, after the tribunal had sentenced Abdalla al-Hudhaif in May 1995 to twenty years in prison, the Ministry of Interior protested the lightness of sentence and demanded a retrial. The judiciary complied, and in the second review, al-Hudhaif was sentenced to death.

The decision to put him to death – which was reported made in early July and ratified by King Fadh on July 10 – was kept secret until August 12, a day after the execution. The beheading was carried out in secret, an exception to the rule of public executions. The authorities reportedly rejected the dead man's family's requests to hand over his body to conduct religious burial services. Instead, he was buried by the government, fueling speculation that he had been tortured while in detention.

Since execution was clearly disproportionate to the attack on the secret police officer, the government justified this unprecedentedly harsh sentence by citing the need to combat dissension and maintain the security and stability of the state. It cited other alleged offenses that the condemned man had committed, including the possession of weapons and his support for CDLR and the distribution of its publications, which are usually highly critical of Saudi leaders.

1. Nine other Islamists, including two university professors and a lecturer, were given lengthy prison sentences by the same tribunal, which cited their support for CDLR among the grounds for the conviction. Human Rights Watch noted in particular that two of the convicted were accused of conspiracy to attack the intelligence officer although they had already been in detention for weeks when the attack took place.

   The intelligence officer, who was not named by the government, is reported to have been Major Saud ibn Shibrin, an interrogator for the Department of General Investigations (the secret police) who in 1994 became notorious after he was named in Islamist leaflets distributed in Saudi Arabia as the most violent of DGI investigators. He reportedly interrogated Abdalla al-Hudhai1, the executed man, during a previous detention. According to a government statement announcing the execution, the attack took place after sunset on Friday, November 11, 1994, as the officer was leaving his home in Riyadh. The attacker, 'who was lying in wait, deliberately threw a caustic acidic substance aiming to kill the officer and resulting in burning a large part of his body.'

2. The others convicted include: Ibrahim al-Hudhaif, brother of executed Abdalla al- Hudhai, sentenced to eighteen years in prison and 300 lashes; Professor Muhammed al- Hudhaif, another brother, sentenced to fifteen years; Professor Muhsin al-Awaji, sentenced to fifteen years; Nasser al-Barrak, sentenced to fifteen years; and Abdel-Rahman al-Hudhaif, a cousin of Abdalla al-Hudhaif sentenced to eight years. These five were convicted of 'supporting the so-called CDLR, communicating with it and spreading its ideas which defame the Commander of the Community [King Fahd] and the Ulema [religious scholars].' They were also accused of conspiracy in the attack on the intelligence officer. Muhammed al-Hudhaif, a professor of mass communications at King Saud University, was convicted of the conspiracy despite the fact that he has been detained since October 5, 1994, more than a month before the attack. Muhsin al-Awaji, a professor at the College of Agriculture of King Saud University, was also convicted of the conspiracy despite the fact that he has been in prison since September 8, 1994, a full two months before the attack.

   Two other activists, Saleh al-Barrak and Sultan al-Suwailem, were each sentenced to five-year prison terms for helping Abdalla al-Hudhaif the alleged attacker, to evade capture by security forces and supporting CDLR. Two others, Khaled al-Yahya (a police officer) and Sultan al-Khamis, were each sentenced to three years in prison for 'supporting the so-called CDLR, attending meetings sponsored by its supporters and distributing the heretical CDLR's leaflets despite their knowledge that the leaflets were banned,' according to a government statement, which did not refer to their involvement in the attack on the interrogation officer.

The stiff sentences represent an escalation in the government's four-year campaign against the opposition, which until now has consisted of arresting key figures, the mass dismissal of Islamist sympathizers, and the blanket bans on assembly and public speech. They also coincided with the increasing intensity of rhetoric by the exiled Islamist opposition group CDLR against corruption in the kingdom. The CDLR's weekly bulletins, which include scathing critiques of the royal family's monopoly of power, are faxed from London to Saudi Arabia where they are reproduced and distributed widely. The CDLR's accusations of corruption and malfeasance, which frequently name allegedly corrupt officials and members of the royal family, are widely discussed in the kingdom, to the government's embarrassment. CDLR's questioning of the religious legitimacy of the government is especially challenging to the Saudi royal family, since its rule is founded on its claim to uphold religion in the kingdom, to promote it worldwide, and to safeguard Islam's holy shrines.

The government's August 12 statement announcing the new verdicts ominously branded the opposition as heretics, referring to the CDLR as a group that has 'strayed beyond the pale of Islam by sowing the seeds of dissension [fitna] when they declared their disobedience to the ruler of the nation to whom they had pledged loyalty and expressed their utter disregard for the Ulema, whom they accused of failing to perform their duty'. The government has already secured an opinion from the Council of Senior Scholars denouncing the CDLR as a heresy. If convicted as heretics, many of the detained Islamist opponents could face severe punishments, including the death penalty.

3. Human Rights Watch calls on the government of Saudi Arabia to set aside these harsh judgments and bring those suspected of participation in the attack on the intelligence officer to a fair and public trial before an independent court. They should be given a sufficient opportunity to defend themselves and have lawyers of their own choosing. Coerced confessions should be rejected as evidence and reports of torture should be vigorously investigated. We call on the government to permit the independent medical examination of the body of Abdalla al-Hudhaif, to determine his condition before he was beheaded, and to investigate his alleged torture. All of those who have been convicted or held without trial solely because of their peaceful expression should be immediately released.

Human Rights Watch/Middle East Page, Internet, New York, USA, 17 August 1995.

8K
Execution and Flogging

Amnesty International expressed concern in August 1995.

One man is officially reported to have been executed and another sentenced to be flogged after a trial of ten political prisoners held behind closed doors in Saudi Arabia. The case has further heightened Amnesty International's fears for up to 200 other political detainees believed to be currently detained without charge or trial.

A statement by the Ministry of Interior announced that 'Abdullah 'Abd al-Rahman al-Hudhayf, in his thirties, was executed on 12 August 1995 in Riyadh. It said he had been sentenced to death after he was found guilty of attacking a security officer with acid and of having links with the leaders of the Committee for the Defence of Legitimate Rights (CDLR), an organization based in London and banned in Saudi Arabia.

Amnesty International received reports in June that 'Abdullah 'Abd al-Rahman al-Hudhayf had been sentenced to 20 years' imprisonment on the same charges by a court in Riyadh. The organization does not know how his prison sentence was increased to the death penalty as the trial had been, and remains, shrouded in secrecy. He had had no access to defence lawyers or any legal assistance since his arrest, possibly in November 1994. He is also said to have been denied family visits and his body has apparently not been returned to his family.

Nine other political prisoners were sentenced to prison terms ranging from three to 18 years. Four were convicted of participating in the planning of the attack on the security officer and of membership of the CDLR. One of them Ibrahim 'Abd al-Rahman al-Hudhayf, has been sentenced to 300 lashes in addition to 18 years' imprisonment. The other three, Dr Muhammad 'Abd al-Rahman al-Hudhayf, Naser Ibrahim al-Barak and Dr Muhsin Hussain al-'Awaji received 15 years imprisonment each.

Two of the remaining five prisoners, 'Abd al-Rahman 'Ali al-Hudhayf and Salih Mansur al-Barak were convicted of providing refuge for 'Abduallah al-Hudayf and were respectively sentenced to eight and five years' imprisonment. The other three were convicted on various charges which included assisting 'Abdullah 'Abd al-Rahman al-Hudahyf in his aborted attempt to leave Saudi Arabia secretly and holding meetings for the CDLR and receiving its leaflets. Two of these, Khalid 'Abdullah Salih al-Yahya and Sultan 'Abd al-'Aziz Suwaylem were sentenced to five years in prisonment each. The other prisoner, Sultan 'Abd al-Muhsin al-Khamis, received three years' imprisonment.

The Ministry of Interior's statement concluded with the warning that 'such will be the fate of anyone who breaches any aspects of our religion . . . or endanger the security enjoyed by this country'. Amnesty International believes that the ten men have been punished for their political dissent rather than the criminal charge of injuries caused to the security officer. As such, some of them may be prisoners of conscience.

The ten are among hundreds of political suspects subjected to arrest and detention since 1994. Most were held for short periods before being released. However, about 200, including the ten, remained in detention. Most of those currently held are reported to be detained without charge or trial and without access to any legal assistance to challenge the lawfulness of their detention.

Amnesty International, International Secretariat, London, 15 August 1995.
AI Index: MDE 23/05/95.

8L
Dialogue on executions

Amnesty International responded in April 1995 to Saudi criticism.

'We apply the laws of God and don't pay attention to "whoever says anything about that".' This is reported (Reuters, 27 April 1995) to have been the Saudi Arabian Interior Minister's reply to reporters' questions about Amnesty International's Urgent Action of 20 April which expressed the organization's concern about the sharply rising number of executions in Saudi Arabia, and about the fate of seven Somalis, reported to be on death row there.

In an earlier Reuters report, dated 21 April, the Saudi Arabian Ambassador to London, Dr Ghazi A. al-Ghosaibi, is quoted as saying, also in response to the Urgent Action, that the recent sharp increase in the number of executions was due to an increase in drug trafficking offences. This explanation was also given by the Saudi Arabian Government in 1987 when it introduced the death penalty for drug trafficking for the first time. The number of people executed for such offences has since been steadily increasing and has accelerated alarmingly in 1995. This situation reinforces the evidence that the death penalty is not an effective means to combat crime.

The Ambassador was also quoted as saying that 'while one appreciates the idealistic motivations of Amnesty, one is struck by the organization's total insensitivity towards the religious beliefs of societies with different value systems, and its total disregard for the plight of the victims and their families'. Amnesty International takes no position on religious beliefs. The organization works for the protection of the right to life for everyone, irrespective of their ethnic origin, colour, sex, language, religious or political beliefs. Amnesty International recognizes the right of states to bring criminals to justice but does not believe that the use of the death penalty is an effective means to combat crimes.

However, neither the Minister of the Interior nor the Ambassador provided any clarification as to why prisoners facing the death penalty are denied the right to be defended by a lawyer or why confessions, even when obtained under torture are apparently accepted by the courts as evidence, and may be the sole evidence on which conviction is based. In addition, the Ambassador failed to provide any clarification regarding the seven Somali nationals reported to have been sentenced to death in 1994 for crimes which they allegedly did not commit. In one case, that of 'Abd al-'Aziz Muhammad ISSE, the crime of which he was found guilty is said to have occurred before his arrival in Saudi Arabia from Somalia. Although this information is obtainable from the airport on his arrival in Saudi Arabia, it was apparently not taken into account during his trial. The other six Somalis are: Muhammad Jamal 'ALI, 'Abd al-Qadir Muhammad MUQ-TAR, Faqay Haji CUSMAN, Sali Id Farah YACQUB, Muhammad Nur MUHAMMAD, Muhammad Abu 'Abd al-Qadir ADE. They are all reported to have been held in Priman and Ruwais Prisons in Jeddah in 1994. Amnesty International has sought clarification of these cases from the Saudi Arabian Minister of Justice but has not received a response.

Amnesty International, London, 27 April 1995,
AI Index: MDE 23/02/95.

8M
Subject to torture – personal account

A personal account by an 'Arab Afghan', arrested and tortured in November 1995.

After the fall of Kabul in April 1992 and eruption of the fires of *fitna* between the various *mujahideen* factions, we refused to indulge in such *fitna* and returned to our land, the Arabian Peninsula to seek *amn* and *aman* (safety and tranquility). I sought treatment for my amputated leg (lost during the Afghan Jihad). I stayed close to the hospital in Jeddah in a small apartment.

After the Riyadh bombing (of a US training facility in November 1995), I was awakened in the middle of the night by someone banging violently on my door. I stood on my canes and went to open it only to see it knocked down. The intruders burst into the apartment. I thought they were thieves. I yelled at them: 'Who are you? What do you want from me?'

There were eleven of them, members of the *Mabaheth* (Saudi Security). They knocked me to the ground and handcuffed me. Then they searched my apartment turning it upside down for about two hours. They did not leave anything or anywhere, including the pipes in the bathroom. Then they took whatever they willed of my books and tapes and took me with them, my hands still tied behind my back. My journey of misery and agony would last eight months.

I could never imagine that such humiliation would be inflicted in *Bilad al-Haramayn* – land of the two Holy Places. [This is a reference to the promise given by Allah in the noble Qur'an [2:125], of *amn* and safety to anyone seeking rescue and protection – *Jiwar al-Haramayn* – in certain parts of Arabia making such places a sanctuary and making the old Arab practice of *Jiwar* – rescue/protection – legally binding in Islam – Ed.]

'The car (which took me along with my belongings) stopped in front of a big building. I knew it was ar-Ruwais Prison where the central *Mabaheth* of Jeddah is located. We passed a large gate and I was given a tour of the compound as if to give me a flavour of the massive complex, which was recently expanded to deal with victims of increasing and continuous security raids.

After the routine 'check-in' procedures, I was taken to a small cell not exceeding 1.5 m by 1 m. I spent three months there. Soon after my arrival, I was taken to *Maktab* (office) No. 1. There I met the interrogator, who went by the alias of Abu Nayef, who was recently promoted to the rank of lieutenant. He was promoted, I believe, for his commitment to humiliating the faithful servants of Allah and because of his creative techniques of torture.

I later discovered that Abu Nayef was the first stop, a low-level interrogation, but he is committed to doing this 'routine' himself. He then passes the case to a subordinate while still following it closely. He also seeks directions from his boss, the prison director, Zagzoug (pronounced Za' zoo' – the name suggests he is Egyptian). He is the leader because of his torture techniques and foul-mouthed attacks on the *deen* of Islam.

I stood in front of him, handcuffed. Two subordinates standing beside him. Their faces had no expressions except those of hatred and enmity. He asked me: 'Were you the one who set up the Riyadh Bomb?' I denied any connection to the bombing. It was the truth – I knew nothing of the bombing except what I read and heard in the media.

They started beating me savagely. No part of my body was spared. My clothes were all torn. During all this, my hands were still cuffed. I was half-naked. Their appetite for torture increased when they saw the state I was in. They started using whips and tools I have never seen in my life. After hours of beating, they were asking the same question again and again: 'Why did you bomb the Riyadh?'

'I could do nothing but deny the charge. I did not do it. I was dizzy and eventually passed out. Every time I fainted, they would throw water at me to bring me back. I could no longer stand, I fell on the floor. Had they not been bored and exhausted of torturing me, they would have finished me that day. They ordered the guards to take me back to the cell. I was like a corpse; I could no longer move.

The next day they took me for more interrogation. They asked the same question again and again. Each time I denied, they lashed me with a whip. Now they tried a new form of torture. My hands were tied at the back and I was hanged from a metal bar like a slaughtered animal ready for roasting.

The interrogation was now a special kind of torture. They hit me with whips and sticks all over. Sometimes they did it all as a group, at others, they took turns. They were making *Jihad fi Sabil as-Sultan* (Jihad in the way of Sultan) and competing as to who will skin me first. It was all legitimate in their eyes. I could not withstand these exotic torture techniques. I was hanging in the air; my head was suspended. The earth started to spin around me. My soul was about to come out seeking the help of its Creator against these beasts.

I was in better shape than most other prisoners. Some had no clothing left during the torture or 'roasting' sessions. Despite the agony of the tortured person, they fondled his private parts and inserted whatever they willed, in his rectum. All this time, while they indulged in these horrible acts, they laughed as if they were feasting at a camp fire like the desert Arabs.

The second day I was taken to my cell. I was in much worse shape than during the 'party' of the previous day. The 'feast' and 'parties' continued until the party animal, Abu Nayef was tired. Then he took me to his boss Zagzoug. He had a worse tongue, and a *kufr* speech. He cursed the *ulama* as well as the righteous ones. Every time I remember how he cursed the *Deen* and *Shar'a* (Islamic law), with horrible words, by Allah, it hurt me more than what was inflicted upon me physically. I felt helpless to call on Allah's Name. Amid all this he even threatened to rape me!

After the interrogators realized that I had no connection to the Riyadh bombing, they started to force me to confess that I was one of the people of *Takfir*, those who not only say that our leaders are disbelievers, but those who go to the point of claiming that the *ulama* and society as a whole are in a state of disbelief (therefore making it legal to wage war against them, according to *Shari'ah*). They wanted to force me to confess to having used weapons to target some civilian areas, such as shopping malls and so forth.

I knew later when I was taken to the collective cell that all the *shabab* (youth) that were under incarceration were forced to confess to *Takfir* and armed action. This is with respect to Saudi citizens. As far as non-Saudis are concerned, they were asked to confess one of two things: either they worked for the intelligence services of their home country or they supported an armed struggle back home. Anyone who thought that either option would save him from torture was mistaken. The torture increased, for the interrogators thought that such confessions were true. They would torture a person until he confessed to matters other than what he was forced to sign.

I realized after having been moved to the collective cell that the number of prisoners of conscience was extremely high. It is as if any youth who displayed some degree of religiosity was incarcerated at ar-Ruwais prison. I discovered that some youths' wives were incarcerated. They were being interrogated by *wuhush ad-dhariah* (savage beasts). I was filled with rage and helplessness. These interrogators have no morals or ethics to indulge in targeting these ladies. I could only seek Allah's help to protect and save them. Some prisoners told me they were threatened with bringing their *Mahrems* (wife, mother or sister) to rape if they did not confess. I discovered also that several prisoners were gathered in one room, all naked, tortured as the others watched to further humiliate and degrade them. I also came to know that the treatment to which I was subjected was nothing compared to what others had been through.

There were those whose toe and finger nails were removed. There were those who were deprived of sleep for consecutive days. One prisoner was denied sleep for nine days. They whipped him every time he sat or tried to sleep. His torturers took turns to make sure that he did not sleep. The poor man lost his nerve and started to cry hysterically. He lost his mental balance and still suffers from it.

In the collective cell, I saw and heard unbelievable things. In *Mu'taqal* (the concentration camp) I saw a group of Arab *Mujahideen* about whom no one in Arabia could speak except by way of honour and respect because of their dedication and courage in the way of Allah. I saw the famed Hassan al-Srihi, of the 'Lion's Den' Operation – who was brought from Pakistan and delivered to the *Mamlakah* (kingdom). He was exposed to the worst kind of torture by the king's minions to confess to the Riyadh bombing. Despite the fact that no connection has been established to his association with the bombing, whether close or far, he is still in prison. No one took up his cause or championed him in the outside world. Neither did the authorities do justice to him.

I knew from my stay there that (Palestinian) Professor Muhammad Yusuf Abbas (alias Abu al-Qassim) who was Shaikh Abdallh Azzam's *khalifa* at *Maktab Khadamat al-Mujahideen* (Al-Kifah Refugee Centre) was there. Abu Abdelaziz Barbaros, the man who was at the forefront of the Jihad in Bosnia, who is almost 50 years old, of which he spent many performing the duty of Jihad for Allah's sake, was also there.

There was a cell called The Trouble-makers' Cell (*Zenzanat al-Mushaghibeen*) prepared especially for those who do not cooperate with the interrogators. The cell is situated outside the main building at ar-Ruwais Complex in the burning sun. It has a toilet which does not have an exit.

Therefore all excrements remain on the spot bringing in insects and the worst kinds of odors. This is for those who pass by it. What about those who are made to live in it? This reminds me of another problem from which we all suffer: bathrooms. The ratio of restrooms to prisoners is very low. We have to stand in line to relieve ourselves at the collective cell in this manner and had to give reasons and excuses for such a dire matter.

Even after being moved to the collective cell, I was not spared the torture. Each of us was taken at least twice a week to the 'roasting' feasts. We were entertainment material for these 'human' wolves.

During the torture session the interrogators created new stories and new allegations – ranging from running weapons smuggling rings, to armed operations to connections with 'x' or 'y' or *Takfir*. All of this was done to find justification for their own crimes of torture which no law, whether revealed or written, has enacted.

Despite all the plots of the torturers and servants of the king, their plans are doomed. It is through trial and sufferance that Allah's victory comes about and His powers are displayed. It is in these times that the sublime *Sakina* and tranquility come. It is through this that we get assurance that Allah's promise will be fulfilled and His will shall come to pass as decreed.

I never heard anyone regret one day spent in Jihad, or consider Jihad as being the source of hurt they were subjected to at the hands of those who do not fear Allah. Some have displayed the best example of resistance and strength. Hassan al-Srihi was the talk of everyone: How under torture he kept on reading our Qur'an and making *dhikr* (remembrance of Allah by way of hymns). He stayed in such a state until the torture ended.

I felt reassured after I saw him. After all this, the 'confessions' on TV, or those that were publicized in the [Saudi and Western] media were nothing but coerced confessions and the work of interrogators who force their victims to sign whatever they write. If you see those subjected to such dehumanizing conditions, there is no way one can believe what the authorities claim.

I ask the Almighty, in all His powers, to remove this adversity imposed on people of the land of Harmayn, for it is now a prison for any one seeking *Islah* (reform), or championing the law of *Shari'ah*, when once, this land was a place of refuge for the oppressed. I asked Him to give victory to the Muslims in general, and the people of the Peninsula in particular, to give them victory over those who have wronged them and to consider what we have been subjected to, me and my brethren, as bounty in our favour on the day we meet Him. *Amen.*

Released through the Internet by 'The Islamic Movement for Reform in Saudi Arabia', London, 11 November 1996, printed in *Crescent International*, Canada, 1–15 December 1996.

8N
The UN on torture

In a report by the Special UN Rapporteur on torture in January 1996, the following was reported on Saudi Arabia.

Information transmitted to the Government and replies received.

578. By letter dated 18 September 1995 the Special Rapporteur advised the Government that he had received information indicating that the torture and ill-treatment of prisoners in Priman prison in Jeddah were widespread. It was reported that the prison had insufficient space for detainees to sleep, that temperatures sometimes reaches as high as 54 degrees Celsius and that it lacked medical facilities to treat prisoners, many of whom were ill.

579. The special Rapporteur also transmitted the individual cases described in the following paragraphs.

580. Four Christian prisoners, with the surnames Garcase (aged 89), Bile, Johanis and Caperey (correct spellings uncertain), were allegedly taken outside the prison on 13 July 1994 and severely beaten for failing to participate in a Muslim prayer session.

581. Muhammed Dahir Dualle, a national of Somalia, was reportedly arrested and beaten in Mecca on 14 August 1994 because he was not in possession of a passport. He was taken to Jeddah, and after failing to locate the house in which he had left the passport, was allegedly beaten severely, causing him to suffer a broken nose and profuse bleeding from his ears and nose. He was treated at hospital and taken to Priman Prison. At the prison, he slipped and fell while carrying some books. In response, a soldier allegedly kicked him in the kidney and, as a result, he had to be transferred back to hospital. A doctor diagnosed a serious injury to his kidney and ordered that he refrain from normal work.

582. Gulam Mustafa, a national of Pakistan, was allegedly tortured on 23 May 1994 in a detention centre for drug offenders in Jeddah. Police personnel allegedly inserted an object into his penis and applied electric shocks, causing him to bleed. He was transferred to Priman prison with his penis bleeding heavily.

583. Osman Gheddi Guled, a national of Djibouti, was transferring planes en route to Cairo when he was detained, reportedly after failing to pay a bribe to the authorities when khat, a herbal stimulant, was found in his luggage. His passport and luggage with a large sum of money were seized and he was placed in detention. Several days later, he was taken for interrogation and asked for his passport. When he replied that is had already been confiscated, he was allegedly beaten unconscious. He spent several months in Priman prison, where he was allegedly subjected to further beatings. He was released more than two months after being found innocent by tribunal.

584. By the same letter the Special Rapporteur reminded the Government of information transmitted on 3 June 1994 concerning the alleged ill-treatment of Iraqi refugees, regarding which no reply had been received. On 27 October 1995 the Government replied that the authorities at the national and local levels had treated the refugees in the same way as Saudi citizens and in some cases had accorded them special privileges to help them to maintain their traditions and preserve their identity. The refugees were treated in accordance with customary international law and the Geneva Conventions concerning the law of war, when they had been considered prisoners of war. After they were recognized as refugees, the Government had treated them according to international instruments concerning refugees or Saudi national law, consisting in the Islamic Shari'a. Initially, there were few incidents involving infringements by some soldiers with little or no experience of refugees problems, but persons responsible for those infringements were invariably punished in accordance with Islamic Shari'a. as a result of which the situation at the camps had been brought under control. Refugees suspected of committing offences were investigated under the normal procedures in force in the country, in accordance with the Islamic Shari'a. Contrary to allegations, no refugees had died as a result of the investigation methods applied. Corporal punishment might have been required under the terms of legal judgements handed down against law-breakers. However, the authorities had endeavoured to restrict and even avoid its application to the refugees in light of their particular status and the penalty had been commuted and was not used against any of the refugees.

585. In its reply, the Government also mentioned several individual cases transmitted by the Special Rapporteur – those of Hadi Nasi Hussein, Abbad Ali Mahawi, Muhammad Hassanm Ali Sabah Ward, Basim Youssuf Ibrahim al-Shaimari and Asaad Ali Hussein al-Bashama. With the exception of Ali Sabah, they had not complained of ill-treatment to the authorities concerned or to the Office of the United Nations High commissioner for Refugees (UNHCR)

Urgent appeals

586. The Special Rapporteur sent three urgent appeals on behalf of the persons mentioned in the following paragraphs, all of whom had reportedly been sentenced to flogging. The dates on which the appeals were sent are mentioned in brackets at the end of each summary.

587. Mohammad 'Ali al-Sayyid, an Egyptian national, was reportedly sentenced to a prison term of seven years and 4,000 lashes after being convicted of theft. He was allegedly removed with his legs shackled once every two weeks from al-Burauda prison in al-Qaseem province and taken to the marketplace, where he would receive from a police official 50 lashes with a bamboo cane of about one metre in length and one half centimetre in diameter. As a result of this treatment, he usually suffered bruised or bleeding buttocks, leaving him unable to sleep or sit for three or four days afterwards. He is said to have this far received 3,400 lashes (2 August 1995).

588. Ibrahim 'Abd al-Rahman al-Hudayf was reportedly sentenced to 300 lashes and 18 years' imprisonment after being convicted in a secret trial of participation in the planning of an attack on a security officer and of membership in the committee for the Defence of Legitimate Rights (17 August 1995).

589. Hamid Bin Nazal Bin Muhbub al-'Anzi, Riad Bin Kuleyb Bin Salim al-Mutay, Morris Bin Sayf al-Sahli, 'Abd al-'Aziz bin Zayd al-Sahli, Abdullah Bin Muhammed al-'Anzi, 'Aday Bin Tayib al-'Anzi, Hamdn Bin Salih Bin Hadi al-Mukhlis, Nawaf Bin Farraj al-Harbi, Nadir Bin Fahis Bin Musfir al-Dawsari, Salih Bin Muslih al-Shahri, and Mohammad Bind Abdullah al-Huta were reportedly convicted of charges in connection with membership of a criminal gang. They were sentenced to prison terms of between two and 15 years and to 200 to 1500 lashes to be carried out 50 lashes at a time (18 September 1995).

United Nations, Economic and Social Council, document E/CN.4/1996/35/
Add.1.Page 111, New York, 16 January 1996.

80
The European Parliament Critique

A resolution by the European Parliament in January 1996 criticized Saudi Arabia.

A. Deeply disturbed at the serious, widespread and increasing violation of basic human rights in Saudi Arabia, including the detention and ill-treatment of political prisoners, and at the growing number of public executions and the range of crimes which carry the death penalty, as reported by Amnesty International and Human Rights Watch.

B. Worried by the reported increases of judicially ordered floggings and amputations.

C. Seriously concerned at the total absence of fundamental freedoms and democratic rights in Saudi Arabia and the limitations on the rights of women and foreign workers.

D. Aware of the situation of complete media censorship.
E. Believing in the right of Saudi citizens living abroad to advocate reforms peacefully, though by no means endorsing the particular viewpoint upheld by Mohammed A.S. al-Mas'ari.
F. Recognizing the dangers to which exiles may be subject if denied political asylum.
G. Deeply aware of the importance of Saudi Arabia as a source of oil and a trading partner for European Union Member States and others anxious to encourage good relations with the Saudi people, but rejecting the idea that concern with human rights should be disregarded or suppressed to safeguard economic interests.

1. Deplores proposals to deport the Saudi dissident Mohammed A.S. al-Mas'ari from the United Kingdom or to isolate him in a distant land, particularly in view of the fact that he was imprisoned and tortured for forming the Committee for the Defence of Legitimate Rights before his escape from his native land; calls upon the UK not to deport him.
2. Calls for the right of asylum for genuine political dissidents to be fully upheld within the European Union as a whole.
3. Calls upon the Saudi Arabian Government to take measures urgently towards the general improvement of the human rights situation in Saudi Arabia.
4. Urges the Council and the Commission to stress this issue in their political contacts with Saudi Arabian Government and in the context of the Gulf Cooperation council.
5. Calls upon all Member States to act in unison to prevent some Member States from benefiting in the event of sanctions being imposed on others for upholding human rights.
6. Views with deep concern the extent to which some states are dependent on arms exports to countries with poor human rights records and urges diversification and observance of the guidelines proposed in its resolutions of 24 March 1994 on disarmament, arms export controls and non-proliferation of weapons of mass destruction and 19 January 1995 on the need for European controls on the export or transfer of arms.
7. Instructs its president to forward this resolution to the Council, the Commission, the Governments of the Member States and the Government of Saudi Arabia.

European Parliament, 18 January 1996, Official Journal of the European Communities 5.2.1996.

8P
Recipients of US Aid

Amnesty International, USA, in Spring 1996 published an account on human rights in countries receiving US Security Assistance. Below is a summary in the case of Saudi Arabia.

Amnesty International's Concerns:

- Arrest and detention of suspected political opponents, human rights activists, and religious minorities
- Unfair trials
- Torture and ill-treatment during pre-trial incommunicado detention
- Long-term detention without trial of Iraqi refugees at Rafha Camp
- Alarming upsurge in numbers of executions
- Wide use of judicial punishments by flogging and amputations . . .

Political parties and trade unions are banned in Saudi Arabia, and strict censorship is enforced. Over the years, a clear pattern has emerged whereby hundreds of individuals suspected of being members or sympathizers of opposition groups have been arrested by the al-Mabahith al-'Amma. Political detainees are not informed of the reasons for their arrest and are held for prolonged periods without trial – in some cases for years – or sentenced following unfair trials. During the first few days or weeks of detention, political suspects are usually held in solitary confinement, routinely tortured or ill-treated, and denied access to family or legal counsel.

Peaceful groups and individuals who have criticized the kingdom's policies, alleged the corruption of members of the royal family, and/or called for political reforms have faced persecution. Scores of political suspects, including prisoners of conscience, were arrested and detained during 1995. The majority of detainees arrested in the past year were suspected Sunni Islamist opponents of the government; in March, Dr. Nasseral-'Umr, professor of religious studies at the University of Riyadh, was arrested and in July, Sheikh 'Abdul-rahman bin Muhammad al-Dakhil was arrested.

Following establishment in 1994 of an office of the banned Committee for the Defence of Legitimate Rights (CDLR) in London, there was a wave of arrests of suspected supporters of that and other opposition groups in Saudi Arabia. More than 20 political prisoners arrested in 1994 were tried and convicted on charges relating to alleged attacks against security officers and of having links with the CDLR. As is typical in Saudi Arabia, none of the defendants was allowed access to lawyers throughout their detention or trial. 'Abdullah 'Abd al-Rahman al-Hudhayf received a death sentence, which the government announced was carried out on 12 August in Riyadh. However, opposition sources claimed that he had died in custody as a result of torture. Ibrahim 'abd al-Rahman al-Hudayf was sentenced to 300 lashes in addition to 18 years of imprisonment. The other defendants were sentenced to prison terms ranging from three to 18 years. All appear to have been punished for their political dissent rather than the criminal charges brought against them; they may be prisoners of conscience.

Up to 200 other political detainees arrested in 1993 and 1994 remain in custody without charge or trial, and without access to legal representation. They include prominent religious figures Sheikh Salman bin Fahs al'Awda and Sheikh Safr 'Abdul-Rahman al-Hawali, who were arrested in 1994 for giving public lectures criticizing the government. In recent years many suspected followers of Salafiyya, a Sunni Muslim doctrine, have been arrested. While the majority of a group arrested in 1993 were reportedly released during 1995, the remainder are believed to still be held without trial.

A large number of Iraqi refugees, who fled from Iraq during and after the Gulf War, or who were prisoners of war (there were 23,000) remain in the desert camp of Rafha in northern Saudi Arabia. Amnesty International continues to be concerned about a pattern of human rights violations in the camp mirroring those practiced against suspected political opponents in Saudi Arabia: they include arbitrary detention, torture and ill-treatment, and lack of fair legal proceedings. Reports received of numerous cases of deaths in custody, apparently as a result of torture, have still not been addressed by the government. The fate of at least 30 Iraqi refugees arrested following a protest in Rafha Camp in March 1993 remains unknown. One such refugee, 'Ali L'aibj Abu Khanjar, son of a prominent tribal leader from southern Iraq, refused when requested by Saudi authorities to identify refugees who had participated in a protest in Rafha in March 1993; he was beaten with cables and taken to an unknown destination.

Public and private non-Muslim religious worship is, in practice, banned in Saudi Arabia. In the aftermath of the Gulf War, religious intolerance has become particularly acute, with hundreds of Christian men, women, and children having been the targets of arrest, detention, torture, flogging, or other cruel, inhuman, and degrading treatment, at the hands of the security and religious forces. In December 1995, seven Tamil Indian nationals were reportedly arrested in the city of Jubayl for conducting Christmas services. Six individuals were released in January 1996, and one was detained until March 1996 before being freed.

Religious intolerance not only applies to non-Muslims; the public expression of Shi'a Muslim beliefs or the performance of their religious rites has also been monitored and generally prohibited. Among those detained in connection with Shi'a religious activities in 1995 were at least six people arrested in the Eastern Province. Zuhair Hajlis, Shakir Hajlis, Ridha al-Huri and Mahdi Hazam were reportedly arrested in March for taking part in a ceremony commemorating the death of the son of the late Ayatollah Khomeini of Iran. In April, Sheikh Ja'far 'Ali al-Mubarak, a leading religious scholar from Safwa, was arrested, apparently for refusing to sign an agreement not to preach. He had been arrested and held without charge or trial on two previous occasions since 1985. The sixth detainee, 'Abd al-Jabbar Habib al Sheikh, is also believed to have been detained in connection with his Shi'a religious beliefs.

Torture and ill-treatment of political prisoners and common law criminals in police stations and prisons is routine in Saudi Arabia. These practices are used to punish or to extract 'confessions', particularly during pretrial incommunicado detention. The most common methods of torture include falaqa (beatings on the soles of the feet), ta'liq (suspension by the wrist from the ceiling or a high window), beatings all over the body, and electric shock. One detainee, an Indonesian national, was reported to have died in custody in 1995; he was reportedly beaten to death by a policeman in the holy city of Mecca following his arrest, apparently for overstaying the limit allowed by his visa to Saudi Arabia. In 1994, Gulam Mustafa, a Pakistani national, was reportedly subjected to electric shocks and had a metal stick inserted into his anus while held in a detention center for drug offenders in Jeddah. Reportedly left bleeding and unable to walk, he received no medical attention. He was subsequently released and deported to Pakistan. Amnesty International has urged the authorities to initiate investigations into allegations of torture and ill-treatment. Courts have repeatedly failed to investigate claims of torture and appear to continue to consider that 'confessions' are the sole evidence on which a conviction may be based. In addition, defendants who are foreign nationals are reportedly not always provided with adequate interpretation facilities during trial.

Judicial punishments by amputation and flogging continue to be imposed for a wide range of offenses, including theft, consumption of alcohol, and sexual offenses. At least nine people had their right hands amputated during 1995. Flogging is widely used. Mohammad 'Ali al-Sayyid, an Egyptian national working in Saudi Arabia, served a sentence of 4,000 lashes in addition to seven years of imprisonment, for burglary. Former prisoners held with him have reported that every two weeks he was taken, with his legs shackled, to the marketplace, where a policeman administered 50 lashes. Each flogging session was said to have left him with bruised or bleeding buttocks and unable to sleep or sit for three or four days. The highest number of public executions ever recorded by Amnesty International in a single year in Saudi Arabia were carried out in 1995. At least 192 prisoners, including seven women, were executed, most by public beheading. The majority of the victims were foreign nationals, including Afghan, Chadian, Egyptian, Filipino, Nigerian, Pakistani, Somali, Turkish, and Yemeni nationals. All victims had been sentenced to death and executed after trials in which international standards for fair trials were violated in contravention of the United Nations safeguards guaranteeing protection of the rights of those facing the death penalty.

The scores of prisoners on death row include 'Abd al-'Aziz Muhammad Isse, a Somali national who claimed during his trial that the crimes with which he was charged had occurred before his arrival in Saudi Arabia. Although this information was available from the airport at which he arrived, it was apparently not taken into account during his trial. Two other Somalis convicted on the same charges were among six beheaded on May 31, 1995, in Jeddah.

This failure to meet international standards for fair trials pervades all legal proceedings involving political or criminal prisoners. Prisoners are not allowed access to lawyers during pre-trial interrogations, and defense lawyers are not formally present during trials. Defendants may be convicted on the sole basis of 'confessions' often obtained under torture or ill-treatment.

Government Response

Over the years, Amnesty International has repeatedly raised specific cases of human rights violations with the Saudi Arabian authorities through reports, confidential communications, embassy visits, and letters from numerous Amnesty International local group members. While blanket denials of the use of torture or of the existence of prisoners of conscience have been issued on occasion through the press, the Saudi Arabian authorities have yet to address any specific concerns.

During the past year, Amnesty International continued to express concern about the detention of people for the peaceful expression of their political or religious beliefs, and called for the immediate and unconditional release of prisoners of conscience and for all other political prisoners to receive a fair and prompt trial or be released. The organization urged the authorities to initiate investigations into allegations of torture and ill-treatment. The Saudi Arabian government has not responded. To Amnesty International's knowledge there has not been one case of reported torture, ill-treatment, or death in custody that has been publicly and independently investigated by the Saudi Arabian authorities.

Amnesty International also continued to express its concern about the alarming increase in the number of executions and to call for an end to the use of the death penalty. In public statements, the Saudi Arabian authorities maintain that the sharp increase in death sentences was related to the increase in drug-related offenses. However, no convincing evidence has been produced to show that the death penalty – in place for drug offenses since 1987 – is an effective deterrent against crime. No clarification has been provided as to why prisoners are denied the right to be defended by a lawyer or why confessions, even when obtained under torture, are apparently accepted as evidence by the courts.

Amnesty International has repeatedly been denied permission to enter the Kingdom of Saudi Arabia for fact-finding missions, trial observations, meetings with government officials, or any other purpose involving the research and monitoring of the human rights situation in the country.

Recommendations

1. Release immediately and unconditionally all prisoners of conscience, that is persons who have been detained for the peaceful exercise of their political and/or religious beliefs.
2. Charge all those detained without fair trial with a recognizable criminal offence and give them a prompt, fair trial in accordance with international standards. Otherwise release them.
3. Ensure that all detainees are given prompt, regular and confidential access to lawyers at all stages of the proceedings. All detainees should be brought without delay before a judge empowered to assess the legality and necessity of their detention, and should be provided with access to a doctor of their choice, if necessary.
4. Enact legislation to combat religious intolerance and protect the right to freedom of religion as recognized in international instruments.
5. Investigate promptly and impartially all reports of torture and ill-treatment. The methods and results of the investigations should be made public. All those responsible for human rights violations should be brought to justice. 'Confessions' obtained as a result of torture should be included as evidence before the courts. These investigations should be consistent with such international standards as the UN Basic Principles on the Effective Prevention and Investigation of Extra-Legal, Arbitrary and Summary Executions.
6. Commute all death sentences, reduce the number of offenses punishable by death, and take steps to abolish the death penalty.
7. Ratify human rights instruments. Saudi Arabia should expedite steps towards ratifying and implementing the International Covenant on Civil and Political Rights, and the UN Convention against Torture and Other Cruel, Inhuman or Degrading Treatment or Punishment.

Amnesty International USA, 'Human Rights Violations in Countries Receiving US Security Assistance', Washington, DC 1996.

8Q
Death penalty and drug offences

Saudi Arabia introduced the death penalty for drugs offences in 1987.
Amnesty International reported 1996.

On 18 February 1987 the Council of Senior 'Ulama (Religious Scholars), the highest religious body in Saudi Arabia entrusted with interpreting Islamic law, issued *fatwa* (religious edict) No. 138. The edict was approved by King Fahd bin 'Abdul-'Aziz in March. The edict provides for a mandatory death penalty for smuggling or receiving drugs from abroad and an optional death penalty for recidivist distribution of drugs. The language of the edict refers simply to 'drugs' and does not specify the amounts or types of drugs with respect to which a person may be sentenced to death. It states that the death penalty is provided for smugglers because of their 'evil work' in 'bringing much corruption and deterioration to the country'.

The first execution under the new law recorded by Amnesty International was carried out in the capital, Riyadh, on 29 July 1987 when Muhaisin bin Falih bin Kami al-Muqati' was beheaded after conviction for smuggling and using drugs, as well as shooting and wounding a member of the patrol which arrested him. By the end of the year at least nine prisoners had been executed for drug offenses, including two Jordanians and three Filipinos.

Cases involving the death penalty in Saudi Arabia are first heard before al-Mahakim al-Kubra (the General Courts) and death sentences passed by such courts are automatically referred to the Court of Appeal, whose decision is referred to the permanent body of the Supreme Judicial Council for review and approval. Final ratification is by Royal Decree. Executions of males are usually by beheading with a sharp sword, carried out in public in major towns and cities, often in a square in front of the provincial governor's palace. Executions of females are believed to be carried out by beheading or by firing squad.

Trials in death penalty cases fail to meet international norms for a fair trial. Defendants do not have the right to have a lawyer formally present during the trial. During hearings of the General Court the presiding judge questions and cross-examines witnesses and the defendants before passing sentence. Defendants who do not speak Arabic are reportedly not always provided with adequate interpretation facilities. Many convictions may be based solely on a 'confession', which in Amnesty International's view creates an incentive for interrogating officials to coerce defendants, including by torture or ill-treatment, in order to force them to 'confess'. Defendants are denied the most basic rights during pre-trial detention which could serve as safeguards against torture, including the right of access to lawyers and independent medical attention, prompt access to a judge, and the ability to challenge their detention before a judge, and are not given adequate time and facilities to prepare their defence. Courts in Saudi Arabia have repeatedly failed to investigate claims of torture. These features contravene international human rights norms and exacerbate the risk of executing the innocent.

Where details of the offence are given in news reports, the prisoners executed are usually said to have smuggled drugs into the country, but there have also been occasional executions for distributing drugs. The reports sometimes mention the type of drugs involved, but the amount is seldom specified. Where the type of drug is named, it is usually heroin or hashish. In

April 1989, for example, two Pakistani nationals were executed in Riyadh for attempting to smuggle hashish into the country. At least two people were executed in 1992 for smuggling hashish and at least 14 for the same offence in 1993. In an unusual case, the official news agency SPA (Saudi Press Agency) reported on 7 August 1995 that a Syrian, Mohammad al-Jabawi, had been beheaded for smuggling hallucinogenic pills into the country. Later in August, four Turks were executed for smuggling amphetamines.

The Saudi authorities have executed nationals of Afghanistan, Pakistan, India, the Philippines, Iraq, Jordan, Syria, Yemen, Chad, Nigeria and Turkey for drug offenses as well as Saudi Arabians. Sometimes international relations have been disturbed when foreigners have been executed. On 14 August 1995 the Turkish foreign ministry issued a statement saying that the Saudi ambassador to Turkey had been summoned to give an explanation of the execution of four Turks despite high-level attempts by Turkey to have their lives spared. The four men had been convicted of smuggling amphetamines into the country; two of them were beheaded on 11 August and the other two on 14 August. The President of Turkey, Suleyman Demirel, had appealed for clemency to the King of Saudi Arabia. Turkish newspapers published photographs of angry friends and relatives of the four beheaded prisoners burning Saudi flags and shouting offensive slogans.

Saudi officials have repeatedly stated that executions have reduced the incidence of trafficking, but to Amnesty International's knowledge they have never released figures to support their claims. In 1988 the Minister of the Interior Prince Nayef Ibn Abdelaziz was quoted by Reuters news agency as saying: 'No doubt the death penalty has achieved its goal and that is evident in the drop in drug-related cases.' Saudi Arabian officials said that drug smuggling into the country had dropped by 40 per cent after beheadings began and that smugglers were thinking twice before trying to bring in drugs, according to Reuters.

In January 1990 Major General Ibrahim Al-Maiman, acting director general for the drug combating department, told SPA that cases of drug abuse and trafficking in the country had dropped by 50 per cent since the introduction of the death penalty. 'The decision to execute drug smugglers and traffickers has had a major impact', he said. Other methods being used to combat trafficking included intercepting drug rings inside and outside the country, searching out known groups of smugglers, surveillance of land, sea and air routes to the country and cooperation with anti-drug efforts in other countries, he said.

In January 1994 General Ahmed Mohammed Bilal, director of the public security department in the Ministry of Interior, told a Saudi-French symposium on narcotics control in Riyadh that the use of the death penalty for drug trafficking had sharply reduced the incidence of drug-related crimes. He said that the country had established a successful record of tackling addiction and peddling as well as halting the flow of narcotic and psychotropic substances largely due to the use of the death penalty, according to a report in the newspaper *Arab News*.

These claims are belied by the increase in the use of the death penalty, especially since 1993. In 1900 Amnesty International recorded nine executions for drug offenses in Saudi Arabia. In 1991 the number of recorded executions for drug offenses dropped to three, but it rose to 13 in 1992 and 53 in 1993. The organization recorded 19 executions for drug offenses in 1994 and at least 62 between 1 January and 18 August 1995. In one eight-day period in April 1995, 25 foreigners were executed for drug smuggling, more than the total number of reported executions for drug offenses the year before.

In an April 1995 statement which implicitly contradicted earlier claims of the efficacy of the death penalty against drug trafficking, the Saudi Arabian Embassy in London said that the increase in executions since the beginning of the year reflected a rise in drug trafficking. 'The increase in the number of executions of drug traffickers simply indicates how this evil international drug mafia continues to spread its evil activities,' Ambassador Ghazi Algosaibi said. The statement was issued in response to an appeal from Amnesty International calling for a halt to executions.

In August 1995, Crown Prince Abdullah bin Adbul-Aziz made a statement which reverted to earlier claims of the efficacy of the death penalty. As quoted by SPA, he told a weekly cabinet meeting that crime rates in Saudi Arabia were 'at their lowest, especially drug [crimes] thanks to the application of capital punishment to smugglers and traffickers'. The country would 'continue, with God's help, to apply capital punishment to drug smugglers and traffickers', he said. He also stated that the Saudi Arabian judiciary was 'independent', 'fair' and 'efficient'.

Amnesty International, *The Death Penalty: No solution to illicit Drugs*, 3 October London 1996.

8R
Muhammed Al-Massari on intellectual freedom

Intellectual freedom and development: Professor Muhammed Al-Massari accuses the Saudi governing family of trying to stop a historic process.

With the critique of corruption at the time of economic decline, things started to move. Lots of questions arose on the social development, the economic development and the direction of the whole society. Questions of modernization and post-modernity; of poetry with debates of classical form contra new loose concepts.

In the late eighties and beginning of the nineties, the debate became fully political; what was wrong with the constitutional system; what was wrong with the organization of the state and the society? When that began taking course in koran schools – in fact you do not have koran schools, but regular schools with korannic lessons added – the government became worried and cracked down on the education system. Now you have all kinds of fixed curricular and circulars and regulations, prohibiting certain discussion, and questionable people have been fired. The intellectual climate in the public domain is very stagnant. The debate has moved underground.

– That does not sound compatible with new educational challenges, new technologies.
Massari: We obviously cannot withstand historic forces. Even so the regime tries to make a crack in history. The number of educationally advanced people is growing virtually by the hour. In every household someone will read and write, demand information and want to use the advantages of satellite dishes. It is a very big business. In the beginning you could demand thousands of pounds for a dish, now it is down.

– But the government tries to regulate and licence the whole business?
Massari: The problem is that they do not permit new [technologies]. Nobody really cares. But then they threaten to remove the old ones with the excuse of clergy, worried of public morale.

– Is that 'un-Islamic' or just repressive?
Massari: Only repressive. I am sure some of the clergy are very sincere. But to the immoral government it only has to do with power. They are so corrupt, so un-Islamic with so many stupid rulings. I am doubtful they can pursue this policy. You probably would find more than 200,000 satellite dishes in the kingdom, and a considerably large number of dishes serve several households. If the government moves with ferocity against so many households, they may face a 'dish revolution' – and they know that. The people have got so used, so addicted to the new satellite channels that you cannot take it away from them.

– But they do try to create an easier-to-control cable system to substitute the satellite dishes?
Massari: This is only an excuse for collecting the dishes. The people are far too intelligent to accept that. They know how to deal with such things. They will have two water tanks on the roof, one for water, the other for a hidden satellite dish. Or they will find other means under the cover of the right to privacy. It is clearly an uphill, losing battle for the regime.

Interview, conducted in London, April 1996.

8S
EU criticism

*Intervention by an EU representative during the Human Rights
Commission, 52nd Conference on 16 April 1996.*

The European Union is very concerned at reports on instances of failure to
observe due process in convictions leading to executions taking place in Saudi
Arabia during the past year and at reports of torture of detainees and other
cruel, inhuman or degrading punishment, and detentions without trial. The
situation of women is also a cause of concern. We are concerned about the
denial of the right to freedom of religion and freedom of expression.

   We call on Saudi Arabia to ratify the main Human Rights Conventions
and cooperate with human rights monitoring bodies.

                              Permanent Mission of Denmark to the UN, New York.

8T
Further EU concern

*In the General Assembly, 3rd Committee, the EU representative on
19 November 1996.*

The overall human rights situation in Saudi Arabia is of grave concern to
the EU. In particular we deplore continuing denials of civil and political
rights as well as violations of the human rights of women. We continue to
be concerned at shortcomings in the administration of justice in Saudi
Arabia and at reports of torture of detainees and of other cruel, inhuman or
degrading treatment or punishment and detention without trial. There
continue to be serious obstacles to the enjoyment of freedom of religion and
expression. We call upon the Saudi authorities to cooperate fully with all
human rights bodies of the UN.

                              Permanent Mission of Denmark to the UN, New York.

8U
Saudi Address to the UN

*A Saudi diplomat in December 1996 addressed the UN General
Assembly, as recorded by the Royal Saudi Embassy in Washington,
DC, on the Internet.*

Saudi Arabia . . . addressed a session of the United Nations General
Assembly devoted to discussing human rights questions. A statement

delivered by Abdul Rahman Al-Rassi, second secretary at the Permanent Mission of Saudi Arabia to the UN, described human rights as 'one of the most important subjects which dominates international debate in this decade because it affects the well-being and dignity of people'.

The various past treaties, conventions and the large number of reports issued on human rights indicate that the international community attaches great significance to this issue, the statement observed. 'But this also is an indication of the many difficulties that impede an agreement on a unified understanding of those rights' and in bringing these rights to reality. The statement added that Saudi Arabia believes that when defining human rights, the international community should take into consideration 'the diverse and specific historical, religious, cultural and social connotations of these rights'.

Emphasizing the importance Saudi Arabia attaches to people and their rights, the statement added that 'human dignity is protected without any discrimination, as it is dictated by the lofty principle of Islam. The Islamic *Shariah* [law] gave us a complete creed built on detailed explanation of human rights. It defines the duties and obligations in all forms of human relations,' as well as the individual's right to pursue an honorable life safe from any attack on his person, private life, property or family. 'These rights and freedoms, which are protected by Islam, are not intended as moral sermons, but rather as legal dictates from God to ensure respect and application.' The statement stressed that Islam does not restrict these rights to a specific religion, race or culture, but extends them to all humanity.

The system of government in the Kingdom of Saudi Arabia, which is based on Islamic Shariah, guarantees for the Saudi citizen all the rights that are [included] in the Universal Declaration of Human Rights,' the statement noted.

The Saudi delegate observed that in order to ensure respect for human rights worldwide, the international community will have to work sincerely and seriously to achieve the following set of objectives:

- Refrain from any attempt to marginalize the role of developing countries in formulating or explaining policies on human rights, and to take into consideration the diversity of social customs, traditions and beliefs;
- Objectively deal with international issues regarding violations of human rights;
- Never use human rights as a pretext for interfering in the internal affairs of other countries;
- Strive to achieve economic and social development as a means of protecting and promoting human rights.

Embassy of Saudi Arabia, Washington, DC, News and Press
on the Internet, 1996.

8V
US State Department Critique

The US Lawyers Committee for Human Rights, in its annual critique
of the US State Department Human Rights Yearbook.

The 1995 report on Saudi Arabia is marred by a very serious overall shortcoming, one that was raised in last year's edition of the Critique. This is the State Department's tendency to cheer for the unrepentantly fundamentalist Saudi government while subtly representing its opponents as extremists. The specious distinction which the report attempts to draw between the benign fundamentalism of an important US ally the Saudi government and the malevolent fundamentalism of the religious opposition spoils an otherwise good discussion of human rights in the Kingdom. This is unfortunate because, in terms of detail, breadth and factual accuracy, this year's report otherwise continues a welcome trend of steady improvement in reporting on human rights in Saudi Arabia. Facts are presented clearly and most of the salient issues discussed frankly. However, the report's insidious attempt to discredit the opposition to the Saudi regime by subtle shadings of meaning and tone has no place in a serious human rights report.

This problem has ramifications for the report's discussions of Islam and Islamic law, two areas which are critical for evaluating the human rights situation in the Kingdom. It also leads the report's drafters to overstate in an irresponsible manner the existence of popular support for the current Saudi government. Finally, and most distressingly for a document that styles itself an objective report on human rights, the partisanship displayed on behalf of the Saudi government subtly imparts the suggestion that governments which support US foreign policy initiatives are held to a lower standard than those that do not.

As in 1994, the introduction to this year's report omits the main item of interest in the Kingdom, namely the appearance of an organized opposition movement. This opposition, until recently represented principally but not exclusively by the Committee for the Defense of Legitimate Rights (CDLR) has a pronounced conservative religious character and apparently comprises a large number of clerics and intellectuals. Clearly it does not include all persons opposed to the government or all persons who urge reform, but it does constitute the one group which continues to speak out consistently against the Saudi government and whose supporters have become special targets of that government's oppressive practices.

Given the unprecedented fact of an opposition group operating within (and now also outside) Saudi Arabia, despite enormous obstacles in the form of Saudi laws prohibiting all forms of free speech and association (which the report describes in detail), it is simply incredible that the report's introduction should fail to mention the CDLR, or at least the phenomenon for which it stands. The introduction should have stated in no uncertain terms that a more or less organized opposition movement has formed, and that the Saudi government has responded to it with a disappointing and brutal pattern of human rights violations. That is a simple and indisputable fact of primary relevance, and precisely the sort of 'key human rights development' that drafters of the Country Reports are instructed to include in their introductions.

If the State Department does not believe that the Saudi government considers the CDLR a serious threat, then its drafters should consider Saudi Arabia's widely reported attempts to have the CDLR's head, Dr. Abdullah al-Mas'ari, expelled from Britain for expressing and publicizing criticism of the Saudi government. Dr. al-Mas'ari was forced to secretly flee Saudi Arabia in 1994 after being detained and tortured for his public criticism of the Saudi government.

In March the British Home Office rejected Dr. al-Mas'ari's asylum application, after British government spokesmen had alluded publicly to the potentially negative effect of Dr. al-Mas'ari's presence in Britain on British exports to Saudi Arabia. In January 1996, the Home Office ordered Dr. al-Mas'ari deported, which order was, however, rejected by Chief Immigration Appeals Adjudicator, Judge David Pearl, in March. Judge Pearl criticized the Home Office for attempting to circumvent the UN Convention on Refugees for 'diplomatic and trade reasons'. In April, after reconsidering its precarious legal position, the Home Office granted Dr. al-Mas'ari exceptional leave to stay in Britain for four years in a move that has been characterized as a grant of asylum in all but name. Furious over Dr. al-Mas'ari's presence in Britain, the Saudi government has publicly threatened to boycott British firms, most recently through its ambassador in London, Ghazi al-Ghosaibi, and its Interior Minister, Prince Nayef. According to one British engineering firm, Saudi Arabia began a de facto boycott of British contractors in November 1995 which was still in effect as of April 1996. Britain's Department of Trade and Industry has denied that British business has been adversely affected. It is possible that the State Department shares the Saudi government's concern about the CDLR.

Although the CDLR is not mentioned in the introduction, many unflattering references to it appear in the body of the report, which gives the following characterizations of the CDLR and other persons: '[The CDLR and Mohamed al-Mas'ari] were associates of Abdullah Bin Abd Al-Rahman Al-Hidaif, who was executed for assaulting a security official with acid . . .' 'The vociferously anti-government CDLR . . .' '[Al-Mas'ari's] publicized views have expressed opposition to peace with Israel and to Saudi support for the peace process.' 'The CDLR does not advocate internationally recognized human rights but takes a rigidly Islamic fundamentalist approach. Statements by CDLR supporters have advocated policies and actions that are anti-women and anti-Shi'a. [The group has expressed] understanding' of the National Guard headquarters bombing.' '[One CDLR founder has] made strong anti-Shi'a statements.' To label CDLR members 'associates' of Mr. Hidaif is nothing less than an attempt to suggest guilt by association.

To label CDLR 'vociferous' is gratuitous and redundant. The CDLR's views on peace with Israel are so egregiously irrelevant to the human rights situation in the Kingdom that it is astonishing that this claim should appear in the report for the second year running. This claim serves solely to underline the (admittedly likely) fact that the CDLR may not agree with U.S. foreign policy objectives in the Middle East, which, it hardly needs saying, has no bearing whatsoever on the state of human rights in the Kingdom. The report might just as well have mentioned that *The Economist*, too, routinely criticizes the current incarnation of the Israeli-Arab peace process. Or, to be fair, it might speculate about how deep support for the Arab-Israeli peace process runs among the members of the Council of Senior Ulema.

In addition, the report could have presented a more balanced description of the trial and execution in mid-August of Mr. al-Hidaif. The report takes two swipes at the late Mr. al-Hidaif. In the first, it notes that he, 'a supporter of [CDLR], was sentenced to death by a Saudi court and executed for the 1994 attempted murder by acid of an Interior Ministry official'. The second is quoted above. As noted already, both passages aim to discredit the CDLR by mentioning it and the word 'acid' in the same sentence. (It bears emphasizing in this context that the CDLR's manifesto expressly eschews violence, though Dr. al-Mas'ari has made public statements which seem to contradict the principle of non-violence.) Neither passage states that the charges against Mr. al-Hidaif included his support for the CDLR, thus ignoring direct evidence of the Saudi government's prohibition of freedom of association and speech in his case.

That fact is stated in more neutral territory where the charges against his co-defendants are mentioned, but where neither the word 'acid' nor the name of Mr. al-Hidaif appear. Now, it is important to condemn violence whatever its source, and if Mr. al-Hidaif attacked a Saudi security official with acid, that act ought rightly to be punished in accord with applicable criminal law, whatever the circumstances. But the circumstances, even if they do not excuse, are not therefore irrelevant, and in this particular case they should have been mentioned in the report. Human Rights Watch/ Middle East reported that the victim of the attack had interrogated and tortured Mr. al-Hidaif during a previous detention and, further, that the Saudi government refused to return Mr. al-Hidaif's body to his family, suggesting that he had been tortured prior to his execution. The fact that Mr. al-Hidaif's alleged accomplices included several of his family members suggests a revenge motive and lends credence to the report by Human Rights Watch. Wholly irrelevant is the claim that the CDLR rejects international human rights norms.

Paragraph 8.G of the State Department's instructions to those drafting the Country Reports requires them to discuss human rights violations by 'guerrilla forces, terrorists or occupying forces of a foreign power' and by 'rebel/insurgent forces'. The CDLR is none of these.

Neither is Saudi Arabia 'affected by serious international or internal conflict', as spelled out in paragraph 12 of the State Department instructions. Thus, the CDLR, being neither a government nor an armed insurrection in progress, is not in a position to violate anyone's human rights. It is true that the distaste for international human rights norms which the CDLR seems to share with the Saudi government represents an interesting facet of political discourse in the Kingdom (although this is ignored in the report, as discussed below). Of primary relevance, however, is that the CDLR's supporters have been victims of human rights violations committed by the Saudi government (as noted in this year's and the previous two reports), which denies the validity of such norms (as noted by this year's report). Mention of the 'anti-women' and 'anti-Shi'a' tendencies of the CDLR is vulnerable to the same criticism of irrelevance. Finally, the allegation that the CDLR exhibits a rigid Islamic fundamentalism presents a particularly pernicious drafting tactic in the report.

Assuming that such a characterization is accurate, it would be relevant only if the report's drafters wished to make the point that the Saudi government holds itself out as a rigidly fundamentalist Islamic regime in the belief that this constitutes an effective claim to political legitimacy (the report could even go further and note that the Saudi government seems to understand its asserted fundamentalism as license to commit certain kinds of human rights abuses in the name of Islam). Then, it would make perfect sense to say that the CDLR challenges the asserted religious legitimacy of the Saudi regime, claiming for itself a more authentic or different form of Islamic fundamentalism (even assuming that 'fundamentalism' is a meaningful term in this context).

However, the report does not proceed in that manner, but rather labels the CDLR as 'fundamentalist' while applying much less loaded descriptions (such as 'rigorously conservative') to the Saudi government. As is apparent from the Saudi government's many human rights abuses in the name of Islam (including torture, maiming, discrimination against women, abuses by the religious police (Mutawwi'in), discrimination against the Shi'a, executions for practicing 'witchcraft' and for apostasy, use of government-sponsored religious organs to have opponents declared heretics, etc., most of which are described in this and past reports), the only meaningful difference between the respective 'fundamentalisms' of the CDLR and the Saudi government is the latter's support of US foreign policy initiatives in the Middle East. The strategy adopted in this year's report to discredit the CDLR violates the spirit of evenhandedness and fairness called for in the State Department's drafting instructions.

The report's kinder and gentler approach to dealing with the Saudi regime's 'fundamentalism' infects its attempts to explain the application of Islamic law and precepts in Saudi Arabia. In its introduction, for example, the report notes that the Saudi government's 'adherence to the precepts of a rigorously conservative form of Islam . . . enjoys near-consensus support among Saudi citizens.' In addition, it states (echoing the unfortunate formulation of last year's report) that: 'Most Saudis respect the legal system, which they believe is divinely inspired.' It is quite obvious that neither of these statements is verifiable, especially in a country which has, as the report very competently notes, neither elections nor a free press, and where anti-government expression is strictly prohibited by law and routinely punished by arbitrary detention and torture.

As the 1994 edition of the Critique pointed out, given the immunity in practice of the royal family before Saudi courts (noted again in this year's report), it is inconceivable that Saudis consider their legal system to be 'divinely inspired', though it is very likely that they consider the shari'a to be so and therefore believe it should be applied. (It hardly needs stating that Islamic law and actual Saudi legal practice cannot be assumed to be identical. The asserted adherence of the Saudi legal system to Islamic precepts is precisely what the conservative religious opposition challenges; that challenge is a fact, but the report ignores it.) Such irresponsible generalizations constitute nothing less than cheerleading on behalf of the Saudi government and should be excised from the report.

This year's report contains further problems along these lines. One is the attempt to explain away the inherent discrimination of the Islamic law of inheritance, in which female heirs receive only half the share of male heirs. The statement that such discrimination reflects the fact that 'men have financial obligations to their mothers and sisters' is entirely inappropriate and misleading. The report apparently means to suggest that such inherent discrimination constitutes a benevolent paternalism, ensuring that women in fact receive their full inheritance via their male relatives, a patently absurd implication. In fact, Islamic law consistently views women as only half as valuable as men, since it is also the case as the report notes that 'the testimony of one man equals that of two women'. Such inherent gender-based discrimination in the Saudi interpretation of Islamic law should be stated as a brute fact without attempts to rationalize it away. The attempted rationalization of legally sanctioned polygamy is similarly fraught with difficulties. The literal sense of the Qu'ranic passage which serves as the basis for this rule is simply that polygamy is allowed, not necessarily that four is an upper limit. The point is that this rule is equivocal, or rather that it, too, is a brute fact requiring no exegesis from the report's drafters. Finally, the characterization of the Sunna as 'authenticated actions and deeds of the Prophet Muhammad' correctly states a theological proposition, not a relevant fact. It would be more accurate to say that Muslims consider the Sunna to be authentic and leave it at that. Also, the discussion of the application of 'ta'zeer' in the case of the execution of Mr. al-Hidaif could have been clearer. Ta'zeer is a punishment left to the discretion of the judge and is ordinarily less severe than the corresponding capital or corporal punishment (hadd). Ta'zeer can be as mild as a verbal reprimand; in Mr. al-Hidaif's case it was, very unusually, death. It is also the prerogative of the sovereign to apply ta'zeer (hence the intervention of the Ministry of the Interior, which demanded that Mr. al-Hidaif receive a stiffer sentence than the prison term originally imposed). Thus, ta'zeer can serve as an instrument of political coercion. The claim that ta'zeer is also applied as a deterrent is correct, as is the accompanying analysis, namely that it was designed in Mr. al-Hidaif's case to 'deter others who might . . . sympathize with acts of political resistance that bring disunity to the community.'

The report could have gone one step further in its analysis and noted this as an instance in which the Saudi government cynically invoked an idiosyncratic interpretation of Islamic law as a pretext for violating binding international human rights norms to serve its domestic political interests. Moreover, inasmuch as it notes problems relating to procedural safeguards in cases of arrest, defendants' lack of legal representation in court, rules of evidence which encourage forced confessions, interference by governors, royal family members and their associates with legal proceedings, and the perception that the royal family is above the law, one wonders how the report can again sanguinely state that 'The independence of the judiciary is . . . usually respected in practice.'

It is not the task of the report to explain Islamic law to its audience. The fact that it does so is pernicious; it represents a subtle exercise in slanting information in such a way as to suggest that reasonable principles underlie the Saudi government's brutal practices. It is both ironic and unfortunate that such rationalizations (even assuming for the sake of argument that they are well-intentioned) appear in a report on a country which seems to view maiming, beheading, and gender-based discrimination as the very essence of Islamic law. Such a drafting tactic insults Islam and, more important, directly undermines the report's own credibility as a serious human rights document.

The above points are important; the shortcomings they outline color the entire report. It is, however, also important to give credit where credit is due, and, the foregoing criticisms aside, this year's report is generally very good when describing concrete cases and general tendencies, excluding the difficulties it has in dealing with the related problems of Islam and the religious opposition. However, the following issues represent areas in which still further improvement is possible and, indeed, desirable.

One case which the report might have mentioned, whether under the rubric of foreign labor, the arbitrary and repressive character of the Saudi legal system, or cruel and inhuman punishment, is that of Egyptian national Muhammad Kamil Khalifa, which was raised in last year's edition of the

Critique. In late 1994, Mr. Khalifa accused the headmaster of his son's school of sexually assaulting the boy, a charge later reportedly confirmed by medical examination. For making this medically supported allegation, Mr. Khalifa was imprisoned and sentenced to be flogged in front of the school's students. This sentence was later commuted to 80 lashes, which Mr. Khalifa received, before the student body, in May 1995. No doubt the students learned their lesson. While the State Department's instructions discourage the report's drafters from presenting a mere laundry list of incidents, the horrific experience of Mr. Khalifa underlines both the complete vulnerability of foreign workers under Saudi law, as well as the flawed and brutal functioning of the Saudi justice system. Since this case cuts across many of the report's different topics, it would have been appropriate to include it. Continuing the unfortunate practice of ignoring UN human rights investigations concerning Saudi Arabia, this year's report also failed to mention the United Nations' interest in Mr. Khalifa's case.

A Special Rapporteur to the UN Commission on Human Rights transmitted an official expression of concern to the Saudi government concerning this case, noting in particular that corporal punishment of the type inflicted on Mr. Khalifa was inconsistent with binding international human rights norms prohibiting torture and other cruel, inhuman or degrading treatment or punishment. The report also ignores important findings of the UN Special Rapporteur Nigel S. Rodley regarding the mistreatment and abuse of Iraqi refugees. For the last two years the drafters of the report have offered a spirited defense of Saudi treatment of Iraqi refugees displaced by the Gulf War. In 1994 this was done in response to a devastating Amnesty International report which provided details of numerous disturbing abuses committed against Iraqi refugees in the Rafha and Artawiya camps between 1991 and 1993. The 1994 report went so far as to directly refute Amnesty's findings.

This year's report ignores the Special Rapporteur's conclusions regarding the mistreatment of such refugees during the same period. The Special Rapporteur outlined the specifics of a number of different cases of mistreatment, torture, collective punishment, death and other abuses violative of international norms of human rights and humanitarian law. The Special Rapporteur concluded, contrary to the assertions made in the last two State Department reports, 'that the allegations of torture and cruel and inhuman treatment and punishment of Iraqi refugees [appeared] well founded'. Another report concerning the same camps by UNHCR is cited by the report without editorial comment in order to refute a 1993 report by Human Rights Watch that such refugees had been forcibly repatriated to Iraq. The State Department instructions to drafters of the Country Reports requires them to 'pay special attention to reports by the various UN human rights mechanisms'. The self-serving and selective use of such sources made by this year's report is deplorable and violates the spirit of this instruction.

The fact that the Saudi government refused to cooperate with the Special Rapporteur regarding his inquiry into abuses against Iraqi refugees also deserved mention since it continues a pattern of disregard in practice of international human rights mechanisms. This fact would make a fitting addition to the report's otherwise adequate discussion of the Saudi government's rejection of international human rights norms as a matter of allegedly Islamic principle.

Another issue which the report continues to ignore, despite repeated urging in previous editions of the Critique, is the Saudi government's relentless efforts to stifle domestic and external criticism by acquiring or thwarting foreign broadcast and other media. The latest casualty in this campaign is a joint Saudi-BBC television venture which the Saudis forced to shut down in early 1996 after it broadcast a documentary featuring Dr. al-Mas'ari. In addition, the Egyptian Organization for Human Rights (EOHR) reported that the Saudi government had successfully pressured the Egyptian government to ban any and all books critical of the Saudi government. Also, in an article in the London *Sunday Telegraph*, noted author Said K. Aburish revealed that in 1993 a Saudi government advisor had offered him $600,000 to cancel publication of a book critical of the Saudi government. Aburish also recounted an incident in which the Saudi government successfully pressured the BBC to cancel an appearance by Aburish on a news program to discuss the November car-bombing in Riyadh of a National Guard training facility.

The Saudi government's censorship extends abroad in order to prevent negative information about itself reaching its citizens at home. Such practices are therefore appropriate for inclusion in the report. It is difficult to divorce the State Department's reluctance to criticize the Kingdom's censorship of media located outside Saudi Arabia from the fact that the US government, through the Voice of America (VOA), now assists the Saudis in broadcasting pro-Saudi propaganda in the Middle East and North America. VOA and Middle East Broadcasting Corp. (MBC), owned by King Fahd's brother-in-law, jointly produce a program called 'Dialogue with the West'. MBC reportedly has editorial control over the program's content. The program runs in the United States over the Arab Network of America, a Saudi-owned radio network noted in last year's edition of the Critique for its censorship of reports critical of the Saudi government.

Aside from the US government's dubious decision to aid dissemination of propaganda by a country routinely identified by the US government itself as one that 'commits or tolerates serious [human rights] abuses', this partnership bodes extremely ill for the many persons in the Middle East who rely on VOA for objective news reports.

Absent from this year's report is the fact that different elements among the Saudi security forces, some of which were responsible for human rights violations (as noted in the report's introduction), seem to represent competing constituencies within the Saudi government. Paragraph 13 of the State Department's instructions to drafters encourages them to note where security forces are not under the complete control of the government. This seems to be the case with the Mutawwi'in, who often overstep their authority and yet are only very rarely, if ever, reprimanded for doing so. In past years, the National Guard, under the command of the Crown Prince, have presented something of a counterbalance to the Mutawwi'in, as suggested by occasional incidents of conflict between the two groups. In any event, the fact that the Mutawwi'in are not entirely under the Saudi government's control should be stated more clearly. On a related note, this year's report is to be commended for correcting last year's questionable assertion that incidents involving the Mutawwi'in were on the decline, and instead noting this year a long-term increase in such incidents of abuse.

The report could improve its section on arbitrary detention by providing an estimate of prisoners of conscience in one place; this is admittedly difficult in a country like Saudi Arabia where information is tightly controlled. However, the report's current approach is confusing. It appears to suggest that it could only confirm the detention of 38 persons for their anti-government activity (27 from an incident in 1994, nine in connection with the execution of Mr. al-Hidaif, and two clerics).

While the report is appropriately cautious in accepting the figures given by the CDLR, it might have mentioned the figure of 200 proposed by Amnesty International. Parts of this year's report were very well done. For example, it offers a fine discussion of capital punishment in the Kingdom, noting the alarming increase in executions, the fact that most persons executed are non-Saudis, and the expansion of capital offenses. It would have been appropriate to note that a number of women were publicly beheaded in 1995 (12 as of mid-October). The beheading of women represents a new development in Saudi penal practice; according to last year's report women were formerly executed out of public view by firing squad.

Aside from the criticisms above, the discussion of women's rights in the Kingdom is detailed and accurate. Issues appropriately raised included: domestic violence; the use of religion as a pretext for legalized discrimination; discriminatory dress codes; harassment by the Mutawwi'in; restrictions on travel and freedom of movement; polygamy; and discrimination in the work place. Similarly complete, again subject to criticisms raised above, is the discussion of discrimination against the Shi'a. However, the report's wording ('Sunni clerics . . . and one CDLR founder have made strong anti-Shi'a statements') could suggest that only the religious opposition encourages such discrimination on the basis of religion. It would be helpful to note that state-sponsored clerics have in the past engaged in virulent public tirades against the Shi'a. That would clarify that the government encourages religiously motivated public expressions of anti-Shi'a sentiment.

Also, the report's discussion of worker rights is thorough, noting among other things that Saudi Arabia has been suspended from the US Overseas Private Investment Corporation for its failure to adhere to internationally recognized worker rights standards. A good summary of the abuses suffered by female foreign domestic servants, a problem of epidemic proportions in Saudi Arabia, appears in the section dealing with women's rights.

Lawyers Committee for Human Rights, 'Critique', New York, 1997.

8X
Capital punishment

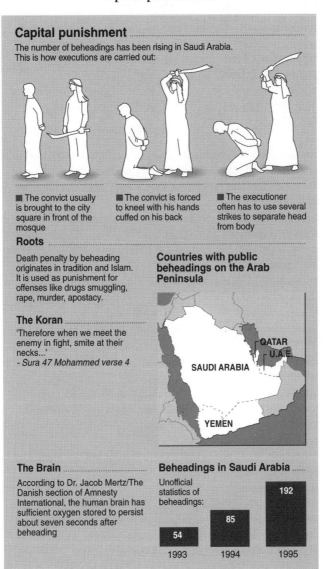

Capital punishment

The number of beheadings has been rising in Saudi Arabia. This is how executions are carried out:

■ The convict usually is brought to the city square in front of the mosque

■ The convict is forced to kneel with his hands cuffed on his back

■ The executioner often has to use several strikes to separate head from body

Roots

Death penalty by beheading originates in tradition and Islam. It is used as punishment for offenses like drugs smuggling, rape, murder, apostacy.

The Koran

'Therefore when we meet the enemy in fight, smite at their necks...'
- *Sura 47 Mohammed verse 4*

Countries with public beheadings on the Arab Peninsula

QATAR
U.A.E.
SAUDI ARABIA
YEMEN

The Brain

According to Dr. Jacob Mertz/The Danish section of Amnesty International, the human brain has sufficient oxygen stored to persist about seven seconds after beheading

Beheadings in Saudi Arabia

Unofficial statistics of beheadings:

1993	1994	1995
54	85	192

8Y
International Human Rights Instruments

According to a UN publication, 'Human Rights, International Instruments, Charts of Ratifications as at 30 June 1996', Saudi Arabia figured low among countries which have signed the 25 most important human rights instruments:

Saudi Arabia had ratified four instruments:

- The Convention on the Prevention and Punishment of the Crime of Genocide
- The Convention on the Rights of the Child
- The Slavery Convention of 1926 as amended
- The Supplementary Convention on the Abolition of Slavery, the Slave Trade, and Institutions and Practices Similar to Slavery

Saudi Arabia had not signed or ratified 21 instruments:

- The International Covenant on Economic, Social and Cultural Rights
- The International Covenant on Civil and Political Rights
- The Optional Protocol to the International Covenant on Civil and Political Rights
- The Second Optional Protocol to the International Covenant on Civil and Political Rights aiming at the abolition of the death penalty
- The International Convention on the Elimination of All Forms of Racial Discrimination
- The International Convention on the Suppression and Punishment of the Crime of Apartheid
- International Convention against Apartheid in Sports
- The Convention on the Non-Applicability of Statutory Limitations to War Crimes and Crimes against Humanity
- The Convention on the Elimination of All Forms of Discrimination against Women
- The Convention on the Political Rights of Women
- The Convention on the Nationality of Married Women
- the Convention on Consent to Marriage, Minimum Age for Marriage and Registration of Marriages
- the Convention against Torture and other Cruel, Inhuman or Degrading Treatment of Prisoners
- the Slavery Convention of 1926
- the 1953 Protocol amending the 1926 Convention
- the Convention for the Suppression of the Traffic in Persons and of the Esploitations of the Prostitutions of others
- the Convention on the Reductions of Statelessness
- the Convention relating to the Status of Stateless Persons

- the Convention relating to the Status of Refugees
- the Protocol relating to the Status of Refugees
- the Convention on the rights of migrant workers and the members of their families

United Nations, New York, 1996.

8Z
US State Department on Human Rights Practices

The US Department of State Report on Human Rights Practices for 1996.

Saudi Arabia is a monarchy without elected representative institutions or political parties. It is ruled by King Fahd Bin Abd Al-Aziz Al Saud, a son of King Abd Al-Aziz Al Saud, who unified the country in the early 20th century. The King and the Crown Prince are chosen from among the male descendants of King Abd Al-Aziz. There is no written constitution. The concept of the separation of religion and state is not accepted by either society or the Government. The Government maintains adherence to the precepts of a rigorously conservative form of Islam.

The Government does not permit the establishment of political parties and suppresses opposition views. In 1992 King Fahd appointed a Consultative Council, the Majlis Ash-Shura, and similar provincial assemblies. The Council began holding sessions in 1994. The judiciary is generally independent but is subject to influence by the executive branch and members of the royal family.

Police and border forces under the Ministry of Interior are responsible for internal security. The Mutawwa'in, or religious police, compose the Committee to Prevent Vice and Promote Virtue, a semi-autonomous agency that encourages adherence to Islamic values by monitoring public behavior. Members of the security forces committed human rights abuses.

The oil industry has fueled the transformation of Saudi Arabia from a pastoral, agricultural, and commercial society to a rapidly urbanizing one characterized by large-scale infrastructure projects, an extensive social welfare system, and a labor market comprised largely of foreign workers. Oil revenues account for 37 percent of the gross domestic product (GDP) and 72 percent of government income. Agriculture accounts for only about 8 percent of GDP. Government spending, including spending on the national airline, power, water, telephone, education, and health services, accounts for 36 percent of GDP. About 37 percent of the economy is in private hands, and the Government is promoting further privatization of the economy. The Government has also undertaken an aggressive campaign to increase the number of Saudi nationals represented in the private and public work forces. This has included restrictions on some categories of foreign workers, for example, limiting certain occupations to Saudis only, increasing fees for some work visas, and setting minimum wages for some job categories designed to increase the cost to employers of non-Saudi labor.

The Government commits and tolerates serious human rights abuses. There is no mechanism for citizens to change their government, and citizens do not have this right. Since the death of King Abd Al-Aziz, the King and Crown Prince have been chosen from among his sons, who themselves have had preponderant influence in the choice. A 1992 royal decree reserves for the King exclusive power to name the Crown Prince. The Government bases its legitimacy on governance according to Islamic law. Security forces continued to abuse detainees and to arbitrarily arrest and detain persons. Ministry of Interior officers abused prisoners and facilitated incommunicado detention in contradiction of the law, but with the acquiescence of the Government. Prolonged detention is a problem. The legal system is subject to executive and royal family influence. The Government prohibits or restricts freedom of speech, the press, assembly, association, and religion. Reports of harassment by the Mutawwa'in decreased in 1995 and 1996, though Mutawwa'in intimidation, abuse, and detention of citizens and foreigners of both sexes continued. Other problems include discrimination and violence against women, suppression of ethnic and religious minorities, and strict limitations on the rights of workers. The Government disagrees with internationally accepted definitions of human rights and views its interpretation of Islamic law as its sole source of guidance for human rights.

RESPECT FOR HUMAN RIGHTS

Section 1.
Respect for the Integrity of the Person, Including Freedom from:
a. Political and Other Extrajudicial Killing

There was one allegation of political or other extrajudicial killings by government officials. In early December, Haytham Al-Bahir, a Shi'a student, reportedly died of complications arising from detention and torture, which aggravated a preexisting medical condition.

On June 25, unknown persons exploded a truck bomb outside a US military housing complex at Al-Khobar. The bomb killed 19 US personnel and wounded hundreds of persons. Authorities arrested dozens of people, and the investigation was continuing at year's end.

On April 22, the authorities announced the arrest of four persons for the November 1995 car bombing of a US-run military training center for Saudi military that killed 7 persons and wounded 60. All four were tried and found guilty in accordance with Saudi judicial procedures, which include several levels of appellate review, and mandatory review by the King prior to their execution on May 31.

b. Disappearance

There were no reports of politically motivated disappearances.

c. Torture and Other Cruel, Inhuman, or Degrading Treatment or Punishment

There were credible reports that the authorities continued to abuse detainees, including citizens and foreigners. Ministry of Interior officers are responsible for most incidents of abuse, which can include beatings and the deprivation of sleep during weeks of interrogation resulting in severe weight loss for the detainee. There were unverified reports of worse abuses. Efforts to confirm or discount reports of worse abuses, including torture, are hindered by the Government's refusal to grant members of diplomatic missions access to the Ministry of Interior detention facilities or allow members of international human rights groups into the country. The Government's past failure to denounce human rights abusers has contributed to the public perception that abuses can be committed with impunity.

Although reports of harassment by the Mutawwa'in decreased, Mutawwa'in intimidation, abuse, and detention of citizens and foreigners of both sexes continued (see Sections 1.d. and 1.e.).

The Government rigorously observes criminal punishments according to its interpretation of Islamic law, including amputation, flogging, and execution by beheading or stoning. No executions were performed during the five-month period from October 17, 1995, to March 14. Executions resumed March 15, and by year's end the authorities had beheaded 40 men and 1 woman for murder, 14 men for rape, 6 men and 2 women for drug offenses, 5 men for armed robbery, and 1 man for witchcraft. In a reversal of previous years, those executed in 1996 were predominantly Saudi (39 men and 1 woman). There were no executions by stoning in 1996.

In accordance with Shari'a, the authorities punish repeated thievery by amputation of the right hand. However, amputation has not been imposed since June 1995. For less serious crimes, such as drunkenness or publicly flouting Islamic precepts, flogging with a cane is frequently the punishment.

Conditions in standard jails and prisons vary throughout the Kingdom. Prisons, particularly in the eastern province, are of generally high quality, with air-conditioned cells, good nutrition, regular exercise, and careful patrolling by prison guards. Some detainees in police station jails, however, have complained of overcrowding and unsanitary conditions. Family members are allowed access.

Boards of Investigation and Public Prosecution, organized on a regional basis, were established by King Fahd in 1993. The members of these boards have the right to inspect prisons, review prisoners' files, and hear their complaints. The Government, however, does not permit visits to jails or prisons by human rights monitors. Some diplomats have been granted regular access to incarcerated foreign citizens.

No impartial observers are allowed access to specialized Ministry of Interior prisons, such as Al-Hair Prison south of Riyadh, where the Government detains persons accused of political subversion.

Representatives of the United Nations High Commissioner for Refugees (UNHCR) are present at the Rafha refugee camp housing former Iraqi prisoners of war (POW's) and civilians who fled Iraq following the Gulf War. According to UNHCR officials, there is no systematic abuse of refugees by camp guards. When occasional instances of abuse surface, the authorities are generally responsive and willing to reprimand offending guards. The camp itself is comparatively comfortable and well run.

d. Arbitrary Arrest, Detention, or Exile

The law prohibits arbitrary arrest. Despite the law, however, officers make arrests and detain persons without following explicit legal guidelines. There are few procedures to safeguard against abuse. However, there was a case in 1995 in which a Saudi citizen successfully sued the Government for wrongful imprisonment and was awarded compensation.

Authorities usually detain suspects for no longer than three days before charging them, in accordance with a regulation issued by the Ministry of Interior in 1983, although serious exceptions have been reported. The regulation also has provisions for bail for less serious crimes. Also, detainees are sometimes released on the recognizance of a patron or sponsoring employer without the payment of bail. If not released, the accused are detained an average of one to two months before going to trial.

There is no established procedure providing detainees the right to inform their family of their arrest. If asked, the authorities usually confirm the arrest of foreigners to their country's diplomats. In general, however, foreign diplomats learn about such arrests through informal channels. The authorities may take as long as several months to provide official notification of the arrest of foreigners, if at all. In capital cases, foreigners have in the past been tried and executed without notification of their arrest ever having been given to their government's representatives.

The Mutawwa'in enforce a strict public code of proper dress and behavior. However, reports of harassment, intimidation, and detention of those deemed to be violating the code declined in 1995 and 1996. The Mutawwa'in have the authority to detain people for no more than 24 hours for violation of behavior standards. However, they sometimes exceeded this limit before delivering detainees to the regular police (see Section 1.f.). Current procedures require a police officer to accompany the Mutawwa'in before the latter make an arrest, although this requirement is sometimes ignored.

Detainees arrested by the General Directorate of Investigation (GDI), which is the Ministry of Interior's security service, are commonly held incommunicado in special prisons during the initial phase of an investigation, which may last weeks or months. The GDI allows the detainees only limited contact with their families or lawyers.

The authorities detain without charge people who publicly criticize the Government, or they charge them with attempting to destabilize the Government (see Sections 2.a. and 3). The authorities continued to detain Salman Al-Awdah and Safar Al-Hawali, Muslim clerics who were arrested in September 1994 for publicly criticizing the Government. Their detention that year sparked protest demonstrations resulting in the arrest of 157 persons for anti-government activities. At the end of 1994, 27 of these persons remained in detention pending investigation; the Government has not announced the release of any of those detainees in the succeeding two years. The thousands of prisoners and detainees released under the annual Ramadan amnesty included no political dissidents. The total number of political detainees is impossible to determine.

The Government does not use forced exile. However, Mohammed al-Masari and Osama Bin Ladin, two critics of the Government who live outside of the country, have had their citizenship revoked.

e. Denial of Fair Public Trial

The independence of the judiciary is prescribed by law and is usually respected in practice. However, judges occasionally accede to the influence of the executive branch, particularly members of the royal family and their associates. Moreover, judicial, financial, and administrative control of the courts rests with the Ministry of Justice.

The legal system is based on Shari'a, or Islamic law. Regular Shari'a courts exercise jurisdiction over common criminal cases and civil suits regarding marriage, divorce, child custody, and inheritance. These courts base judgments largely on the Koran and on the Sunna, another Islamic text. Cases involving relatively small penalties are tried in summary courts; more serious crimes are adjudicated in general courts. Appeals from both courts are heard by the appeals courts in Mecca and Riyadh.

Other civil proceedings, including those involving claims against the Government and enforcement of foreign judgments, are held before specialized administrative tribunals, such as the Commission for the Settlement of Labor Disputes and the Board of Grievances.

The military justice system has jurisdiction over uniformed personnel and civil servants charged with violations of military regulations. Court-martial decisions are reviewed by the Minister of Defense and Aviation and by the King.

The Government permits Shi'a Muslims to use their own legal tradition to adjudicate noncriminal cases within their community.

There is a Supreme Judicial Council, which is not a court and may not reverse decisions made by an appeals court. However, the Council may refer decisions back to the lower courts for reconsideration. Its members are appointed by the King, as are most senior jurists, called muftis. Only the Council may discipline or remove a judge.

There is also the Council of Senior Religious Scholars, which is an autonomous body of 15 senior religious jurists, including the Minister of Justice. It establishes the legal principles to guide lower court judges in deciding individual cases.

Defendants usually appear without an attorney before a judge, who determines guilt or innocence in accordance with Shari'a standards. Defense lawyers may offer their clients advice before trial or may attend the trial as interpreters for those unfamiliar with Arabic. The courts do not provide foreign defendants with translators. Public defenders are not provided. There is no licensing procedure for lawyers. Individuals may choose any person to represent them by a power of attorney filed with the court and Ministry of Justice. Most trials are closed. A woman's testimony does not carry the same weight as that of a man. In a Shari'a court, the testimony of one man equals that of two women.

In the absence of two witnesses, or four witnesses in the case of adultery, confessions before a judge are almost always required for criminal conviction – a situation that repeatedly has led prosecuting authorities to coerce confessions from suspects by threats and abuse.

Sentencing is not uniform. Foreign residents often receive harsher penalties than citizens. Under Shari'a, as interpreted and applied in Saudi Arabia, crimes against Muslims receive harsher penalties than those against non-Muslims. In the case of wrongful death, the amount of indemnity or 'blood money' awarded to relatives varies with the nationality, religion, and sex of the victim. A sentence may be changed at any stage of review, except for punishments stipulated by the Koran. Provincial governors have the authority to exercise leniency and reduce a judge's sentence. In some instances, governors have reportedly threatened and even detained judges over disagreements on their decisions. In general, members of the royal family, and other powerful families, are not subject to the same rule of law as ordinary citizens. For example, judges do not have the power to issue a warrant summoning any member of the royal family.

The King and his advisors review cases involving capital punishment to ensure that the court applied the proper legal and Islamic principles. The

King has the authority to commute death sentences and grant pardons except for capital crimes committed against individuals. In such cases, he may request the victim's next of kin to pardon the murderer – usually in return for compensation from the family or the King.

There is insufficient information to determine the number of political prisoners because the Government does not provide information on such persons or respond to inquiries about them. Moreover, the Government conducts closed trials for persons who may be political prisoners and in other cases has detained persons incommunicado for long periods while under investigation. At year's end, at least nine persons were serving prison terms for their connections to the rigidly fundamentalist Committee for the Defense of Legitimate Rights (CDLR), an opposition group based in London (see Section 3), and their alleged involvement in a 1994 assault on an Interior Ministry official.

f. Arbitrary Interference with Privacy, Family, Home, or Correspondence

The sanctity of family life and the inviolability of the home are among the most fundamental of Islamic precepts. Royal decrees announced in 1992 include provisions calling for the Government to defend the home from unlawful incursions.

The police must generally demonstrate reasonable cause and obtain permission from the provincial governor before searching a private home, but warrants are not required.

Customs officials routinely open mail for contraband including material deemed pornographic as well as non-Muslim religious material. They regularly confiscate materials deemed offensive. The authorities also open mail and use informants and wiretaps in internal security matters.

The Government enforces most social and Islamic religious norms, which are matters of law (see Section 5). Women may not marry non-Saudis without Government permission; men must obtain approval from the Ministry of Interior to marry women from countries outside the six states of the Gulf Cooperation Council. Although women are prohibited from marrying non-Muslims, men have the right to marry Christians and Jews, in accordance with Islamic law.

Both citizens and foreigners were targets of harassment by members of the Mutawwa'in and by religious vigilantes acting independently of the Mutawwa'in, though on a lesser scale than in 1995. The Government enjoins the Mutawwa'in to follow established procedures and to offer instruction in a polite manner; following especially egregious altercations, the authorities have exerted tighter control over the Mutawwa'in (see Section 1d). The Government, however, has not condemned the actions of religious vigilantes but has sought to curtail their activities.

Mutawwa'in enforcement of strict standards of social behavior included the closure of commercial establishments during the daily prayer observances, insistence upon modest dress in public, and harassment of patrons of videotape rental shops. They remonstrate with Saudi and foreign women for failure to observe strict dress codes and for being in the company of males who are not their close relatives. They also harassed and arrested non-Muslims attempting to conduct religious services (see Section 2c).

Section 2.
Respect for Civil Liberties

a. Freedom of Speech and Press

The Government severely limits freedom of speech and the press. The authorities do not countenance criticism of Islam, the ruling family, or the Government. Persons whose criticisms align them with an organized political opposition are subject to arrest and detention until they confess their crime or sign a statement promising not to resume such criticisms, which is tantamount to a confession.

The print media are privately owned but publicly subsidized. A 1982 media policy statement and a 1965 national security law prohibit the dissemination of criticism of the Government. The media policy statement urges journalists to uphold Islam, oppose atheism, promote Arab interests, and preserve the cultural heritage of Saudi Arabia. The Ministry of Information appoints, and may remove, the editors in chief. It also provides guidelines to newspapers on controversial issues. The Government owns the Saudi Press Agency (SPA), which expresses official Government views.

Newspapers typically publish news on sensitive subjects, such as crime or terrorism, only after it has been released by the SPA or when it has been authorized by a senior government official. Two Saudi-owned, London-based dailies, Ash-Sharq Al-Awsat and Al-Hayat, are widely distributed and read in Saudi Arabia. The authorities continue to censor stories about Saudi Arabia in the foreign press. Censors may remove or blacken the offending articles, glue pages together, or prevent certain issues of foreign publications from entering the market. However, the Ministry of Information continued to relax its blackout policy regarding politically sensitive news concerning Saudi Arabia reported in international media, although press restrictions on reporting of domestic news remain very stringent. The terrorist bombing of a US military facility in Al Khobar on June 25 was promptly reported by the government media.

The Government's policy in this regard appears to be motivated in part by pragmatic considerations: Saudi access to outside sources of information, especially Cable News Network and other satellite television channels, is widespread.

The Government tightly restricts the entry of foreign journalists into the Kingdom but admitted a markedly increased number into the country in 1996.

The Government owns and operates the television and radio companies. Government censors remove any reference to politics, religions other than Islam, pork or pigs, alcohol, or any sexual innuendo from foreign programs and songs. Reflecting competition from outside satellite television networks, Saudi television has introduced some program changes, including 'Face to Face', a weekly live talk show in which ministers and other senior officials interact with a moderator and answer phone and facsimile questions from citizens.

There are as many as 300,000 satellite receiving dishes in the Kingdom that provide citizens with foreign broadcasts. The legal status of these devices is ambiguous. The Government ordered a halt to their import in 1992, at the request of religious leaders who objected to foreign programming available on satellite channels. In March 1994, the Government banned the sale, installation, and maintenance of dishes and supporting devices, but the number of dishes continues to increase and residents may legally subscribe to satellite decoding services that require a dish.

The Government censors all forms of public artistic expression. The authorities prohibit cinemas and public musical or theatrical performances, except those that are strictly folkloric.

Academic freedom is restricted. The authorities prohibit the study of evolution, Freud, Marx, Western music, and Western philosophy. Some professors believe that government and conservative religious informers monitor their classroom comments.

b. Freedom of Peaceful Assembly and Association

The Government strictly limits these freedoms. It prohibits public demonstrations as a means of political expression and the establishment of political parties or any type of opposition group (see Section 3). By its power to license associations, the Government ensures that groups conform to public policy.

Public meetings are segregated by sex. Unless meetings are sponsored by diplomatic missions or approved by the appropriate governor, foreign residents seeking to hold unsegregated meetings risk arrest and deportation. The authorities monitor any large gathering of people, especially of women.

c. Freedom of Religion

Freedom of religion does not exist. Islam is the official religion, and all citizens must be Muslims. The Government prohibits the practice of other religions. There are isolated reports of harassment and arrest of foreign workers conducting clandestine worship services, particularly around non-Muslim religious holidays. One Christian worship service was broken up by police and Mutawwa'in, and the man who hosted the service was punished by lashing.

Conversion by a Muslim to another religion is considered apostasy. Public apostasy is a crime under Shari'a law and punishable by death.

Islamic practice is generally limited to that of the Wahhabi sect's interpretation of the Hanbali School of the Sunni branch of Islam. Practices contrary to this interpretation, such as visits to the graves of renowned Muslims, are discouraged.

The Ministry of Islamic Affairs directly supervises and is a major source of funds for the construction and maintenance of almost all mosques in the country. The Ministry pays the salaries of all imams and others who work in the mosques. A governmental committee is responsible for defining the qualifications of imams. The religious police, or the Mutawwa'in, receive their funding from the Government and the general president of the Mutawwa'in holds the rank of minister.

The Shi'a Muslim minority (roughly 500,000 of over 13 million citizens) lives mostly in the eastern province. They are the objects of officially sanctioned social and economic discrimination (see Section 5). Prior to 1990, the Government prohibited Shi'ite public processions during the Islamic month of Muharram and restricted other processions and congregations to designated areas in the major Shi'ite cities. Since 1990, the authorities have permitted marches on the Shi'a holiday of Ashura, provided the marchers do not display banners or engage in self-flagellation. In May Ashura commemorations in the eastern province passed without incident.

The Government seldom permits private construction of Shi'ite mosques. The Shi'a have declined government offers to build state-supported mosques because Shi'ite motifs would be prohibited in them.

The Government does not permit public or private non-Muslim religious activities. Persons wearing religious symbols of any kind in public risk confrontation with the Mutawwa'in. The general prohibition against religious symbols applies also to Muslims. A Muslim wearing a Koranic necklace in public would be admonished. Non-Muslim worshippers risk arrest, lashing, and deportation for engaging in any religious activity that attracts official attention.

d. Freedom of Movement Within the Country, Foreign Travel, Emigration, and Repatriation

The Government restricts the travel of Saudi women, who must obtain written permission from their closest male relative before the authorities will allow them to board public transportation between different parts of the country or travel abroad (see Section 5). Males may travel anywhere within the country or abroad.

Foreigners are typically allowed to reside or work in Saudi Arabia only under the sponsorship of a Saudi national or business. The Government requires foreign residents to carry identification cards. It does not permit foreigners to travel outside the city of their employment or change their workplace without their sponsor's permission. Foreign residents who travel within the country are often asked by the authorities to show that they possess letters of permission from their employer or sponsor.

Sponsors generally retain possession of the workers' passports. Foreign workers must obtain permission from their sponsors to travel abroad. If sponsors are involved in a commercial or labor dispute with foreign employees, they may ask the authorities to prohibit the employees from departing the country until the dispute is resolved. Some sponsors use this as a pressure tactic to resolve disputes in their favor, or to have foreign employees deported.

The Government seizes the passports of all potential suspects and witnesses in criminal cases and suspends the issuance of exit visas to them, until the case is tried. As a result, some foreign nationals are forced to remain in the country for lengthy periods against their will. The authorities sometimes confiscate the passports of suspected oppositionists and their families. Some husbands of women who participated in a 1991 motorcade through the streets of Riyadh in protest of government restrictions on female driving reported that, five years later, they still have not had their passports returned. The Government prevents Shi'a Muslims believed to have pro-Iranian sympathies from traveling abroad.

Citizens may emigrate, but the law prohibits dual citizenship. Apart from marriage to a Saudi national, there are no provisions for long-term foreign residents to acquire citizenship. However, foreigners are granted citizenship in rare cases, generally through the advocacy of an influential patron.

The 1992 Basic Law provides that 'the State will grant political asylum if the public interest mitigates' in favor of it. The language does not specify clear rules for adjudicating asylum cases. In general, the authorities regard refugees and displaced persons like other foreign workers: They must have sponsors for employment or risk expulsion. Of the 35,000 Iraqi civilians and former prisoners of war allowed refuge in Saudi Arabia at the end of the Gulf War, none has been granted permanent asylum by the Saudis; however, the Government has underwritten the entire cost of providing safe haven to the Iraqi refugees, and continues to provide excellent logistical and administrative support to the United Nations High Commissioner for Refugees (UNHCR) and other resettlement agencies.

At year's end, approximately 25,000 of the original 35,000 Iraqi refugees had been resettled in third countries or voluntarily repatriated to Iraq. Most of the remaining 10,000 refugees are restricted to the Rafha refugee camp. The UNHCR has monitored over 2,800 persons voluntarily returning to Iraq from Rafha since December 1991 and found no evidence of forcible repatriation.

The Government has temporarily allowed some foreigners to remain in Saudi Arabia in cases where their safety would be jeopardized if they were deported to their home countries.

Section 3.
Respect for Political Rights: The Right of Citizens to Change Their Government

Citizens do not have the right to change their government. There are no formal democratic institutions, and only a few citizens have a voice in the choice of leaders or in changing the political system. The King rules on civil and religious matters within certain limitations established by religious law, tradition, and the need to maintain consensus among the ruling family and religious leaders.

The King is also the Prime Minister, and the Crown Prince serves as Deputy Prime Minister. The King appoints all other ministers, who in turn appoint subordinate officials with cabinet concurrence.

In 1993 the King appointed 60 members to a Consultative Council, or Majlis Ash-Shura. This strictly advisory body began to hold sessions in 1994, but the Council has maintained a low profile and is not regarded as a significant political force by the citizenry or those in power.

The Council of Senior Islamic Scholars is another advisory body to the King and the Cabinet. It issues decisions based on Shari'a in its review of the Government's public policies. The Government views the Council as an important source of religious legitimacy, and takes the Council's opinions into account when promulgating legislation.

Communication between citizens and the Government is usually expressed through client–patron relationships and by affinity groups such as tribes, families, and professional hierarchies. In theory, any male citizen or foreign national may express an opinion or air a grievance at a majlis – an open-door meeting held by the King, a prince, or an important national or local official. However, as governmental functions have become more complex, time-consuming, and centralized, public access to senior officials has become more restricted. Since the assassination of King Faisal in 1975, Saudi kings have reduced the frequency of their personal contacts with the public. Ministers and district governors more readily grant audiences at a majlis.

Typical topics raised in a majlis are complaints about bureaucratic delay or insensitivity, requests for personal redress or assistance, and criticism of particular acts of government affecting family welfare. Broader 'political' concerns – social, economic, or foreign policy – are rarely raised. Complaints about royal abuses of power would not be entertained. In general journalists, academics, and businessmen feel that avenues of domestic criticism and feedback to the regime are closed.

An opposition group, the Committee for the Defense of Legitimate Rights, which advocates a rigidly fundamentalist Islamic viewpoint, was established in 1993 by six citizens. The Government acted quickly to repress the CDLR following its formation. In 1994 CDLR spokesman Mohammed Al-Masari secretly fled to the United Kingdom, where he sought political asylum and established an overseas branch of the CDLR. Al-Masari continued to criticize the Government, using computers and facsimile transmissions to send newsletters back to Saudi Arabia. In March internal divisions within the CDLR spawned the rival Islamic Reform Movement (IRM), headed by Sa'ad Al-Faqih. Al-Masari has expressed the group's 'understanding' of two fatal terrorist bombings of American military facilities and sympathy for the perpetrators. The IRM also implicitly condoned the two terrorist attacks in Saudi Arabia, arguing that they were a natural outgrowth of a political system that does not tolerate peaceful dissent.

In April the Saudi Ambassador in the United Kingdom stated publicly that his Government would withdraw from large contracts for British weapons unless the United Kingdom expelled Al-Masari. The British Government denied Al-Masari's initial request for asylum, due to the circumstances of his illegal entry, but eventually Al-Masari was granted permission to remain in the United Kingdom for four years, with the option of applying for permanent residency at the end of that period. There is no evidence of Saudi Government retribution against the British Government for this decision.

Women play no formal role in government and politics, and are actively discouraged from doing so. Participation by women in a Majlis is restricted, although some women seek redress through female members of the royal family. Only one of the 60 members of the Majlis Ash-Shura is a Shi'a.

Section 4.
Governmental Attitude Regarding International and Nongovernmental Investigation of Alleged Violations of Human Rights

There are no publicly active human rights groups, and the Government has made it clear that none critical of government policies would be permitted.

The Government does not permit visits by international human rights groups or independent monitors, nor has it signed major international human rights treaties and conventions. The Government disagrees with internationally accepted definitions of human rights and views its interpretation of Islamic law as the only necessary guide to protect human rights. Citations of Saudi human rights abuses by international monitors or foreign governments are routinely ignored or condemned by the Government as assaults on Islam.

Section 5.
Discrimination Based on Race, Sex, Religion, Disability, Language, or Social Status

Systematic discrimination based on sex and religion are built into the law. The law forbids discrimination based on race, but not nationality. The Government and private organizations cooperate in providing services for the disabled. The Shi'a religious minority suffers social, legal, and religious discrimination.

Women

The Government does not keep statistics on spousal or other forms of violence against women. Hospital workers report that many women are admitted for treatment of injuries that apparently result from spousal violence. Some foreign women have suffered physical abuse from their Saudi husbands, who can prevent their wives from obtaining exit visas.

Foreign embassies receive many reports that employers abuse foreign women working as domestic servants. Embassies of countries with large domestic servant populations maintain safe houses to which citizens may flee to escape work situations that include forced confinement, withholding of food, beating and other physical abuse, and rape. Often the abuse is at the hands of female Saudis. In general, the Government considers such cases family matters and does not intervene unless charges of abuse are brought to its attention. It is almost impossible for foreign women to obtain redress in the courts due to the courts' strict evidentiary rules and the women's own fears of reprisals. Few employers have been punished for such abuses. There are no private support groups or religious associations to assist such women.

By religious law and social custom, women have the right to own property and are entitled to financial support from their husbands or male relatives. However, women have few political and social rights and are not treated as equal members of society. There are no active women's rights groups. Women, including foreigners, may not legally drive motor vehicles and are restricted in their use of public facilities when men are present. Women must enter city buses by separate rear entrances and sit in specially designated sections. Women risk arrest by the Mutawwa'in for riding in a vehicle driven by a male who is not an employee or a close male relative. Women are not admitted to a hospital for medical treatment without the consent of their male relative. By law and custom, women may not undertake domestic and foreign travel alone (see Section 2d).

In public women are expected to wear the abaya, a black garment covering the entire body. A woman's head and face should also be covered. The Mutawwa'in generally expect women from Arab countries, Asia, and Africa to comply more fully with Saudi customs of dress than they do Western women; nonetheless, in recent years they have instructed Western women to wear the abaya and cover their hair.

Some government officials and ministries still bar accredited female diplomats in Saudi Arabia from official meetings and diplomatic functions.

Women are also subject to discrimination in Islamic law, which stipulates that daughters receive half the inheritance awarded to their brothers. In a Shari'a court, the testimony of one man equals that of two women (see Section 1e). Although Islamic law permits polygyny, it is becoming less common. Islamic law enjoins a man to treat each wife equally. In practice such equality is left to the discretion of the husband. Some women participated in al-Mesyar (or 'short daytime visit') marriages, where the women relinquish their legal rights to financial support and night-time cohabitation. Additionally, the husband is not required to inform his other wives of the marriage, and the children have no inheritance rights. The Government places greater restrictions on women than on men regarding marriage to non-Saudis and non-Muslims (see Section 2d).

Women must demonstrate legally specified grounds for divorce, but men may divorce without giving cause. If divorced or widowed, a woman normally may keep her children until they attain a specified age: 7 years for boys, 9 years for girls. Children over these ages are awarded to the divorced husband or the deceased husband's family. Divorced women who are foreigners are often prevented by their former husbands from visiting their children after divorce.

Women have access to free, but segregated, education through the university level. They constitute 55 percent of all university graduates but are excluded from studying such subjects as engineering, journalism, and architecture. Men are able to study overseas; women may do so only if accompanied by a spouse or an immediate male relative.

Women make up only 5 percent of the work force. Whereas salary and other benefits are the main concerns for men seeking employment, for women the primary goal is merely establishing some toehold in the private or public sector. Most employment opportunities for women are in education and health care, with lesser opportunity in business, philanthropy, banking, retail sales, and the media. Women wishing to enter nontraditional fields are subject to discrimination. Women may not accept jobs in rural areas if they are required to live apart from their families. All workplaces where women are present are segregated by sex. Contact with male supervisors or clients is allowed by telephone or facsimile machine. In 1995 the Ministry of Commerce announced that women would no longer be issued business licenses for work in fields that might require them to supervise foreign workers, interact with male clients, or deal on a regular basis with government officials.

Children

The Government provides all children with free education and medical care. Children are not subject to the strict social segregation faced by women, though they are segregated by sex in schools starting at age 7. In more general social situations, boys are segregated at age 12, and girls at the onset of puberty. It is difficult to gauge the prevalence of child abuse, since the Government keeps no statistics on such cases and is disinclined to infringe on family privacy. Societal abuse of children does not appear to be a major problem.

People with Disabilities

The provision of government social services has increasingly brought the disabled into the public domain. The media carry features lauding the public accomplishments of disabled persons and sharply criticizing parents who neglect disabled children. The Government and private charitable organizations cooperate in education, employment, and other services for the disabled. The law provides hiring quotas for the disabled. While there is no legislation for public accessibility, newer commercial buildings often include such access.

Religious Minorities

Shi'a citizens are discriminated against in government and employment, especially in national security jobs. Several years ago the Government subjected Shi'a to employment restrictions in the oil industry and has not relaxed them. The Sunni majority discriminates socially against the Shi'a minority.

Shi'a face restrictions on access to several services, despite efforts by the Government to improve the social service infrastructure in predominantly Shi'a areas of the country. Since the Iranian revolution, some Shi'a suspected of subversion have been subjected periodically to surveillance and limitations on travel abroad.

National/Racial/Ethnic Minorities

Although racial discrimination is illegal, there is substantial societal prejudice based on ethnic or national origin. Foreign workers from Africa and Asia are subject to various forms of formal and informal discrimination and have the most difficulty in obtaining justice for their grievances.

Section 6.
Worker Rights

a. The Right of Association

Government decrees prohibit the establishment of labor unions and any strike activity.

In 1995 Saudi Arabia was suspended from the US Overseas Private Investment Corporation insurance programs because of the Government's lack of compliance with internationally recognized worker rights standards.

b. The Right to Organize and Bargain Collectively

Collective bargaining is forbidden. Foreign workers comprise about half of the work force. There is no minimum wage; wages are set by employers and vary according to the type of work performed and the nationality of the worker.

There are no export processing zones.

c. Prohibition of Forced or Compulsory Labor

Forced labor is prohibited by a 1952 royal decree that abolished slavery. Ratification of the International Labor Organization (ILO) Conventions 29 and 105, which prohibit forced labor, gives them the force of law. However, employers have significant control over the movements of foreign employees, giving rise to situations that might involve forced labor, especially in remote areas where workers are unable to leave their place of work.

Sometimes sponsors prevent foreign workers from obtaining exit visas to pressure them to sign a new work contract or to drop claims against their employers for unpaid salary (see Section 2.d). In another pressure tactic, sponsors may refuse to provide foreign workers with a 'letter of no objection' that would allow them to be employed by another sponsor.

The labor laws do not protect domestic servants. There were credible reports that female domestic servants were sometimes forced to work 12 to 16 hours a day, seven days a week. There were numerous confirmed reports of runaway maids (see Section 5). The authorities often returned runaway maids to their employers against the maids' wishes.

There have been many reports of workers whose employers have refused to pay several months, or even years, of accumulated salary or other promised benefits. Nondomestic workers with such grievances have the right to complain before the labor courts, but few do so because of fear of deportation. The labor system abets the exploitation of foreign workers because enforcement of work contracts is difficult and generally favors Saudi employers. Labor cases can take many months to reach a final appellate ruling, during which time the employer can prevent the foreign laborer from leaving the country; alternatively, an employer can delay a case until a worker's funds are exhausted and the worker is forced to return to his home country.

d. Minimum Age for Employment of Children

The minimum age for employment is 13 years of age, which may be waived by the Ministry of Labor with the consent of the juvenile's guardian. There is no minimum age for workers employed in family oriented businesses or in other situations that are construed as extensions of the household, e.g., farmers, herdsmen, and domestic servants.

Children under the age of 18 and women may not be employed in hazardous or harmful industries, such as mining or industries employing power-operated machinery. While there is no formal government entity charged with enforcing the minimum age for employment of children, the Ministry of Justice has jurisdiction and has acted as plaintiff in the few cases that have arisen against alleged violators. In general, however, children play a minimal role in the work force.

e. Acceptable Conditions of Work

There is no legal minimum wage. Labor regulations establish a 48-hour workweek at regular pay and allow employers to require up to 12 additional hours of overtime at time-and-a-half pay. Labor law provides for a 24-hour rest period, normally Fridays, although the employer may grant it on another day.

Many foreign nationals who have been recruited abroad have complained that after arrival in Saudi Arabia they were presented with work contracts specifying lower wages and fewer benefits than originally promised. Other foreign workers have reportedly signed contracts in their home countries and were later pressured to sign less favorable contracts upon arrival. Some employees report that at the end of their contract service, their employers refuse to grant permission to allow them to return home.

The ILO has stated that the Government has not formulated legislation implementing the ILO Convention on Equal Pay and that regulations that segregate work places by sex, and limit vocational programs for women, violate ILO Convention 111.

Labor regulations require employers to protect most workers from job-related hazards and disease. Foreign nationals report frequent failures to enforce health and safety standards. Workers in family operated businesses, farmers, herdsmen, and domestic servants are not covered by these regulations. Workers would risk their employment if they were to remove themselves from hazardous work conditions.

United States Information Service (USIS) 1997, American Embassy, Strandvagen 101, 115 89 Stockholm.

Chapter Nine

THE PRESS AND FREEDOM OF SPEECH

9A
The Press and Publication Law

A 'Royal decree for Printed Material and Publications', no. M/17 issued 7 February 1982 (13.4.1402) by King Khaled, outlines the legal system for printing and publishing in Saudi Arabia.

Article One: The following must conform to the rules of this legal system:

(a) Printing presses.
(b) Printed matter and newspapers.
(c) Bookstores which engage in the sale of books and newspapers.
(d) Places of business for design, photography, and calligraphy.
(e) Places of business for printing, recording, selling and renting of films, records, and duplicating tapes.
(f) Institutes for artistic production.
(g) Offices of news agencies and information correspondents.
(h) Offices for advertising, publicity and public relations.
(i) Publication and distribution houses.

Definitions

Article Two: The following terms, wherever they may appear in this legal system are defined thus:

(a) Printing press: any apparatus equipped for printing of words, figures or pictures on paper, clothing or any other material for the purpose of circulation.
(b) Printer: official responsible for the printing press regardless of whether he is the owner or one who represents him.
(c) Printed matter: any device for expressing the real or symbolic in what is printed by mechanical or chemical means regardless of whether it is

original, is written, drawn, photographed, or oral if the objective is to adopt it for circulation.

(d) Newspaper: any periodic publication which appears regularly at specified times such as newspapers, magazines, and bulletins.

(e) Journalist: anyone who adopts journalism as a profession and pursues it professionally or semi-professionally. Journalistic work includes writing and production of newspapers, editing of articles and supplying news, results of investigations, articles, pictures, and drawings.

(f) Bookstore: place of business which engages in the display and sale of publications among them books, newspapers, and magazines.

(g) Public library: library which is under any government body.

(h) Publication house: institution which undertakes the preparation, production, distribution, and marketing of publications.

(i) Publisher: whoever undertakes to publish some intellectual production for himself or others and offers it for circulation with or without compensation; it includes editor-in-chief, producer of broadcast materials, office director of a news agency and information correspondents.

(j) Director: administrative official responsible for any of the activities aforementioned in the first articles of this legal system.

(k) Distributor: person who undertakes to offer publications for circulation regardless of whether they were published in or outside the Kingdom.

(l) Ministry: Ministry of Information.

Licensing

Article Three: The opening of any places of offices or practicing of any professional activity indicated in Article 1 of this legal system is not permitted except after obtaining a license from the Ministry of Information; this licensing does not prevent the seeking of any other licenses which other observed regulations require.

Article Four: It is necessary that whoever is granted licensing for any work or activity aforementioned in Article 1 and the responsible office director fulfil the following conditions:

(a) to be a Saudi citizen with legal capacity; it is permissible to exclude foreign information correspondents from the requirement of citizenship by a decision from the Minister of Information.

(b) not to be less than 25 years of age; the Ministry of Information has the right to decrease the age requirement for specific activities to no less than 20 years.

(c) to be of good character and reputation without a criminal record or conviction for immorality or dishonesty as long as he has not been rehabilitated in accordance with the regulations and instructions related to it.

(d) any other condition which the Ministry considers necessary for the practice of a professional activity in itself.

Article Five: In addition to the conditions mentioned in the preceding article, it is necessary that every publisher and director of publishing press with office for publicity and public relations must be the holder of professional qualifications acceptable to the Ministry. The Minister of information may grant an exemption from this condition to anyone who qualifies with appropriate or equivalent experience.

Article Six: The printing of any publication which is against the law or public morals in the Kingdom is prohibited:

Article Seven: The printing, publishing, or circulation of printed matter which contains any of the following [is prohibited, Ed.].

(a) All that violates any basic law or infringes upon the sanctity of Islam and its tolerant law or offends public morality.

(b) All that is incompatible with state security and public order.

(c) All that infringes upon directives and regulations with its secretiveness except when special permission is granted by the competent authorities.

(d) Reports and news which infringe upon the safety of the Saudi Arabian armed forces except after the approval of proper authorities.

(e) All that is intended to expose armed forces personnel or their weapons and equipment to danger.

(f) The publication of regulations, agreements, treaties, or official government statements, before their official announcement, as long as it was done without the approval of proper authorities.

(g) All that infringes on the honor of presidents of countries or heads of diplomatic missions who are accredited by the Kingdom or harms relations with such countries.

(h) All that is attributed of false news to officials of the state, institutions, and local organisations, public and private, or to individuals for the sole purpose of harming them or undermining their authority or infringing upon their honor.

(i) Calling for destructive ideologies, shaking public confidence, and spreading divisiveness among citizens.

(j) All that lead to the advocation of or calling for criminal behaviour or instigating attacks upon others in any way.

(k) All that is defamatory or slanderous to individuals.

(l) Extortion by threatening any person (physical or juridical) by publishing any secret with the intent to compel compensatory payment, real or incorporal, or to force providing benefit to the perpetrator or any other person, or to prevent the exercise of legal rights.

Article Eight: There should be compiled in every (printing) press a special paginated record affixed with the Ministry's seal. All relevant data should be recorded in it, especially titles of books prepared for publication, names of authors and publishers (if available), their addresses, and the number of copies requested for printing. It is also incumbent upon the director of the printing press to make available such a record to the appropriate inspector upon request.

Article Nine: There should be recorded on the first page of each publication printed internally the title of the publication, name of the author, the publisher, if available, date of publication and the number of the printing press.

Article Ten: The publisher and author are responsible for any violation that may appear in a publication if it is circulated prior to obtaining approval. If either of the two pleads ignorance, then the director of the press becomes responsible; if he pleads ignorance on behalf of the press, then the distributor or whoever is in possession of the publication is responsible.

Article Eleven: Every author, publisher, or distributor who desires to print a publication for circulation must present two copies of it to the Ministry for its approval before printing or offering it for circulation. The Ministry within a thirty-day period from the date of submisssion of the request will either approve the publication by affixing its seal on the two copies submitted and return one of them to the person concerned or reject it with a statement of reasons. A complaint against the rejection decision may be lodged with the Minister of Information whose decision in this case is final.

Article Twelve (a): An author, publisher, or distributor must, before circulating any publication printed in the Kingdom, deposit in the National Publishing House in Riyadh five free copies of books and three free copies of other matter; the deposit should be made immediately upon their publication. As for newspapers the deposit should be made within three days of their publication.

External publication

Article Thirteen: Publications arriving from outside the country must be devoid of any prohibited items specified in this law.

Article Fourteen: No publication arriving from outside the country is allowed circulation except after submitting two copies of it to the Ministry for its approval. The Ministry under normal circumstances will either approve the publication within a period of thirty days from the date of submission by affixing a seal on the two copies, one of which is returned to the office concerned or will reject it with a statement of reasons. A complaint against the rejection decision may be lodged with the minister of information whose decision in this case is final.

(b) The revocation of newspapers and periodicals arriving from outside will be applied in accordance with the instructions which are issued by the Ministry of Information.

Article Fifteen: The Ministry has the right in facilitating permission for circulation to develop an agreement with the official concerned to remove objectionable pages or to blot out what it deems necessary in an appropriate way.

Article Sixteen: The Ministry has the right to confiscate any prohibited or unapproved publication and to destroy it without compensation or to retain it or give permission to re-export it. The Minister of Information has the right to determine whether compensation is to be arranged in the event of retention of a publication.

Article Seventeen: Every Saudi who has publication printed outside of the country [is obliged, *Ed.*] to deposit in the National Publishing House Riyadh five free copies of books and three copies of other printed matter immediately upon publication.

Article Eighteen: An exception to the above is the censorship by the Ministry of any publications procured by universities, public libraries, and government agencies, provided that the Ministry of Information is specially advised of such procurement. However it is not permitted to circulate any publication for information as long as it has not been originally authorized for circulation.

Article Nineteen: The Minister of Information or his representative [is authorized, *Ed.*] to issue individual licenses, permanent or temporary, to allow researchers to examine unlicensed publications.

Literary Rights

Article Twenty: Rights of authorship, printing, translation and publication are safeguarded for all Saudi owners, their heirs, and the authors of these publications printed inside the Kingdom and for the national subjects of states whose laws safeguard such a right for Saudis.

Article Twenty-one: The Ministry must prevent any infringement upon the aforementioned rights in the preceding article. The committee referred to in Article 40 of this law has the authority to investigate any infringement upon these rights and hand a judgement of compensation to the concerned person for any material and spiritual harm may have befallen him.

The concerns of the Local Press

Article Twenty-two: Licensing for the publication of newspapers is granted in accordance with the rules pertinent to it.

Article Twenty-three: Among the aims of local newspapers is the call to the Islamic Religion, noble characteristics, guidance, and raising consciousness to all that comprises goodness, progress, righteousness, the dissemination of culture and knowledge, and objective treatment of matters. Newspapers should comply with the restrictions laid down in this system of rules.

Article Twenty-four: The freedom of expressing an opinion by various means of publication is guaranteed within the preview of enacted, and religious rules and local newspapers are not subjected to censorship except during emergency circumstances which are determined by the council of ministers.

Article Twenty-five: Every person has the right to pursue journalistic work in accordance with the provisions of this system of regulations and executive rules.

Article Twenty-six: It is not permissible to issue a magazine or publication outside the purview of journalistic institutions be it governmental, civil or individual except through licensing by the Minister of Information; this licensing is not granted except with the approval of the prime minister. Exempt from licensing are journals and publications which are issued by universities, institutes and schools; their publication takes place after an agreement concerning them is reached between the ministry and the concerned party; and the supervision of the publication and the director of the issuing administrative agency are responsible for guaranteeing what is published is in accordance with the provisions of this system of regulations.

Article Twenty-seven: Whoever applies to obtain in his own name a license, as aforementioned in the preceding article, must fulfil the conditions laid down in the fourth and fifth articles of this system of rules.

Article Twenty-eight: Whoever applies for a license to issue a journal or a publication in accordance with the two preceding articles must submit the following statement:

(a) The name of the editor-in-chief with a statement of his qualifications; the Ministry has the right to accept or reject him.
(b) The name of the journal of publication, place and dates of publication, and the subjects and specialities to be dealt with.
(c) The language(s) in which it is to be published.
(d) The name of the printing press in which it will be printed, and the name and address of its owner.
(e) Any other information requested by the Ministry.

Furthermore, the Ministry should be supplied with information about modification made in the statements.

Article Twenty-nine: The names of the licensed official and editor-in-chief, place of publication and date of publication and subscription, as well as the name of the press in which it was printed, should appear in clear form in a conspicuous place in the newspaper.

Article Thirty: The name of any previously published newspaper which subsequently closed publication cannot be used except after the elapse of ten (10) years after it has ceased publication as long as those who are affiliated with it or their heirs do not give up the name; likewise, the name cannot be adopted for a newspaper or a new printed matter which leads to confusion with the name of another.

Article Thirty-one: The Ministry has the right to establish annual subscription fees for newspapers, magazines, and publications as well as the price of a single issue just as it has the right to administer matters of advertisement and their rates.

Article Thirty-two: The Minister of Information has the right to withdraw a license if the newspaper or publication ceases publication for a continuous period which exceeds three months or if it continues publication sporadically and irregularly.

Article Thirty-three: The Ministry of Information has the right to confiscate or destroy any issue of any newspaper published in the Kingdom without reimbursement if it contains what may affect negatively the religious feeling or peace or general morals or general regulations. The responsible party will be punished according to law.

Article Thirty-four: The Minister of Information has the right to stop any publication in the Kingdom for a period which does not exceed thirty days. Any extension must be approved by the Prime Minister.

Article Thirty-five:

(a) Neither a publication nor its employees are permitted by law to accept bribes from foreign sources directly or indirectly, within or outside the Kingdom.
(b) Advertisements for foreign countries or institutions, governmental or private, are not permitted unless approved the Ministry of Information.
(c) Investigative reports of an advertising nature are not permitted publication unless they indicate clearly their nature.

Article Thirty-six:

(a) The editor assumes full responsibility for what is published in his publication.

(b) The Writer of an article is responsible for what he writes if he signs his legal name or pseudonym. In the absence of the name, the editor will assume responsibility.

Article Thirty-seven: If a newspaper [is] publishing wrong information, it must publish the correction, in its first issue after the request is made in the same location of the original publication or in a noticable location. The following conditions must be observed:

(a) Publication will only be of the corrected part.
(b) If the corrected publication was not made properly before.
(c) The correction must be in the same language as the original publication.
(d) The correction must not include the publication of any violation of rules.

Article Thirty-eight: Without prejudice to any severe punishment, a violation of any of these regulations will receive a punishment of one year imprisonment and/or 30,000 Riyals.

Article Thirty-nine: Upon violation of Article 35 a. mentioned above, the bribe must be confiscated in addition to the punishment stated in Article 38.

Article Forty: Upon a resolution from the Minister of Information, a committee of three members is formed to look into all violations. One of the members must be a legal advisor; and all decisions are made by vote of the majority. Decisions are made after hearing the offer or his representative or any other person the committee deems to summon. All Decisions become effective after approval by the Minister of Information.

Article Forty-one: A violater who receives a jail sentence or a charge which exceeds 1,000 Riyals may file an appeal before the Court of Appeals during the thirty days following this notification of the verdict. The sentence will not be carried out until the Court of Appeal makes its decisions.

Article Forty-two: If the nature of a violation is beyond the limits of this code, the Ministry will submit it to the Prime Minister for his consideration and decision.

Concluding Provisions:

Article Forty-three: Any individual who is practising now any of the activities specified in section (1) of this law, must rectify his status according to this law and to obtain the necessary license.

Article Forty-four: The information minister shall issue the Executive Ordinance for this law with exception of the executive provisions of sections (12.17) which must be issued in conjunction with the Minister of Education.

Article Forty-five: This law will replace the printing and press law which was issued by the royal decree no. (15), dated 8/8/1378, and cancel whatever contradicts with its provision.

Article Forty-six: This law and its executive ordinance will be published in the official gazette and shall be effective after 30 days from the date of its publication.

> Ministry of Information, 'The Saudi Media, Evolution and Progress', Riyadh, Kingdom of Saudi Arabia, June 1993.

9B
The Gulf War Press

The Gulf war did nothing to ease strict controls on the Saudi press – quite the contrary, according to Reporters Sans Frontieres. Censorship and self-censorship work hand in hand.

1. Death, the ultimate censorship

No journalists have been murdered in the course of their work in recent years.

2. Torture and imprisonment to silence journalists

Freelance journalist Zuhair Issa Muhammed Al-Safwani was arrested at the passport office in Dammam on 18 January 1992. He had just returned from London, where he had been studying computer technology, to get married. He was sentenced to four years in prison and 300 lashes. Although the journalist was not informed of the charges against him, he thought his sentence might be linked to articles he had written for Arabic-language newspapers in London – such as the Kuwaiti Al-Ahdath – or to his connections with the Saudi opposition. His family, who had no news of him for five months, were finally allowed to visit him in mid-June.

3. Seizing and banning troublesome newspapers

There were hardly any seizures of newspapers because the press is already muzzled by the government.

4. Economic and legal censorship

Article 39 of Saudi Arabia's new Fundamental Law, promulgated on 1 March 1992 by King Fahd, sums up the countless interdictions to which Saudi journalists have been subjected for decades. 'The media and publishing houses, as well as all other forms of expression, must respect the word and law of the State', it says. 'They must contribute to state education and defend the unity of the nation. Publication of anything that might lead to internal rifts or struggle, or that might harm state security or foreign relations, is forbidden, in accordance with the law.' This new legislation attempted to fill any gaps in the law on publications of 2 July 1982, Articles 6 and 7 of which list 18 taboo subjects, for instance: 'Anything that may harm the dignity of heads of state or leaders of diplomatic representations accredited in Saudi Arabia, or that may adversely affect relations with other countries.' The new law certainly tightened the straitjacket in which the Saudi press works. Moreover, the law on private press companies of 1 August 1964, which is still in force, allows the government to close down any company 'if interests of the country so demand' (Article 8), and the editor of a publication can be dismissed at any time. In December 1992, Mohammed Salah al-Din, editor of the daily *al-Nadwa*, was dismissed for writing an article criticising US President George Bush. Some newspapers even have a censor with special responsibility for religious issues to ensure that Islamic Law and the Koran are strictly and unequivocally observed.

Since broadcasting is under the direct control of the information ministry – private radio and television stations were banned 30 years ago – there is little if any room for freedom of speech in the Saudi media.

5. When outsiders are unwelcome

Journalists of the international media who turn up in Saudi Arabia are systematically given a hard time. Armed with scissors and thick black felt-tips, the censors make sweeping cuts. And any reporter who decides to travel within the country is followed by an official from the information ministry.

The Saudi press also hit out at the 'paradiabolic' aerials 'that have invaded our Islamic countries and are insidiously threatening our values and traditions.' In December 1992, the privately owned weekly *Al-Muslimun* published a series of features entitled 'The invaders are coming in through the roofs of our homes' listing the 'dangers' of programmes broadcast by international television and picked up from satellites by parabolic aerials. 'These programmes are debasing our faith, ridiculing our culture and, in a clever and tantalizing way, helping to shake the basis of our society', one journalist wrote, condemning the 'unequal media conflict between the Arab-Islamic world and the West, with its arsenal of diabolic methods'.

6. Telling it like it is

Here are just few examples of the way Egyptian television series are censored before they can be broadcast in Saudi Arabia:

- Two actors playing the parts of husband and wife are not allowed to share a bed – unless they are married in real life.
- Actors who are not married cannot be shown sitting in the same room with the door closed.
- A father cannot be shown kissing his daughter, or a mother kissing her son, unless they really are related in this way.
- Women cannot be shown singing or dancing.
- No woman is allowed to appear on Saudi television during the month of Ramadan.
- Scenes that show a crime being committed are banned.
- Statues or figures representing a human or animal cannot be shown, because sculpted images are banned by Islamic law.

Reporters Sans Frontieres, 'Censored', Vienna, 14–25 June 1993.

9C
Banning satellite dishes

The Interior Ministry of Saudi Arabia on 27 June 1994 according to Saudi Arabia TV1, Riyadh, issued a statement, banning satellite dishes.

In accordance with Resolution No. 128 of the Council of Ministers issued on 25th Sha'ban 1414 AH regarding the regulation of the reception of foreign satellite television broadcasts in Saudi Arabia, which banned dealing in [satellite] dishes and their auxiliary equipment and decoding systems and their auxiliary equipment, and in accordance with the rules stipulated by the resolution within the context of the alternative service which will be provided by the state and supervised by the Information Ministry, and which banned queries received by the concerned authorities from brother citizens on this issue, the Interior Ministry would like, in the following clarification, to announce everything related to defining the bases and rules which will be followed in all the issues related to satellite television and broadcasts in the light of the regulations referred to in the resolution. They are as follows:

1. With regard to the unused satellite dishes and all their auxiliary equipment which are already in the possession of shops and individuals in warehouses and depots, the owners will be allowed to export these dishes and

equipment officially outside Saudi Arabia via all air, land and sea outlets to anywhere abroad in accordance with wishes of the beneficiary with a maximum period of one month from the issuance and enforcement of this statement. Otherwise, after the end of the period specified in the first article, any equipment found in the possession of either individuals or shops will be immediately confiscated and the offender will be liable to the fines stipulated in the resolution of the Council of Ministers.

2. The words receiver and auxiliary equipment include the following equipment:
   (a) All sizes and types of satellite dishes.
   (b) All types and sizes of receivers used for satellite TV reception.
   (c) Decoders.
   (d) Low Noise Block Down Converters or LNBs.
   (e) Feed-horn equipment.
   (f) All other necessary and technical equipment related to installing and operating the receiver.
3. It should be particularly emphasized that citizens should not get involved in any kind of trading or dealing in the banned equipment stipulated in this statement or in the original resolution.

   May God guide us.

BBC, Summary of World Broadcasts, London, 21 July 1994.

9D
The Economist censored

Like most European and American publications, *The Economist* is often banned in Middle Eastern countries. The Saudi authorities, according to that publication, are by far the most severe censors closely followed by Kuwait and Bahrain. Specific issues of The Economist, banned 1991–96, included the following articles:

Dec 21, 1991:	'Weak at the top'
June 12 1993:	'Seeds on stony ground'
July 09 1994:	'Islam survey'
Sept 17 1994:	'Spare a billion'
Oct 08 1994:	'Challenge to the House of Saud'
Dec 24 1994:	'Xmas double issue'
Feb 04 1995:	'Silent revolution'
March 18 1995:	'Living with Islam'
Aug 12 1995:	'Saudi new cabinet'
Nov 18 1995:	'Chairman Fahd'
Jan 07 1996:	'Saudi Royals'
Jan 13 1996:	'M Al Massari'

Although easy to spot, the Ministry of Information will never confirm or reveal the offending article. Except for the prolonged ban of December 1991 which went on for almost 18 months all other occasions of censorship are one-week bans.

Provided by The Economist Publications, London, 1997.

9E
Promoting independent media

Arab and International media experts, meeting at a UNESCO-seminar in Yemen, January 1996, called for Arab governments to ensure the development of independent and pluralistic media.

We, the participants in the United Nations/United Nations Educational, Scientific and Cultural Organisation Seminar on Promoting Independent and Pluralistic Arab Media, held in Sana'a, Yemen, from 7 to 11 January 1996;

Bearing in mind Article 19 of the Universal Declaration of Human Rights, which states that 'Everyone has the right to freedom of opinion and expression; this right includes freedom to hold opinions without interference and to seek, receive and impart information and ideas through any media, and regardless of frontiers';

. . .

Noting with satisfaction resolution 4.6 of the twenty-eighth session of the General Conference of UNESCO (1995), which stressed the outstanding importance of, and endorsed, the Declaration adopted by the participants of the Seminars, held in Windhoek, Namibia (29 April–3 May 1991), in Almaty, Kazakstan (5–9 October 1992), and in Santiago, Chile (2–6 May 1994), and which expressed its conviction that the joint UNESCO/United Nations . . . regional Seminar on Promoting Independent and Pluralistic Arab Media to be held in Sana'a, Yemen in early 1996 will contribute to creating conditions that will enable pluralistic media to develop and participate effectively in the democratization and development processes in the Arab religion;

. . .

Noting the vital need and the importance of access by women to free expression and decision-making in the field of media;

. . .

Welcome the world-wide trend towards democracy, freedom of expression and press freedom, recognize efforts by a number of Arab countries in this direction and urge all Arab states to participate in this historic process;

Believe that the advent of new information and communication technologies contributes to genuine cooperation, development, democracy and peace; acknowledge, however, that these technologies can be used to manipulate public opinion; and note that some governments do exploit the perceived threat of such technologies to justify curtailing of press freedom;

Deplore that, in the Arab World, journalists, publishers and other media practitioners continue to be victims of harassment, physical assault, threats, arrest, detention, torture, abduction, exile and murder. They are also subject to economic and political pressures, including dismissal, censorship, curbs on travel as well as passport withdrawals or visa denials. In addition to limitations on the free flow of news and information, and on the circulation of periodicals within countries and across national borders, the media is also subject to restrictions in the use of newsprint and other professional equipment and material. Licensing systems and abusive controls limit the opportunity to publish or broadcast;

Believe that arrest and detention of journalists because of their professional activities are a grave violation of human rights and urge Arab governments that have jailed journalists for these reasons to release them immediately and unconditionally. Journalists who have had to leave their countries should be free to return and to resume their professional activities. Those who have been dismissed abusively should be allowed to regain their positions.

Declare that:

Arab States should provide, and reinforce where they exists, constitutional and legal guarantees of freedom of expression and of press freedom and should abolish those laws and measures that limit the freedom of the press; government tendencies to draw limits outside the purview of the law restrict these freedoms and are unacceptable.

The establishment of truly independent, representative associations, syndicates or trade unions of priority in those Arab countries where such bodies do not now exist. Any legal and administrative obstacles to the establishment of independent journalistic organizations should be removed. Where necessary, labour relations laws should be elaborated in accordance with international standards.

Sound journalistic practices are the most effective safeguard against governmental restrictions and pressures by special interest groups. Guidelines for journalistic standards are the concern of the news media professionals. Any attempt to set down standards and guidelines should come from the journalists themselves. Disputes involving the media and/or the media professionals in the exercise of their profession are a matter for the courts to decide, and such cases should be tried under civil and not criminal codes and procedures.

Journalists should be encouraged to create independent media enterprises owned, run and funded by the journalists themselves and supported, if necessary, by transparent endowments with guarantees that donors do not intervene in editorial policies.

International assistance in Arab countries should aim to develop print and electronic media, independent of governments in order to encourage pluralism as well as editorial independence. Public media should be supported and funded only when they are editorially independent and where a constitutional, effective freedom of information and expression and the independence of the press are guaranteed.

State-owned broadcasting and news agencies should be granted statutes of journalistic and editorial independence as open public service institutions. Creations of independent news agencies and private and/or community ownership of broadcasting media, including in rural areas, should also be encouraged.

Arab governments should cooperate with the United Nations and UNESCO, other governmental and non-governmental development agencies, organizations and professional associations, in order to:

(I) enact and/or revise laws with a view to; enforcing the rights to freedom of expression and press freedom and legally enforceable free access to information; elimination monopoly controls over news and advertising; putting an end to all forms of social, economic or political discrimination in broadcasting, in the allocation of frequencies, in printing, in newspaper and magazine distribution and in newsprint production and allocation; abolishing all barriers to launching new publications and any form of discriminatory taxation;

(II) initiate action to remove economic barriers to the establishment and operation of news media outlets, including restrictive import duties, tariffs and quotas for such things as newsprint, printing equipment, typesetting and word-processing machinery and telecommunication equipment, and taxes on the sale of newspapers or other restrictions on the public access to news media;

(III) improve and expand training of journalists and managers, and other media practitioners, without discrimination, with a view to upgrading their professional standards, also by the establishment of new training centres in the countries where there are none. . .

Seek the assistance of national, regional and international press freedom and media professional organizations and other relevant NGOs to establish national and regional networks aimed at monitoring and acting against violations of free expression, to create data banks and to provide advice and technical assistance in computerization as well as in new information and communication technologies. . .

Sana'a, Yemen, 7–11 January 1996, in the records of UNESCO.

9F
In the Saudi pocket

The Saudis are not the first to invest in the Arab media, wrote Index on Censorship in 1996. An international Arab press has existed under foreign patronage since the last century. From the 1970s, the migrant Arab press began to take on additional significance, sponsored or controlled by Lebanese, PLO, Libyan and later Iraqi interests. The Saudis turned the Arab exile press into a high-tech operation, featuring some of the most professional Arab journalists, but according to Index risking payment of a heavy price in terms of dependency. The magazine interviewed Jihad Khazen, editor-in-chief of the daily al-Hayat (Life) and Abdul Bari Atwan, editor-in-chief of the daily al-Quds (Jerusalem), both London-based.

Abdul Bari Atwan: A quick look at the map of the Arab media shows that the Kingdom of Saudi Arabia dominates 95 per cent of the Arabic-language newspapers and magazines, radio and television stations in the Arab countries and abroad. This domination is either direct, such as total ownership by members of the royal family and their relatives or indirect.

The Saudi desire to dominate the Arab media may be traced back to the propaganda war conducted by Gamal Abdel Nasser in Egypt against the Saudis in the 1960s, and the tremendous wealth generated by the oil booms of the 1970s. Under the guise of moderation, the Saudis began in 1978 to acquire a media empire to combat revolutionary ideologies (Communist, Arab nationalist or Islamist) and to stifle any criticism of the Kingdom and its ruling family. This allowed the Saudis to set the rules for press coverage of their affairs, both through the press they owned and the power of their massive wealth over the domestic press of other Arab countries.

The Saudi government signed 'media protocols' with the ministries of information of several Arab states, including Egypt. Under these protocols, the publication of any material critical of Saudi Arabia and its internal situation and the domination of its affairs of state by the princes and their acquisition of public funds was prohibited. One Egyptian editor-in-chief said he had received clear instructions from the Egyptian ministry of information not to criticise either King Fahd, his government, his family and his policies or the Egyptian president, Hosni Mubarak, and his sons. Criticism of anything else was permissible.

Through its dominant position in the Gulf Co-operation Council, Saudi Arabia was able to impose its media policy on the smaller Gulf states. It was instrumental in getting the Conference of Gulf Ministers of Information to issue resolutions to ban the few newspapers and magazines that attempted to criticise it, and to blacklist and isolate certain writers and journalists, prohibiting any dealings with them whatsoever.

Facilitated by the entry of Egypt and Syria into the coalition, the efficacy of the Saudi media empire and the role it is intended to play became abundantly clear during the (Second) Gulf War when it succeeded in preventing the expression of views other than those of the anti-Iraqi coalition. In Saudi Arabia the media is like a veiled woman. Beneath the veil you may have the finest dressing – the best technology, the best writers and journalists, the finest offices. But it is veiled, completely covered in black. It is censored.

Jihad Khazen: The Arabic press has very different characteristics from the western press. The two chief distinctions being the relatively limited financial resources and the very limited freedom of the Arab press. Limited resources have resulted in a system of patronage.

Compared to papers in the West, Arabic newspapers also have limited circulations. Only in Egypt with its large and urbanised population, do national newspapers enjoy circulations in excess of 100,000 copies. *Al-Ahram* (*The Pymamids*) and *al-Akbar* (*The News*) both sell over 500,000 copies of their daily editions and more than one million copies of their weekend editions. However, in most Arab countries national newspapers sell no more than between 5,000 and 10,000 copies a day. Revenues from sales as well as advertising are a fraction of those in the West.

Estimates made recently by a subsidiary of Saatchi & Saatchi put total advertising expenditure for 1994 in the Gulf and other important Arab press countries such as Jordan, Lebanon, Yemen, Egypt and Morocco, in the region of US$900 million, a meagre one third of one per cent of global advertising, which totalled US$330 billion. Advertising in Israel alone reached nearly US$800 million in the same year.

Saudi Arabia's role as sponsor of the Arab press results from its position as the country where almost all advertising in the Arab world is concentrated. Industrialists from Boeing in Seattle all the way to Datsun and Toyota in Japan are all interested in the single Saudi market. Their advertising budget is allocated in proportion to newspapers sales in the Kingdom. Without the Saudi market *al-Hayat* could not survive. It sells all over the Arab world except in Iraq and Libya. It earned about US$ 13 million in advertising revenues last year, of which US$12.5 million came from Saudi Arabia.

This holds for the international Arabic press in general. Two years ago, probably under pressure from the ulema (religious establishment), the Saudi information minister decided to ban all women's magazines. The next day, 19 out of 24 magazines folded because they were dependent on the Saudi market for advertising. The only way to survive is to sell more copies in Saudi Arabia and get more advertising. The sponsorship is really indirect. I don't mind my paper being banned anywhere for one day – in fact it's good publicity to show that we are not toeing the line of this Arab government or that. But when the ban is indefinite, particularly in Saudi Arabia, it can be really dangerous. We were once banned indefinitely by Saudi Arabia. It lasted 20 days and cost us nearly US$1 million. Had we been banned for another month or two we might have folded. Not only did we lose 21 days' advertising but we lost ads that were part of campaigns: banned in February, we lost advertising right through April.

If we are going to be banned in Saudi Arabia I have to make the decision myself. I want to know if this one line in an editorial is worth US$40,000. We consciously went after stories that got us banned. We interviewed Iraqi foreign minister Sahhaf last year and were banned. We interviewed the Iraqi oil minister and were banned. I told my staff to go after the story because it was worth the US$ 40–50,000.

Despite all the problems, we never ever publish a story on request. We commit sins of omission. There was a very important story about an Egyptian doctor arrested in Saudi Arabia which heightened tensions between the two countries. I refused to take the line of the Egyptians or the Saudis. Rather than risk alienating two of the most important countries for the paper I ignored the whole story. No-one forced my hand, but I couldn't put what I wanted in the paper.

Atwan: The Saudis dominate the press in a number of ways. Their newspapers have become very influential – the importance of a story is confirmed only if it appears in the Saudi-sponsored press. One day I was called by the BBC-TV Arabic Service: 'There's a story on your front page today, saying such and such. Is it true?' I asked why he should doubt it and he replied: 'It's not published in *al-Hayat* or *al-Sharq al-Awsat*.'

They definitely want to cover up their domestic affairs. The Saudi press doesn't discuss anything about Saudi Arabia. No-one has any sense of how many people are in prison or any statistics on road accidents for fear that such reporting might be construed as a criticism of the king or his government. Saudi newspapers don't talk about Saudi affairs, Arab newspapers don't. British newspapers don't, so who does? The British in particular are intimidated by the Saudis. UK foreign secretary Malcolm Rifkind used his first meeting in Saudi Arabia recently to criticise Mohammed al-Mas'ari. Who is Mas'ari? Rifkind did it because the Saudi authorities are upset about a Saudi opposition movement in Britain.

We are banned in Saudi Arabia and, as a result, are completely deprived of advertisements. The last meeting of Gulf information ministers decided to ban any Arab newspapers critical of any of the Gulf Co-operation Council countries. There was only one newspaper banned: *al-Quds*.

To shape a paper around a market that represents some 2 percent of the Arab people is disastrous. We would like a paper that caters for the whole of the Arab world, for the 98 per cent. As journalists we have championed freedom of expression and freedom of the press. If, as in Saudi Arabia, you cannot question a minister, nor talk about women driving cars, nor about commissions and corruption, if you can't talk about deals for arms that are never used, then what is the purpose of journalists here? We don't have as much at stake as *al-Hayat*, we don't publish 50,000 copies but sometimes you lose your pride, sometimes you lose your principles. I wouldn't want to be editor of *al-Hayat*. At least I can say we are 95 to 96 per cent independent. And we have the freedom to write any story tomorrow.

Khazen: This is really the problem. You can publish and be damned and sell to a few friends and a few Arabic readers in London and Paris: or you can be more careful and sell to a number of Arab countries; or be even more careful and sell to all of them – and not have a newspaper. You have to draw a line somewhere. *Al-Quds* definitely has more touchy stories than *al-Hayat*, but as a result it sells in five or six countries while we sell in 18 out of 20. We are totally free to support or oppose the peace process, but we have to be very careful talking about Saudi domestic affairs or religious matters. I don't know what is better. It's a personal decision more than anything else.

Index on Censorship, March/April 1996, Vol. 25, No. 2.

9G
Princes of the media

Saudi Research and Marketing Company. Incorporated in 1978, the London-based SRMC currently publishes over 15 daily, weekly and monthly publications. Chief among them the green-paged daily, *Al-Sharq al-Awsat* (225,000 copies), and the political weekly *al-Majalla* (120,000 copies) The organisation is owned by Prince Salman bin 'Abd al-Aziz, sixth in line to the Saudi throne; the chairman of the board of directors is his son, Prince Abmad bin Salman. All SRMC editors-in-chief are Saudi nationals.

Al-Hayat Press Corporation: Based in London with branches in Riyadh, Jeddah, New York and Paris, the corporation publishes the influential Arabic daily *al-Hayat* (110,000 copies), edited by Jihad Khazen, a Lebanese of Palestinian origins and a political weekly magazine, *al-Wasat* (100,000 copies) edited by another Lebanese national, George Sim'an. Since 1990 the corporation has been owned by Prince Lt Gen Khalid bin Sultan bin Abd-al-'Aziz, who served as Commander-in-chief of the Arab forces in the Gulf War.

Middle East Broadcasting Centre: Created in September 1991 by Saudi billionaire Salih Kamil, the London-based MBC was the first Arab satellite TV station. It broadcasts to Europe and the Middle East. It was bought in

1993 by Walid and 'Abd al-'Aziz al-Barahim, brothers-in-law law of King Falid and uncles of the king's youngest son, Prince 'Abd al-'Aziz bin Fahd, counsellors at the Royal Palace with ministerial rank. It is rumoured that the Saudi monarch is the real owner of MDC with first and last say in the management of its affairs. The channel is free to viewers.

Arab Media Corporation: Owns the Rome-based Arab Radio and Television (ART) network, which is set to expand from its current fours satellite TV channels to 14. Co-founded by Salih Kamil who is said to own up to 90 per cent of AMC, and a nephew of the king. Prince Walid bin Talal bin 'Abd al-Aziz, who reportedly owns some 30 per cent of the shares in ART. Prince Walid is also connected, through a 4.1 per cent shareholding in Mediaset, to the Fininvest Group of Silvio Berlusconi.

Orbit Television: A subscription satellite TV network of 28 chains based in Rome and broadcast to 23 countries, Orbit is owned by Prince Fahd bin 'Abdullah al-Rahman, a nephew of King Fahd. The network is rumoured to be losing money in its competition with rival MBC. In June 1994 Orbit concluded a contract to transmit the BBC Arabic Service television. The network provoked a storm of criticism in January 1996 for censoring all BBC coverage of Saudi dissident Mohammed al-Mas'ari's controversial extradition order.

Index on Censorship, London, March/April 1996, Vol. 25 No. 2.

9H
BBC: Death of a Service

John Tusa, managing director of the BBC World Service 1986–93, from the beginning found it risky to cooperate with Saudi Arabia, which in April 1996 decided to make its satellite media company stop transmitting the BBC Arabic Service, following the transmission of a documentary on human rights in the Kingdom.

The words 'Saudi' and 'editorial freedom' sound more like a contradiction in terms rather than natural partners. The decision by the Saudi media company Orbit and BBC Worldwide (the holding company for commercial operations) to start an 'orderly rundown' of the two-year-old joint venture BBC World Service Television in Arabic is a reflection of the fundamental contradiction at its heart and acknowledges that what was always an editorial gamble on the BBC's part has not paid off. It is a blow to the BBC's attempt to find a 'third way' of funding its international television project, and could signal a setback for those tendencies within Saudi Arabia itself that seek more open, modernising policies.

Anyone involved in the Arabic Service television project on the BBC's side must – or should – have been well aware of the World Service's long-running difficulties with the Saudi government during the Gulf war. The Saudis behaved true to their cautions from the very start by not broadcasting news of the Iraqi invasion of Kuwait in their own media for several days. By then, Saudi citizens knew all about it from the BBC in Arabic or English, or from the VOA or CNN. Reluctantly perhaps, but certainly slowly, the Saudi media followed where others led.

The Saudi government turned its attention to what it was convinced were heavily biased broadcasts from the BBC Arabic Service. Accusations – channelled through the British ambassador in Riyadh and passed on by the Foreign Office – started landing on my desk at Bush House. That the coverage was distorted; that the Arabic Service was staffed only by Palestinians or by Iraqi-sympathising Jordanians; that more news stories originated from Baghdad than from 'friendly' allied capitals; that the language was loaded, the tone sneering, and that even if sympathy for Saddam Hussein was not overt, the tone of voice indicated that it was. There was only one way to deal with these allegations – by disproving them. I told the Arabic Service staff that I doubted that these charges were accurate. But if I was to defend them confidently I had to be able to do so on the basis of firm evidence. I asked the then head of the Arabic Service, Sam Younger, now managing director of the World Service, to carry out a series of detailed monitoring exercises on the service's output. They established beyond question that Saudi charges of direct or indirect bias or distortion were totally untrue. A distinguished Arab academic listened to hours of broadcasts on my behalf and assured me that neither tone of voice nor use of language had the effect of introducing a distortion words alone might not reveal.

Even so it took some months for Saudi grumbling to die down and FCO suspicions to be allayed. That experience must have been fully weighed in the difficult decision to start up a BBC Arabic TV Service with Saudi money. There were many voices, not least from within Bush House itself, warning against the wisdom any partnership with Saudis no matter how many editorial safeguards were written in. It would be good to think that the new executives in BBC World-wide, most with no experience of the perils of international broadcasting, listened to those anxieties. On one side, they had to consider the risk to the BBC World Service's reputation if it tailored its output to suit Saudi sensitivities; or the opposite risk, that has now occurred, of being shown the door because they did not. On the other side, BBC Worldwide was driven by a need – imposed from Broadcasting House – to be commercial, entrepreneurial, thrusting, and global as part of the 'new' BBC's public positioning. . . .

Among the journalists who pioneered the service, a few thought it was doomed from the start but had to be attempted; others knew it was on a knife edge; few were cheered by the knowledge that the Saudi royal family watched the service and enjoyed it. No doubt the 'Lady Chatterley' factor played a part; you can view it, but not the servants.

So what are the conclusions from this sad affair? First, that it represents another battle of honour for the World Service – it has paid the price of exclusion from an audience because it stayed true to the needs of that audience for truthful and accurate information. (Other satellite broadcasters, please note.) Second, that the risk analysis of taking part in the joint venture with the Saudis after the Gulf war was insufficiently rigorous . . .

The advocates of openness and modernisation within the Saudi royal family have lost a battle. Both they and the BBC World Service must devise new strategies to win their respective wars.

John Tusa, *The Guardian*, 10 April 1996.

9I
The US on Saudi Media

The United States Information Service in Riyadh issued a paper on the Saudi Media in 1996.

All domestic Saudi electronic media in the Kingdom are either directly or indirectly controlled by the government. Pan-Arab Saudi owned media, most of which is London-based, is privately-owned but usually associated with top members of the Royal family and respectful of Saudi domestic and foreign policy interests. Local TV news heavily reports the 'comings and goings' of various senior royalty but features a good deal of international news. Saudi TV also has correspondents in various capitals.

Because of continuing government interference, religious pressures, and technological advances, which are widening informational choices available to Saudi media consumers, the Saudi domestic media are steadily losing market share in the increasingly competitive local information market.

Radio is not a particularly influential medium of communication in Saudi Arabia due to poor quality programming by Saudi Radio and strong signals of the major international radio broadcasters (MBC and the BBC, in particular). The Saudi-owned commercial radio station, MBC FM, began broadcasting in London in 1994 and by the end of the year was claiming 1.2 million listeners for its mix of Arabic language news, music, and entertainment. Like its main competitor, the BBC Arabic Service, MBC is available via satellite as well as on short and medium wave.

Surveys indicate that Saudis are inveterate TV watchers and get most of their international information from television. Because of the pallid programming offered by domestic television, most Saudis who can afford satellite dishes now get their news from outside the Kingdom. Only a few years ago, the number of owners of satellite dishes in Riyadh could be counted on the fingers of one hand. Despite a 1994 law banning the importation, manufacture or sale of satellite dishes, sales of these dishes continue to boom. A well-informed trade source recently estimated that by the end of 1994 there were 200–300,000 dishes in the Kingdom and that several million people now have access to satellite by the day for an increasing numbers of Saudis, and USIS Riyadh has been actively including the London-based Middle East Broadcasting Center (MBC) in its information programming. ART broadcasts five channels via satellite out of Cairo. The orbit TV Satellite Service carried the BBC Arabic TV Service until April 1996, when Orbit terminated its contract because of a BBC TV program on human rights in Saudi Arabia.

New programming on Bahraini television gives Eastern Province viewers access to CNN, BBC, and international Arabic TV channel, MBC, even without a dish. Viewers in the Hejaz similarly have long been accustomed to watching Egyptian TV, while Asiris frequently watch Yemeni TV. The satellite dish revolution has given Saudi Arabia many new options, although CNN and BBC television continue to be the most common choices for English-language news and MBC the most common choice for Arabi-language news.

Officials at Saudi TV acknowledge the 'two-tiers' of Saudi TV viewership – one for the wealthy, the middle class and the expatriates, who tend to view foreign or London-based Saudi channels via their satellite dishes, and Saudi programming for that portion of the population that cannot afford a dish. While some at Saudi TV would like to compete more actively for viewers, they acknowledge that religious pressures are likely to forestall positive change.

Print Media

Newspapers and magazines are also controlled by the government. They depend heavily on government subsidies that take the form of advertising and government-ordered hajj supplements. Ministry of Information censors have lists of proscribed subjects and people, e.g., no criticism of the King and his brothers is permitted, no discussion of the ban on women driving, nothing touching Islam, etc. In general, the censors focus more on sex than on politics. Editors are kept apprised of what is not permitted. Saudi publications are also told by the Ministry of Information what they must include, e.g., that a photo of the King must appear on page one, a photo of the Crown Prince on page two and so fourth. Such censorship makes it hard for local publications to compete, and several are clearly losing readers to publications such as *Al Hayat* and *Al Sharq Al Awsat* that are edited and printed abroad so as to avoid the worst excesses of Ministry of Information control.

Daily newspapers are widely distributed and read. The two most important newspapers are the Saudi-owned, but London-based newspapers, *al-Sharq al-Awsat* and *al-Hayat*, which are both distributed through the Arab world and the Arab expatriate population of Europe. *Al-Sharq al-Awsat* generally follows Saudi Ministry of Information guidelines on subjects relating to the Kingdom and is simultaneously published in Riyadh, Jeddah, and Dhahran. *Al-Hayat* is printed in Bahrain and is subject to censorship, but generally follows a Saudi line only on issues of paramount concern to the Kingdom. The quasi-international status of these two papers enables them to escape the Ministry of Information's positive control, i.e. they do not have to appear each morning with a photo of the King or some other royal family member on the front page, which gives them a different, more inviting look on the newsstands.

In addition, there are nine Arabic and three English newspapers published for domestic consumption in the Kingdom. *Ukaz* is the most important in the Hejaz and somewhat influential in the Najd, competing against its more aged and tired competitors, *al-Madian*, *al-Bilaad*, and *an-Nadwa*. (*Al-Nadwa* enjoys a special niche, however, thanks to its reputation for comparatively good editorial writing and its status as Makkah's hometown newspaper.) *Ar-Riyadh* is increasingly beating *al-Jazira* in the Najd. *Al-Yawm* acts as a daily newspaper for the Eastern province. The sole afternoon paper in Saudi Arabia, *al-Masa'iya*, has limited readership and importance. *Al-Iqtisadiya*, and commercial reader; it has a solid readership base in the urban areas. The English press is read predominantly by South Asian, Filipino and Western expatriates, but Western-educated Saudis also turn to it for international news and features. The *Arab News* is the market leader, but both the *Saudi Gazette* and the *Riyadh Daily* are aggressively seeking to expand their market share.

There are twenty-two weekly or monthly periodicals in Saudi Arabia, although only two, London-based *al-Majalla* and *al-Yamama*, are of any particular importance either as 'newsmakers' or vehicles for intelligent policy debate. For business and commerce, *al-Tijara* has considerable influence as the leader in its field in Saudi Arabia.

Also of recent importance in Saudi Arabia are unofficial media, mostly in the form of cassette tapes and faxed newsletters. Generally, these communications are the only way to widely disseminate views critical of Saudi governmental policy. The content of tapes sold openly in stores can range from innocuous discussions of purely religious matters to criticism of 'Westernization' and 'secularism' or wild tales of Western, Zionist and Masonic conspiracies against the Arab/Islamic world. More strident attacks on the West and the Saudi government circulate informally and illegally. The Committee for the Defense of Legitimate Rights a London-based opposition group, faxes its anti-regime, anti-Western views on a regular basis to hundreds of Saudis, as does a new splinter group, the Islamic Movement for Reform.

United States Information Service (USIS), Riyadh, 1996.

9J
Action alert

'IFEX', a part of the 'International Freedom of Expression Exchange Clearing House', issued on 25 September 1996 an 'Action Alert' on behalf of the weekly Middle East Times, banned in Egypt from publishing an interview with a Saudi dissident.

On 12 September 1996, officials from the [Egyptian] Ministry of Information's Foreign Press and Publications Bureau informed the English-language weekly *Middle East Times* that it would not be permitted to publish a featured interview with Saudi dissident Mohammad Maasari in its 15–21 September 1996 issue. The newspaper was subsequently forced to replace the interview with another article.

According to the newspaper, this latest case of censorship against it marks at least the eighth time in 1996 that one of its articles has been banned by the Ministry of Information. It is also the second time this year that an article deemed critical of Saudi Arabia has been forbidden.

IFEX, 25 September 1996.

Chapter Ten

REFUGEES

10A
Refugees abused

Amnesty International in May 1994 complained about the Saudi treatment of Iraqi refugees in the kingdom.

Hundreds of Iraqi refugees who sought shelter in Saudi Arabia after the 1991 Gulf War have been arbitrarily arrested, tortured and ill-treated, deliberately killed or forcibly returned to Iraq during the past three years, according to Amnesty International.

In a report published today, the worldwide human rights organization said that the refugees held at Rafha camp and, until its closure in December 1992, Artawiyya camp, 'have been subjected to treatment unacceptable by any international standards for the treatment of refugees'. In most cases, the refugees are abused for a wide range of perceived offenses, including criticising the camps' authorities, protesting against living conditions, being 'disobedient' or in order to extract 'confessions'.

Some 23,000 Iraqi refugees remained in Saudi Arabia as of April 1994. They include former members of the Iraqi armed forces who surrendered to the allied forces at the end of the Gulf War and who refused to be repatriated, and civilians who fled southern Iraq in the aftermath of the crushing of the March 1991 mass uprising. Following widespread condemnation by a number of international non-governmental organiza-tions, the Saudi Arabian authorities made improvements in the refugees' living conditions and said large amounts of money were invested in new facilities. . . .

Amnesty International has evidence of a pattern of torture and ill-treatment, including the systematic use of various forms of collective punishments – such as denying the refugees food and water – particularly in response to protests about living conditions and treatment at the hands of the camp authorities.

None of the reports of torture or deaths in custody have been investigated by an independent judicial authority according to Amnesty

International. Indeed, available evidence indicates that the Saudi Arabian government has turned a blind eye to torture and ill-treatment and has allowed it to take place with impunity.

Amnesty International, International Secretariat, London, 10 May 1995
AI Index: MDE 23/WJ 01/94.

Chapter Eleven

LABOUR

11A
Restrictions

King Faisal in 1969 by decree M/21 issued the 'Labour and Workers Regulation', still in force. The decree outlines a number of punishable acts.

Article 189:

1. Any individual shall be punishable with imprisonment from one month to one year or with a fine from SR 1,000 to SR 3,000 or with both such penalties, who with a group of persons goes on strike with the intent to bring a standstill the following:
   (a) transportation within the various parts of the Kingdom and between the latter and the other countries;
   (b) postage, telegraphic and telephonic communication;
   (c) any of the public utilities, particularly those which pertain to the distribution of water, electricity or primary foodstuffs.
2. The contractor of any of the aforesaid utilities shall be liable to the same punishment if he suspends, without lawful cause, the functioning thereof.
3. If the offence is accompanied by violent acts against persons or things, by threats or other intimidation, by acts of fraud or false pretences that tend to influence psychologically, by crowding in streets and public squares or by occupation of the places of work, the perpetrators of such acts shall be punished with imprisonment from six months to two years, or with a fine from SR 1,000 to SR 3,000, or with both such penalties.

Labour and Workers Regulation, M/21 of 6/9/1389 A.H. (15.11.1969).

11B
Employment of Foreigners

Import of expatriate labour is only allowed, if no Saudi national is available, according to the Saudi Labour and Workers Regulations.

Article 48: Work is a right of the Saudi national and no other person shall be allowed to exercise this right unless the conditions laid down in this chapter shall have been fulfilled. Saudi workers shall have equal rights to work in all areas of the Kingdom without distinction.

Article 49: It shall not be allowed to import foreigners to work or permit them to do work with private companies and firms, except pursuant to the Minister of Labour's approval and the obtaining of a work permit as per the pro-forma proceedings and rules laid down by the Labour Ministry; the said permit shall not be given unless the following conditions have been satisfied:

1. The worker shall have entered the country legally and satisfied the conditions prescribed in the Residence Regulation.
2. He must possess the occupational proficiencies or academic qualifications needed in the country, provided that no Saudi national holds the same or that the number of the available Saudi nationals does not satisfy demand.
3. He shall have entered into a contract with a Saudi employer or a non-Saudi employer who is authorized under the Investment of Foreign Capital Regulation and under the guarantee of the employer, or if he is a liberal professional guaranteed by a Saudi national or is on contract with and guaranteed by any of the concessionary companies.

Work, in this Article, shall mean any industrial, commercial, agricultural or other work, as well as any service, inclusive of domestic service.

Article 50: Every employer shall improve his Saudi workers' level of technical proficiency in work carried out by non-Saudi workers in order to enable them to be sufficiently qualified in their occupation so that they can replace non-Saudi workers; he shall prepare a register wherein he shall enter the names of Saudi workers who have replaced non-Saudi workers, according to the terms, rules and time limits prescribed by the Labour Minister . . .

Labour and Workers Regulations, M/21 of 6/9/1389 A.H. (15.11.1969).

11C
Treatment of Foreign Workers

The Minnesota Lawyers International Human Rights Committee in their 1992 report 'Shame in the House of Saud' dealt with the conditions of international labour in Saudi Arabia, starting with a quote from the Cairo Declaration on Human Rights in Islam.

'The employee shall have the right to safety and security as well as to all other social guarantees. He may neither be assigned work beyond his capacity nor be subjected to compulsion or exploited or harmed in any way. He shall be entitled – without any discrimination between males and females – to fair wages for his work without delay, as well as to the holidays allowances and promotions which he deserves.'

The frenetic pace of development in Saudi Arabia since the start of the oil boom has required many foreign workers. In fact, foreigners employed as guest workers in Saudi Arabia now account for a significant share of the resident population. One 1985 account estimated Saudi Arabia's labor force at 4.4 million, of which 2.7 million were foreign workers. A more recent appraisal estimates that 3.5 to 4 million of Saudi Arabia's current labor pool of 7 to 8 million are foreigners, most from developing nations; another estimates 4 to 5 million of such foreign workers.

Saudi Arabia, however, is a society with significant xenophobic tendencies and the presence of millions of foreign workers is therefore politically controversial. The Saudi Government periodically attempts to limit the size of the foreign work force in an effort to restrict the foreign cultural and political influence. During the Second Economic Development Plan, launched by Saudi Arabia in 1975, there was an attempt to limit the foreign work force to an annual growth rate of not more than 1.2%.

In addition to attempting to limit foreign labor, the Saudis have switched from a preference for importing primarily Arab foreign labor to a preference for Asian labor because of the perceived political threat from the influence of other Arab nations. Indeed, by 1980 Asia had become Saudi Arabia's main source of foreign labor. One report estimates that Asians account for more than 60 percent of the 7.6 million foreign workers in the gulf region. In the wake of the 1990–91 gulf war, Saudi Arabia has continued to reduce the number of Arab foreign workers, particularly those from countries friendly to Iraq, such as Jordan, Sudan, and Yemen. In September 1990, for example, the Saudi Government issued restrictive employment regulations that resulted in the mass exodus of an estimated 800,000 Yemeni workers. There were also mass terminations of employment for Palestinians and Jordanians.

Despite the Saudi Government's efforts to limit the number and influence of foreign workers, by most estimates foreign workers in Saudi

Arabia now account for at least 50 per cent of the total work force. An analysis of the treatment of these workers and their living conditions is therefore essential to a comprehensive study of the situation of human rights in Saudi Arabia.

A. Working Conditions and Abuses

The Minnesota Lawyers Committee's study of the human rights situation of foreign workers in Saudi Arabia found that most foreign workers receive poor treatment. Continuing patterns of societal prejudice in Saudi Arabia, however, based on sex or national or ethnic origin, create an especially bad situation for workers from developing countries, generally, and for female workers, in particular. The Committee conducted most of its research on foreign laborers from the Philippines. It is estimated that in 1989, over one million Filipinos worked as contract laborers in Saudi Arabia.

Nearly everyone interviewed by the Committee regarding the treatment of foreign workers noted that workers from Western countries receive better treatment from Saudi citizens and the Saudi Government than do workers from Asian, African, and other Arab countries. This situation is aggravated by the need of the workers' countries of origin to maintain the flow of foreign currency from their workers abroad. As a consequence, those governments traditionally have overlooked the abuses committed against their nationals working in Saudi Arabia.

The 1990–91 gulf war also exacerbated the human rights abuses inflicted on these foreign workers. There were widespread reports of Saudi employers refusing to allow Asian foreign workers to leave the country by withholding their passports and tickets. Asian foreign workers were the last to receive gas masks.

1. Contract Substitution

The most widespread abuse which foreign workers suffer upon entry into Saudi Arabia is contract substitution. Contract substitution occurs when, after arrival in Saudi Arabia, the employer presents the worker with a contract different from the contract signed at the recruitment agency in the sending country. Some substituted contracts purport already to bear the worker's signature.

Often the Saudi employer forgoes the formality and simply tells the foreign worker that the new (lower) wage will apply and the new job duties will be performed while in Saudi Arabia. Frequently the original employment contract provides for overtime pay and rest and leisure. In practice, these contractual safeguards are either ignored or unilaterally stricken from the contract once the worker arrives in Saudi Arabia.

Often, when the workers learn of the contract substitution, they already have surrendered their passports and are at their employer's place of business. Because foreign workers may not seek employment with anyone but their sponsor, and because the workers already have paid travel expenses and recruitment agency fees, many accept the lower wages without complaint. The workers who do demand to return home because of contract substitution often do not have the money for their return travel.

2. Long Hours and Delay in Payment

Delay in payment of wages for periods of weeks and months is commonplace for foreign workers in Saudi Arabia. Two Filipino interviewees reported engaging in informal collective action because they and fellow workers were not being paid by their employers. One worker was fired and the other resigned. Both were stranded in Saudi Arabia for an additional two months before their employers would provide them with exit visas. Neither received any wages for the two month delay.

Their treatment is not unusual. One man stated that each time he or a coworker aired a complaint to their employer it was considered a 'violation', and each violation was considered justification for a deduction in salary. In another documented case, a Filipino was paid for only four of the seven months he worked for his employer. Saudi Government decrees forbid the formation of labor unions and strike activity. Dismissal, imprisonment, or expulsion follow most attempts at organizing by foreign workers.

Many foreign laborers work extremely long hours. In particular, the domestic servants interviewed by the Minnesota Lawyers Committee all reported working seven days per week, sometimes 12–18 hours per day. Most other Filipino workers, many of whom work in construction or other heavy industry, also work long hours without overtime, six days per week.

3. Lack of Redress

'Should workers and employers disagree on any matter, the State shall intervene to settle the dispute and have the grievances redressed, the rights confirmed and justice enforced without bias' (Cairo Declaration on Human Rights in Islam).

Although the Saudi Labor Code prohibits many of the abuses inflicted on foreign workers, the worker who is victimized by contract substitution or overtime and hour violations of the Saudi Labor Code is offered little assistance by the Saudi Government. Most of the workers the Committee interviewed were not even aware they had any right to lodge complaints with Saudi labor officials.

When foreign workers do complain to Saudi labor officials about contract substitution, delay in receiving salary, or physical abuse, the results are mixed. Often, the Saudi labor officials refuse to speak English or to provide a translator for the foreign worker. Two workers interviewed by the Committee did receive some assistance from Saudi authorities when their employers refused to pay their wages.

One worker's contract called for her to work for a family in Taif as a seamstress at $258 per month. When she arrived at her employer's residence in Taif, she learned that her salary was only $150 per month and that, in addition to her sewing duties, she was expected to work as a domestic servant. When she complained to her employer's daughter, she was beaten by her employer.

The worker left the family home one day and made her way to what she referred to as the 'Saudi Labor Office' in Taif. The labor official with whom she spoke wrote a letter to her employer informing the employer she must stop beating the worker and that she must pay her proper wages. The letter was followed by a visit from a Saudi labor official who cautioned the employer that she would be taken to jail if she did not stop beating her employee. There was, however, no further follow-up and nothing changed for this worker, who left Saudi Arabia never having received her full wages. In addition, the woman had to suffer sexual propositions from two of the officials with whom she spoke at the Saudi Labor Office.

In another case, a worker brought his complaint regarding delay of payment to the Saudi Labor Office. In his later statement to the Philippines Overseas Employment Administrations he alleges that, as a consequence of a conciliation meeting arranged by the Saudi Labor Office, his employment contract was torn up by the employer's representative. He further alleges he was imprisoned for three days and deported because of fabricated criminal charges. He paid his own airfare upon deportation.

Some Filipino workers lodge complaints about their working conditions and payment problems with their own embassy officials in Saudi Arabia. Others simply do not know where to direct their complaints or are afraid of retribution. Indeed, one interviewee who complained to the Philippine embassy about the delay in receiving his salary was deported when his employer found out about his complaint.

Another interviewee complained to the Philippine embassy when his employer deducted from his salary the hospital expenses incurred from a work-related accident. The time he spent out of work and in the hospital also was deducted from his salary. After hearing about the complaint, his employer called the police. The police arrested the worker who spent two days in jail before he was deported.

Another worker told of complaining to his employer when he did not receive his salary. He also went to the Riyadh office of the agency that recruited him. After complaining, he was locked in his room for an entire month by his employer. He also was forced to sign a release before his employer would give him an exit visa and pay for his ticket home, as required by his contract.

B. Living Conditions

Generally, foreign workers from developing nations live in communal or dormitory settings while in Saudi Arabia. Some live in camps; others live in small apartments or barracks. Living conditions commonly are crowded and dirty. One interviewee working as an auto mechanic described his living quarters as a twelve-square-meter concrete shelter shared by three workers. Domestic servants live in the employer's dwelling, isolated from friends and other workers. Some domestic servants have their own room while others are forced to live in the pantry or laundry area. Many domestic servants tell of being locked inside their rooms at night, and locked inside the house when the family leaves.

1. Separation by Sex and Nationality

Foreigners working for large corporations in Saudi Arabia usually are segregated by nationality. Filipinos live with other Filipinos, Pakistanis with other Pakistanis, and so forth.

Upon arrival at the international airport in Riyadh, officials immediately separate by sex the Filipino and other Asian foreign workers. During their entire stay in Saudi Arabia, sometimes for several years, foreign workers are strictly forbidden even to converse with members of the opposite sex. The Mutawwi'un harass and sometimes beat male foreign workers who dare to speak with a female in public. Some foreign workers report instances in which male and female foreign workers are jailed for speaking to one another in public.

One man reported he was arrested after making eye contact with a Saudi woman who walked past him on the street in a small town near the Saudi Arabia–Jordan border. The police warned him that he must never look at a woman on the street again. On another occasion, the same man was beaten by an agent of the Mutawwi'un after he attempted to converse with a Filipino woman in a store.

2. Restrictions on Travel and Exit

The movement of foreigners is very restricted in Saudi Arabia. All workers interviewed by the Committee had to relinquish their passports to their employers, or 'sponsors', upon arrival at the airport. Foreign workers essentially become wards of their employer during their stay in Saudi

Arabia. Many Saudi employers regularly abuse this system to exploit their economically vulnerable foreign employees. Hence, despite Saudi labor laws which ostensibly offer protection to both native and foreign workers, 'situations that could be described as forced labor can occur, especially in remote areas where workers are unable to leave their place of work'.

Foreign workers are subject to arrest and deportation if caught on the streets of Saudi Arabia without a valid residency permit, or 'iqama', which they rely on their employer to provide.

In addition, employees must receive permission from their employer and a travel permit if they wish to travel outside of the sector in which they work. Many women working as domestic servants are not permitted even to leave the home of their employer during their entire stay in the country.

Exiting Saudi Arabia is as difficult as entering. Foreign workers must obtain exit visas from their Saudi employers. These workers sometimes languish in deportation centers or hide with friends, at times for months, until they can obtain an exit visa. Several interviewees spoke of having to ask their employers for 'permission' to leave the country. Permission is not always granted.

3. Prohibition of the Practice of Religion

Non-Muslim foreign workers are not permitted to practice their religion while working in Saudi Arabia. Many foreign workers attempt to bring religious mementos and artifacts into Saudi Arabia. Several persons interviewed reported that Saudi border officials confiscated all religious artifacts including crosses, rosary beads, and holy cards. Those foreign workers who attempt to smuggle in religious artifacts or scripture risk arrest and deportation.

Practicing any non-Muslim religion while in Saudi Arabia will subject the foreign worker to arrest, detention, and deportation. In addition, according to a Filipino who worked as a nurse's aide in a hospital in Medina, all overseas contract workers sent to the holy cities of Mecca and Medina are required to convert to and practice Islam while in Saudi Arabia. Foreign workers in other Saudi cities are sometimes forced to attend Islamic religious services with their employer.

C. Abuses by the Security Forces

Virtually all foreign workers interviewed by the Committee expressed great fear of the Saudi police. According to some interviewees, beatings and floggings in Saudi jails regularly occur every Friday – the Islamic Day of United Prayer.

Summary arrest and detention of foreign workers by Saudi authorities also is commonplace, without any apparent check on the discretion of the police to arrest for the slightest perceived impropriety. Saudi police, including the Mutawwi'un, frequently arrest foreign workers first and ask questions later – particularly those workers from developing nations. All foreign workers interviewed by the Committee told of friends and colleagues who had been arrested while in Saudi Arabia. Some related accounts of their own arrests.

One man told of being jailed for not reporting to the police a theft he allegedly had witnessed. He was hit in the face and jailed for 18 hours before being released. Another worker reported that his friends were whipped and beaten while in a Saudi jail.

Another man was arrested after a Saudi driver crashed into his car. He was arrested at the scene after the wife of the Saudi driver accused him of being at fault because 'if [he] had not been in Saudi Arabia, there would not have been an accident'. His employer paid his bail after he had spent two days in jail and suffered a beating by three policemen. The employer deducted from his salary both the amount of the bail and the time he missed from work because of injuries from the police beating.

One worker reported that his friend was arrested merely because Saudi authorities found a letter he wrote in the apartment of another Filipino who also had been arrested. While in jail, Saudi authorities whipped him on the soles of his feet.

One interviewee reported that a friend had been arrested merely for having reported a stolen tote bag to the authorities. The Saudi authorities hit the man, and when the his US supervisor complained about the treatment, the supervisor also was arrested and jailed for two weeks.

It is common for Saudi employers to threaten their foreign workers with police involvement in work-related disputes. One Saudi employer taunted his ill-treated employees by reminding them they would not receive any help from the Saudi authorities because he was well-connected and they were merely foreigners.

D. Domestic Servants

Most female foreign workers in Saudi Arabia are domestic servants, or 'maids', who work in the private confines of an employer's home. The lack of legal protection for these women, combined with the private nature of their work environment, put them at even greater risk of abuse than other foreign workers.

Domestic servants returning from Saudi Arabia routinely complain of being overworked, underpaid, and underfed by their employers. They also complain of beatings and sexual harassment, adding that there is nowhere to turn to remedy their situation. Many workers interviewed spoke of being locked inside their employer's house, even when the rest of the family was gone. The great majority of these women, moreover, do not receive an iqama and thus cannot leave the house of their employer even when the doors are not locked.

Most domestic servants may not meet with or otherwise associate with anyone other than their employer, including other domestic servants in the area. Association with men is strictly prohibited, with stiff penalties ranging from beatings to deportation for being caught with an unrelated male.

Typically, the foreign domestic servant in Saudi Arabia is the first to rise in the morning and the last to retire at night. Although specific responsibilities vary from case to case, she generally performs all household chores, including cooking, cleaning, child care, and sewing. It is not uncommon for a domestic servant to be forced to perform these duties for more than one family or household. There are reports that domestic servants sometimes must work 12–16 hours per day, seven days per week.

One young woman worked as a domestic servant in Dammam from March until November 1990. She worked from 7:00 a.m. until 1:00 a.m. doing a variety of household chores, but was not allowed rest breaks during the day. When she would request a rest, her employer would respond, 'You are not allowed to rest because I am paying you.' She was allowed only one full meal of rice and chicken per day at 2:00 p.m., although occasionally she was given tea and a piece of bread for dinner.

The young woman slept on the floor in a stock room without air conditioning. Her employer paid her for the first time after four months of work, and then once again after two months. When she complained about her working conditions and asked to return to the Philippines, the employer withheld three months salary to pay for the airline ticket.

Her employer never permitted her to leave the house alone. When her employer left, she was locked inside the house. Her employer told her that if she went outside the house alone the police would arrest her. She was not permitted to fraternize or speak with other Filipino domestic workers living in Dammam.

Other domestic servants allege they received regular beatings if their employers were dissatisfied with their work or in a bad mood. Stories of beatings, sometimes with objects such as a hairbrush or a spike-heeled shoe, are not uncommon. Representatives of the Minnesota Lawyers Committee reviewed in Manila the affidavits of many Filipino women after they had returned from Saudi Arabia. A sampling of these affidavits paints a grim picture of their life as Saudi Arabian domestic servants:

Case No.1. Contracted to be a seamstress; upon arrival in Saudi Arabia, forced to work as a seamstress and a domestic servant; made to work overtime without pay; allowed to eat once a day; paid less than contracted amount; after escaping from employer to Philippine embassy, handed over to the Saudi authorities; languished in deportation cell in the Social Welfare Administration ('SWA') for one month.

Case No.2. Employer failed to meet her at airport in Riyadh; arrested and placed in a deportation cell for four days; different employer fetched her from deportation cell; did not receive any salary; escaped from her employer; languished in a cell at SWA for one and a half months.

Case No.3. Contracted to be a seamstress; upon arrival informed that she would be a domestic servant; not compensated during early months of her stay; employer did not give her sufficient food and would beat her; escaped and deported after spending time in a cell at the SWA.

Case No.4. Contracted to work as a seamstress; worked from 9:00 a.m. until 11:00 p.m.; not permitted to sit down during working hours; required to perform domestic chores in employer's house from 5:30 a.m. until 8:30 a.m.; letters from the Philippines were destroyed; blindfolded while being transported from home to the shop; her left foot became inflamed; rather than give her medical treatment, employer sent her home.

Case No. 5. Paid $50.00 less per month than contract required; worked from 5:00 a.m. until 2:00 a.m. each day; verbally harassed and threatened with being sent into the desert; after escaping from her employer, she was sent to the SWA before being deported.

Case No.6. Contracted to be a seamstress; upon arrival, presented with a forged contract to be a domestic servant; worked as a domestic servant for Prince Saad ibn Abdullah Al Saud; worked 18 hours per day, no days off; employer refused to take her to a doctor when she was sick; escaped to Philippine embassy whereupon embassy officials turned her over to a representative of her employer; her employer beat her severely upon her return.

The Philippine Government is aware of the poor treatment of domestic servants in Saudi Arabia. A 1987 internal report from the Philippine embassy in Saudi Arabia describes the treatment of domestic servants:

'Women who are going to Saudi Arabia to work as domestic helper have no protection whatsoever. . . It was our experience that female domestic helpers are helpless and subject to abuses because of the culture being practised in The Kingdom. The Kingdom's concept of domestic helpers is still that of slave, having no rights whatsoever. They can be given away as presents. They can be maltreated and when they complain they are under the police jurisdiction and immediately land in jail even if they are the complainants. We were able to document abuses committed to our Filipina domestic helpers and reports to this effect were submitted praying the temporary banning of deployment to this kind of category. The arguments that were advanced by some proponents who are against the banning was financial support to our government through the earnings of these domestic helpers. We are still saying that their earnings are not worth the problems encountered. Although we imposed $200 to $250 as their salaries, their employers are only giving them $100 to $150. There is no way they can complain if they are already here as they are not allowed to talk to anybody while in the home of their employers. Their passports, by law in Saudi Arabia, remains with their employer. Exit visa can only be secured by their employers and when they are lucky to [e]scape and complain to our embassy, our hands were tied up by the Ministry of Foreign Affairs of Saudi Arabia, through the issue of a note ordering us to immediately turn over all runaway workers to the police authorities and ultimately to the Social Welfare Administration, which is the equivalent of women's jail. Thus, it is almost a no-win situation for these type of workers and they have to accede to the decision of their employers. Per our records we have documented 230 cases of abuse whether physical or sexual. (Philippine Embassy, Riyadh, 1987)

We reiterate our strong recommendation to impose the total ban in the sending of female domestic helpers in the Kingdom of Saudi Arabia.

In addition to complaints of sexual harassment, there is also ample evidence of physical abuse of domestic servants. In one recently reported case, a Filipino woman was repatriated after brutal abuse by her employer. The woman stated that her employer:

always punched me in the ears until they became infected and changed form. They also hit me until I bleed with the rope they tie around their head. . . When they were hitting me with the cord of the flat iron, it hit my left pointed finger which got infected and had to be cut off by a doctor. They also burned my face with a flat iron, including my arms and legs . . . They would pull my hair, they would not feed me until I lost all energy in my body. Even my teeth had fallen off because of the constant beating I got (*Philippine Star*, 23 February 1991).

She arrived in the Philippines looking malnourished, with thinning hair, burns on her face, and with ears deformed from burns:

Women who find the courage and the means to run away from their employers quickly learn that there is little help to be found either at the Philippine embassy or with the Saudi authorities. An agreement made between the Philippine and Saudi Governments describes the procedure for handling cases of domestic servants who escape their place of employment and seek refuge in the Philippine embassy with complaints of ill-treatment. The agreement provides that the Filipino officials are required to turn the women over to the Saudi authorities within twenty-four hours of their arrival at the embassy. The women are then taken to the Social Welfare Administration ('SWA', a jail for women) until 'resolution' of the case.

A Philippine embassy official, speaking anonymously, stated that many women were either sexually harassed or abused by SWA officials at the SWA facility. It is not uncommon for SWA officials to require that the

Filipinos provide sexual favors in exchange for making a telephone call to the Philippine embassy.

Some women remain in the SWA for months. Others stay until their employers are contacted and come to return them to the abusive environment. In cases where the women are forcibly returned to their employers, they tend to be punished or otherwise harshly treated for running away and lodging a complaint. In other cases the women are deported.

According to the complaints of 17 women who were held at the SWA in 1989 and later deported, the time spent in the jail ranged from 3 days to 3 months. The women originally sought refuge at the Philippine embassy complaining of abuses such as attempted rape by an employer or employer's relative, ill-treatment, physical assault or abuse, no salary for periods as long as 2 years and 2 months, overwork, lack of food, and contract substitution.

During the time that the women are locked away in the SWA, the embassy officials have only limited access to them, if they are granted access at all. In most cases, only immediate family members are allowed access to the women confined at the SWA, which for Filipinos means no visitors at all.

E. International Protection of Migrant Workers

A new international treaty approved by the United Nations General Assembly, including the Saudi delegation, provides for the international protection of migrant workers. The International Convention on the Protection of the Rights of All Migrant Workers and Members of Their Families is the first comprehensive document to address the need to make further efforts to improve the situation and ensure the human rights and dignity of all migrant workers. Although Saudi Arabia is not yet a party to the Migrant Workers Convention, its General Assembly vote to adopt the Convention indicates its approval of the emerging international norms in this area. It is only Saudi practice which has departed from those norms.

The treaty defines migrant worker as a 'person who is to be engaged, is engaged or has been engaged in a remunerated activity in a State of which he or she is not a national'. Among other provisions, the treaty protects rights of migrant workers in areas such as movement, torture, slavery, thought, conscience, religion, privacy, property, liberty and security of person, conditions of arrest and detention, equality before national courts, no punishment for contract breaches, travel documents and work permits, access to consular and diplomatic authorities, and employment conditions.

The treaty further establishes a Committee on the Protection of the Rights of All Migrant Workers and Members of their Families (Part VII) to receive and comment upon periodic reports of State Parties on the legislative, judicial, administrative and other measures taken to give effect to the Convention's provisions.

The Migrant Workers Convention incorporates and expands upon an already established body of labor standards, and, due to the growing transnational movement of workers, is one of the most important new human rights treaties to be adopted by the United Nations. The Migrant Workers Convention should set the standard in Saudi Arabia for the rights of foreign workers and the obligations of the Saudi Governments to protect those rights.

> Minnesota Lawyers International Human Rights Committee (now the 'Minnesota Advocates for Human Rights'), *Shame in The House of Saud*, 1992. (See original for footnotes.)

11D
Top Destination

Filipinos flock to Saudi Arabia according to the POEA, the Philippine Overseas Employment Administration, quoted in an NGO newsletter in July 1996.

Saudi Arabia remains the top destination for Filipino migrant workers. In 1995 alone, total deployment reached 160,604, according to a recent issue of the *Saudi Gazette*.

POEA chief Felicisimo Joson Jr. predicts that deployment to Saudi will continue to grow despite the 'Saudization program'. Saudization means Saudis would replace foreign workers. Joson noted that in spite of Saudization, the demand for Filipinos continues to rise. This is no longer surprising. Filipinos will endure any hardships to earn a living. They must, for their families' survival in the Philippines.

Remittances from workers in the Middles East serves as the primary support for the Philippine economy. According to the National Statistics Office (NSO), of the P16.6 billion remittances last year, P5.2 billion was from Filipinos in Saudi.

> Newsletter of the Kanlungan Center Foundation for migrant workers, Kamias, Quezon City, The Philippines, July 1996.

11E
The Sponsor system

The Egyptian Organization for Human Rights (EOHR) in April 1995, issued a document of concern of the rights of Egyptian (international) Labors in the Arab Gulf, Saudi Arabia included.

The EOHR believes that there are several factors, as well as legal and political considerations which, combined and interrelated, represent the main cause of the problems faced by Egyptian workers in the Gulf countries. In some cases they have led to serious violations and it is possible that they could open the floodgates at any moment and cause an increase in such cases, even though these cases might appear at first to be exceptional, affecting only a limited number in each country.

The main elements of these violations and the most important considerations concerning them can be summed up as follows:

1. The level of human rights protection in the Constitutional and legal structure of the Gulf countries

The protection of human rights in Arab countries is generally highly controversial due to governmental practices as well as the degree of human rights embodied in the constitutions. It is completely different, however, in the Gulf countries because they have refrained from becoming party to the main international human rights conventions, notably the International Covenant on Civil and Political Rights and the International Covenant on Economic, Social and Cultural Rights. Furthermore, two countries of the Gulf Cooperation Council, namely Saudi Arabia and Oman, lack any constitutional framework.

All the Gulf states have stated their oppositions to the freedom of trade unions and the right to strike. These countries have ignored the agreements of the international community concerning the mechanisms of the judicial system and the safeguards which ensure the right to a fair trial. For instance, in Saudi Arabia, which contains the largest number of Egyptians of all the Arab countries, trials in most cases lack both publicity and the right to a defence. The formation of courts is done through decisions by the Minister of Justice who has the right to appoint judges and to transfer and promote them.

The legal framework in these countries lacks the standard safeguards against false imprisonment and arbitrary detention. It is to be pointed out in this respect that the security forces in Saudi Arabia have wide powers of arrest, detention and interrogation. The regulations for precautionary detention in the kingdom permits the governors of the emirates to forward an application to the judiciary to extend the three-week detention, pending an investigation by another 30 days. The governor has the power to extend this detention until the Minister of the Interior makes the final decision concerning the detainee. Under these regulations, the detainee has no right to contest the extension of his detention before a special judiciary body as the regulations only provide for the detention to be reviewed by a committee made up of a legal expert and a representative of the police.

2. The sponsorship system

The increasing need for workers in the Gulf states due to the widening of economic activities there and concerns in the countries over the residency of foreigners, have led to the rise of the economic and social role of the sponsor. To work in these countries one must have a contract, a sponsor or both. When the state is the contractor, it acts as a sponsor. On the other hand, in the private sector the sponsorship system is the most prevalent. Foreign businessmen who wish to begin a project on their own must find a sponsor from the country concerned to be their partner in order to make their business legal. In return, the sponsor procures more than half of the profits. A sponsor might import workers and then present them to local businessmen for a percentage of their wages. The sponsor also offers his signature to permit Egyptian workers to enter the receiving country. These Egyptians would then try to find work for themselves on their own. In this case they pay a certain amount to the sponsor. The legal responsibility of the sponsor towards the government and the sponsored persons is unclear. He may be responsible for the general behaviour of the sponsored person. For this reason he keeps their passports and documents under his control. This prevents their freedom of movement in and outside the country and it denies them the freedom to work for others without his approval.

A report by the 'Citizens and Complaints Service' in the Ministry of Foreign Affairs summarises the problems caused by the sponsorship system for Egyptian workers, as follows:

(i)   The worker is dependent on the sponsor, just as a slave is to his master.
(ii)   The sponsor sets severe conditions, to the extent of forbidding the worker from bringing his family with him, thus denying him the right to family life.
(iii)   The sponsor might make a deal with a contractor guaranteeing a larger number of workers than the business requires. He then tells them to look for another job and asks for a monthly commission, sometimes amounting to 50% of their salary. In many cases, the sponsor comes to Egypt and sells the contract or the visas to Egyptian workers through a travel agent for many thousands of pounds.
(iv)   This system offers rights to the sponsor without duties and commitment to the guaranteed person. The termination of the contract and deportation is a sure consequence of any perceived mistreatment of the sponsor by a worker he has contracted. In such a case, the sponsor would annul the contract and have the worker returned to Egypt, whatever the cost or the consequences.
(v)   The slackness of the sponsor in carrying out the procedures for renewing the residency of Egyptians can lead to interrogations and fines.
(vi)   Some sponsors stubbornly refuse to return passports to the workers once their contracts have expired so as to compel them to relinquish their financial rights towards them.
(vii)   In case of the transfer of sponsorship, the sponsor may use his power to blackmail the worker to relinquish some of his financial rights.
(viii) Some sponsors hand the worker over to the police, claiming fears that he might escape. This can lead to his imprisonment until the procedures

for ending his residency and his subsequent deportation are completed. Sometimes false accusations are forged against the worker and he is imprisoned to prevent him from claiming money owed to him.

The organization states that the sponsorship system, especially in Saudi Arabia, as evidenced by the complaints it has received, has led to forged cases against Egyptians and imprisonment after trials that lack the minimum guarantees of a fair trial, sometimes leading to severe sentences, such as flogging . . .

(The EOHR concluded:)

. . . The EOHR has no doubts that the sponsorship system, by imposing harsh restrictions on workers which prevent them from moving from one job to another, from changing their sponsor and from leaving their job and returning to their countries without obtaining the sponsor's consent or being forced to renounce part or all of the money owed to them, constitutes a fraudulent way of avoiding the provisions of the previously mentioned convention.

The EOHR would like to point out that both Saudia Arabia and Kuwait have ratified the Supplementary Convention on the Abolition of Slavery. Under this Convention, they are committed to take all the necessary legislative and non-legislative measures to put an end to slavery and other similar customs and practices.

The EOHR is convinced that any attempt to solve the problems of Egyptians working in the Gulf area must deal with both the unique conditions imposed by the sponsorship system and the general context in which Egyptians' human rights – whether in the Gulf countries or other Arab countries receiving Egyptian worker – are violated.

In this context, the EOHR makes the following recommendations and believes that if they are collectively adopted, the problems of Egyptians working in Arab countries, notably the Gulf states, will be greatly reduced.

Firstly: Recommendations forwarded to the governments of the Gulf Cooperation Council:

1. The abolition of the sponsorship system.
2. The prompt joining and ratification of the international conventions on human rights, notably, the International Covenant on Economic, Social and Cultural Rights, the International Covenant on Civil and Political Rights, and its Optional Protocol and the Convention against Torture and Other Cruel, Inhuman or Degrading Treatment or Punishment.
3. Reviewing the existing legislative structures to ensure their consistency with international human rights principles and the relevant international conventions. Also, to guarantee the protection of all people against arbitrary arrest, torture and ill-treatment, as well as to adopt the internationally recognised safeguards for an independent judiciary and the right to a fair trial.

4. Launching a dialogue between representatives of these countries and human rights organizations, replying to their correspondence and allowing these organizations to send fact-finding missions to examine human rights conditions in these countries . . .

EOHR, Cairo, 2 April 1995

11F
Victim of a sponsorship system

The Egyptian Organisation for Human Rights in April 1995 raised the case of an Egyptian labourer in Saudi Arabia.

Amin Abdou Khalil. On 5 October 1994 he went to work in Saudi Arabia as a chauffeur (as indicated on his visa) for a Saudi sponsor. On 10 October 1994 his sponsor took him to his farm, where he asked him to work as a farmer. He rejected the offer since agriculture was not his profession, adding that he came to work as a chauffeur, as indicated in his contract and visa. The sponsor told him he must choose between working as a farmer or returning to Egypt. The Egyptian chauffeur expressed his willingness to return to Egypt but asked the sponsor to pay him the sum of 3,500 LE, since he had paid 2,000 LE to the sponsor's brother when they signed the contract in Egypt and 1,500 LE to the employment agency who had started to insult him and kick him. When the chauffeur resisted, an Indian driver who was there held him down whilst the sponsor beat him severely. He was left at the farm with no shelter or covers. At midnight the sponsor came back accompanied by this brothers who started to beat him again until he passed out. When he came round, Amin Abdou Khalil found himself lying on the side of a main road. A Pakistani driver took him to El A'mar police station where he was transferred to El a'mar Hospital on 11 October 1994. The hospital registered his injuries but refused to give him an official report.

When he went back to the Saudi sponsor with a letter summoning him to the police station, the latter lost his temper and he and his brothers took the chauffeur in their car to a destination outside the city. They hung him by his feet, inserted a club into his rear and stubbed out cigarettes on his body. They then took him to El A'mar police station. The Saudi sponsor was also a police officer and at the police station the officers attacked Amin Abdou Khalil violently. He was beaten by all of them and was detained for a week, during which time he suffered all kinds of physical and psychological torture. He was then transferred to El Mouzanab police station where he was redetained. They asked him to sign a statement saying that he had received all the money owed to him by his sponsor. When he refused, he was beaten by the police. They were aided by a brother of the sponsors who is sergeant at El A'mar police station. He was subjected to electric shocks and was also caned. This torture lasted for two days. On 5 November 1994 he was deported by land. His passport was only given back when he crossed the border.

He filed a complaint to the Department of Consular Affairs for citizens within the Egyptian Ministry of Foreign Affairs on 20 March 1995 and also contacted the EOHR. When its lawyers examined the torture marks on his body, they noted cigarette burns on his arms, as well as brown lines across his back, in addition to bruises on his shoulders.

EOHR, Cairo, 2 April 1995.

11G
Saudization of labour

Emphasized by Prince Nayef in May 1996.

Prince Nayef Bin Abdul Aziz, Minister of Interior and President of the Council for Manpower, during a speech on the occasion of the vocational day recently organized by King Abdul Aziz University in Jeddah, underscored the importance of Saudization of the labor force, saying that the percentage of nationals employed by the public sector has reached 99.9 in several government departments. Noting that at present 65 percent of the jobs at Saudia, the national airline, are occupied by Saudis, he said the company is planning to complete the Saudization of its employees by the end of the current sixth five-year development plan.

In underlining the significant role to be played by the private sector in the national economy, Prince Nayef said the Saudi private sector was the biggest importer of expatriate manpower to the Kingdom with more than 500,000 visas issued last year. As a major pillar for the process of development, it should shoulder its share of responsibility towards Saudization of employment in the country.

Press release, Embassy of Saudi Arabia, Washington, 11 May 1996.

11H
Migrant conditions

The Philippines Overseas Workers Welfare Administration has made a 'primer' for citizens, contemplating a future as an 'Overseas Contract Worker' (OCW) in Saudi Arabia. On 'Working Conditions', it states the following:

As an OCW in Saudi Arabia, you can earn a better wage than you would in the Philippines. You can buy things that are not readily available in the

Philippines, such as appliances, imported items, gold and fine jewelry. And you can improve the lot of your family by the money you send.

But work in Saudi Arabia is not easy. If you think you are embarking for paradise, forget it.

An OCW should come prepared for the worst. He should expect a hostile climate, a different working environment, and a strange and seemingly confusing way of life. Above all, he should expect bouts of loneliness and homesickness. The feeling of loneliness and homesickness begins when you arrive at the airport.

To overcome them, the OCW must learn to appreciate activities like reading, playing solitaire, listening to music, watching video tapes, window shopping, doing household chores, writing or preparing recordings for loved one, etc. Blot out the discos, beerhouses, movies, concerts, and dates from your mind.

The employer holds tremendous power over the OCW. The OCW cannot leave Saudi Arabia without his employer's consent. The OCW's visa is the complete responsibility of the employer; the OCW can do nothing about it. Only the employer may secure exit papers for the OCW. Persons other than the employer may sign for the exit documents but only with the consent of the employer. Thus, the OCW is well advised to maintain good relations with his employer even under the most trying circumstances.

Working conditions vary according to the employer. If you are employed in an established company, you will enjoy good wages and accommodation. Your worksite will generally have modern equipment, good lighting and ventilation, and safety devices. It is best that you go to Saudi Arabia as a skilled worker since you will be asked to do only what your job requires. This is not so for unskilled ones, or those who agree to do a broad range of tasks.

Workers in hospitals also enjoy modern facilities and good accommodation. But the women staff have been known to complain of strict regulation by management of their activity even on their free time.

If you work for a small company whose operation budget depends on its income, particularly from government contracts, you can expect to have a hard time. Your pay may not come on time, if at all. The worksite will not have adequate facilities and will very much resemble the sweatshops in Manila.

The oil glut several years ago has not only shrunk work opportunities in Saudi Arabia but has made working conditions especially bad. Wages and benefits have fallen and the small companies constantly suffer from financing problems. They are normally not able to pay their workers on time.

More than this, OCWs going to work for these companies must deal with the problem of 'contract substitution'. This practice is widespread. What happens is that an OCW who leaves Manila after signing a contract is presented with a new one as soon as he lands in Saudi Arabia. The new contract gives the OCW a raw deal. But many OCWs end up accepting the new contract since they are already in Saudi Arabia and have no wish to go home empty handed. Others complain, but, not uncommonly, the result of this is that the OCW is sent home after a long and complicated hearing.

Generally, workers are entitled to a month's vacation, fully paid, after two years service. If they are coming back, employers give them round-trip tickets. Company workers are housed in work camps whose conditions vary. Workers in well-established companies are generally comfortable while those in small ones complain of wretched accommodation. One assistant veterinarian said he slept in a room with sick animals.

OCWs who are dissatisfied with their work and wish to terminate a contract may complain to the Labor Office. The Philippine Embassy and other agencies may help them prepare their statements – which have to be written in Arabic – but may not interfere in the proceedings. The results vary according to the merits of the case.

In Riyadh, if a worker is terminated or refuses to continue to work, he/she is referred to the OWWA/Filipino Workers Social Center. An OCW can only stay at the OWWA center for 24 hours, after which a female worker shall be turned over to the Social Welfare Administration (SWA) while a male OCW shall be brought to the immigration or deportation office. An OCW will await the completion of his/her deportation papers, exit visa by the employer and return ticket in the SWA or deportation office.

If the worker is accused, he is referred to the police to answer complaints by employers, usually concerning theft.

The Governor of Makkah in Jeddah has recently promulgated a new policy requiring runaway workers to serve a minimum detention of 45 days at their detention centers, whether or not they have plane tickets.

Maids, or domestics, in particular, live an austere life in Saudi Arabia. The job is not for secretaries, nurses, midwives and other professionals who are not used to doing heavy household chores daily. Even those who are used to it have cause to complain. It is not always true that maids will have machines to help them do their work. Indeed, the norm is that maids wash clothes, walls, and floors with their hands, without protective covering. Runaways often show hands full of wounds or rashes from constant and long exposure to clorox and other powerful detergents.

The work, which carries no definite hours, can last up to 18 hours a day. The food is often meager and served less than three times a day. During Ramadan, maids must be prepared not to eat the whole day. But they must also be prepared to serve their masters the whole night long when they break their fast and entertain guests. And still, they must be prepared to start work the next day at 6:00 a.m. Thus, they have coined the phrase, 'no meals and no end to work'.

Family drivers fare in the same way. They, in particular, should be very careful during the Ramadan since they tend to be in a foul mood, being unable to eat, drink and smoke during the day. Many tend to hurry home to break the fast while others tend to get carried away by the merrymaking in the night and fail to adjust to the somber mood in the morning.

If you are a maid, you must cope further with being a woman. You have to ward off advances by your master, his brother, son, and other male members of the household. You may also have to bear pinching, slapping, and scratching from your mistress. Mistresses get jealous of their maids for no reason at all and punish them for it. You may not get to bathe everyday as this is a luxury and is, in any case, considered unhealthy.

Forget about your beauty needs. The work is heavy and unglamorous. Be prepared to wash clothes even after ironing. You will not be allowed to rest even when sick and you may be asked to pay the bill if you see a doctor. You may not even have time to comb your hair from all the work you need to do. In any case, improving your looks may prove an invitation to sexual harassment.

Never write to a male pen pal. Your master will suspect you of having an affair and may cause you to be detained by the police using the letters as a proof. Do not write to any male acquaintance or relative in Saudi Arabia whose family name is not the same as yours. Upon being suspected of immorality, your friend or relative may also be arrested, interrogated, and detained by the police.

Do not expect to be given rest days or shopping time by your masters. If you are, your movements will be strictly supervised. At the least, you will be accompanied by your mistress or a female member of the household. In part, this is so because your master will be held accountable for your behavior. Indeed, masters explain their seemingly harsh treatment of maids in this way. As head of family, they must punish the maids in the same way that they must punish their own wife and children for wrongs they commit. Often, they say, the maids show loose morals.

Finally, do not go to Saudi Arabia if you are pregnant. Your employer will not take your frail condition into account. Worse, he may suspect you of having an affair with a man and have you arrested. It is hard enough working as a maid in Saudi Arabia without a child. It is far worse doing so with one. And, of course, you have to have proof that your child is legitimate. Failure to produce the necessary papers could mean jail.

Survival Tips

- Always bring your iqama, or ID card, with you. Routine police checkpoints require the showing of the iqama. Failure to show it will land the offender in the Deportation Detention Center.

- Observe religious laws to the letter. Respect the prayer times. Practice your own faith privately. Do not use the term Mohammedan. The proper term is Moslem. Never stare at a praying Arab or pass in front of him. Never step on his prayer rug.
- Be prepared, in particular, for the Ramadan. Eating, drinking, and smoking in public are prohibited. Obey the law, or face jail and deportation.
- *For women.* Remember that there are separate rules for men and women. Men and women never intermingle in social or public gatherings. Do not smile at men you do not know. Do not travel alone, especially in a taxi. Do not drive. Dress modestly, and wear a black veil over your dress when walking out. Steer clear of gossip or any situation that may give rise to gossip. As a rule, be polite rather than friendly. The polite but firm way for women to stop an Arab's advances is to say 'haram', which means 'not allowed'.
- Do not get involved in political activities and refrain from making political commentaries about Saudi Arabia.
- Travel outside the place of work requires a travel permit, to be given by the employer. Otherwise, the traveller could be detained by the police.

Leaving Saudi Arabia

To exit from Saudi Arabia, OCWs need the following:

a. Workers who have completed their two-year contracts:
   (1) Notice from the worker of the termination of contract, with no intention of renewing it,
   (2) The iqama, which is turned over to the employer so that he may secure an exit visa from you,
   (3) An exit visa from the Immigration Office, and
   (4) Your passport.

b. Workers who have not completed their contracts, including illegal workers, stranded workers, and runaways:
   (1) Police certificate, for those detained at the deportation center or in police stations,
   (2) Non-objection certificate from employer (the employer will normally charge the worker with the cost of bringing him over from Manila),
   (3) Plane ticket (those who have been detained and have no friends or relatives in Saudi Arabia are normally aided by the Embassy and Labor/OWWA),

(4) Documents of identification (those who have lost their passport or whose passports have been turned over to the Immigration Office which has lost them), and

(5) Deportation paper, with official stamp.
The exit visas may not be used beyond two months after issue.
Good Luck!

Prepared by the Overseas Workers Welfare Administration in the Department of Labor and Employment, Manila, the Philippines as a hand-out, 1997.

11I
Fate of a labourer

A Philippine guest worker, Sarah Jane Dematra, is waiting and fearing execution in Dammam, Saudi Arabia. The Philippine 'Kanlungan Center Foundation' for migrants rights, in 1997 explained her story.

Sara Jane, after four days of setting foot in Dhahran, Kingdom of Saudi Arabia, was sent to jail. She was arrested for the alleged murder of her female employer, Lalah Saleh al Humaidi. She has been languishing in jail since 15 November, 1992.

A high-school graduate, Sarah Jane went abroad to augment her family's meager income. Her mother, a factory worker, is the sole source of her family's survival.

A released co-prisoner related Sarah Jane's account of the event: after four days in her employers' house, her male employer asked Sarah to pull Lalah's body to the basement. Sarah was in the act of pulling the body when the police arrived. Sarah was fingerprinted and detained. She was accused of killing Lalah with a 'pipe'.

In her letter, Sarah narrated the difficulties of prison life. She said, 'hirap na hirap na ako, wala man lang akong makausap na maaaring makatulong sa akin' ('I mourn my affliction. I do not have anybody to turn to for help'). Sarah said that one of her co-prisoners, who was at her age, was beheaded last May 1993. She fears she will be the next one to die.

A Saudi Court in 1994 deemed that Sarah is 'responsible for the murder of Lalah Saleh Humaidi', and she would have to stay in jail and 'wait for the youngest child of the victim (about five years old now) to reach the age of 18 years' to be able to join the other heirs in requesting for her execution . . .

Kanlungan Center Foundation: 'Movement to Free Sarah Jane Dematra' folder,
Kamias, Quezon City, Philippines 1997.

11J
ILO on labour and globalization

The Director-General of the ILO in April 1997 urged the member states to ensure that 'social progress' and 'humane conditions' proceed apace. An executive summary for International Labour Conference, 85th Session 1997 follows.

The ILO, standard setting and globalization

Despite the hopes it raises and promises it makes, the liberalization of international trade might well flounder if its beneficial effects are slow in making themselves felt for workers or if, on the contrary, it is associated in the mind of the general public with an increase in inequalities or precarious conditions. Globalization cannot be left to its own devices. Rather, economic progress resulting from the liberalization of trade should be accompanied by social progress. In order to live up to the expectations placed in it, the ILO should guarantee a greater universality in the application of its fundamental standards and be more selective in its new standards.

The Report submitted to the Conference sets forth a series of specific measures likely to guarantee that the standard-setting action of the ILO will be more relevant in the forthcoming years. All these measures may be taken within the framework of constitutional provisions in force. Acting in this area is therefore mainly a matter of political will.

Although the 'debate' over the link between the liberalization of trade and the protection of workers' rights at first took the form of mutual accusations of social dumping and protectionism, it has made significant headway, due to a great extent to the impetus of the ILO and the work of its various groups and committees examining the issue. Today, nobody can claim that developing countries are not entitled to the advantages they derive from their wages and levels of social protection which are comparatively lower.

But if this approach is to be formalized, it presupposes the universal respect of certain fundamental human rights of workers: freedom of association and collective bargaining (Conventions Nos. 87 and 98); the prohibition of forced labour, including forced labour of children (Conventions Nos. 29 and 105); equality of treatment and non-discrimination (Conventions Nos. 100 and 111); minimum age of employment (Convention No. 138). These fundamental rights, which must be acknowledged as such as being universally binding, are of a particular significance in the context of globalization because they are instruments enabling workers to claim their fair share of the economic progress generated by the liberalization of trade.

The Heads of State attending the Social Summit at Copenhagen agreed on the need to promote the fundamental Conventions of the ILO, which has since then been carrying out a successful ratifications campaign. Furthermore, the particular significance of these fundamental rights was officially acknowledged in the Singapore Ministerial Declaration which stressed that the ILO was 'the competent body to set and deal with these standards'.

The question must now be what particular form this political will, so clearly expressed, should take within the ILO.

Although the ratification of ILO Conventions is voluntary, as in the case of any treaty, not everything is contingent upon the good will of the States. Indeed, the Constitution of the ILO allows it to request States which have not ratified an instrument to give explanations on their attitude. In this respect, the Governing Body has already decided to request each year reports on the reasons for failing to ratify fundamental Conventions. These reports might in the future be used to examine regularly the situation of countries which have not ratified these Conventions.

Another approach – moreover complementary – would be to raise the question of whether, even in the absence of ratification of the relevant Conventions, all member States, by virtue of their acceptance of the Constitution, and the objectives of the principles of the ILO, are not bound to a minimum of obligations with respect to fundamental rights. The supervisory machinery for the application of Conventions and principles on freedom of association provides an interesting reference and experience in this area. Under this procedure, governments or workers' and employers' organizations may submit complaints concerning violations of trade union rights by States, irrespective of whether or not they have ratified the Conventions on freedom of association.

A declaration or any other text enshrining principles adopted by the Conference might help to define the universally acknowledged content of the fundamental rights which should be respected by all Members of the Organization, whether or not they have ratified the corresponding Conventions, and to establish a mechanism to guarantee their promotion. Discussions on this matter have already started in the Governing Body and will continue at the Conference on the basis of the Report.

A system of mutual encouragement to attain social progress.

A regular report on social progress in the world?

The guarantee of fundamental rights is a prerequisite for social progress – but it is not enough. As Members of the ILO, the States undertake to try to attain actively social progress in all its forms. Although it is up to the States to act in accordance with their possibilities and preferences, it is important that any efforts they make to turn the benefits of globalization to good account in terms of social progress should be encouraged and evaluated. In this respect, the ILO has the legal means and necessary mandate to set in motion once again the virtuous circle of social progress. It might, in the light of the present discussions, start by gathering and determining a number of basic principles or objectives which should guide the action of States in the area, for example: (i) that a comparative advantage linked to a certain level of wages or social protection is legitimate, if it is a factor of economic growth, provided that it is not artificially maintained or used as a mere means of winning markets; (ii) that there is, in addition to fundamental rights, a minimum programme that each State should try to achieve; (iii) more generally speaking, that all workers, and not only those producing export goods, should be able to have a fair share of the fruits of globalization and that, to attain this objective, a system of tripartite consultation should be envisaged at the national level.

The ILO Constitution and the Declaration of Philadelphia provide the Organization with the means and mandate allowing it to supervise the implementation of these basic principles. By accepting the commitment to work towards the ILO's objectives in good faith, its Members have acknowledged amongst other things the necessary interdependency of their efforts – and consequently a reciprocal right to see what other Members are doing. Although introducing a social conditionality would be nonsense because the opening up of markets constitutes to a great extent a kind of precondition to social progress, it would be just as inconsistent to claim that all partners, in the name of social progress, should have access to all markets without having to give account to anyone on their practices in this field.

On this basis, the Conference could, by means of a text enshrining principles or even a Recommendation, draw up a list of basic principles and establish a follow-up mechanism, for example in the form of a regular report by the Director-General on social progress in the world – followed by a tripartite discussion. In this way, all the Members of the ILO – and more generally national and international public opinion – might have an overall and objective view of the efforts made by each State to turn the economic benefits resulting from the liberalization of trade to good account in terms of social progress.

The mobilization of non-governmental actors to promote social progress

Social progress is no longer the prerogative of States. An increasing number of enterprises are concerned about the social or environmental repercussions of their activities; consumers are also increasingly aware of the responsibilities they undertake when they make a certain choice of product or services. This two-pronged converging movement is giving rise to an abundance of charters, codes of practices or 'labels', which are supposed to guarantee the respect of various criteria – social and others – in the manufacturing of a particular article.

Although at first sight the objectives of these voluntary arrangements and the ILO might seem to be the same, they risk being arbitrary, singling out a particular right or product or being put to improper use. The main disadvantage of these labels, however, is that they concern exclusively, through the products they address, workers producing for the international market and certain aspects of fundamental rights. They do not come to grips with the reasons for the situation. To contribute in a more rational and consistent way to the ILO's objectives, it might be envisaged to award an 'overall social label' to countries complying with a set of fundamental principles and rights and agreeing to have their practices supervised by an international inspection on the spot which is reliable and legally independent. It would be perfectly feasible to provide for such a system of inspection under an international labour Convention which, because of its voluntary nature, would allow each State to decide freely whether to give an overall social label to all goods produced on its territory – provided that it accepts the obligations inherent in the Convention and agrees to have monitoring on the spot. The ratification of such a Convention would be attractive in terms of real economic interests – and not only from a moral standpoint.

More Targeted Standards for a Greater Impact

In its second part, the Report rules out the idea of taking a break from standard setting and advocates strengthening the relevance and efficiency of the standard-setting machinery by making a more judicious choice of subjects and exploiting better the variety and flexibility of the means of action provided for under the ILO Constitution.

A wider and more targeted choice of subjects

In attempting to be more selective in its choice of subjects, the ILO should try to gather more information on the real needs of its constituents by making greater use of its decentralized structures. This information would help the Governing Body constitute a wider, regularly updated portfolio of proposals, enabling it to make strategic choices which correspond to actual needs. It must then make a stricter choice from among the subjects envisaged for standard setting, taking into account the added value that each standard might contribute to the existing instruments. The Report puts forward detailed proposals on the criteria which would help guide better the choice of new standards, for instance the considerations of whether or not a subject lends itself to standard setting, or whether it would make more than an ephemeral contribution, etc.; it suggests an unofficial codification which would give a more coherent summary of existing instruments; it also raises the question of whether it might not be preferable to rely on principles of responsibility rather than accumulate protective provisions. Finally, the Report proposes a number of ways in which adjustments could be made to the procedure in force so that the Organization might have an overall view of the possible content of the instruments envisaged before making an irreversible choice.

A greater recourse to Recommendations

The drop-off in the number of ratifications is undoubtedly inevitable and linked not only to globalization but also to other factors, particularly the proliferation of international instruments. This should not, however, hamper the ILO's standard-setting action because Recommendations are an extremely efficient means of action, provided that their full potential is exploited. If Recommendations are to regain their rightful place, they should once again be considered as instruments in their own right; they should then, and this is of paramount importance, be followed up on a regular basis as provided for by the Constitution. By definition, Recommendations do not impose obligations but they can still have a strong influence on social policy and legislation if they are subject to a real and efficient follow-up, which has not been the case until now.

Overall evaluation mechanism

It is indispensable that the ILO should have a self-correcting mechanism for its standard setting to be able to ascertain the impact and relevance of standards and thus draw lessons for the future. This evaluation would attempt not only to measure the success achieved in fulfilling the specific objective set forth in the instrument, but also to identify any possible indirect or adverse repercussions there might be with respect to other ILO objectives – for example that of employment. It will be up to the Governing Body, as the case may be, to choose the appropriate body and procedure for evaluation.

International Labour Organization (ILO), Geneva 1997.

Chapter Twelve

GENDER

12A
American Women's advisory

During the Gulf crisis 1990/91, the American Army in a 'Dhahran Area Guide' advised its women soldiers to beware of local conditions.

Local laws are more stringent than ours. One individual received 200 lashings for touching a female's breast. More serious offenses can carry a death penalty.

Do not take justice into your own hands. If you do, you may be subject to host nation law. Let their system work for you.

Another major difference you'll find is that women are not permitted to drive in this country. Because the duties of many military women require them to drive, the host nation has agreed to allow women to operate vehicles with the following restrictions:

- Women may only drive on base, including trips to the main exchange, post office and commissary.
- Women driving must be in uniform and wearing a hat. This includes driving in Khobar Towers and the short transit between the two base areas and the Oasis.
- Women are not permitted to drive in any other areas. They may not drive downtown, in the local community, on public highways or enroute to any other military installation.

Transportation for Women

It is forbidden by Saudi Arabian law for women to drive motor vehicles or to ride bicycles or motorcycles in public. Women are also advised not to ride in the front seat of chauffeur-driven cars.

Women should not use taxis alone, unless it becomes absolutely necessary. If it becomes necessary to use a taxi, it is important for people to be able to give directions in Arabic and determine the price of the trip before entering the cab. If you do not like the driver for any reason, stop the taxi, pay the driver, and get out immediately.

There are several limousine companies in the Dhahran area which will provide transportation for women. The drivers speak English and the companies' managements request patrons report discourteous or unsafe drivers. Hotels and restaurants generally have the taxi companies' telephone numbers and can assist in obtaining their services.

The city bus system, while very reasonably priced, is not recommended due to frequently changing routes and potential language difficulties. Women riding the bus are required to sit in the rear of the vehicle.

> Dhahran Area Guide, published by 4404th Wing (Provisional) Public Affairs
> Office, Eastern Province of Saudi Arabia, 1990.

12B
Appeal for women

The Saudi 'Committee for the Defence of Human Rights/Saudi Arabia' in December 1990, protested against the government's handling of the famous women's demonstration in Riyadh in November, claiming the right to drive their own cars.

Following the women's demonstration which took place in Riyadh, the capital of Saudi Arabia on November 6th of this year, which was an expression to the social condition from which our country suffers as a result of oppressing to public freedoms, the unjust practices towards our people, the complete absence and prevention of our people from women, their historical responsibilities for their Country and people, in consequence of this demonstration, the Saudi authorities took unjust measures towards those demonstrators for, after their release, the authorities took the decision to expel them from their jobs and prevented them from travelling abroad, and their husbands were harassed. This was accompanied by a defaming campaign against them when the authorities gave full reign to the conservative spiteful groups to express their contempt, and through the distribution of spiteful leaflets, which included false accusations and insults to the honour of the heroic demonstrators.

However, the situation did not end at this point. The Saudi authorities continued to be led by this unjust campaign, which was represented by the Minister of Interior, against those women whose only demand was to be granted what would be the minimum legal rights to ensure dignified life for them as human beings.

The Saudi Arabian authorities arrested the well-known writer and journalist Saleh Al-Azaz and imprisoned him regardless of his deteriorating health, and confined him incommunicado, for no other reasons than that he is the husband of one of the demonstrators.

The Committee for the Defence of Human Rights appeals to your living conscience, and to all of human rights organizations, and to all political parties and organisations, patriots parliamentarians and all who value human freedom and dignity, to demand of the Saudi authorities the immediate release of Saleh Al-Azaz. To stop all oppressive measures taken against the women who demonstrated against the desperate situation which our country lives, and to support them against the cheap campaigns defamation.'

Committee for the defence of Human Rights, Saudi Arabia, 5 December, 1990.

12C
Gender and Education

In a comprehensive essay on 'Female Education in Saudi Arabia and the Reproduction of Gender Division', Nagat El Sanabary, researcher at the Center For Middle Eastern Studies, University of California, concluded:

Despite the remarkable expansion of women's education in Saudi Arabia during the first 30 years of its existence, the education system continues to function as a conservation force that helps reproduce gender divisions and power relations in the wider society. This is accomplished through vertical gender division in the educational hierarchy: an education policy that emphasizes women's reproduction and nurturing functions: a vast network of gender-segregated schools and colleges; and several forms of curriculum differentiation at the various educational levels.

Gender-segregated Saudi Arabia draws upon Islam and its oil wealth to maintain a highly gender-segregated education system that reflects and reproduces the gender divisions in the wider society. The country's wealth has enabled it to provide schooling for most of its current school age population, male and female, in a highly centralized and controlled education system which steers students toward socially acceptable educational and employment options. The Saudi education system is a microcosm of Saudi society; it echoes the prevailing class and gender structures and conforms to the society's socio-economic and political expectations and control mechanisms. Hence, education's role as a conservation force supersedes its function as a force of social change.

There is no doubt that Saudi women have been both participants and beneficiaries of the sweeping educational and employment changes in their country. The handful of Saudi women who agitated for female education in the 1950s have made it possible for over a million Saudi girls and women to take advantage of the expanding educational opportunities, and for thousands of them to play an active role in the country's gender-segregated economy. Saudi women have made remarkable progress in many areas, but they still have a long way to go in order to achieve their full potential and contribute fully to the development of their country.

The gender segregation that characterizes Saudi Arabia of the early 1990s is definitely different from that of earlier periods. The transformation of the Saudi economy and its accompanying educational expansion has had major effects on the situation of Saudi women in their homes and communities. Despite its limitations and restrictions, female education has opened new options for Saudi women. On the private level it has increased women's negotiating power within the family. It has also given them greater mobility: hundreds of thousands of girls and women go out daily to either school or work, although they still cannot drive a car or travel alone. On the public level, education has made it possible for thousands of Saudi women to enter the labor force.

In 1985, according to government statistics, 50,000 Saudi women were in paid employment, mostly in the public sector. They made up 5% of the Saudi work-force. These include thousands of Saudi women teachers, hundreds of school and college administrators, university and college professors, doctors and nurses, and others in women's welfare associations serving the needs of their less fortunate sisters and their families. A relatively small number of women have entered non-traditional jobs such as banking in special women's banks, journalism, radio broadcasting, and private business. Saudi working women receive equal pay for equal work and enjoy generous maternity and sick leave benefits. Several education institutions provide low-cost on site child care facilities for the children of women students, teachers, and staff, many of whom are young and experience many pregnancies and births during their education and employment.

Undoubtedly, the situation of Saudi women has changed drastically since the opening of the first public girls' schools in 1960. Educated working women are helping raise the educational, health, and cultural standards of the Saudi population. They also help reduce their country's dependency on expatriate women, especially in school teaching and administration.

Yet, these developments in female education and the consequent rise in female employment have not changed the prevailing gender division in the Saudi work-force and in society generally. Saudi working women remain largely in traditional female occupations where women serve other women such as teaching, medicine, nursing and social work. This occupational segregation has made it difficult for women graduates to find employment. Consequently, the country suffers from a major problem of unemployment among the educated, especially the females. Thousands of women graduate every year from Saudi universities – 3500 in 1985 and 5000 in 1988. The lucky ones find jobs, but the majority cannot be accommodated by Saudi Arabia's segregated work-force. The Government has tried to open up new employment opportunities for women, but the biggest obstacle is deciding which jobs are appropriate for a Muslim woman. Women's work is hotly debated in Saudi newspapers and magazines, and discussed by educators and planners. Yet no solution has yet been found. And the question is often asked, 'has education been wasted on women?' The efficiency-minded economists and cost-benefit analysts say 'yes', and they question the value of women's higher education in particular.

But the women do not agree. They seek education for its intrinsic value, the status it conveys, and the prospect, however dim it may be, of a fulfilling job: a luxury for some, an economic necessity for others. Women in leadership positions propose various alternative solutions ranging from the establishment of feminine secondary vocational education, to the opening of special sections for women in every government agency that serves the public such as hospitals, utilities, immigration, and social welfare agencies. These women complain that the Government's policy on women's education and employment is vague and in need of clarification. They press for an urgent solution to a worsening educational and social problem.

Unlike their Western sisters who have to struggle with the image of alleged inferior intellectual abilities, what Saudi women have to battle with is not whether or not they can handle intellectual and professional pursuits, but spatial barriers. Their battle may not be easier than that of their Western sisters, but it is definitely different. This paper also suggests that what is happening with Saudi women is not isolated from issues of the East–West discourse. The Saudis tighten the restrictions on their women to protect them from Western influences, and they continue to use Western technologies to maintain gender divisions.

Reforms are badly needed in both education and employment sectors to provide greater equity for women. Previous trends in female educational development indicate that women's access to education will continue to expand to achieve numerical parity with male enrollment, probably within the next 10 years. I would even venture to suggest that females may outnumber males in Saudi higher education as has been the case in Kuwait. But gender segregation and curriculum differentiation will continue. Nonetheless, as the country diversifies its economy and expands the service sector, it will probably liberalize its employment policies by broadening the scope of occupations that are considered suitable for women. This will be necessitated by the existing shortages of indigenous labor and the continuing influx of female graduates from secondary and higher education. But gender role divisions and curriculum differentiation and stereotypes will persist. This is not only because the reproduction of gender divisions and differentiation is deeply rooted in education and in other social institutions and structures, and because not enough women are involved in the educational policy-making process, but also because of a keen desire to preserve traditional Islamic and cultural values, and to check the onslaught of Westernization.

Quoted from 'Gender & Education', Vol 6, No. 2, 1994.

12D
Call to Reject the UN

Dr A. Majid Katme, president of the Islamic Medical Association in London, presented an open letter to the press and NGOs at the UN Women's conference in Beijing in September 1995.

Muslim women of the world: keep to your own religion and culture for your sexual health. Reject the disease-ridden proposals of the UN!

- Virginity is *the* norm among muslim men *and* women before marriage, and this stage *in life* is healthy and free from diseases.
- Adultery/fornication and sex before and outside marriage *are* forbidden in Islam, as a result Aids and a large number of sexually transmitted diseases are prevented.
- Sex is only in Islam between a man (husband) and a woman (wife), no sex in any other form is allowed!
- Anal intercourse and homosexuality are forbidden in Islam so the majority of HIV infection and Aids cases are prevented in Islam.
- Sex is a natural gift from the Creator for both man and woman and is for procreation and recreation.
- Every woman has an equal and similar right for sexual satisfaction (sexual empowerment).
- It is forbidden to project women as sex objects as it is done today and all types of prostitution (forced or *voluntary*) are forbidden in Islam, thus making a great health precaution for women as well as men.
- Only the parents are responsible for the 'sexual education' of their children and no doctor or clinic or a UN can take from the parents this basic right!
- The present sex education is immoral, anti-God and anti-morality and anti-family and full of diseases, problems and misery!
- It is forbidden in a government law or a UN decision to distribute to the adolescents (and our Muslim youth) all types of contraception like the pills and condoms in order to practice sex adultery before marriage!
- No government and no UN has the right to interfere with the natural private sexual relation between the husband and his wife by forcely avoiding pregnancy or limiting the number of one's children (as in population control)!

- There is only one type of sexual orientation and one sexual right – heterosexuality and natural attraction between a man and a woman. Sexual attraction between two men or two women are forbidden in Islam!
- Only one type of *gender*, fixed by the Creator for ever and can not change by social development or by time.
- A man/masculine/husband and a father is attracted only to a woman/feminine/ wife and a mother.
- To make the woman like the man is stupid and very irresponsible and anti-sexuality and anti-woman!
- By doing full blind equality/gender quotas will be harmful to every woman and will cause: hormonal changes, men's diseases and will destroy the natural precious attractive gift of woman: femininity, womanhood, gender and natural beauty and attraction!
- Sexual mutilation to women as well as to men are prohibited in Islam. Circumcision is only recommended for boys as it is very healthy and hygienic.
- All means to cause sexual arousal to man or woman outside marriage are forbidden in Islam!
- Sex segregation and modesty of women are essential for sexual health.
- The Holy Book Al Qur'an and the Ahadiths (Sayings of the last Prophet Muhammad, peace be upon him) contain many references to sexual matters and data given in the context of marriage, morality and family life.
- As a result of disobeying all the Divine and moral teachings of our Creator, the women especially in the west are suffering a hell of diseases and problems related to the sexual chaos and loss like: Aids and sexually transmitted diseases, sexual harassment, rape, homosexuality, unwanted pregnancy, teenage mothers, abortion, illegitimate children, cancer of the cervix, of the uterus and of the breast, high divorce rate, children in care and delinquent children and sexual abuse of the children!

We see clearly today: (Muslims and Christians) that the Proposals of the UN in connection of sex are to give a bigger dose of all the above mentioned problems and diseases with the huge finance to be spent on all these epidemic of diseases and problems!

And all these terms in the UN Document like: sexual orientation, sexual right, reproductive right, reproductive health, sex education, gender, human right, etc., are to be opposed and to be rejected as they are code words for abortion, homosexuality, adultery and all the diseases and problems mentioned before! Muslim women should *speak up* and be proud of their own Islamic culture and heritage at least for their own sexual health! And reject all the disease-ridden proposals of the UN!

Issued at the UN Womens Conference 1995 by Dr. A. Majid Katme, President, Islamic Medical Association, London.

12E
Women's rights

The General Federation of Jordanian Women prepared an 'Information Kit on Women in the Arab World' for the UN Women's Conference in Beijing 30 August–8 September, 1995.

There are two separate but interrelated issues related to women's rights. The first, is women's constitutional right and, the second, is the status of women under Islamic laws. While some countries depend purely on Islamic *Sharia* (Islamic laws) others have adapted to a mixture of both. In the latter, family laws tend to extend itself mostly from Islamic *Sharia* while all other issues depend on a larger variety of civil laws.

The constitutions of Egypt, Syria, Lebanon, Jordan, Libya, Morocco, Tunis, Bahrain Yemen, and Sudan affirm unconditionally the equality of men and women and the right to live without discrimination. Despite this, however, not all of these countries have ratified and/or signed the convention on the elimination of all forms of discrimination against women. This is because despite the affirmations of equality various restrictions upon women's lives exist. The restrictions are mostly based on the patriarchal nature of society. Examples include the fact that no Arab country grants nationality through the mother. Also, as a means to control women's freedom of movement, women in several countries cannot obtain passports without consent of male guardian.

Besides constitutional rights the Islamic *sharia* grants women various rights. For example, under the *Sharia* laws, women can sign contracts, control financial assets and own property separately from their husbands or fathers. Despite this however, the laws governing business transactions and ownership are granted to women in only 10 out of the 21 Arab states.

Other laws that depend on Islam *sharia* include laws that govern marriage, divorce, custody and inheritance. In principle, the Islamic sharia has empowered women to control such aspects of their lives through the marriage contract that can accommodate any set of legally binding conditions between two spouses. Yet there are intrinsic gender disparities. Polygamy is such an example. Men can marry up to 4 wives. To date, it has only been Tunisia and Iraq that have prohibited this practice. Men can easily divorce while women should either state this right clearly in the marriage contract or go through complicated legal proceedings and risk losing their rights for financial support or child custody. In terms of child custody young children automatically stay with their mothers but upon puberty stay with their fathers. In other words, mothers are the nurturers but the children belong to fathers families.

In short, Women, through Islamic laws, have a variety of rights – the main problem in most Arab countries is women's awareness of these rights.

Furthermore, besides women's limited legal awareness, they have limited access in enacting these rights as a result of social restrictions. Therefore, there are two separate issues in terms of women's rights in Arab countries. The first is the legal systems and women's roles within it and the second is women's access and utilization of the legal systems.

Women and Politics

Women's participation in public life in most Arab countries remains limited. Women hold only 4% of parliamentary seats in the region, which is well below the 10% average for the developing countries. The political participation of women can be measured through their right to vote, the right to run for office and their presence at decision making levels in the governmental bodies and judiciary system.

Women's political right largely reflect the political system under which they live. Women's right to vote and run for office in Jordan, Syria, Lebanon, Yemen, Egypt, Algeria and Tunisia is part of the constitution. In these countries women, are represented in legislative, parliamentary and local municipal bodies. Yet despite these constitutional rights representation of women in these countries varies. Examples range from Syria which has 21 women (8%), Egypt which has 10 women (2%), Tunisia which has 11 women (7%) Jordan and Lebanon has 3 women (3% and 2% respectively) and Yemen which has 2 women (1%).

Other countries, like Kuwait, does not grant women any political rights, whether to vote or be selected for public office. Recently, however, Kuwaiti women have been actively campaigning to gain their political rights. Other countries such as Saudi Arabia, Bahrain, Qatar, and Oman, democratic elections are non-existent and therefore men and women do not have the right to vote. In these cases, individuals are nominated to office and in the case of Oman, two women were recently nominated for the legislative council.

Women's political rights in Arab countries, however, are not reflective of women's participation in political activity. Women have always played active roles in various political movements starting from the nationalist movements against colonial rule in Egypt, Syria and Algeria to the more recent Palestinian and Lebanese resistance movements. In these settings, women have moved into the political arena as organizers and activists. Unfortunately, this has not been translated into effective political participation at the stages of nation-building or during institution building. Women's movements at these stages somehow becomes restricted to women's unions or organizations and their focus shifts from resistance to providing social welfare.

Women's presence in most Arab countries in decision making levels within government bodies is limited. Women ministers, ambassadors, judges or in any of the higher echelons of the government administration remains meager. This has been a major obstacle for enhancing the integration of women in the development process and has limited their influence on policy making and legislative change. Within this context, it has to be mentioned that in some countries there has been recent changes and women's visibility in public office and decision making is increasing. In 1994, there were 7 women ministers in Syria, 4 in Tunisia and Algeria and 2 in Jordan.

General Federation of Jordanian Women, Beijing, China, 30 August 1995.

Chapter Thirteen

TERROR

13A
King Fahad Letter to President Clinton

King Fahad on 14 November 1995 sent a letter to American President Bill Clinton.

Dear Mr. President:

I wish to convey my condolences and those of the people and Government of the Kingdom of Saudi Arabia to you and to the families of the American victims who were killed as a result of the bombing that occurred in Riyadh on Monday, 13 November 1995. I would also like to convey my sympathies and those of the people and Government of the Kingdom of Saudi Arabia to you and to the families of the injured for whom we bestow the best care possible during their recovery.

I would like to assure you that the appropriate security services in the Kingdom of Saudi Arabia are working tirelessly to expose whoever is behind this criminal explosion, which is adverse to our community, and to disclose all its dimensions and background. You may be assured that all necessary action will be taken against the perpetrators who will be punished severely.

With best regards,

Your friend, Fahd Bin Abdul Aziz, Custodian of the Two Holy Mosques, King of the Kingdom of Saudi Arabia.

King Fahad: 20/6/1416 H, distributed on the Internet 15 November 1995, by the Saudi Arabian Embassy, Washington, DC, USA.

13B
A Questionable confession

The Committee for the Defence of Legitimate Rights (CDLR) on the 24 of April 1996 objected to the official presentation of the responsibility of a terrorist bomb attack in Riyadh which killed American servicemen.

Four 'Saudi' nationals confessed to the Riyadh bombing on Monday the 22nd of April 1996 on state television. They also admitted planning further attacks. The confessions were 'almost identical', as Reuters stressed. The four also are reported to have said that they had been: 'influenced by Islamic groups outside the kingdom, including dissident Dr. Al-Mass'ari'.

There are a few points worth noting about this interestingly timed broadcast, they are:

1. It is well established that confessions in 'Saudi' Arabia are obtained regularly by torture and other illegitimate means. Possible involvement of royals and their cronies is usually covered up and final formulation of such confessions is usually so phrased and 'spiced' to suit various purposes of that oppressive tyranny. This is proven beyond doubt by our immediate experience in the political prisons of the 'Saudi' security authorities and numerous corroboration reports and news programmes (see, for instance, the Panorama programme on the 1st of April this year). Therefore it should be prudent to view these 'confessions' in the light of these facts and not accept them at face value. We believe that further information and independent corroboration must be awaited and subjected to the utmost anxious scrutiny before any reasonable analysis could be made.

2. The four are quoted by Reuters as having fought in Afghanistan and one as having fought alongside the Bosnian Muslims as well. All are of relatively young age and limited experience for such a sophisticated operation like the Riyadh bombing. It is well known that several intelligence services, specifically the Saudi General Intelligence headed by prince Turki Al-Faisal, have deeply penetrated such inexperienced, highly emotional and zealot Afghanistan fighter groups, misguided and redirected them for their evil ends. We have the right to enquire about the role of Turki Al-Faisal in this mess!

3. The main sympathy and support for the CDLR is in the circles of young scholars of Islam, intellectuals, university professors, university and high school students, professionals and other sections of the business community and middle class. The purely ideological, intellectual and political message of the CDLR could not find any following in circles adopting the use of force to change state and society or to advance political goals. CDLR has been described by such circles as 'deviating' and 'heretical' because of its position on violence.

4. The CDLR's publications are read regularly by tens of thousands of households in the Arab Peninsula (including the Gulf). Further hundreds of thousands read them from time to time. It is also read and distributed worldwide. The overwhelming majority of those readers are rational peaceful sympathisers and supporters using only intellectual and political means in their struggle for the establishment of an elected and accountable government system in Arabia. We challenge the Saudi

regime, and every one else, to bring even one sentence from our literature advocating or calling for hatred, violence or bloodshed.

5. The fact that Dr. Al-Mass'ari, and other dissident personalities and groups, has been named is a further proof of such 'spicing' of invalid 'confessions' obtained by torture and other illegitimate means. This could be only a part of the two years long smearing campaign against opposition figures in a futile attempt of the Saudi regime to demonise them. This is further confirmed by the press release of the Al Saud embassy dated 22nd April 1996. That remarkable press release consisted of three paragraphs. The first one of them, 33 words, described the TV broadcast in a slightly sensational language, the second paragraph of 21 words quotes them saying they have been influenced by the thoughts of extremist groups, including the messages sent by 'Mohamed Al Mass'ari', and the last paragraphs of 16 words repeats the old lie: Following the explosion, Al Mass'ari said publicly that he thought the explosion was against 'a legitimate target'. It is obvious that the press release was rather to smear Professor Muhammad Al-Mass'ari and not so much to inform the public.

Committee for the Defence of Legitimate Rights (CDLR) London, 24 April 1996.

13C
Judicial murder

The CDLR in London condemned the execution in May 1996 of four suspects of the Riyadh bombing in November the previous year.

The Saudi regime executed the four suspects of the Riyadh bombing suddenly and without warning on Friday 31 May 1996. Some analysts believe that the Saudi regime panicked because of US secret requests of an independent American interrogation and a possible extradition of the young men. The Saudi tyranny feared that such an investigation might expose extremely sensitive background information and unveil the regime's cover-up. Moreover, a trial on US soil would definitely 'degenerate' into scandal and a trial of the corrupt Saudi regime itself.

CDLR must accept the following facts and principles:

First: The armed American presence under American sovereignty and flag contradicts the sovereignty of Islam which cannot be tolerated in any Muslim Land. Moreover, it violates the specific Islamic injunctions about the Arab Peninsula. This presence is henceforth devoid of any Islamic legitimacy.

Second: This presence lacks any popular approval, direct by popular vote or indirect through a duly elected body. It lacks any *democratic legitimacy* at all.

Third: This presence is in violation of two established principles of international law, the right of self-determination of peoples and the right of sovereignty of states. The approval of that presence by the current Saudi regime, which is formally recognised internationally, cannot take precedence over essential principles of international law.

These facts are well known to Al Saud and their Masters in the ruling capitalist oligarchy of America, therefore both are keen to keep them hidden from their own people. Al Saud claim, falsely, that the American presence consists of a few experts, training and military personnel under Saudi sovereignty, while the American oligarchy is misleading the American public by the claim of countering the Iraqi and Iranian threats and that the American forces are duly invited and welcome (!) by the general public.

Fourth: The four young men did not enjoy any fair process. Their confessions were extracted by torture. Their trial, if any, was secret and lacked any safeguards of due process or rule of law. A comparison between this incident and last year's Oklahoma bombing shows the vast difference between Aal Saud's harsh treatment, unfair trial and summary execution of the suspects, obviously with approval of their American masters, and the American treatment of their own 'terrorists'. This shows how the American oligarchy views the world: here a master race with all rights and privileges, and the slaves!

CDLR warns that the US is viewed by the public at large as an accomplice of the Saudi tyranny in this tragedy and as an unjust racist imperial power in general. Many young disappointed men and women may resort to violence and bloodshed, which cannot be prevented by harsh 'security' measures. Only justice, equality and respect for human dignity can be a reliable base for peace, development, co-operation and brotherly exchange of benefits between peoples and nations.

The CDLR condemns this judicial murder in the sharpest possible form and denounces the American silence, their support and cover-up of the Saudi tyranny.

CDLR, London, 4 June 1996.

13D
Statement by President Clinton's

President Bill Clinton on explosions in Saudi Arabia on the 25th of June 1996.

An explosion occurred this afternoon at the United States military complex near Dhahran in Saudi Arabia. Our best information at this time is that there are many injuries. There have been fatalities. We do not yet know how many.

The explosion appears to be the work of terrorists. If that's the case, like all Americans I am outraged by it. The cowards who committed this murderous act must not go unpunished.

Within a few hours, an FBI team will be on its way to Saudi Arabia to assist the investigation.

Our condolences and our prayers go out to the victims, families and their friends.

We're grateful for the professionalism shown by the Saudi authorities and their reaction to this emergency. We are ready to work with them to make sure those responsible are brought to justice.

Let me say again: We will pursue this. America takes care of our own. Those who did it must not go unpunished.

CNN, through the Internet, 25 June 1996.

13E
A Political explosion

The opposition movement CDLR, asked the US government to consider the background of the bomb explosion in Riyadh in November 1995.

The media has reported the bombing in the heart of Riyadh, targeting a building used by US military forces. The bombing has resulted in a number of casualties of US personnel and other nationalities.

Despite the fact that CDLR is opposed to violence and has no information on the responsible group with regard to the bombing, CDLR was not surprised by the incident. The CDLR had warned in the past that such events are to be expected due to policies and attitudes of the Saudi regime.

The CDLR has indicated in many bulletins and communiqués that what happened is a natural end result of the complete lack of freedom of speech and assembly and oppressions of reformers. One of the main reason for this development is the detention of hundreds of credible community leaders who had played an effective role in controlling the populace and channelling their anger through peaceful means. In addition, the regime resorted to practices which proved irritating to the frustrated and alienated youths, who had already had the capabilities of obtaining and using all types of firearms and weapons.

The CDLR had also indicated the growing anti-US sentiment among the Saudi populace due to the involvement of US supporting and abetting the Saudi regime and helping in the cover-up of its crime. The US exploited the vulnerability of the Saudi regime by confiscating the country's resources to US interests.

The CDLR pointed out that the US government has deliberately kept the American people in the dark regarding the true situation in Saudi Arabia. The CIA and US state department reports did indicate the great resentment of the people of Saudi Arabia against the regime and US forces and the potential danger that the American personnel in Saudi Arabia are likely to face. The US authorities classified all those reports and tried to give a rosy picture of the Saudi regime. The US specifically tried to give false impressions of the so called 'sound stability of Saudi Arabia and the great satisfaction of Saudi people with their Royal Family'. The aim of this cover-up and misleading policy of US government is to avoid the outcry of American people who would otherwise demand a review of the US – Saudi relationship.

The recurrence of such events will not be prevented by strengthening of security measures and increasing the military grip of the people. The only preventative measures are proper support of this dictatorial and cruel regime and consideration of the people's view towards their presence in the Arabian peninsula.

The CDLR believes that the first step in this direction is the immediate and unconditional release of all political prisoners and then the restoration of the legal rights of the people including the rights of freedom of speech and assembly and the right to choose their accountable leaders.

CDLR, Saudi Arabia, London, Tuesday 14 November 1995.

13F
Warning to American citizens

The US Department of State, in November 1995 warned its citizens in Saudi Arabia of new terror.

Officer of the Spokesman, 25 November 25th 1996: Following the November 13 bombing of the Saudi Arabia National Guard training program building in Riyadh in which Americans were killed and wounded, threats have been made against American citizens in Saudi Arabia. The US Embassy in Saudi Arabia has advised Americans in Saudi Arabia to exercise caution, keep a low profile, reduce travel within Saudi Arabia, and treat mail received from unfamiliar sources with suspicion. Some US military personnel in Saudi Arabia have had their travel and activities within the country restricted. Americans in Saudi Arabia should be especially vigilant at all times and under all circumstances of their personal security and surroundings and should report any suspicious activities to the nearest US embassy or consulate. The government of the United States and the government of Saudi Arabia are cooperating closely to investigate the tragic incident and to assure the security of all Americans in Saudi Arabia.

US Department of State, Office of the Spokesman, 25 November, 1996.

13G
US concern

The office of the spokesman of the US Department of State made a public announcement on 25 February 1997.

The American Embassy in Riyadh and the American Consulates General in Dhahran and Jeddah are issuing the following warden message:

'The Embassy notes with deep concern a recent interview aired on London television on February 20 with well-known terrorist, Usama Bin Ladin, in which he not only threatened again the US military in Saudi Arabia but also called for the expulsion of American civilians. At the same time, the Embassy continues to receive reports indicating possible surveillance or probes of US military and government facilities suggesting that planning for terrorist action against US interests in Saudi Arabia continues unabated. This current period is considered particularly dangerous, since at least one public threat declared that attacks would occur in the Kingdom should certain detained individuals not be released prior to the end of Ramadan.

The upcoming month of Hajj (pilgrimage) also is a period of concern because the large inflow of pilgrims of all nationalities places a heavy burden on the entire Saudi government, but most particularly the security forces.

These statements and reports reinforce the Embassy's view of the need for the private American community in Saudi Arabia to heighten its level of vigilance and alertness. Over the last several months, the Embassy, Consulates General, and the US military elements throughout the country have reviewed their security postures and made improvements wherever possible to lessen their vulnerabilities. We strongly encourage all Americans resident in Saudi Arabia to likewise take appropriate steps to increase their security awareness and lessen their vulnerability.

The private American community should continue to exercise extreme caution in matters concerning personal security. Americans should maintain a low profile, reduce travel within the Kingdom, vary travel routes and times for all required travel, and treat any mail from unfamiliar sources with suspicion. In addition, it is imperative that any suspicious activity, individuals, or vehicles be reported to the Embassy or nearest Consulate. License numbers of vehicles and descriptions of individuals are extremely helpful. Saudi Arabian officials continue to cooperate closely with the Embassy to ensure the safety of all Americans.

The Embassy encourages all American citizens to register their presence in Saudi Arabia with the Consular Section at the Embassy in Riyadh or the Consulates General in Jeddah or Dhahran. To hear a recorded message of the latest information concerning Saudi Arabia, you may call the Embassy in Riyadh at 966-1-488-3800 and press 7.'

Department of State, February 25th 1997, Washington, DC, USA, on the Internet.

Chapter Fourteen

SECURITY AND STABILITY

14A
Armed Forces

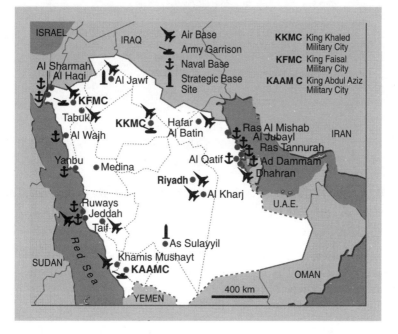

Armed Forces of Saudi Arabia

Army: 70.000 regular troops
- The force has grown from 40.000 before the Gulf War to 60.000 after the war. The current force structure according to 'Janes Intelligence Review' (November 1994) would require around 100.000 to be fully manned, but the authorities 'have faced difficulties in recruiting the necessary personel, especially in technical roles'.

National Guard: 77.000, of which 57.000 active regulars, 20.000 tribal levies
- Consists of tribal volunteers; according to 'Janes Intelligence Review' (November 1994) it serves as 'a counterweight to the regular army and a balance to the Sudairy brothers, who control the throne and the military establishment.' The guard has been used to quell internal unrest in the Eastern Province, but apprantly is building up a conventional army structure.

Air Force: 18.000 regular
- Has developed intensely into the best, most modern Saudi Defence force due to massive investments. Performed surprisingly well during Gulf War along its Western cooperation partners. Only Saudi force believed to be able to cover all national territory.

Navy: 13.500 regular
- Based at Jubail and Jeddah, it serves to secure the Red Coast and the Gulf. Due to lack of manpower, ships and aircraft, it remains highly dependent on foreign navies, i.e. American or British and French forces.

Foreign forces: France 130, US 5.000, UK 200 plus 1 infantry Brigade fom GCC states.

Source of numbers: IISS, London, 1997

14B
Prospects for stability

Dr Gregory Gause III, Assistant Professor at the University of Vermont, outlined in March 1997 the challenges to stability in the Gulf oil states.

The link between oil and political stability in the cases of the Gulf Cooperation Council is at a general level obvious, but specifically more difficult to pin down. These states have built their 'ruling bargains' on oil revenues. Those revenues allow the Gulf governments to:

1. Support large government bureaucracies that provide employment to citizens and monitor their political behaviour.
2. Provide subsidised or free public services to citizens with little or no taxes.
3. Build capital-intensive militaries that link their security to the interests of important world powers.
4. Provide for the rulers' most important constituency, their own families. Without oil revenues, this 'ruling bargain' would collapse.

On the other hand, all these regimes predate the discovery of oil in the Gulf. They have substantial ideological and historical resources – independent of oil – upon which they can draw to tie them to at least some of their citizens. All survived the precipitous downturns in oil prices in the mid-1980s as well as the political and security challenges presented by Nasir [Egyptian president, *Ed.*] in the 1960s, Khomeini in the 1980s and Saddam Hussein in 1990. Their stability is thus not directly threatened by every fluctuation in the oil market or strategic chance in the region.

The challenge that all these governments now face, however, is substantially different from those mentioned in the previous paragraph, which all emanated from outside their borders. With rising populations and no prospect for vastly increased oil prices in the near future, the Gulf governments confront the need to slim down their welfare states without disrupting their 'ruling bargain' with their citizens. How they negotiate this transition, on both the economic and the political fronts, will define their politics for the next generation.

Stability depends not only on governments but also on oppositions. Islamist oppositions now dominate the political field in the Gulf states, but they are very dissimilar from country to country. In some, the 'opposition' basically accepts the political system and campaigns publicly for a greater role in it. In others, opponents seek the downfall of the regime and acts secretly and violently against it. The dynamic between government and opposition and the strength of that opposition is unique in each of the six Gulf monarchies.

Serious challenges to the stability of any of the Gulf regimes are only likely to emerge from a conjunction of crises, any one of which by itself would not be difficult to master. Such crises could include: economic downturn, regional ideological-political-military pressure, an upsurge in domestic opposition activity, splits within the ruling elite.

Dr. F. Gregory Gause III, Assistant Professor, Department of Politics, University of Vermont, Burlington, at an academic Middle East Conference south of London, 17 March 1997.

Chapter Fifteen

INTERNATIONAL RELATIONS

15A
Damage to friendship

Acting Secretary of State, Lawrence Eagleburger, in a letter to senator Patrick J. Moynihan, 30 September, 1992, expressed concern over allegation of torture of US citizens in Saudi Arabia.

Dear Senator Moynihan:

I am writing to say that the Department of State shares your deep concern over the alleged mistreatment of American citizens in Saudi Arabia.

Various members of the Senate Foreign Relations Committee have made it clear that allegations by Americans, including Scott Nelson, that they were tortured or otherwise abused by Saudi officials are causing very serious damage to our bilateral relations. Because this is a matter of such serious import, I can assure you unequivocally that we will convey to King Fahd the Committee's concern over this particular case and others and our own strong view that the Saudi Government should resolve these cases. Because it is so much is the interests of Saudi-American comity, we will explain that the United States Government places a high priority on the swift and equitable resolution of the Nelson case and other similar cases involving American citizens.

Since we are aware of your strong and continuing interest in these matters, we would also undertake to inform you of any progress being made in resolving the Nelson case and other similar cases.

Sincerely,

Lawrence C. Eagleburger, Acting Secretary

Department of State, Washington DC, 30 September 1992.

15B
US arms sales considerations

Richard F. Grimmett, specialist in national defence, listed a number of 'questions related to future major US Arms sales to Saudi Arabia' in a report to Congress in Washington, DC, 1993.

Various questions are likely to arise when future arms sales are proposed for the Saudis, particularly if they include highly advanced combat systems. While the following list of questions is by no means exhaustive, it indicates the range of issues that could be posed regarding such prospective new Saudi arms proposals. The questions fall into four main categories.

Absorptive capacity

Can the Saudis absorb the major new items proposed in light of the numbers of items of new equipment they have already received? Do they have or *can* they develop the skilled manpower necessary to operate and maintain the various Army and Air Force weapons systems proposed? Do the Saudis have enough trained pilots capable of effectively utilizing the fighter aircraft and helicopters they currently have? Will the arrival of additional advanced fighter aircraft and helicopters place a critical strain on their ability to use all the systems they would then have? Do the Saudis have sufficient maintenance, technical, and logistical personnel to support the operation of the advanced weapons systems they would have if the prospective sales are approved? Since the Air Force has been the Saudi service that has received the greatest attention over the years, can the Saudis develop sufficient trained personnel to utilize the tank and land forces equipment they have and may receive in the near future?

Security of Israel

Would the weapons proposed in any new arms sales threaten Israel's security? Could the United States be called upon to fund expensive new weapons for Israel to offset quantitative or qualitative military capabilities the Saudis may gain from further major US weapons sales? By what means would such new weapons transfers for Israel be financed? If the US does not sell a particular weapon system to the Saudis, can they obtain equivalent systems from other arms suppliers? If so, what would be the implications of such alternative Saudi arms acquisitions for Israeli security?

Political vulnerabilities

Is Saudi Arabia vulnerable to a political upheaval such as occurred in Iran, where American military equipment was seized after Khomeini overthrew the Shah's government? Is the present Saudi government stable and secure in its position? Is it vulnerable to attacks from Islamic fundamentalists or poorer and nationalist elements of its society who oppose its cooperation with the United States and its permitting the deployment of non-Arab and non-Muslim forces inside Saudi Arabia?

Security threats

Even if major new weapons systems are sold to Saudi Arabia, could the Saudis protect themselves without significant military forces from outside states such as the United States in the event of an invasion? What are the serious military threats to Saudi security that the prospective sales would address?

Richard F. Grimmett, 'Arms Sales to Saudi Arabia: 1990–1993', a CRS Report for Congress, 17 December 1993.

15C
Valued customer

Arms Sales Monitor, Washington, DC, in March 1996, issued a list of the top US Arms Customers 1991–95.

Saudi Arabia:	$38,423,769,000
United Kingdom:	$19,147,038,000
Japan:	$17,572,474,000
South Korea:	$12,057,626,000
Turkey:	$10,623,317,000
Germany:	$10,317,566,000
Israel:	$9,632,840,000
Taiwan:	$9,603,594,000
Classified sales:	$8,949,468,000
Egypt:	$8,890,882,000

Arms Sales Monitor, Federation of American Scientists, No. 32, Washington, DC, 5 March 1996.

15D
Commitment in the Gulf

Assistant Secretary of State, Robert Pelletreau, explained in the House of Representatives in June 199the 4, US commitment in the Gulf.

Chairman Hamilton: What is our commitment to defend the Gulf countries?

Mr. Pelletreau: We believe that the Gulf is an area of vital strategic interest to the United States; and we have entered into agreements with a number of the Gulf countries that would commit us to consult with them in times of crisis and to act together in deterring threats or in facing threats but always, in our case, we would do so in accordance with our constitution and its requirements.

Chairman Hamilton: Are we committed to defend those countries in the event of attack?

Mr. Palletreau: We are committed to consult with them about how we might assist in defence and in acting together in such contingencies.

Chairman Hamilton: Your use of the word 'vital' is interesting, Mr. Secretary. 'Vital' is a very important word.

Mr. Pelletreau: It was first used by President Carter.

Chairman Hamilton: We have a vital interest in all of the Gulf states. That is what you are saying?

Mr. Pelletreau: In the Gulf area and in access by ourselves and our allies and friends to the petroleum resources of that region and on reasonable commercial terms. The United States is, as you know now, a large importer of oil; and some of our friends are even larger.

Chairman Hamilton: But the word 'vital' is about as strong as you can state the American commitment, is it not?

Mr. Pelletreau: I think the strongest example of the American commitment in a sense is to go to war to correct an aggression. We did so just a short while ago.

Chairman Hamilton: Is the perception of the countries in the Gulf that if they are attacked by Iraq or by Iran or by any other country – that we would come to their defense?

Mr. Pelletreau: I believe that perception does exist.

Chairman Hamilton: Yes.

Mr. Pelletreau: I think there is a very strong feeling that that would be in the interests of the United States. But it is very much in our interests to work with the Gulf countries to build the type of security framework and deterrent framework that would prevent such a treatment from coming to actuality.

Chairman Hamilton: Well, of course, one of the things that impressed us during the Gulf War was that despite all of our efforts to build such a security framework, when push came to shove, and the invasion came, those countries were not able to defend themselves for 24 hours. Is it any better today?

Mr. Pelletreau: I think it is somewhat better than it was then; but it is far from reaching its full capability.

Gulf Security Regime

Chairman Hamilton. There was a lot of talk right after the Gulf War about forming this Gulf security regime. I think even the possibility of using Egyptian troops or other troops from other countries that had a large manpower base. And forming a genuinely cooperative defense arrangement. Has that happened?

Mr. Pelletreau: That has not happened. There is an ongoing consultation mechanism between members of the Gulf Cooperation Council and they have taken a certain number of decisions in this respects; but those decisions have not yet been fully carried out.

Mr. Hamilton: It is a difficult situation, I understand. My sense of it is that those countries believe, as you indicated a moment ago, that if any aggressor did come upon them, that we would come immediately to their aid and, therefore, there is no great pressure or urgency on them to do very much themselves in the way of collective self-defense.

Mr. Pelletreau: We have emphasized to them that collective security really has several dimensions. First of all, there is the dimension of the individual country and its effort and its commitment to be willing and able to defend itself in a crisis.

On second level, there is the ability of the GCC countries to act together and coorperate together in a collective security environment.

Chairman Hamilton: Are you disappointed in their efforts at collective security?

Mr. Pelletreau: Yes.

'Developments in The Middle East', Committee on Foreign Affairs, House of Representatives, 103 Congress, 2nd Session, 14 June 1994.

15E
Export of torture devices

FAS, the Federation of American Scientists Fund, in July 1995, made a
statement on the US export of torture devices.

It would probably surprise most Americans to learn that their government licenses instruments of torture for export to countries around the world.

From September 1991 to December 1993, the Commerce Department approved over 350 export licenses, worth more than $27 million, for torture and police equipment under commodity category OA82C. According to the *US Export Administration Regulations*, this broad-ranging category includes: 'saps, thumbscrews, keg irons, shackles, and handcuffs; specially designed implements of torture; straight jackets, plastic handcuffs, police helmets and shields; parts and accessories.' (see p. 2.)

Another category, OA84C, combines electric shock batons and cattle prods with shotguns and shells. Over 2,000 licenses were granted for these items. We obtained the information under a Freedom of Information Act request for data on gun exports. These licenses represent the government's permission for the export to go forward; they do not indicate actual delivery.

By lumping controversial items (like thumbscrews) together with non-controversial ones (like helmets) into broad general categories, the Commerce Department effectively ensures public oversight. This makes many suspect the worst, especially when these commodities are licensed for export to governments with well-documented records of human rights abuse. For example, the Commerce Department approved $10.5 million of such exports to Saudi Arabia, where government officials 'continued to torture and otherwise abuse detainees, including citizens and foreigners', according to the State Department's latest human rights reports.

FAS, the Federation of American Scientists Fund, Arms Sales Monitor, No. 30, 20
July 1995, Washington, DC.

15F
Saudi Arabia and the UN

Prince Saud al-Faisal, Minister for Foreign Affairs of Saudi Arabia
talked to the 50th session of the General Assembly of the United
Nations, 10 of October 1995, in New York.

In the name of Allah, most compassionate, most merciful.
Mr. President:
As we embark upon the Fiftieth Session of the United Nations General Assembly, it is with pleasure that I convey to Your Excellency, on behalf of

the Kingdom of Saudi Arabia, our sincerest congratulations on the occasion of your election to the presidency of this important Session which marks the Fiftieth Anniversary of this international organization. Your presidency also reflects the appreciation of the international community for the role your country plays in the international arena. We wish you success in the pursuit of your mission and wish to assure you of the desire of our country, as one of the original signatories of the UN Charter, to cooperate with you in achieving the desired objectives of this important Session.

On this occasion, I also take this opportunity to congratulate your predecessor, H.E. Mr. Amara Essy, for his effective conduct of the affairs of the General Assembly during its previous Session.

I also wish to take this opportunity to note the sincere efforts of H.E. the Secretary General of the United Nations, Dr. Boutros Boutros-Ghali, to enhance peace and strengthen security in many parts of our world which continue to experience tension and face challenges.

Mr. President:

Fifty years have elapsed since the historic San Francisco Conference which culminated in the signing of the United Nations Charter and the dawning of a new era in international relations, based on certain principles which may be regarded as the gist of the lessons learned from the experience of two devastating World Wars causing immense suffering to humanity.

In spite of the fact that the principles of the Charter have not always been fully adhered to by all the members of the United Nations, the fact remains that its ability to continue to exist and function throughout half a century, during which great contributions in the humanitarian, cultural, and social fields were made through its various bodies and specialized agencies, makes it deserving of our full appreciation and support.

Although the Agenda for the current Session does not differ greatly in its content from that of previous Sessions, the international community looks at this Session with special interest. It is our hope that the Fiftieth Anniversary of the establishment of this Organization will have a positive impact on strengthening the fundamentals upon which it is based, in a manner that enables us to deal with a number of pressing issues which remain on the Agenda from previous Sessions. We should utilize the festive spirit of this Session to crystallize ideas and adopt decisions that meet the hopes and expectations of our states and peoples.

Mr. President:

The United Nations Organization has, over the past fifty years, experienced multiple crises which have, as a result of their intensity and complexity, threatened international peace and security. We are all keenly aware of the fact that the ability of this international organization to deal with global problems and crises relies very much on the political will of member states to abide by the principles of the Charter.

As the intense rivalry that prevailed during the Cold War era afflicted this organization with impotence in dealing with issues of war and peace, the changes we have recently witnessed have reinforced our hope in asserting the basic role of this organization, namely the preservation of international peace and security. Regardless of whether the present situation constitutes a new international order or not, what is certain is that we are facing new realities and experiencing fundamental changes in the conduct of international relations. The international changes which have occurred over the past years were so dramatic as to make us encounter a new international reality with a host of new challenges. They also offered a new opportunity to reinforce the principles enshrined in the Charter for the benefit of strengthening international legitimacy, including justice and equality among nations, the rejection of the use of force in the settlement of conflicts, as well as the preservation of the dignity of man, and providing security and prosperity for all mankind.

Mr. President:

The brutal Iraqi aggression against the State of Kuwait in 1990 constituted, by all accounts, a clear challenge to all the principles upon which the UN Charter is based, and signaled a flagrant violation of the dynamics of the prevailing system. The immediate and courageous decision of the international community to confront this aggression was a unique example, which must be emulated every time the international community faces a similar aggression. The principled position of the international community was manifested in a series of historic resolutions passed by the Security Council, which called for the reversal of the Iraqi aggression, and the restoration of legitimacy and sovereignty to the State of Kuwait along with measures to prevent a recurrence of that tragedy. We have always considered these resolutions as a cohesive legal structure in which the comprehensive and total implementation of the contents of all the resolutions pertaining to that brutal aggression represents a basic requirement before entertaining the possibility of easing or lifting the sanctions imposed by the Security Council.

We are fully aware of the difficulties and suffering experienced by the fraternal Iraqi people as a result of the continuation of the sanctions, and have repeatedly expressed our sympathies for the Iraqi people in this regard. Nonetheless, everyone is aware that the responsibility for this suffering lies solely with the Iraqi regime, which continues in its policies of maneuvers and deceptions in connection with UN Security Council Resolutions, particularly its refusal to accept Resolutions 706, 712 and 986 dealing with the humanitarian needs of the Iraqi people.

Our experience with the Iraqi regime and its aggressive intentions, as the reports by Mr. Rolf Ekeus, the Chairman of the UN Special Commission for the Elimination of Iraq's Weapons of Mass Destruction (UNSCOM) so clearly indicate. Moreover, the recent revelations by one of the pillars of the Iraqi regime who defected to Jordan were so alarming as to justify our insistence on the need to unmask the nature of the intentions of the Iraqi regime as a basic requirement prior to any review of these sanctions. We greatly appreciate the efforts of Mr. Ekeus and his esteemed team in their efforts to achieve this goal, yet we have noticed that the serious information provided by the Iraqi defector vastly exceeds the information gathered by UNSCOM during five years of continuous work. It is, therefore, incumbent upon us to start searching for ways and means to enhance the scope and performance of this commission so as to enable it to fulfil its important task in the various aspects of inspection, verification, and observation.

We look forward to the return of Iraq to the fold of the international community, with its noble and industrious people, where it can play a constructive role. The suffering of the Iraqi people will remain a source of concern for us, and we remain committed to the preservation of the unity, sovereignty and territorial integrity of Iraq.

Mr. President:

Distinguished Delegates:

We continue to follow, with keen interest, the developments in the Middle East peace process in both the bilateral and multilateral tracks. The Kingdom of Saudi Arabia has supported this process since its inception at the Madrid Peace Conference in 1991, and has actively worked to advance the bilateral talks between the Arab parties and Israel. It has also participated, through its delegations, in the various working groups stemming from the multilateral talks.

This interest, coupled with the effective participation of the Kingdom of Saudi Arabia, reflects the genuine desire of the Arab parties in the achievement of a just and comprehensive peace in the region. We have repeatedly emphasized that the multilateral talks are part and parcel of the peace negotiations which began in Madrid, and that they are complementary to the bilateral talks, and not a substitute thereto. It was on the basis of this understanding that we participated in the working groups. We believe that any progress in the multilateral talks is necessarily linked to progress in the bilateral talks between the parties most directly concerned.

The signing of the Declaration of Principles between the Palestine Liberation Organization and the Israeli Government in Washington in September of 1993, raised hopeful expectations, and signaled the first step toward the achievement of a just and permanent settlement of the question of Palestine. However, the Palestinian-Israeli agreement faced a number of obstacles as a result of Israeli intransigence, which curtailed the ability of the Palestinian National Authority to exercise its responsibilities and expand its authority throughout the West Bank, in accordance with the principles of the agreement.

The continued construction of settlements by Israel in the Occupied Territories, and its detention of large numbers of Palestinians, as well as its imposition of various restrictions on the Palestinian people, are among the practices that violate the text and spirit of the agreement. It is incumbent upon the two co-sponsors of the peace process to compel the Israeli Government to abide by its commitments by refraining from placing obstacles in the course of the negotiations and during the actual implementation of the second phase of the Declaration of Principles, which was signed recently in Washington. This should lead to the redeployment of Israeli occupation forces, prepare for the first Palestinian elections, and transfer more authority to the Palestinians. It is clear that further progress in the peace process will depend on fulfilling the legitimate rights of the Palestinian people. Conversely, any disregard of these rights will result in blocking the peace efforts.

With regard to the Agreements reached between Jordan and Israel, my country has already expressed its welcome of the progress realized on this track. However, we fail to see any noticeable progress on the Syrian and Lebanese tracks. The issue of the occupied Syrian Golan Heights is quite clear, and is related to the principle of the sanctity of international borders. On its part, Syria has demonstrated a willingness to meet the objective requirements for peace. It has raised the level of its representation in the bilateral talks and embarked upon a positive and serious effort to reach a settlement. Its constructive efforts, however, have not been matched by the Israeli side. With regard to the Lebanese-Israeli track, it is governed by UN Security Council Resolution 425, which calls for the immediate and unconditional Israeli withdrawal from occupied Lebanese territory.

Mr. President:

The question of Jerusalem – al-Quds al-Shareef – is at the heart of the Arab-Israeli conflict, and is of utmost concern for the Arab and Muslim world. The manner in which this issue is handled could determine the future of the peace process. The decision to delay negotiations on Jerusalem until the final stage of the peace talks should not be taken as indicative of the lessening of its importance, but rather as to give the peace process a chance to create the proper environment for the required good-will that would help in the successful resolution of this highly sensitive issue.

We regret that the Israeli authorities continue to take steps whose purpose is to change the demographic character and create new realities in the status of Jerusalem, with the intention of prejudicing the negotiations on the final status of the city. Our position remains that any settlement of this issue must take into account the resolutions of international legality, and in particular UN Security Council Resolution 242 which calls for Israeli withdrawal from the territories occupied in 1967, and UN Security Council Resolution 252 regarding Jerusalem.

Any permanent and comprehensive settlement must also address the issue of the return of Palestinian refugees, and the release of Palestinian prisoners, as well as the issue of settlements created by Israel in the Occupied Territories, in violation of the letter and spirit of the Declaration of Principles and in breach of international law and the Geneva Conventions.

Mr. President:

The Government of The Custodian of The Two Holy Mosques has given great attention to efforts to remove the danger of weapons of mass destruction from the Middle East. It has worked to make this sensitive region of the world free of all weapons of mass destruction, whether nuclear, chemical or biological. It is on this basis that the Kingdom of Saudi Arabia participated in the United Nations conference on the future of the Nuclear Non-Proliferation Treaty earlier this year in New York.

This position conforms with our announced support for the efforts to eliminate weapons of mass destruction from the Middle East. We believe in the necessity of tightening the safeguards system of the International Atomic Energy Agency. We view as necessary the establishment of controls and measures that will help in achieving progress in all aspects of this issue in accordance with General Assembly Resolution No. 1 of 1946, which addresses, inter alia, the issue of eliminating weapons of mass destruction.

Mr. President:

The occupation by the Islamic Republic of Iran of the three United Arab Emirates islands (Abu Musa, the Greater Tunbs and Lesser Tunbs) is a source of great concern not only to the United Arab Emirates, but also to the states of the Gulf Cooperation Council as a whole, who desire to have the best possible relations with their neighbor, Iran. We have repeatedly urged the Islamic Republic of Iran to respond to the call of the United Arab Emirates to settle this problem peacefully through serious bilateral negotiations. However, we have not yet seen any response to these calls, which leaves no choice but to refer this matter to the International Court of Justice.

Mr. President:

The firm stand of the international community during the Iraqi invasion of Kuwait is the kind of example that should be evoked to verify the credibility of our organization. By contrast, the equivocation and weakness that characterized the international community's response to the Serbian aggression against the Republic of Bosnia and Herzegovina is a most negative example of how things could worsen and deteriorate as a result of the unchecked aggression waged by the Serb forces and their supporters in Serbia and Montenegro against the unarmed Bosnian people.

Hopefully, this war of genocide and ethnic cleansing seems to have finally made the international community seize the opportunity to put an end to this human tragedy, by demonstrating our ability to take strong and resolute positions in the face of Serb aggression.

The situation created by NATO air strikes against military sites of the Bosnian Serbs, located near Sarajevo, has provided a real opportunity for extracting this war-torn nation from its tragic situation, and placed it on the road to a meaningful settlement. Any just and durable settlement of this conflict must ensure the rights of the Republic of Bosnia and Herzegovina to sovereignty, independence and unity within its recognized international borders. It is also of the utmost importance to prosecute war criminals and subject them to trials for their war crimes and crimes against humanity.

We would like to express our appreciation for the efforts of President Clinton to reach a just settlement between the conflicting parties. We also appreciate the efforts made by H.E. President Jacques Chirac of France in promoting cooperation and coordination between the International Contact Group and the Islamic Contact Group. We hope that any settlement pertaining to the status of minorities in Bosnia and Herzegovina also comprises the situation of the Albanian minority in Kosovo.

Mr. President:

Somalia continues to experience instability and political chaos complemented by acts of terrorism and bloodshed. In spite of all the efforts expended to extract this nation from its dilemma, instability and lack of security remain a feature of this troubled land. The Kingdom of Saudi Arabia has attempted many times to contain the conflict in Somalia and to bring about national reconciliation between the various factions. It has extended a helping hand and provided humanitarian assistance and relief to the Somali people, and urged all factions to allow reason to prevail and place the interests of the Somali people above all else and work toward national reconciliation.

It is in this spirit that we appeal to the Mujaheddin in Afghanistan, who have not been able to reap the fruits of their victory against foreign occupation as a result of the conflicts between their various factions. Since the outbreak of this conflict, the Kingdom of Saudi Arabia has endeavored, under the guidance of The Custodian of The Two Holy Mosques, King Fahd bin Abdul Aziz, to put an end to this fratricide. These efforts were crowned with the Makkah Agreement, signed in 1993. We continue to urge all factions of the Afghani Mujaheddin to immediately put an end to the fighting by complying with the Makkah Agreement in letter and spirit, in order to move in the direction of reconstruction and development to enable their nation to resume its proper place in the international community.

Among the conflicts that continue to rage in Asia is the Pakistani-Indian dispute over Jamu and Kashmir. We believe that the appropriate solution to this conflict lies in implementing the resolutions of the United Nations and in following the course of negotiation and dialogue, which could lead to an end to this long-standing dispute.

We also regret the continuation of another conflict, namely, Nagorno-Karabakh. The problem of Nagorno-Karabakh, which emerged as a consequence of the Armenian occupation of part of the territory of Azerbaijan, is still unresolved, in spite of all the efforts expended thus far. We see in this occupation a departure from the principle of peaceful resolution of conflicts, and it is therefore incumbent upon Armenia to withdraw its forces from Azerbaijani territory, and transfer this issue to the negotiating table for the purpose of arriving at a peaceful settlement, which assures the legitimate rights of the Azerbaijani people.

Mr. President:

This brief overview of some of the problems which continue to exist in the international arena, whose resolution depends on the commitment of the members of this organization to the principles of the Charter, is not intended to diminish the important role this organization has played in the settlement of other problems; thus enhancing our hope for a better future for the United Nations.

The recent resolution of long-standing problems in Cambodia, the Middle East, and Northern Ireland, as well as the historic changes in South Africa, will contribute to affirm the international trend, which the Secretary General of the UN was keen to emphasize in his two reports, 'An Agenda for Peace' and 'An Agenda for Development'. These two reports focused attention on a new approach for the United Nations, based on the principles of the UN Charter and international legality.

We are confident that the ideas contained in these reports render important contributions to the General Assembly's efforts to strengthen the role and effectiveness of the United Nations. In this connection, the primary role of the Security Council, as the body most directly concerned with the maintenance of international peace and security, has to be asserted. Any efforts aiming at increasing the ability of the Security Council to act in accordance with the UN Charter must have as its goal the improvement of the effectiveness of the Council, and the avoidance of any measures that could lead to the erosion of its prescribed role.

Mr. President:

A cursory review of world economic problems, and the role played by the United Nations in international economic cooperation, would demonstrate that the success of our organization in dealing with economic issues, and promoting international development, has also been tied to the commitment of member states to the UN Charter.

Although the international community has so far managed, through serious negotiations, to iron out many of the difficult issues, and thus scored unprecedented breakthroughs in very sensitive areas, as in the establishment of the World Trade Organization, we are still concerned about the continuing phenomenon of trade protectionism. The barriers emanating from this policy pose serious challenges to our belief in the importance of allowing market forces to play their natural role in economic affairs. The way to rectify this situation is through serious international efforts to remove these barriers, especially restrictions under the guise of protecting the environment. These restrictions undermine the development efforts of the developing countries whose, process of development is the cornerstone for peace and stability.

The development plan presented by the Secretary General is greatly appreciated and we should all strive to transform it into a real tool for promoting economic and social development on the global level. We believe that the developed countries can play an important role in this area, which will be beneficial to all countries, rich and poor.

Mr. President:

As we prepare to celebrate the Fiftieth Anniversary of the signing of the UN Charter, the Kingdom of Saudi Arabia, a founding member of this international organization, confirms its commitment and continues its efforts to enhance the role of the United Nations and strengthen its capability to preserve international peace and security, and to promote international cooperation within the framework of international legality.

We hope, with all sincerity, that all other member states will share this desire when dealing with the issues before this historic Session, so as to arrive at a successful conclusion that meets the aspirations of our countries and peoples for peace and security. To quote a verse from the Holy Qur'an: 'Allah will not change the situation of a people until they change what is in their souls.'

May peace and the blessing of Allah be bestowed upon you.

Embassy of Saudi Arabia, New York, 10 October 1995, via the Internet.

15G
Consumer report

Profile of a leading customer, by the Arms Sales Monitoring Project, 1996.

Saudi Arabia is the world's top buyer of US arms. Since 1985, the United States has approved foreign military sales to Saudi Arabia totaling some $38,649,307,000. An additional $730 million commercially sold military equipment and services was delivered between FY1985 and FY1990 and the State Department approved commercial export license for another $9,463,573,00 during FY1991-FY1995. Some systems on order, such as M-1A2 Abrams tanks and M-2A2 Bradley armored vehicle, F-15E Strike Eagle attack aircraft and Patriot surface-to-air missile, have only been delivered to US forces in recent years.

Why is Saudi Arabia spending so much on the Military? The three large Gulf states – Iran, Iraq and Saudi Arabia – seem to think that arms will bring security and regional strength. Saudi Arabia, Iraq, Iran spent $55.6 billion, $22.7 billion and $13.9 billion respectively on weapons between 1986 and 1993; nearly forty percent of all arms deliveries to the Third World during this time (Richard F. Grimmett, Congressional Research Service, 'Conventional Arms Transfers to the Third World, 1986–1993' *CRS Report for Congress* [94- 612F], 29 July 1994). Yet recent history demonstrates that arms purchases do not construct 'security'.

Arms Purchases have not brought Security

Saudi Arabia military expenditures totaled some $240 billion during the period 1983–1993, according to US, Arms control and Disarmament Agency estimates (*World Military Expenditures and Arms Transfers,* various years). But big budget deficits brought on by low oil prices and high spending (including at least $60 billion for the Gulf War) have forced the Saudis to slow all government spending (*Washington Post,* 13 August 1994, p.A14). A top Saudi financial advisor has said that he doesn't think the United States 'knows what it's doing by shoving weapons down the Saudis' throats', since the arms purchases increase the Saudis' debt and dependence on Americans (*New York Times,* 23 August 1994, p.A6).

Low oil prices and large budget deficits have forced the Kingdom to revise payments of $25–30 billion in American arms. The 1994 budget has been cut 20 percent (*Washington Post,* 13 August 1994, p.A14). A member of the Saudi Chamber of Commerce and Industry complains that it is the 'defense bill that is killing us'. (*Washington Post,* 13 August 1994, p.A14). Saudi financial reserves, valued at $140 billion ten years ago, may be as low as $30 billion, and one Saudi official has said liquid reserves may be as low as $7 billion. (*New York Times,* 22 August 1993; *Washington Post,* 13 August 1994, p.A14).

A January 1994 deal between the United States and Saudi Arabia extends payment and delivery schedules for outstanding orders; less important orders may be postponed. The Saudis also hope to use US-financed Export-Import Bank loans to purchase 50 US commercial aircraft for about $6.2 billion. Saudi financial problems will grow when the embargo on Iraqi oil is lifted.

Despite high military spending, Saudi Arabia remains unable to defend itself. US naval intelligence has said that, regardless of 'long-term plans to expand their military with the purchase of equipment. . ., it is doubtful that the Saudis would have to be able to counter threats from Iran and Iraq completely. The United States, or a coalition, would have to be called upon again to provide protection or to repel aggression.' A prominent Saudi official has said the Gulf War demonstrated that 'no matter how built-up we become, we can't replace the US . . . The US is our protector.'

The Saudi inclination to buy security may have included attempts to acquire nuclear weapons, according to a Saudi defector. Mohammad Khilewi, first secretary at the Saudi mission to the United Nations until July 1994, said that the Saudis have sought a bomb since 1975. According to Khilewi, the Saudis sought nuclear reactors from China, supported Pakistan's nuclear program, and contributed $5 billion to Iraq's nuclear weapons program between 1985 and 1990. If true, these actions would violate Saudi commitments under the Nuclear Nonproliferation Treaty, which Saudi Arabia signed in 1988 to ease concern over their purchase of Chinese ballistic missiles.

Relations with smaller neighbors have also been difficult on occasion, even with the fellow monarchies of the Gulf Coorperation council (GCC). Qataris and Saudis clashed over a disputed border post in September 1992, leaving two dead. Qatar boycotted several GCC meetings after the skirmish. Qatar and Saudi Arabia have also been at odds over the war in Yemen.

In Yemen, victorious northern forces have accused the Saudis of sending arms, money and mercenaries to breakaway southern forces. Saudi Arabia tried, and failed, to conquer Yemen during its consolidation of the Kingdom in the 1930s. James Wyllie of the University of Aberdeen suggested in 1992 that 'Yemeni democracy presents a sharp and embarrassing contrast to Saudi Arabia's deep-seated political conservatism (*Jane's Intelligence Review*, June 1992, p. 268) Yemen's 1993 elections, which women participated in, were the first ever on the Arabian peninsula. Wyllie reaffirms this opinion in a later article, and adds that Yemen's military, weaker in aircraft but stronger in armored vehicles, also 'had to be accorded some respect'. After unification, seven million (mostly) Sunni-Muslim Saudis faces twelve million (mostly) Shia Yemenis (*Janes Intelligence Review*, August 1994, p. 366).

Saudi Arabia expelled between 500.000 and 800.000 Yemenis in 1990 and 1991 to punish Yemen for its opposition to non-Arabs on the Arabian peninsula. Before the war, it is estimated that Yemeni workers in Saudi Arabia sent home $1.3 billion in remittances annually (*Jane's Intelligence Review*, August 1994, p. 370).

Although Saudi Arabia is vocal in its support for the Palestinians, the Saudis cut off aid and oil supplies to Jordan because of King Hussein's stance during the 1991 Gulf War. Jordan is home to some two million Palestinians. This came at a time when oil supplies from Iraq were drying up; Iran provided more than 80 percent of Jordan's oil before August 1990. King Hussein's great-grandfather, Sherif Hussein, was chased out of Arabia's holy sites by the Saud family seventy years ago.

International Security

Since the Kingdom's founding in 1932, the Saudis have maintained their rule by embracing allies and punishing rivals, both foreign and domestic. The 'invasion' of Saudi Arabia by hundreds of thousands of Western soldiers during Operation Desert Storm caused a backlash among Saudi conservatives, and some liberals, who want to preserve Arabian culture and fear domination by the West. Some secular Saudis dislike the Saud family's domination of the state and the corruption it breeds. More radical Muslims assail the royal family for allying itself with the infidel United States. For decades, the Saudis avoided publicly associating themselves too closely with the United States unless absolutely necessary.

In November 1995, a bomb was detonated at the headquarters of the US Army office that manages the training and equipping of the Saudi Arabian National Guard. Eight people, including five Americans, were killed. Two little-known Islamic groups claimed responsibility for the bombings (*Jane's Defence Weekly*, 25 November 1995, p. 25).

Liberal Saudis criticize the royal family's domination of the state and despise the lack of freedom in the country. In 1992, a consultative council (majlis al shura) of sixty business, academic and religious leaders was established, as were similar provincial councils. The council advises the King, but has no real political power. New written laws will supplement the Shari'a, or religious law, Saudi Arabia's religious legal code since the Kingdom's founding. The current legal system is based on the Koran, interpreted by judges who are appointed by the King.

Political participation will come, apparently, on the royal family's terms. The committee for the Defense of Legitimate Rights, a Saudi opposition group, was banned in May 1993, ten days after it was formed, on the grounds that it violated the Shari'a. When some fifty Saudi women defied tradition in 1990 by dismissing their chauffeurs and driving their own cars, Saudi authorities, within week, reiterated the ban on female drivers.

The 1993 State Department human rights report says that the 'lives of women in Saudia Arabia are rigidly circumscribed; they have 'few political and social rights and are not equal members of society'. Some Islamists advocate the 'strict disciplining' of women, including some degree of physical force. The report also says of Saudi Arabia:

> Human rights continued to be pervasively abused [in Saudi Arabia]. Principal human rights problems include torture and other abuses of prisoners and incommunicado detention; prohibitions or severe restrictions on the freedoms of speech and press, peaceful, assembly and association, and religion; the denial of the right of citizens to charge their government; and systematic discrimination against women and ethnic and religious minorities and suppression of worker's rights.

The 'Government's failure to punish human rights abusers is a salient factor in the climate of impunity that prevails' according to the report. Section 502B of the foreign Assistance Act requires that 'no security assistance may be provided to any country the government of which engages in a consistent pattern of gross violations of internationally recognized human rights'.

'This is not a popular regime,' says William Quandt of the Brookings Institution. 'It's a huge patronage system that has spread the wealth around. If you take that away, you could contribute to a political crisis,' warns Quandt (*New York Times*, 23 August 1993). A major fear of U.S. officials must be the possibility that Saudi Arabia could become 'another Iran', 'falling to anti-American forces as did the Shah's Iran in 1979'. Patrick L. Clawson, a senior fellow at the National Defense University, told the *New York Times* that Saudis can 'slide for the next two or three years, but their underlying structural problems are enormous. . . Combine that with the fact that your ally is an absolutist monarchy that has moved very slowly to democratization of a society in which political opposition is expressed in a way that can easily turn into anti-Westernism, you really have to worry.' (*New York Times*, 22 August 1993).

Adherence to US Laws/Non Proliferation Policies

The Saudis have also been accused of retransferring US military equipment or technology without US approval in violation of obligations under the Arms Export Control Act. The Saudis allegedly gave Iraq 1.500 US 2,000-pound bombs during the Iran–Iraq War. (*Los Angeles Times*, 14 September 1992, p. 8) 'Inadvertent' transfers of bombs and vehicles to Syria and Bangladesh during the Gulf War have also been reported (*Arms Control Today*, May 1992, p. 20). Another 'inadvertent' transfer almost took place when an asylum-seeking Saudi F-15 pilot flew his aircraft to Sudan in November 1990. The plane was returned. (*Washington Post*, 15 November 1990, p.A30.)

Mr. Khilewi, who accused the Saudis of trying to buy access to a nuclear weapon, also says Saudi Arabia has supported terrorism, and has spied on Jewish-American groups and on US military installations. A couple weeks after Khilewi defected, Ahmad Zahrani, deputy consul at the Saudi consulate in Houston, said he would seek asylum in Britain. Zahrani said in London: 'I joined my voice to the increasing number of the moderate academics from our great nation who are no longer able to tolerate the breaches of basic human rights including the right to freedom of expression and political association by the present regime. . . (*Washington Times*, 1 July 1994, p.A19).

Prince Bandar Bin Sultan, Saudi Ambassador to the United States and a member of the royal family, dismissed such criticism, saying that the 'problem, as the infamous Rodney King case in California dramatizes, is in handling the occasional inevitable exceptions to responsible law enforcement'. Bandar assures Americans in a Washington Post editorial entitled 'Modernize, But Not Westernize,' that 'Saudi Arabia is very stable as it moves steadily ahead.'

> FAS (Federation of American Scientists), Arms Monitoring Project, Consumer Report: Profiles of America's leading Customers, on the Internet, 1996.

15H
The UK: A warm relationship

The Foreign Secretary of the United Kingdom, Malcolm Rifkind, gave an interview to the BBC World Service en route to Jedda on 1 July 1996.

Asked if the Al-Masari episode was now over, Mr Rifkind said that 'Mr Masari continues to make some very disagreeable statements, statements that cause very genuine concern, which were well reported last week. But I don't think they have any significance with regard to the United Kingdom's relations with Saudi Arabia. I believe that Britain and Saudi Arabia have an exceptionally good, close and constructive relationship and it is going from strength to strength.' The Government had 'no time for the remarks that he makes. I believe some of the recent comments have been both distasteful and appear to have been equivocal, to say the least, about the atrocity in Dhahran last week. So I believe his remarks are pretty appalling and in that sense we believe that he is a very negative force.' Clearly, they would pay 'a great deal of attention to what he says. If he breaches the laws of the United Kingdom then, as would happen with anyone who breaks the law, action would be taken against him.' However, he believed that Mr Al-Masari appeared 'to have become less significant in recent weeks. He is being increasingly seen in Britain, as well as elsewhere, as a rather extreme figure with little authority'.

Asked why he was visiting Saudi Arabia, Mr Rifkind said that Britain had ' for many years [had] a very good, warm and constructive relationship because Saudi Arabia is a force for stability in the Middle East. The Saudi Arabian and United Kingdom governments have co-operated very closely on not only defence issues, in the Gulf war for example, but also on other matters since then.'

The interviewer said that some major defence and construction companies were complaining that they had lost vital contracts because of Mr Al-Masari. Mr Rifkind said that there was no evidence for this. 'What one can see is what has happened to overall British exports to Saudi Arabia actually went up by eight or nine per cent. In the first three months of this year they went up by further 20 per cent. And the bulk of these exports are not even military matters or matters related to the armed forces, they are normal exports of civilian goods. So at a time when our exports are increasing substantially, I don't think there is any evidence to point to any discrimination against British companies.'

He went on to say that he would like to see 'and I am sure our Saudi friends would like to see . . . a continuing warm relationship whereby we co-operate closely on matters where there is a common interest. We work along with other responsible governments for progress in the Middle East on the peace process, where we work very closely with governments throughout the world in combating the international scourge of terrorism. Saudi Arabia has experienced some savage, vicious, terrorism; so has the United Kingdom. We must have the maximum co-operation because terrorism is international.'

He would be discussing 'ways in which the international community can act more closely and more effectively to deal with terrorism. One of the proposals that we have put to a number of countries, which is being quite well received, is that there should be a new instrument added to the 1951 Convention of Refugees whereby anyone who is aiding and abetting terrorism should not be entitled to claim the normal right of asylum as a refugee under that convention. The convention was never designed to be a help to terrorists in evading their proper responsibilities. This is a proposal which is being seriously looked at by the international community.' This would deal 'with people who are inciting terrorism and are either funding terrorism or actively supporting it in a way that clearly would be incompatible with the normal refugee status'.

Survey of Current Affairs, London, July 1996.

15I
The EU and the GCC

The EU Commission in 1995 issued a brief of EU (EC) relations with the countries of the Gulf Cooperation Council.

1. Introduction

Historically, soon after the formation in 1981 of the Gulf Cooperation Council by the original and present 6 member countries (Saudi Arabia, Kuwait, Bahrain, Qatar, United Arab Emirates and Oman), the GCC took the initiative to establish a close relationship and free trade agreement with the European Community. The Community's response was positive, recognising the vital importance of these countries for the supply of oil to its economy and, more widely, of their role as energy suppliers to the international economy. The Community also recognised the significance of a regional grouping of these countries for promoting stability in the strategically vital Gulf area.

The institutional framework for EC–GCC relations was provided in 1988, when the European Community and member countries of the GCC concluded a Cooperation Agreement. The EC–GCC Cooperation Agreement was the first of a new generation of EC international agreements which included provisions for complementing and strengthening relations by providing for the negotiation of a free trade agreement. With the conclusion of the Cooperation Agreement the two sides recognised the objective importance of their relations based on economic and energy interdependence.

Confirming the EC's commitment to developing free trade relations with the GCC, the Commission obtained from the Council a first negotiating directive in 1990. The Gulf War in 1990/91 was a traumatic experience for the GCC countries. It prompted immediate European solidarity and participation in the international alliance which enabled the liberation of Kuwait. Following the Gulf War, at the request of the GCC countries, the European Community modified its first negotiating directive to provide more balance and a reduced transitional period. The second negotiating directive included comprehensive provisions on tariff dismantling and transitional measures to take account of particularly sensitive sectors in the EU, and of infant industries in the GCC.

However, since the adoption of the second negotiating directive, the negotiations for a free trade agreement have not progressed at all. The GCC side have not offered a comprehensive response to the EC proposals. In April 1993, they insisted instead that the free trade negotiations should concentrate first on priority sectors and put forward proposals for the energy sector, the effect of which would have limited the EC ability to introduce a carbon energy tax, a proposal which the GCC side considers would harm their energy interests.

In parallel to the free trade negotiations, concrete results deriving from the Cooperation Agreement have been slow and limited to:

- Cooperation in the field of customs and from this year in the field of standards.
- Energy cooperation with the holding of a number of EC–GCC Energy Working Group meetings, an EU–GCC Energy Symposium in Muscat in April 1994, and the EU–GCC Ad-Hoc Group's Joint Report on Interrelated issues of Energy and the Environment.
- EC–GCC Industrial Conferences (Granada, 1990; Doha, 1992, and in Muscat from 16–18 October 1995).

- Environment cooperation with the setting up of a marine and wildlife sanctuary in Jubail (Saudi Arabia).

This year's scheduled Joint Council-Ministerial Meeting was postponed and a first-ever EU–GCC Troika Ministerial meeting was held in Granada on 20 July 1995 to assess relations between the two groups. In agreeing to hold this meeting, the two sides recognised, in effect, that special attention was required if new political impetus and momentum were to be given to their relationship.

2. The importance of EU–GCC relations

The original premises of EU–GCC cooperation, namely a high degree of economic and energy inter-dependence, have not changed.

2.1. The importance of the GCC for the EU

Despite a small total population of just over 21 million inhabitants, the GCC is the 5th largest market for EC exports, larger than China and the CIS and the only one of the 5 with which the EC has, consistently, an export surplus. Total EC–GCC bilateral trade reached over 30 billion ECU in 1994. EC exports amounted to 19.3 billion ECU and the EC trade surplus was 7.9 billion ECU. It is important to recognise, however, that since crude oil represents 70% of EC imports from the GCC, the level of the EC trade surplus is to a large degree a reflection of low oil prices. The weakness of the US dollar compared to EC currencies is another factor influencing the size of the EC trade surplus.

Oil continues to be the most important component of EC energy consumption: 45%. In 1994 the GCC countries were the single most important source of EC oil supplies, accounting for 23.7% of total imports. EC external energy dependence is estimated to increase from 50 to 60% by 2010. By then, oil and gas will be the most important components of energy consumption. GCC countries have the largest oil reserves in the world, 47%, and 14.5% of world natural gas reserves. EC energy dependence on the GCC in the medium term is therefore bound to increase.

2.2 The importance of the EU for GCC countries

Although Asia is the single most important destination for GCC oil exports, the EC is the second most important market, accounting for some 15% of GCC oil exports in 1992. Whereas some minor spot LNG sales to some Member States took place recently, the GCC does not yet supply natural gas to the EC on a contractual long-term basis, but as EC demand for gas increases, GCC gas production plans will inevitably lead to significant GCC gas exports to the EC in the future. Overall, and leaving aside the question of future EU enlargement, the importance of the EC energy market for the GCC should increase in relation to increasing EC external energy dependence.

In terms of diversification of GCC exports, the EC absorbs a major share of GCC exports of refined petroleum products, petrochemical products and aluminium.

EU Member States are also the second most important foreign investor in the GCC, ahead of Japan and second only to the US. In contrast to US investment, which is concentrated in one sector, petrochemicals, EU Member States investment is widely spread through industrial sectors. For example, in Saudi Arabia the EU Member States are the principal foreign investor in 6 out of 7 industrial sectors and second in the one sector, petrochemicals, in which the United States leads. On the other hand, the EU Member States are the second destination of GCC outward investment. While there is considerable direct GCC foreign investment in the Member States, in particular in refining and distributing automotive fuels, the bulk of GCC investments in the EU Member States are portfolio investments in deposits, bonds and equities.

3. EU–GCC Inter-Dependence and the need for a stronger relationship

As the above paragraphs indicate, the key word in describing EU–GCC energy, trade and investment relations is inter-dependence. An annex provides full statistical details. But close relations cannot be based simply on a strong trade and investment foundation, although this is a vital pre-requisite. To ensure progress towards a dynamic, mutually beneficial and strategically important relationship, it is necessary that EU–GCC relations should be based on shared political and security interests, a framework for their strong trade, energy and economic interests, good cultural relations and cooperation between civil societies. The Granada Troika Ministerial meeting of 20 July 1995 addressed all three areas and made the following recommendations:

- to strengthen the EU–GCC political dialogue;
- to increase economic cooperation and propose solutions for unblocking the ongoing free trade negotiations;
- to develop instruments of cooperation which will promote increased reciprocal knowledge and understanding, especially in the cultural and scientific fields.

These recommendations were endorsed by EU and GCC Foreign Ministers meeting in New York on 29 September 1995. The two sides are now committed to decide on the implementation of these recommendations on the occasion of the 6th EU–GCC Joint Council-Ministerial Meeting which it has been agreed to hold under Italian Presidency on 22 and 23 April 1996 in Luxembourg.

It is the purpose of this Communication to review these recommendations and prepare for their successful implementation.

4. *Strengthening the EU–GCC political dialogue*

Events in the political and security spheres in recent years ought, if anything, to have strengthened the objective, economic basis for a stronger EU–GCC relationship. During the Iran-Iraq war EU countries helped ensure, by their naval presence, that the Gulf, through which 45% of world oil supplies pass, remained secure for shipping oil to export markets. More dramatically, in 1990–91, the important role of EU countries in the US-led alliance to liberate Kuwait from Iraqi invasion demonstrated Europe's commitment to GCC security and independence. Joint EU–GCC support for the Middle East Peace Process, and a common desire to see a balanced approach to resolving the most dangerous and recurrent cause of conflict in a region directly bordering on GCC territory, ought also to have confirmed the underlying convergence of EU–GCC political and security interests.

One of the shortcomings of the EU–GCC relationship, however, has been the absence of a forum, apart from annual, formal ministerial meetings, where these common interests could be acknowledged, discussed and effectively developed. On the EU side there is, correspondingly, the absence of an appropriate place for relations with the GCC in the Common Foreign and Security Policy (CFSP). Lack of active affirmation at an EU level of interest in GCC security has led to the impression in the GCC that the United States plays an almost exclusive role in the political and security spheres. This impression is erroneous. Experience has amply demonstrated, that no international alliance in support of the GCC would be complete or effective without the backing of EU countries. Lack of active affirmation of EU interest in GCC security has also helped companies in the United States to benefit economically from the perceived US position as sole champion of GCC security, not only with regard to military sales but also in key sectors such as civil aviation and telecommunications.

The establishment of a regular, senior-official level, reinforced 'political dialogue', as recommended by the EU–GCC Ministerial Troika in Granada on 20 July 1995, should therefore provide an opportunity for both sides to better appreciate the extent of their shared political and security interests. The EU should in this context consider GCC security concerns. Events of the past decade have identified the GCC–Iran–Iraq triangular relationship as one of the key issues for international security. The EU should therefore use the machinery of CFSP to study the issues and examine them with its GCC partners in the framework of the strengthened EU–GCC political dialogue.

Another area in which both sides should benefit from a reinforced political dialogue is the Middle East Peace Process. The important roles played by the EU and the GCC in the Peace Process, notably the economic aspects, demonstrate that a new Middle East region requires an active economic role by both the EU and the GCC. GCC energy and capital combined with EU Member States private investment and the large EU market will be decisive elements in determining the economic future of the region. These roles and shared interests should be subject to much greater discussion and exchange and, where possible, co-ordination. The reinforced political dialogue should greatly assist such a process.

A further area in which the EU should seek to benefit from a reinforced EU–GCC political dialogue is in relation to EU Mediterranean policy. As the above discussion of security issues underlines, an EU vision to promote security and stability in the Mediterranean should not stop at the frontier of Saudi Arabia and the edge of the Arabian Peninsula. Equally, GCC political and security interests cannot be confined exclusively to the geographic area of the Gulf. The GCC countries are as much interested in the Mediterranean area between them and Europe as Europe is. They stand to gain as much from our efforts to create a vast Euro-Mediterranean free trade area as Europe and the Mediterranean countries themselves. Strengthened political dialogue will enable the two sides to better appreciate their common interests in the Mediterranean area.

The importance of the GCC in the political field is not confined to the Gulf and the Mediterranean regions. The GCC countries play a major role in international organisations such as OPEC and the Islamic Conference Organisation. They have important energy markets in Asia. They have been actively interested in developments in Central Asia since the end of the Soviet Union and they have followed with great concern events in former Yugoslavia. It is for this latter reason that the EU wishes to enlist their support for the reconstruction of Bosnia. All of these issues could be usefully discussed in the framework of a strengthened political dialogue.

Finally, a strengthened political dialogue would enable the two sides to discuss questions of human rights and democracy which are of importance both at the international level and the level of relations between the EU and GCC. Discussion of these questions and others such as prevention of terrorism is essential if the two groups are to establish a closer political relationship. Frank and constructive discussion would also promote increased reciprocal knowledge and understanding as recommended by EU and GCC ministers in Granada.

To implement the recommendation to strengthen the EU–GCC political dialogue the EU should quickly propose modalities for holding twice-yearly meetings at senior official level to discuss all aspects of EU–GCC and international political and security issues of common interest.

5. Strengthening the framework of EU–GCC Energy and Economic Interests

By virtue of its importance to national economies and the international economy generally, oil is not just a commodity like any other. Its key role requires that EC–GCC energy inter-dependence should be accorded its full significance. Because EC–GCC relations have not developed the full potential of early aspirations, the significance of this inter-dependence has been sidelined in recent years by other considerations. The GCC countries have tended to consider that by means of its European Energy Charter initiative, the EC and its Member States are giving priority in its external energy policies to Russia and the former Soviet Union. The EC has tended to consider GCC objections to issues, such as a possible EC-carbon energy tax, as concerns with the shadows rather than the substance of energy inter-dependence.

Energy policy is intimately connected with economic policy. For example, there is no doubt that the underlying realities of energy inter-dependence would be reinforced by greater cross-investments, with more GCC investment in EU refining and downstream activities, accompanied by EU countries investment in GCC upstream and downstream energy and energy-related activities. Already important downstream investments in Europe, in particular in the refining industry, have been made by Kuwait, Saudi Arabia and the United Arab Emirates. Furthermore, European companies have carried out upstream investments in several GCC countries (UAE, Qatar and Oman, in particular) and in the refining industry in Saudi Arabia. However, this process would be greatly assisted by an improved framework for EC–GCC energy and economic relations.

Regarding future trade trends, GCC countries are as concerned today, or possibly even more concerned, to diversify their industrial base and prepare for the post-oil age as they were when taking their initiative to approach the EC for a preferential trade agreement in the mid-1980s. An EC–GCC free trade agreement would give duty-free access for the products of GCC industrial diversification to a huge, geographically close market of some 500 million inhabitants by early next century.

For the EC, given the continuing importance of the GCC market as described above, a free trade relationship is as much in our interest today as it was at the time of the adoption of the first negotiating directives in 1989. It is obviously of interest to secure duty free access for EC exporters in the 5th most important EC export market. In terms of reciprocal concessions which would be made to secure a free trade agreement, the basic considerations are as follows:

On a larger volume of trade, EC exporters pay GCC duties which are on average higher than EU duties, whereas 79 percent of GCC exports to the EC enter duty free under MFN arrangements and a further 15% could currently benefit from GSP advantages.

Finally, for both the EC and the GCC, a free trade relationship would provide their economic operators a permanent framework for developing cross-investments, vertical integration and industrial alliances which it is clear from experience that the EC–GCC Cooperation Agreement alone does not provide.

The key to strengthening the framework of EC–GCC economic interests therefore could lie in the conclusion of a free trade agreement. Such an agreement could be, objectively, in the interest of the two sides. As to the World Trade Organisation the Community would ensure that such an agreement would comply with its requirements and in particular ensure that it would cover essentially all trade between the two parties and all sectors. Since the harmonised reduction of duties on petro-chemical products in the Uruguay Round, the concerns of this important European industry should also be more easily met. Finally, with the progressive graduation of GCC countries from the EC's Generalised System of Preferences, it is urgent to avoid what could become, in future, increasing trade frictions between the two groups.

Among GCC countries, Kuwait, Bahrain and Qatar are members of the WTO. The UAE are still negotiating their accession. Saudi Arabia has applied for WTO membership and Oman has declared its intention to do so.

The group of Commission and GCC experts proposed at the Granada meeting to study the unblocking of the ongoing negotiations should make every effort to overcome the obstacles which have so far prevented progress in these negotiations. Concrete proposals should be finalised by April 1996 to enable decisions by ministers at the 6th EU–GCC Joint Council. If these proposals lead to the conclusion of a free trade agreement, this would be perhaps the single most important contribution possible to ensuring a close permanent EC–GCC relationship. Of course, the speed and the concrete steps with which we wish to achieve a Free Trade Zone, must always depend on careful examination of the advantages and disadvantages that could occur with each further step in those industrial sectors of both sides which must be seen as particularly affected.

6. Promoting increased reciprocal knowledge and understanding

The GCC countries have long enjoyed good bilateral relations with EU Member States and of course a number of GCC countries gained their independence from the United Kingdom just over 30 years' ago. Despite these advantages, EU–GCC bilateral and regional relations have not promoted sufficient contacts and exchanges to accompany and assist the development of official links between the two regions. In particular, the younger generations are not fostering bonds of contact and understanding which previous generations have done by virtue, mainly, of shared historical and educational backgrounds and experience.

The EU–GCC Troika Ministerial Meeting in Granada therefore rightly stressed the need to open new areas of cooperation and promote reciprocal knowledge and understanding. The scope for action at the EC level to correct these deficiencies is, of course, limited. Bearing in mind the principle of subsidiarity and the considerably greater opportunities for action at national level, it is mainly for Member States to adopt policies to expand the scope of contacts and exchanges with GCC countries.

Nonetheless, at the EU level, the Granada recommendations will be significant. As mentioned above in Section 4, strengthening political dialogue will contribute to these objectives by a more substantial discussion of human rights and democracy.

A commitment to human rights and fundamental freedoms is at the heart of EU policy world-wide. The EU believes that the espousal of international standards of human rights and their respect are essential for long-term social and political stability. In this framework, GCC countries should be encouraged to become signatory parties and fully apply international instruments in relation to human rights. The EU is ready to help the GCC countries to establish a civil society founded on the primacy of law in conformity with the Declarations and Action Programmes of United Nations conferences such as Vienna (June 1993), Copenhagen (March-April 1995) and Beijing (September 1995).

These subjects have not been adequately discussed at ministerial level and there has tended to be a dangerous silence on sensitive matters which, if not properly handled, could affect the progress of relations. More openness and transparency on these issues would help counter reflexive European media and parliamentary critics of GCC practices. The EU should seek through its relations with the GCC countries, which have a special position in the Islamic world, to obtain better insight and judgement on how traditional Islam can accommodate modern concepts of human rights. The official political dialogue should also be used for understanding and appreciating democratic and constitutional developments. The breadth and diversity of EU experience could be valuable to GCC countries which are having to realise constitutional changes which have taken decades and longer in European systems.

But a key new area of cooperation to which Troika ministers referred in Granada was not at the official level but at decentralised levels of cooperation, involving civil society and non-governmental organisations. The possible participation of GCC countries in some horizontal programmes of cooperation on the model of those established for the Mediterranean countries could be very positive. They could lead to greatly increased grass root contact and cooperation in education, training and youth, as well as science, local government and press and television which is an essential accompaniment to the promotion of good official relations. This type of regional, decentralised cooperation would undoubtedly contribute to better regional relations and understanding.

The GCC countries should also be natural partners for collaborating with the Euro-Arab Management School in Granada. Economic development and diversification of GCC economies is producing the need for an increased supply of well-trained managers. Moreover, rapid GCC population growth makes it imperative to create productive job opportunities for new generations.

Information and communication technologies constitute a vital sector for modern economies and key conditions for the emerging information society. They are of particular relevance for the GCC countries due to the high technological level they have already reached and the challenges they face for the setting up of a post-oil economy. Such areas should offer a new field of cooperation focusing on the dialogue of the premises of the information society and aiming at the realisation of pilot projects to demonstrate the feasibility and the concrete benefits of the applications of these new technologies.

The intention of Troika ministers in Granada to increase scientific cooperation merits special attention. GCC scientific capacity is already significant in several sectors but could be strengthened in cooperation with European scientific institutions. Common interests are numerous, ranging from global warming to urban and industrial pollution. Energy related subjects could be prominent, including renewable energy. The Arabian peninsula offers among the best available sites world-wide for the production of solar energy in the 21st century. Consequently, there are vast untapped opportunities for future cooperation between Europe and the Gulf in the field of solar energy. Scientific and technological cooperation between the EU and the GCC should start as of now to make these new resources fully available in due time. The Institute for Prospective Technological Studies in Seville could provide the framework for this cooperation.

Finally, it is essential to underline the fact that the pursuit of sustainable development is a factor underpinning EU relations with all third countries (or regional groupings). More specifically, four of the six GCC states (except UAE and Qatar) have ratified the Convention on Global Climate Change, which calls – inter alia – for a reduction in global emissions from fossil fuels. There is therefore a direct link between the GCC states' principal means of achieving economic growth – the export of oil – and the concern they and the EU share (with others) for the global environment. All GCC states formed part of the consensus at the Rio Conference in 1992 which adopted the Rio Principles.

Topics in the field of the environment where preliminary discussions indicated that the mutual interest could be further explored include marine pollution, hazardous waste management, nature protection, air pollution and international environmental cooperation policies.

If a joint commitment exists to cooperate together in these regional, decentralised, scientific and other programmes it should not be difficult for the EU and GCC to work out modalities and methods of co-financing as recommended by Troika ministers in Granada. The EU has experience of cooperating in such programmes with countries which have similar or higher levels of per capita income. Shared experience in these and similar EC–GCC cooperation activities should help significantly to consolidate and extend official-level relations.

The European Commission could itself make an important contribution to strengthening EC–GCC cooperation and promoting increased contacts and understanding by opening a Delegation in Riyadh, capital of Saudi Arabia and seat of the headquarters of the Secretariat of the Gulf Cooperation Council. A Commission Delegation would be accredited to the governments of all six GCC countries.

In this third, general area, implementation of the Granada recommendations provides many possibilities:

- promoting mutual understanding by discussing questions of democracy and human rights in the strengthened official political dialogue;
- including the GCC countries in EC programmes of regional, decentralised cooperation to increase contacts and grass roots cooperation in education, training and youth matters; and in science, local government, business education and the media.
- improving transport links and strengthening cooperation;
- scientific cooperation, especially in areas of common interest such as energy.
- cooperation in the field of management training, both private and public, through initiatives such as the Euro-Arab Management School;
- as a result of establishing a Commission delegation in the GCC region, the EC could effectively promote these programmes of cooperation and effectively introduce a number of instruments to strengthen economic cooperation such as the Business Cooperation Network (BC Net), Bureau de Rapprochement des Entreprises (BRE) and the European Community Investment Partners (ECIP).

7. Towards a qualitative improvement in relations

The intention of EU–GCC Troika ministers in Granada in making recommendations to strengthen political, economic and cultural and scientific relations was to provide for a qualitative improvement in EC–GCC relations. Indeed, strong economic inter-dependence and shared political and security interests, support the view that the two regions should develop, over time, a strong, strategically important relationship.

This view of an evolving, strong relationship is not one which puts in question the present, predominant role of the United States in GCC military security. This is a fact. It should not obscure, however, the role which Europe has played, and will, no doubt, continue to play in the broader context of GCC security in particular economic security. It is also a fact that since the original EC–GCC commitment to establish close relations, the EU is giving new emphasis to relations with countries to the south. This new emphasis in EU external policy, a direct result of the end of the Cold War and a desire to balance the EU's East and South policies, implies increased importance for the EU of the GCC. The view of an evolving, strong EU–GCC relationship continues, of course, to be most firmly based on the present and future importance of EU–GCC economic and energy interdependence.

The above analysis has shown, however, that an important relationship, such as the EU–GCC relationship, cannot be taken for granted and left to take care of itself. All important relationships must be worked at and given the correct attention and priority by both sides. In the case of the EU and GCC member states, there has been a tendency to look at the trade figures and at bilateral relations and to leave everything at the regional level to take care of itself. The EU–GCC relationship provides complementary, regional added value to bilateral relations. But if regional relations are neglected, or become the source of irritants, then region-to-region relations can spill over and have harmful effects on bilateral relations.

Of course, the development of the region-to-region relationship depends on the development of the regional structures and competences of the two sides. It is therefore essential that the process of GCC cooperation and integration continues as its member countries have resolved. An economically, politically and militarily strong GCC, constituting a firm, independent pillar in the sensitive and strategically important Gulf area security system is of major interest to the European Union. A weak and divided GCC would add dramatically to the potential for instability in the area and the potential for interference by the GCC's powerful neighbours. In the context of the follow-up to the Granada Troika Ministerial Meeting and the desire for a qualitative improvement in EU–GCC relations, it is, therefore, important that the GCC should go on with its policy commitments to strengthen integration and the role of the GCC. This does not mean that, in parallel, bilateral relations with each of the Gulf countries should not be pursued and encouraged according to each country's specific characteristics.

Implementation of the recommendations of the Granada Troika Ministerial Meeting will constitute a test case for EU–GCC relations.

Reinforcing the political dialogue, finding solutions to problems obstructing progress towards strengthening economic relations and developing new cooperation and a meaningful cultural dimension to relations, is a realistic agenda. It is in line with the approach followed in the Euro-Mediterranean partnership framework. It does not require, either, a shift in GCC policies or orientations. If the agenda is implemented, it would provide for the desired qualitative improvement in relations. The EU should therefore make a maximum effort to ensure that, in accordance with the recommendations of the Granada Troika Meeting, the relevant decisions can be prepared for a successful 6th Joint Council-Ministerial Meeting.

8. Conclusions and recommendations

In the light of the above review of EU–GCC relations, the Commission recommends that the Council should:

- reaffirm the strategic importance of a strong GCC regional group capable of playing a progressively more important role in the economic, political and security spheres;
- reaffirm its commitment to the development of strong, mutually beneficial EU–GCC relations;
- confirm the need to include the GCC countries in the EU's global strategy for improving relations with partners from other regions and in particular with the Mediterranean area;
- reaffirm its commitment to follow-up and implement successfully the recommendations and conclusions of the Granada Troika Ministerial Meeting and thereby achieve a qualitative improvement in EU–GCC relations;
- in particular, the Council should agree to reinforce EU–GCC ministerial level political cooperation by holding twice-yearly meetings at senior official level to discuss all aspects of EU–GCC, and international, political and security issues of common interest.

For its part, the Commission will :

- in accordance with the Granada Troika Ministerial meeting recommendations and its negotiating directive, identify with its GCC counterparts obstacles to progress in the ongoing EC–GCC free trade negotiations with a view to re-launching these negotiations, ensuring that a resulting agreement would be in conformity with the requirements of the WTO;
- in liaison with its GCC counterparts and in the framework of the 1989 Cooperation Agreement, make proposals for a significant expansion of cooperation in areas of mutual interest;

- make proposals for increasing contacts and understanding in the fields of regional, decentralised cooperation, scientific and management cooperation and programmes to strengthen economic cooperation;
- study the suitability of presenting to the Council a complementary mandate for negotiation concerning services in line with the OMC dispositions after having carried out the appropriate research into the legal and economic impact on the Free Trade Zone and taking into account the offers presented by the GCC within the GATS framework.

The Commission will keep the Council fully informed of its actions in following up the recommendations of the Granada Troika Ministerial Meeting, including developments in the free trade negotiations and make appropriate proposals in time for the preparation of a successful 6th EU–GCC Joint Council-Ministerial Meeting to be held on 22/23 April 1996 in Luxembourg.

European Union Commission Communication, M (1995) 541/7.

15J
The US Policy

Statement of Robert H. Pelletreau, Assistant Secretary for Near Eastern Affairs, to the House Committee on International Relations, September 1996.

Mr. Chairman, distinguished members of the Committee, I am pleased to appear before you to review recent developments in the Middle East and North Africa. I would like to focus my remarks on the central elements of US policy in the region: the Middle East peace process, our response to Iraq's aggression and international terrorism, and our cooperation with our allies in the Persian Gulf.

An extraordinarily wide range of US national interests converge in the Middle East. Among the crucial national interests are:

- Achieving a just, lasting and comprehensive peace between Israel and its neighbors;
- Maintaining our long-standing commitment to Israel's security and well-being;
- Combating terrorism and countering the spread of weapons of mass destruction;
- Nurturing close relations with our Gulf allies and ensuring the United States' access to the area's vital petroleum reserves;
- Promoting democracy and respect for human rights and for the rule of law; and
- Enhancing business opportunities for American companies.

Promoting these interests requires that we continue our active political engagement in the region and back it with American military power – with the support and cooperation of our allies whenever possible. We are putting special energy into containing the disruption from rogue regimens in Iraq, Iran and Libya, and into denying the benefits of membership in the community of nations to extremists who foment conflict . . .

The GCC

Our Persian Gulf policy consists of two elements, of which countering Iraqi and Iranian hegemonic aspirations is only one. The second is to sustain close political, economic and security relations with the states of the Gulf Cooperation Council.

The US works closely with the six states of the GCC to contain the military threat from Iran and Iraq. Working with US Central Command, we have made steady progress in improving security cooperation with these states since Desert Storm. Our approach has three dimensions. First, we help each Gulf state strengthen its own defense forces through our defense sales and training programs. Second, we encourage regional defense cooperation among the Gulf states through the GCC collective security arrangements. Third, we promote bilateral US Security cooperation with individual states.

In this last area, we have made dramatic strides since 1991: increasing US forward presence in the region in a careful, non-permanent way, prepositioning equipment in Kuwait and Qatar, and carrying out an expanded program of land, sea and air training exercises with GCC states. We are also steadily increasing our regional consultation and intelligence exchanges.

As the heinous bombing of our troops in Khobar, Saudi Arabia, reminds us, security has many dimensions, including security from terrorist attack. In many parts of the Gulf, local and foreign extremists work against US interests as well as those of our friends. As we respond to this threat, we must weigh measures to preserve security and order against their potential to inflame domestic extremism. We believe that our current efforts to increase security and economic cooperation both advance US national interests and increase stability among Gulf states.

Although internal tensions exist in many GCC countries – notably Bahrain – the GCC states are politically stable overall. All the GCC states are able to work with internal opposition effectively. The rulers of the GCC states are acutely aware of the need to address the reasons for internal dissent of a portion of their populations. While this internal political concern may affect the scope of bilateral cooperation in some areas, it is not evidence of a serious lack of internal stability.

The US has considerable economic and commercial interests in the Gulf states, and we are working hard, particularly within the framework of the US–GCC economic dialogue, to expand this aspect of our relations. We encourage Gulf states to privatize and open up their economies, and to promote free trade through easing investment restrictions and protecting intellectual property rights. Four of the six GCC members have joined the World Trade Organization (WTO); applications for the other two are under active consideration. Economically, as well as politically, the GCC states are important partners for the United States and linchpins of the peace process . . .

The State Department, Washington, DC, 25 September 1996.

15K
Torture friends

A Comment: 'Getting Away with Torture, or US – Business as Usual':

A comment in the *Washington Post* and the *International Herald Tribune* by lawyer Leonard Garment.

Washington. Almost 10 years ago, after working on torture issues as US representative to the UN Human Rights Commission, I acquired two American clients who had been tortured.

One, Scott Nelson, had been an engineer in a hospital in Saudi Arabia, where he blew the whistle on superiors who failed to correct a major hazard. He was arrested by Saudi police, imprisoned and tortured in a manner that left him permanently crippled. After 39 days he was released with the help of Senator Edward Kennedy.

The other American, James Smrkovski, a language instructor in Saudi Arabia, was arrested on a false charge of smuggling alcohol. He was confined in a cell the size of a large coffin. Six of his toenails were pulled out. After 454 days of confinement, he was released with the help of Senator Bob Dole.

The reader is left to imagine the physical and emotional scars that the two men took away with them.

Because the torture took place in Saudi Arabia, which lacks a judiciary independent of the rest of government, it is not possible to bring the torturers to justice by suing them in the country where the torture occurred. So my colleagues and I tried to sue in American courts.

We faced a large obstacle. The Foreign Sovereign Immunities Act generally prohibits suits in the United States against foreign governments. But there are exceptions – for instance in situations involving commercial transactions by foreign governments in America.

By last spring we had a bill passed by the House and under consideration in the Senate. The State Department objected – there would be frivolous lawsuits, other countries would retaliate. The Senate passed a bill with its heart cut out.

In it, American citizens could sue in the United States for acts of state violence against them – but only if the crime occurred in a country on the State Department's 'terrorist state' list. The designated countries were Cuba, Iran, Iraq, Libya, North Korea, Sudan and Syria – places so unappetizing that few Americans venture there. The riskier places, palatable enough to attract US citizens for work and trade but repressive enough to pose dangers, were let off. Vertebrae broken by North Korea, it seemed, were morally distinct from those pulverized by Uganda.

This fall we were back on the Hill. The new version of our measure answered the State Department's professed objections. It allowed a suit only if the foreign regime in question had no extradition treaty with the United States; that is, it aimed the amendment only against countries whose legal systems provided no adequate remedies. The new version also guarded against frivolous claims, saying that people who wanted to sue must first offer to have their claims arbitrated.

The House again passed the measure. Senators Relen Specter and Daniel P. Moynihan introduced it in the Senate as part of Foreign Operations Appropriation bill; it passed without audible objection.

On the day the measure was accepted by the House-Senate conference committee, I called my colleague Ralph Oman, who had worked hard on the project, to congratulate him. 'Not so fast', he said. He explained that the administration could now list the conditions under which President Bill Clinton would sign the bill – what provisions he could stay and what had to go. Because Congress was anxious to get a bill through and go home, the White House had the whip hand.

White House and State Department representatives went to the conference committee's leaders, Senator Mitch McConell and Representative Robert Livingstone, and demanded deletions. Our amendment was high on the administration hit list, so it was scrapped.

When we began our efforts to get relief for Americans tortured by foreign governments, President George Bush was in office. His administration opposed the idea, and we were not surprised. But why did the avowedly idealistic Clinton administration treat this amendment as such a threat, especially after it had been redrafted with care to meet reasonable objections?

In part it did so because this administration, like many of its predecessors, takes its sense of foreign and diplomatic threats from the State Department. For years State has been known to harbor an institutional urge to maintain stable relations with its foreign 'clients' states, including unappetizing ones, not infrequently at the expense of Americans at odds with these governments.

The fate of the torture amendment demonstrates that America faces the new post Cold War world with the same old foreign policy apparatus, which will, if unchecked, generate the same old problems.

More interesting the power of foreign money in this debate was more pervasive than even a fairly cynical observer would have expected. In this round because Saudi cases were at issue, it was mainly the Saudi doing the buying. At every step of the process we had to contend not just with the power of Saudi Arabia as an oil-producing ally but also with Saudi resources of a different sort.

The Saudis purchase billions of dollars worth of aircraft, munitions and services in the United States. Saudi diplomats and lobbyists do not let American officials forget this.

The Saudi also spend millions providing employment to influential people on the Hill, like ex-staff aides to important members of Congress. In addition US companies that depend heavily on Saudi trade are enlisted to lobby on the behalf of Saudi political goals.

At the start of the next legislative term, Senator Moynihan and Specter will reintroduce the amendment to protect Americans abroad from violence by foreign governments. This time the light of public debate and political exposure will be brighter, and we will see how the torture measure faces.

The writer, a lawyer, was a special presidential assistant in the Nixon administration. His article was printed in The International Herald Tribune, 29 October 1996.

15L
GCC Communiqué

The 17th GCC Summit Communiqué, 1996.

Crown Prince Abdullah Bin Abdul Aziz, Deputy Prime Minister and Commander of the National Guard, led the Saudi delegation to the 17th session of the Supreme Council of the Gulf Cooperation Council (GCC). The three-day summit, held in Doha, Qatar, was chaired by Qatari Emir Sheik Hamad Bin Khalifa Al-Thani. The following are excerpts of the final communiqué issued on December 9, 1996.

After reviewing GCC achievements in the political, security, military, economic, social, information, and legal arenas, as well as reports and recommendations of the ministerial council, the GCC reiterated its determination to advance the welfare march and to reinforce security, stability, and prosperity to meet the aspirations of its peoples.

Regarding the Iraqi compliance with the UN Resolutions pertaining to its aggression against Kuwait, the Supreme Council regretted the continued

Iraqi manipulation over the implementation of its international obligations including: elimination of weapons of mass destruction, release of the Kuwaiti detainees as well as those of other countries, mechanisms for compensation for and restoration of Kuwaiti belongings, and refraining from aggressive and provocative acts against neighboring countries in compliance with UN Resolution 949. In this context the Council confirmed anew its support for the UN committee assigned to eliminate Iraq's weapons of mass destruction, declared the GCC ready to provide financial and political support for that committee, and called upon the international community to follow suit.

While sympathizing with the Iraqi people, the Council held the Iraqi government fully responsible for the deterioration in the living and health conditions of its people. In this regard the council calls on the Iraqi government to show serious and sincere cooperation with the UN to ensure accurate implementation of Resolution 986. Regarding the recent developments in Northern Iraq, the Council expressed concern over their possible implications for the region, and confirmed an unwavering stand of maintaining the independence, sovereignty, territorial integrity, and safety of Iraqi lands against the intervention of neighboring countries.

Regarding relations with Iran, the communiqué deplored the successive Iranian measures affecting the three islands belonging to the UAE and expressed concern over the Iranian determination to impose a de facto policy in violation of UAE rights, thereby endangering the security and stability of the entire region. The Council expressed full support for all measures and peaceful means to be adopted by the UAE to restore sovereignty, calling on Iran to end occupation of the islands, refrain from unilateral measures, and pursue a peaceful settlement of the conflict based on the principles of international law. The Council also expressed grave concern at Iranian deployment of land-to-land missiles in the Arab Gulf including the three islands, as well as at its continuing efforts to possess and build weapons of mass destruction and enhance conventional and non-conventional arms capabilities beyond its legitimate defense needs. The Council again called on the international community and organizations to exert efforts to transform the Gulf region into a zone free from weapons of mass destruction.

On the Middle East, the Council viewed and rejected the policies of the Israeli government as a threat to peace prospects and warned that should there be a return to tension and violence the GCC would reconsider steps taken towards Israel. The Council also stressed the importance of realizing a just and comprehensive peace in line with UN Security Council Resolutions 242, 338 and 425 and reiterated its support for the land-for-peace formula, and called on the Israeli government to honor its agreements and commitments with the Palestinian side and resume talks on the final status stage. The Council also called on the Israelis to withdraw from

Jerusalem and refrain from demolishing houses, changing the nature of Islamic sanctuaries, and expanding settlements in consolidation of the occupation. The Council also called for the resumption of talks on the Syrian track and full Israeli withdrawal from Golan and from southern Lebanon, and wished success for the European efforts in the economic and political sphere.

Concerning terrorism, the council renewed its condemnation and rejection of fanaticism and violence as dangerous to regional peace and stability, calling on the international community to coordinate efforts in that regard, to ensure that those who commit these acts are brought to justice, and to deny fundamentalist groups the use of the land of any country for financial or armed purposes or for exploiting the media to incite terrorism.

While denouncing terrorist acts in Al-Khobar and in Bahrain, the Council avowed not to allow such acts to jeopardize the security and the progress witnessed by the member states.

In the defense and security arenas, the Council approved recommendations from the defense ministers regarding military cooperation and the building of a collective capability targeting defense integration among member states. The council also expressed satisfaction at the distinguished levels of cooperation and coordination in the security field in view of recommendations made by the interior ministers.

Concerning economic cooperation within the Gulf region, the Council resolved to meet the goal of a customs union and a unified tariff towards a common Gulf market, and approved measures including standardization of commodities. Regarding the mobility of manpower between member states the Summit approved the resolutions of the ministerial committees in that regard. The Council also approved measures to check smoking risks, the amended formula of the GCC joint agricultural policy, and the Muscat document passed by the GCC justice ministers on a unified legal system on personal status as a guiding law for a four-year period.

Finally, the council pointed to the importance of the GCC media continuing to keep up with international developments in the field, using them as a unifying factor and to transmit an accurate image about member states.

Embassy of Saudi Arabia, document published on the Internet, Washington, DC, 9 December 1996.

Chapter Sixteen

THE MASSARI AFFAIR

16A
Decision to deport Massari to Dominica

The British Immigration and Nationality Department, 3 January 1996, informed Saudi Arabian asylum seeker, Professor Mass'ari, of a decision to deport him to Dominica.

Dear Sir,

You have applied for asylum in the United Kingdom on the grounds that you have a well-founded fear of persecution in Saudi Arabia for reasons of race, religion, nationality, membership of a particular social group or political opinion.

However, the Secretary of State notes that Saudi Arabia is not the only country to which you may be removed. You arrived in the United Kingdom on 18 April 1994 on board a Yemen Airways flight from Sana'a, Yemen. You were found to be in possession of a Yemeni passport to which you were not entitled. Subsequently you have been notified that you are an illegal immigrant as defined in Section 33 (1) of the Immigration Act 1971.

Following the hearing before the independent Special Adjudicator on 21 February 1995 the determination, delivered in 7 March, directed that you were not returnable to the Yemen. However, the Secretary of State is now aware that under paragraph 8 (1) (c) (iv) of Schedule 2 to the Immigration Act 1971 and Paragraph 345 (ii) of the Immigration Rules (HC 395) you can be removed to Dominica which is a signatory to the 1951 United Nations Convention relating to the Status of Refugees, and is a country that has provided him with clear evidence that you will be admitted there and which would also be prepared to grant you asylum. The secretary of State takes this view following receipt of the attached letter from the Prime Minister of Dominica.

The Secretary of State, on the basis of his knowledge of the immigration policies and practices of Dominica, has no reason to believe that, in the circumstances of your particular case, the authorities there would not comply with their obligations under the Convention. The Secretary of State therefore has decided to refuse your application without substantive consideration of your claim. Furthermore, he hereby certifies that your claim that your removal from the United

Kingdom would be contrary to the United Kingdom's obligations under the Convention is without foundation as removal to Dominica does not raise any issue as to the United Kingdom's obligations under the Convention.

Yours faithfully,

Russell Swann, B3 Division, Home Office, London, United Kingdom

16B
Blackmail

In an editorial, The Guardian called on the British Government not to give in to Saudi Arabian 'blackmail'.

There is no mystery about the real reason for deporting the Saudi dissident Mohammed al-Mas'ari to Dominica instead of considering his application for asylum. He has not breached any condition for political refugee status. It is not suggested that he is breaking British law or promoting terrorism. No one has cast doubt on his claim to have a well-founded fear of persecution if he returns to Saudi Arabia. Indeed his application for asylum has not been examined at all: it has been refused 'without substantive consideration of the claim'.

The reason why Mr Mas'ari is being banished to a Caribbean Elba was set out with total clarity yesterday by the Home Office minister Ann Widdecombe in following terms: 'We have close trade relations with a friendly state (i.e. Saudi Arabia) which has been the subject to considerable criticism by Mr Mas'ari.' Are Ms Widdecombe's listeners to recoil with shock and horror? So an applicant for British asylum has ventured to criticise this wholly undemocratic repressive state which has arrested hundreds for their political or religious activities and routinely inflicts cruel and inhumane punishment. How dare he! No, even Ms Widdecombe cannot expect such a response. There is no reason why applicants for asylum (or those granted such status) should refrain from political activity, so long as it is non-violent and is not illegal in Britain. Neither the 1951 UN convention nor the subsequent UHNCR guidance to states make any such stipulation. Nor can it be regarded as 'self-serving' – a bogus performance to strengthen Mr Mas'ari's claim. He was jailed and tortured for political protest in Saudi Arabia and is continuing to protest in the same vein.

The answer, simply, is that the government is scared witless by the prospect of upsetting the Saudis. There was some surprise yesterday that Ms Widdecombe should have confirmed this so openly, but her only alternative was to keep quiet. There was no other plausible reason for the Home Secretary's arbitrary act. Deporting Mr Mas'ari to a third country is not, as it happens, a breach of international law though the practice has been expressly opposed in a recent document from the UNHCR. But the expected approach is for the host country to consider an application for asylum, and then either accept or reject it. Instead Britain has refused consideration while, illogically, finding another country, which will not only receive Mr Mas'ari's application but has promised in advance to accept it. The result is that Britain looks ludicrous and craven at the same time.

The blatant admission of a political motive behind this decision may strengthen Mr Mas'ari's case for appeal or judicial review. The nature of Mr Mas'ari's views as an Islamist who advocates Shari'a law is beside the point – and not only because Saudi Arabia is already an Islamic state where the same law is abitrarily applied. Asylum is not granted only to those whose views we applaud.

There remains the Government's appeal to self-interest of the narrowest kind. Protection of British jobs would be more noble cause if it had been pursued elsewhere with equal enthusiasm to prevent the run-down of our manufacturing industry. Besides the linkage of trade and politics – normally opposed by the Government – creates a dangerous precedent. Britain will be seen as more open to blackmail by trading partners who object to political criticism – and there are plenty of them. Nor do massive arms sales to Saudi Arabia do anything to promote a wider stability. Surely the lesson of the Gulf War was that the region needs fewer guns, more democracy.

The Guardian, London, 5 January, 1996.

16C
Rule of law

In an editorial, the Financial Times called on the British Government to respect the freedom of Professor Massari as well as on the Saudi government to deal with the lack of accountability in the kingdom.

Saudi Arabia is a state which likes to keep its international affairs out of the international news. Considering its importance to the rest of the world, notably as the possessor of one quarter of the world's known oil reserves, it is on the whole remarkably successful in doing so.

This week, however, it has been in the headlines thanks to two apparently unrelated events, both which prompt speculation about its future stability.

First, King Fahd, who has been in poor health for some months, officially handed over power to his half-brother and designated successor, Crown Prince Abdullah: ostensibly a temporary move, but expected by many observers to be permanent. Secondly, the British government, bowing to intense if discreet pressure from the Saudi authorities, informed

Mohammed al-Massari, the best known Saudi exile, of its intention to remove him to the Caribbean island of Dominica on January 19.

The latter decision calls for comment quite apart from its Saudi context. By sending Mr al-Massari to Dominica, a 'safe third country', Britain escapes the obligation to examine substantively his claim for refugee status. Hitherto this device has been used only to return asylums seekers to 'safe countries' through which they had already passed on the argument that they should have exercised their right to claim asylum at the first opportunity. That argument has never been very convincing, but the argument for sending Mr al-Massari to a part of the world he has never even visited is weaker still.

Rule of Law

Moreover, the decision has serious implications for Britain's national interests. The fact that there has been strong pressure from the Saudi authorities, and in particular the fact that British businessmen have been told they risk being discriminated against so long as Mr as-Massari is allowed to continue his activities in the UK, should if anything have prompted the British government to treat him with conspicuous fairness. The only sensible, as well as the only honourable, position for a democratic government when faced with this kind of pressure, is to say 'we regret any offence caused, and we by no means endorse Mr X's opinions or ambitions, but order and prosperity in our country depend on the rule of law, and so long as he respects our laws we are obliged to respect his freedom'. Once that position is abandoned, foreign governments are in effect invited to interfere with British legal procedures by threatening to harm Britain's commercial interests.

Doubly painful

What makes the situation doubly painful is that Mr al-Massari's activities, which consist essentially of subjecting the Saudi kingdom to a flow of scurrilous faxes, cannot in themselves pose any serious threat to its stability. The Saudi government's sensitivity to them betrays a troubling insecurity, related certainly to its suppression of even moderate voices calling from within the kingdom for a more representative form of government. Inevitably, a period of budgetary constraint sharpens resentment among middle-class Saudis about the vast commissions for government contracts taken by members of the ruling elite, and about wealth many members of the royal family derive from their appropriation of building and development land.

Crown Prince Abdullah, variously described as a 'traditionalist' or even 'nationalist', is believed by some members of the opposition to be more sympathetic to this kind of grievance than his elder brother. If he is, that should not be seen as contrary to western interests, even if it leads him to influences more firmly at arm's length than his brother has done. He would be right to recognise that conscious self-indulgence and lack of account-ability on the part of his own family and its associates pose greater threat to the kingdom's stability – which is a matter of real concern to the West as well as to Saudis themselves – than any number of faxes emanating from London. Anyway, he may soon discover that there are fax machines even in Dominica.

Financial Times, 5 January 1996.

16D
Letters

On 17 January 1996, Human Rights Watch wrote a letter to Sir Colin Chandler, Chief Executive Officer of Vickers Defence Systems in Newcastle-upon-Tyne, England.

Dear Sir:

Please find enclosed a copy of a letter that Human Rights Watch has sent to Prime Minister John Major protesting the decision to expel Saudi dissident Muhammad al-Mas'ari from the United Kingdom. We believe that in expelling Mr. Mas'ari because of his peaceful speech activities, the United Kingdom would become an accomplice to the Saudi government's intolerance of dissent. This would also violate the United Kingdom's obligation under international law to examine substantively Mr. Mas'ari's asylum application.

Statements made by British government officials as well as press coverage of the case make clear that the expulsion effort is due in large part to pressure from British companies that fear that Mr. Mas'ari's continued activism in the United Kingdom could adversely affect their business dealings with Saudi Arabia. As you know, Vickers was mentioned prominently in this context.

Human Rights Watch, which has worked with corporations operating in many parts of the world, believes that the business community has a responsibility not to become complicit in governmental human rights violations. We are therefore deeply troubled by the role that some British companies have reportedly played in pressing for Mr. Mas'ari's expulsion from the United Kingdom on account of his peaceful criticism of one of the most repressive regimes on the Middle East, and before he has enjoyed his right to a substantive hearing on his clarification from you on Vickers' role in this matter.

I thought you might also find of interest the enclosed chapter on human rights developments in Saudi Arabia during 1995 from our recently released *Human Rights Watch World Report 1996*.

Thank you for your consideration. We look forward to your reply.

Sincerely yours,

Kenneth Roth, Executive Director

Following letter: On 7 February 1996, Human Rights Watch followed up on their earlier letter to Sir Colin Chandler:

Dear Sir,

I am writing to you to follow up on my earlier communication of January 17, 1996, concerning Vicker's part in the decision of your government to expel Saudi dissident Muhammad al-Mas'ari from the United Kingdom. It is the position of Human Rights Watch that such a step would violate the United Kingdom's obligation under international law to examine substantively Dr. Mas'ari's application for asylum.

We wrote to you on January 17 because of news reports contending that your company has been prominent among those placing pressure on the British Government to take this distressing step. *The Guardian* newspaper has published a memorandum from yourself to Mr. David Hastie indicating that you have written to Mr. Michael Heseltine, The Deputy Prime Minister, in connection with Dr. Mas'ari's asylum application.

Human Rights Watch works with corporations operating in many parts of the world, and it is our belief that private firms have a responsibility to avoid complicity in governmental human rights abuses. In this instance, we are deeply troubled by the reports that some British companies, including Vickers, have pressed for Dr. Mas'ari's expulsion from the United Kingdom on account of his criticisms of the government of Saudi Arabia, one of the most intolerant and repressive regimes in the Middle East.

We renew here our request for clarification from your office concerning Vickers' role in this matter. Thank you in advance for your attention to this request. We look forward to your reply.

Sincerely yours,

Kenneth Roth, Executive Director, Human Rights Watch.

Vickers reply: Vickers P.L.C. answered Human Rights Watch on the 22 February 1996:

Mr. Kenneth Roth, Human Rights Watch, New York,

Dear Mr. Roth,

Thank you for your letters dated January 17th and February 7th, receipt of which was acknowledged during my recent absence from the office.

For your records, please note that I am the Chief Executive of Vickers P.L.C. and not the Chief Executive of Vickers Defence Systems. I am aware that, throughout much of the media coverage concerning Dr. Al-Mas'ari, Vickers has been essentially portrayed as an 'arms dealer'. In fact, Vickers is an international engineering company with a turnover of £1.2bn (US$1.9bn) of which less than 30% is devoted to defence operations.

So far as the Kingdom of Saudi Arabia as a potential market for Vickers is concerned, we have opportunities for Rolls-Royce and Bentley motor cars manufactured by one of our subsidiaries and also for equipment from our Medical Division. These prospects are in addition to those for our Challenger 2 Main Battle Tank produced by another of our subsidiaries, Vickers Defence Systems.

Like any other Chief Executive Officer, I have to be concerned that my colleagues and I do all that we can to maximise our sales in order to provide benefits to our shareholders, employees and suppliers. Any obstacle to sales of products from this Company to Saudi Arabia – or, indeed, any other market – leads me to try to use any proper and legal means to try to overcome that obstacle.

Knowing the Saudi Government's strong feelings on the activities of Dr. Al-Mas'ari in the United Kingdom, expressed on many occasions to several British companies, and in the light of Vickers' legitimate commercial interest in Saudi Arabia, I brought that concern to the attention of the British Government. My actions were simple and straightforward.

In your letter you expressed some concern about the role some British companies reportedly played in seeking the expulsion of Dr. Al-Mas'ari. I did not, and indeed could not have pressed for Dr. Al-Mas'ari's expulsion, having no knowledge of or expertise in the laws of asylum of the United Kingdom. I merely pointed out the Saudi Arabia Government's concern as I understood it, and its possible adverse effect on business opportunities for Vickers. It was then a matter for the British Government to decide whether there was a legitimate means of dealing with this concern.

Yours sincerely,

Colin Chandler, Vickers P.L.C., Millbank Tower, Millbank, London.

Reply: On 8 March 1996, Human Rights Watch thanked Sir Colin Chandler, Vickers P.L.C.:

Dear Sir,

Thank you for your letter dated February 22, 1996, responding to ours regarding the role of Vickers in the decision of the British government to refuse to consider the application of Dr. Muhammad Mas'ari for asylum in the United Kingdom. We appreciate your clarifications regarding Vickers' corporate structure.

Human Rights Watch understands your responsibility to maximize business opportunities for your firm, and your interest in removing obstacles to product sales. In this case, our concern is not that you may have used improper or illegal means in pursuit of business opportunities. Rather, we are troubled by your reduction of Dr. al-Mas'ari's right to a fair hearing in his asylum application to the status of an 'obstacle' to Vickers' sales to Saudi Arabia.

There is an important issue of corporate social responsibility for human rights at stake here. Dr. al-Mas'ari had applied to the government of the United Kingdom as a political dissident. His own government, Saudi Arabia, is well-known for its comprehensive intolerance of non-violent political dissent and free expression, and its comprehensive repression of those who would exercise their rights in this regard. It was Dr. al-Mas'ari's attempt to do so which brought about his arrest and reported mistreatment in Saudi Arabia, and led him to flee that country. It is his exercise of these same rights in the UK which has generated Saudi government pressures on Whitehall, in part via yours and other firms, to have Dr. al-Mas'ari deported to a third country.

In the view of Human Rights Watch, it is the responsibility of international corporations to avoid being party to human rights violation by governments with whom they have a commercial relationship. Catering to Saudi Arabia's 'strong feelings on the activities of Dr. al-Mas'ari' places your company at odds with the human rights standards to which Britain and most other nations are State Parties. In this instance, Vickers has allowed itself to be complicit in the Saudi government's effort to suppress Dr. al-Mas'ari's right to freedom of speech.

Human Rights Watch does not question the legitimacy of Vickers' commercial interests in Saudi Arabia. We are concerned, however, that Vickers pursue those interests in a manner that comports with universally recognized standards of international law. In this regard, we urge Vickers and other corporations to make clear to governments with which they have dealings that they will not assist those governments in any way in their efforts to deny fundamental civil and political rights to their citizens.

Human Rights Watch hopes that your company will cooperate in efforts to widen and strengthen the rule of law in countries in which you do business. To that end, I am suggesting that Joe Stork, from our Middle East division, give your office a call next week when he is in London, to see if there might be a mutually convenient time to discuss this issue further.

Thank you again for yours, and I look forward to hearing from you again.

Yours sincerely,

Kenneth Roth

Archives of Human Rights Watch, Washington, DC, 1996.

16E
The House of Commons

British interests and morals as well as indirect attitudes towards Saudi Society were aired in a short dialogue in the House of Commons following the government decision to deport Saudi Arabian Professor Muhammed Al-Massari.

Mr. Neville Trotter (MP for Tynemouth): Is it not in the interests of Britain that Saudi Arabia should continue to have a stable government? Has not Mr. Al-Mas'ari abused his position as a guest in this country? And don't the thousands of people whose jobs he puts at risk, especially in the north of England, feel he's very fortunate to be offered a home in a Caribbean island, rather than being sent back where he came from?

Mr. John Major (Prime Minister): 'The UK has a long and an honorable tradition of protecting those who seek asylum . . . of helping those who seek asylum. But if people abuse that hospitality, I don't believe we should ignore that. The stability of the Saudi Arabian government is a matter of importance throughout the Gulf and to stability more generally, and I do not believe we should give comfort to those who seek to undermine it.'

House of Commons, London, 16 January 1996.

16F
The price

The Middle East Times in an article viewed the deportation of Professor Mass'ari as a British 'sacrifice' in its dealings with Saudi Arabia.

Mohammed Al Masaari – a leading Saudi dissident who has claimed political asylum in Britain – was told by the authorities in London that he would have to leave for the Caribbean backwater of Dominica. To sweeten the pill, Britain quadrupled its aid to Dominica to two million pounds sterling for each of the next two years.

The move followed months of pressure on the British government from leading members of the defence industry, intelligence forces and the Saudis to find a way of silencing Masaari – whose Committee for the Defence of Legitimate Rights has waged a propaganda campaign against the Saudi ruling family – or face harming Britain's lucrative arms deals with the desert kingdom.

'His [Masaari's] activities have been complicating our relations with the Saudis', admitted British Home Office Minister Ann Widdecombe. 'We've had various representations from people in British business and from the Saudis about the situation.'

One representation was from Andrew Green, the newly appointed British ambassador to Riyadh – who just happens to be a non-executive director at Vickers, the arms manufacturer hoping to pull off a three-billion-pound tank deal with the Saudis.

The affair also highlighted the controversial twenty-billion-pound Yamamah deal under which London provides arms in exchange for 600,000 barrels of oil per day.

Critics say that in deciding to deport Masaari – who was tortured in Saudi Arabia – the government has sacrificed Britain's long-cherished asylum rights. . .

Middle East Times, 14–20 January 1996.

16G
Calling for new decision

His Honour Judge David Pearl at Wood Green, 5 March 1996, heard the appeal of Mohammed A.S. al-Massari vs the Immigration Officer of the Secretary of State for the Home Department. In his decision, the judge said the following.

It is necessary to set out the evidence of Professor Al Mass'ari's activities, both past and present, because they have a bearing on the issues I need to decide. There is a detailed statement in the appellant's bundle which sets out Professor Al-Massari's claim for asylum. This document sets out how the appellant and six of his colleagues decided to publicly set up and declare the formation of a committee which according to Professor Al-Mass'ari, had as its object 'to protect human rights' in Saudi Arabia. The committee, with the appellant as spokesperson, was called the Committee for the Defence of Legitimate Rights (which I shall refer to as CDLR). The CDLR was formally announced on 3rd May 1993. In his evidence before me, Professor Al-Mass'ari gave an account of what then transpired; namely he lost his job as a Professor of Physics on 13th May 1993, he was kept in detention for six months and ten days, and whilst in detention he was ill-treated. The following extract from his evidence sets out what he said happened to him whilst in detention:

'I was deprived of sleep, interrogations through the night, beaten on the back, abuse and threats all the time, shoes thrown at me, beaten with a cane on the back of my body and on the soles of my feet.'

In his statement, which he confirmed in evidence, he said that he was eventually released after being forced to sign a document to say that there would be no celebration held on his release and that he would not tell anybody about his time in prison. He recounted also that he was taken before a Sharia Court (an Islamic religious court) where, according to him, an agreed form of words was negotiated which would have satisfied both himself and his accusers. In fact, he said that the published decree ignored the agreed form of words and omitted any mention of the formula which he said had been entered on the Record Book of the Court. He felt that the inaccurate published decree was made for political reasons, and he brought a legal counterclaim. His appeal request was set for hearing, but before this came about, he was again picked up by the Security forces and told that his appeal had been reviewed in secret and that it had been dismissed. He was given a document to sign which he said he signed under duress, in the sense that if he had not signed it he would have been returned to detention. He then left Saudi Arabia clandestinely and travelled to Yemen. He obtained a false Yemen passport, then using that passport he obtained a UK visit visa, and he landed in UK on 18th April 1994.

In answers to questions from me, the appellant explained what activities CDLR were involved in from his base here in London. He said that he sends 850 faxes a week to Saudi Arabia, and 700 faxes to USA and Canada. These faxes are translated into English and sent to the media around the world. The recipients of the faxes would include individuals, institutions, and even the King of Saudi Arabia. He said he also uses Email facilities although this is obviously confined to the English language. His campaign is directed at 'removing injustice, supporting the oppressed and defending the rights that were given to man by the Shari'a (the Islamic law)' (Declaration of the CDLR; 3rd May 1993). It is common ground that in these activities, the appellant has committed no act which can amount to a criminal offence under English law. It is also common ground that his activities are designed to embarrass the government of Saudi Arabia.

The UK's response

The UK Government's response to the activities of the appellant are conveniently set out in the particulars served pursuant to the Order that I made in the preliminary hearing on 1st February 1996. The second set of Particulars deals with information made available by HMG to the Government of Dominica as to the appellant's claim for asylum. It states as follows:

'2. Particulars of information made available by HMG to the government of Dominica as to the Appellant's claim for asylum

(a) At the meeting on 18th December 1995, between the Secretary of State and the Dominican Prime Minister, the Dominican government was informed that the Appellant was conducting a campaign against the Saudi Arabian government by fax and the Saudi Arabian government was extremely anxious about the Appellant's activities, and that HMG's attempt to remove the Appellant to the Yemen had failed because of the risk that the Appellant would suffer persecution there.

(b) The following background information on the Appellant's presence in London and the nature of the Appellant's claim for asylum was supplied to the Dominican government.

The Appellant was born in Mecca in 1946 and is a Saudi Arabian national. He was educated at Cologne University and became an associate professor of physics at the King Saud University, Riyadh. In 1993, he was linked to the foundation of a new group designed to oppose the Saudi government, which was named 'The Committee for the Defence of Legitimate Rights' ('CDLR'). The Appellant's father was one of the six founding members of the group. As a fluent speaker of English, the Appellant became the group's spokesman.

The group's name was carefully chosen to lead external commentators to believe that it was concerned with human rights and liberal values. In fact, 'legitimate' equates to 'relating to the Sharia (Islamic law)'; the CDLR calls for a more rigid and rigorous implementation of Islamic law than exists in Saudi Arabia at present. The group's agenda would significantly reduce the freedoms currently available to Saudi Arabian citizens.

Shortly after the group's foundation, the Saudi Arabian government ordered that it be disbanded and dismissed all its members from their jobs. The Appellant, along with a number of other members of the group, was arrested. After a period in detention, during which the Appellant claims to have been mistreated, the Saudi authorities released him. The Appellant later evaded their surveillance and escaped to the Yemen, where he acquired a Yemeni passport in a different name, which he used to obtain a visa for the United Kingdom and to travel to London.

He arrived in the United Kingdom on 18th April 1994. Three days later his solicitors lodged a claim for asylum with the Home Office. The Appellant also set up an office. On 20th April 1994 he sent a fax to Saudi Arabia announcing the resumption of the group's activities. Since then, he has sent thousands of faxes to government and non-government fax numbers in Saudi Arabia. These faxes have contained personal abuse of members of the Saudi royal family, and have sought to undermine the stability of the Kingdom of Saudi Arabia.

In November 1994, the Home Secretary decided that the Appellant should be returned to the Yemen, as a safe third country through which he had passed on his way to the United Kingdom. However, an independent Immigration Special Adjudicator allowed the Appellant's appeal. Consequently, the Appellant's case awaits a further decision.

During his period in the United Kingdom, the Appellant had not broken the law of the United Kingdom. There had been no evidence of direct involvement with terrorism or with individuals actively involved in terrorist groups.

It will be seen that there are some differences between the account given to me by the appellant of his activities and his aims, and the account given by HMG to the Government of Dominica. These differences, however, are not substantial in character. It is clear however from these particulars, and from the additional statement in paragraph 1(e) of the particulars, that EMO thought that the removal of the appellant from London 'would be well received in the Arab world and particularly in Saudi Arabia'. That same paragraph discloses that 'although HMG could not give any assurances on the question whether decisions on aid could be speeded up, HMG acknowledged that one good turn deserved another'.

(i) *Evidence that the Saudi regime has in the past taken violent action against its opponents both within Saudi Arabia and elsewhere*

I heard a great deal of evidence on the issue of the activities of Saudi Arabia, in particular with regard to evidence that they were involved in violent action against opponents both within Saudi Arabia and extra-territorially. The main witness called by the appellant was Mr Said K. Aburish. He is the author of a book *The Rise, Corruption and Coming Fall of the House of Saud*. The title itself provides a flavour of the contents. Mr Aburish gave evidence in the earlier hearing before Mr Care. In his determination Mr Care said: 'Mr Aburish gave valuable testimony and, as far as one can ever expect any certainty, I think that his evidence came close to it. In any event, he gave his evidence convincingly.' Of course, Mr Care was considering the safety of Yemen and I must make my own independent assessment of Mr Aburish's evidence.

Mr Richards submitted that I should treat Mr Aburish's testimony with considerable caution. He suggested that it was based on second, third or even fourth hand reports and he reminded me of the risks of accepting at face value hearsay evidence. Mr Aburish referred in his evidence to a number of incidents; in particular those concerning Selim Louzi, Nasser Al-Said, Muhammad Mirri, Muhammad Al Fassi, and a journalist whom he did not name whose arms were broken in Marbella. In all these incidents Mr Aburish identified Saudi Arabian agents, or those working on behalf of Saudi Arabia, as being responsible for violent acts against individuals outside the borders of Saudi Arabia. He was subjected to very close cross examination by Mr Richards. It is suggested by Mr Richards that the incidents have no certain basis.

The last alleged incident of violence is in 1991. In his book, Mr Aburish said that 'the use of violence backfires' and therefore the Saudis resort now to more subtle techniques. When questioned on this apparent inconsistency, he said that policy changes all the time, and he felt that the danger of violence could reoccur 'now that the cat is out of the bag'.

Against Mr Aburish's view there is the Memorandum of the Home Office which reads as follows:

'The Government assessed that it would be contrary to Saudi Arabia's interests that an attack on Dr al-Mass'ari should take place. Whoever was responsible for such an attack Saudi Arabia would be blamed. The Kingdom's reputation and interests would be gravely damaged. Nevertheless in the light of all the factors relating to Dr al-Mass'ari's safety, and the allegations of threats to him, HMG sought assurances from the Saudi Government. The Saudi Government assured HMG that it was not, and never had been', the policy of the Saudi Government to seek to cause harm to the person of Dr al-Mass'ari.'

There has also been disclosed a letter from the Ambassador of the Royal Embassy of Saudi Arabia to the Court of St James, Mr Ghazi Algosaibi. This letter is dated 20.2.96 and is addressed to the Assistant Under Secretary for the Middle East, FCO. It reads as follows:

'In the light of claims made by Dr Mohammad al-Mas'ari you asked me for assurances regarding his safety. On instructions from my Government, I hereby confirm to you that causing physical harm to Dr al-Mas'ari, or others, has never been the policy of the Saudi Government in the past or the present, and will not be its policy in the future. Any such actions would be contrary to the principles and beliefs of the Saudi Government.'

Mr Richards asked me to prefer the view of the FCO backed up by the letter written by the Ambassador to what he referred to as the 'highly speculative and unsubstantiated assertions' of Mr Aburish.

Mr Nicol submitted that I should treat the Ambassador's letter with caution. I must say that I agree with him on this matter. I have heard evidence of how the appellant was incarcerated in Saudi Arabia and how relatives of his have also been arrested and imprisoned. I also have had cited to me reports from Amnesty International, Human Rights Watch and the US State Department. This independent evidence, the thrust of which I accept, would appear to contradict the evidence of past behaviour in the Ambassador's letter. As a statement of future policy, of course, the letter carries little weight. So far as the HMG memorandum is concerned, this also can only be an assessment which is to be viewed in the light of the respondent desperately trying 'to find a way of disposing of the Mass'ari problem', as Mr Nicol put it.

Mr Nicol in his submissions urged me, when considering Mr Aburish's evidence, to bear in mind that his evidence was the product of considerable research over many years. He submitted that it was not necessary, when making an assessment of the risk, to produce convincing evidence sufficient to satisfy a criminal court.

There is of course an inherent difficulty in assessing this evidence by its very nature, in the 'half light' of intrigue which has accompanied Middle Eastern politics for many years, it is not certain where the truth lies. A great deal of the 'evidence' is inference, hearsay, and mere speculation. The first of this type of evidence might be acceptable if the issue came before an English court; the last certainly would not; and the middle category would require some corroboration before conclusions could be drawn. I do not know where the truth lies in the incidents given in evidence by Mr Aburish. Suffice it to say that I am convinced that Mr Aburish believes that the incidents occurred in the way he described in evidence, and the appellant also believes that they occurred in that way; namely that the Saudi regime was behind all the acts of violence described.

I have looked at this evidence very carefully, and I have arrived at the conclusion that Mr Aburish's evidence can be viewed in the following sense. It goes towards the argument that the appellant represents, so long as he continues his campaign, a continuing threat to the Saudi Arabian Government. There is some evidence that Saudi Arabian agents, or those acting under orders from Saudi Arabia, have been involved in extra-territorial violence. This evidence would not satisfy a criminal court; or indeed even satisfy a test 'more probable than not'. However, I do find that there is 'some' suggestion, which is in no way fanciful, that the Saudi Government has been involved in extra-territorial violence in the past. I do not put it any higher than that.

(ii) *Evidence of threats to the appellant in the UK*

I have heard evidence of threats to the appellant in the UK. In his statement, the appellant states as follows:

Because of the effectiveness of the CDLR's campaign for democracy and political rights I believe the Saudi royal family will go to great lengths to silence me. I have received plausible threats to my life while in the United Kingdom. For example one was in December 1994 as a result of which I met with an officer from Scotland Yard Special Branch at my solicitor's offices on 15 December 1994 to pass over the information and to receive advice on personal physical safety here. On another occasion there was a threatening telephone call to me and a tape of the call was passed to Special Branch who continued to review their safety advice, talking to my solicitors at intervals and I met the officer concerned again at my solicitor's offices on 11 May 1995 and had a long discussion and he came to review security at my home and CDLR premises on 17 May 1995 and saw me again at my solicitor's offices on 9 October 1995.

On two other occasions threats were strongly reported to CDLR. I have also seen in the past newspaper reports referring to death threats and hit squads, for example in the *Mail on Sunday* of 13 November 1994. A copy of that item is included in my bundle of documents. I believe measures taken against me so far by the Saudi royal family have included enormous diplomatic pressure on the British government not to offer me a place of refuge in the United Kingdom. This is clearly reflected in the newspaper clippings, in my bundle of documents, already referred to above included in my bundle of documents.

There is in the documentation, an article from the *Mail on Sunday* dated 13.11.94 headed 'Saudi squad hunts rebels in Britain' which suggests that a Saudi death squad is in Britain on a secret mission to assassinate exiled Saudis living in UK, and that one of the two men most at risk is the appellant. I have been shown attendance notes between the solicitors and a Special Branch officer which concern the appellant's safety. In one of the notes, Mr is reported as saying: 'There is obviously no doubt that the authorities in Saudi Arabia are extremely annoyed about the whole thing and they have made representations to the authorities here about your continued presence here . . . it is obvious that you have annoyed King Fahd and this is why I am concerned about your safety here. I have discussed with my colleagues, we have never known of any occasion when the Saudis have taken direct action here. . . although they have never taken action before – they could use others to do so – I'm worried because I don't recall any other occasion of a Saudi dissident having so much publicity in six months.'

I heard evidence of abusive and threatening phone calls to the appellant on 23rd April 1995 which were left on the ansaphone. I have seen an English translation. The first message starts: 'A curse may damn your father and mother! You are a whore, a pimp. You will be slaughtered right in your place this week.'

The third message says: 'You will be slaughtered, yes that is easy; but before you will be tortured. Be sure you will be kidnapped, then tortured and publicly denounced and then killed. You deserve nothing except this. Go to your end, son of a bitch!'

It would seem that the Government has kept under review the possibility that the appellant might be at physical risk in the UK. He has been provided with police advice on security matters, although it has not been judged necessary to offer him special protection. It is the Government's assessment that there would be no increase in risk by virtue of his removal to Dominica. However, Scotland Yard Special Branch have been involved in providing the appellant with security advice, and there is therefore some evidence which suggests that the appellant's safety in this country is a matter of concern. There is evidence which suggests that the Special Branch believe that the Saudi regime could use illegal measures against this appellant given his high profile.

All this evidence added together leads me to the conclusion that there is some risk, perhaps not very high by itself, but nevertheless there, that the respondent fails to discharge the onus of proof. But it is now necessary to consider the other aspect of the question relating to safety, namely the position of Dominica.

Dominica

I turn therefore to the evidence relating to the safety of the appellant if he were removed to Dominica. The Commonwealth of Dominica is situated in the Windward Islands group. English is the official language. It is primarily an agrarian economy which depends on earnings from banana exports to the UK. It has a total population, according to the US State Department Report, of 72,000. Of this total there are some 3,000 Carib Indians who live on a 3,700 acre reservation. It became independent in 1978. The present Government is headed by the United Workers Party and the Prime Minister is Mr Edison James. According to the 1995 *Europa Yearbook*, Dominica's history has not been entirely free from strife. In 1979, two people were killed by the Defence Force at a Demonstration, and this was followed by a General Strike; in 1986 the former Commander of the Defence Force was hanged for the murder of a police officer during a coup attempt; a programme introduced in 1991 granting citizenship in return for a minimum investment of $35,000 caused controversy and there were demonstrations; and it is reported by the US State Department Report that during campaigning for a new chief of the Carib indigenous territory in June 1994, a policeman shot and killed a man. The policeman said that he was protecting himself and others, but witnesses claimed the shooting was unprovoked and stemmed from a lingering feud. The authorities reduced the charges to manslaughter, suspended the policeman and released him on bail pending trial.

It is clear to me from all the evidence I have read and heard that there is considerable local opposition to the arrival of the appellant. For instance, the leader of the opposition Labour party, Mr Douglas, is reported as saying at a News Conference: 'The last thing the people of Dominica needed with the economy at the point of collapse was to bring in a controversial figure whose presence may well lead to threats on his life. The local police force was small and badly resourced. It could hardly protect Professor Al-Mas'ari.'

It is my finding, therefore, giving the matter the most anxious scrutiny in an area of factual information which is surrounded by uncertainty, that the Secretary of State has not established that Dominica is a safe third country within the meaning of the Immigration Rules such that he is entitled to refuse the appellant's asylum claim without substantive consideration. Accordingly, he was not entitled to certify the claim as without foundation.

I make a strong recommendation that the Secretary of State considers the substance of the asylum claim expeditiously and, in any event, within one month of today's date. My reason for making this recommendation is that I believe that the continued uncertainty that would otherwise be produced would be detrimental to the interests of the appellant, the public at large, and also the claims of other asylum seekers.

Thus my findings are:

1. That the Secretary of State was not entitled to certify the appellant's asylum claim as being without foundation.
2. That the case be referred to the Secretary of State for reconsideration.
3. That I recommend strongly that the Secretary of State considers the substantive claim to asylum as expeditiously as possible and in any event within one month of today's date.

His Honour Judge David Pearl, Chief Adjudicator, London, 6 March 1996.

In April Mohammed al-Massari was granted four years permission to stay in Britain.

Chapter Seventeen

GULF WAR

17A
Desert Shield

President Bush in a letter to the Congress, August 9th 1990, announced his decision to defend the kingdom of Saudi Arabia:

Hon. Tomas Foley, Speaker of the House of Representation Washington, DC.

Dear Mr. Speaker: On August 2, 1990, Iraq invaded and occupied the sovereign state of Kuwait in flagrant violation of the charter of the United Nations. In the period since August 2, Iraq has massed an enormous and sophisticated war machine on the Kuwaiti-Saudi Arabian border and in southern Iraq, capable of initiating further hostilities with little or no additional preparation. Iraq's actions pose a direct threat to neighboring countries and to vital U.S. interests in the Persian Gulf region.

In response to this threat and after receiving the request of the Government of Saudi Arabia, I ordered the forward deployment of substantial elements of the United States Armed Forces into the region. I am providing this report on the deployment and mission of our Armed Forces in accordance with my desire that Congress be fully informed and consistent with the War Powers Resolution.

Two squadrons of F-15 aircraft, one brigade of the 82nd Airborne Division, and other elements of the Armed Forces began arriving in Saudi Arabia at approximately 9:00 a.m. (EDT) on August 8, 1990. Additional U.S. air, naval, and ground Forces also will be deployed. The Forces are equipped for combat, and their mission is defensive. They are prepared to take action in concert with Saudi forces, friendly regional forces, and others to deter Iraqi aggression and to preserve the integrity of Saudi Arabia.

I do not believe involvement in hostilities is imminent; to the contrary, it is my belief that this deployment will facilitate a peaceful resolution of the crisis. If necessary, however, the Forces are fully prepared to defend themselves. Although it is not possible to predict the precise scope and duration of this deployment, our Armed Forces will remain so long as their presence is required to contribute the security of the region and desired by the Saudi government to enhance the capability of Saudi armed forces to defend the Kingdom.

I have taken these actions pursuant to my constitutional authority to conduct our foreign relations and as Commander in Chief. These actions are in exercise of our inherent right of individual and collective self-defense. I look forward to cooperation with the Congress in helping to restore peace and stability to the Persian Gulf region.

Sincerely,

George Bush

Communication from the President of the United States of America, 101 Congress, 2nd Session, House Document 101-225

17B
Defending Justice

President Bush in a message to the Congress elaborated on principles of US policies in the Gulf Area and Internationally, September 11th 1990:

A new partnership of nations has begun.

We stand today at a unique and extraordinary moment. The crisis in the Persian Gulf, as grave as it is, also offers a rare opportunity to move toward an historic period of cooperation. Out of these troubled times, our fifth objective – a new world order – can emerge: a new era – free from the threat of terror, stronger in the pursuit of justice, and more secure in the quest for peace. An era in which the nations of the world, east and west, north and south, can prosper and live in harmony.

A hundred generations have searched for this elusive path to peace, while thousand wars raged across the span of human endeavour. Today that new world is struggling to be born. A world quite different from the one we've known. A world where the rule of law supplants the rule of the jungle. A world in which nations recognize the shared responsibility for freedom and justice. A world where the strong respect the rights of the weak.

This is the vision I shared with President Gorbachev in Helsinki. We, and other leaders from Europe, the Gulf and around the world, understand that how we manage this crisis today, could shape the future for generations to come.

The test we face is great – and so are the stakes. This is the first assault on the new world we seek, the first test of our mettle. And had we not responded to this first, provocation with clarity of purpose; if we do not continue to demonstrate our determination; it would be a signal to actual and potential despots around the world.

America and the world must defend common vital interests, and we will.

America and the world must support the rule of law, and we will.

American and the world must stand up to aggression, and we will.

And one thing more – in pursuit of these goals America will not be limited.

Vital issues of principle are at stake. Saddam Hussein is literally trying to wipe a country off the face of the earth.

We do not exaggerate.

Nor do we exaggerate when we say: Saddam will fall.

Vital economic interests are at risk as well. Iraq itself controls some ten percent of the world's proven oil reserves. Iraq plus Kuwait controls twice that. An Iraq permitted to swallow Kuwait would have the economic and military power, as well as the arrogance to intimidate and coerce its neighbours – neighbours who control the lion's share of the world's remaining oil reserves. We cannot permit a resource so vital to be dominated by one so ruthless. And we won't.

Recent events have surely proven that there is no substitute for American leadership. In the face of tyranny, let no one doubt American credibility and reliability.

> Message from the President of the United States of America to the Congress, 101 Congress, 2nd Session, House Document 101-235.

17C
The Gulf War

A Fact list on Operation Desert Shield and Desert Storm, prepared by the United States Central Command:

Air war begins: 3 a.m./17 Jan 91 (7 p.m./16 Jan EST) Ground war – 4 a.m./ 24 Feb (8 p.m./23 Feb EST)

Cessation of hostilities – 8 a.m./28 Feb 91
        (1 a.m/27 Feb 91 EST)

Safwan Cease-fire talks - 11 a.m./3 Mar 91
        (4 a.m./3 Mar 91 EST)

Cease Fire – 11 April 91

Personnel:
Number of U.S. forces at start of ground war: 541,425
        (total 35,146 women)

Army	303,500
Marines	92,800
Navy	83,600 (incl. 800 Coast Guard)
Air Force	54,700
CENTCOM hdqtrs	1,200
SOCCENT	5,300
JCSE	325

Number of coalition forces at start of ground war: 257,900

Number of countries with troops supporting coalition: 31

Afghanistan:	300
Argentina:	300
Australia:	700
Bahrain:	400
Bangladesh:	2,200
Belgium:	400
Canada:	200
Czechoslovakia:	200
Denmark:	100
Egypt:	33,600
France:	14,600
Greece:	200
Hungary:	50
Italy:	1,200
Kuwait:	9,900
Morocco:	13,000
Netherlands:	600
Niger:	500
Norway:	50
Oman:	6,300
Pakistan:	4,900
Poland:	200
Qatar:	2,600
Saudi Arabia:	100,000
Senegal:	500
South Korea:	200
Spain:	500
Syria:	14,500
UAE:	4,300
U.K.:	45,400

Casualties

Total Killed in Action:	244
U.S.:	146
Saudi Arabia:	47
United Kingdom:	25
Egypt:	12
UAE:	10
Syria:	2
France:	2

Total Wounded in action:	894
U.S.:	467
Saudi Arabia:	220
Egypt:	95
U.K.:	45
France:	38
UAE:	17
Senegal:	8
Bahrain:	2
Syria:	1
Oman:	1

Friendly Fire:

U.S.	35
U.K.	9

Number of tons equipment shipped/flown to Southwest Asia at height of war:

3.6 million short tons of equipment & material

Number of gallons jet/diesel/gas used by U.S. from Aug 90–Mar 91:

1.8 billion U.S. gallons (used in AOR, not enroute)

Number of MAC passengers/MAC cargo:

509,129 passengers & 594,730 tons of cargo (as of 7 June 1991)

Total number of combat sorties: 126,645

Total tons of bombs dropped: 96,000 tons

Tons of bombs dropped by U.S.: 88,500 tons

Total number of U.S. combat aircraft:

Air Force	1,203
Navy	444
Marines	364
Army	1,358 (all as of 17 Jan 91)

Number of total sorties flown by Saudi Air Force: 7,018

Number of coalition countries with combat aircraft supporting war: 11

Bahrain:	36
Canada:	24
France:	61
Italy:	10
Kuwait:	41
New Zealand:	2
Qatar:	18
Saudi Arabia:	351

South Korea:	3
UAE:	50
U.K.:	100

Iraqis
Number of Iraqi forces in Kuwait:
- estimated 623,000 in Kuwait Theater of Operations
Number of Iraqi fixed wing/helicopters downed: 36/6 (air to air)
Number of Iraqi fixed wing/helicopters destroyed: 68/13 (on the ground)
Number of Iraqi aircraft flown to Iran (all types): 137
Number of Iraqi main battle tanks destroyed: 3,700 of 4,280
Number of Iraqi armoured vehicles destroyed: 2,400 of 2,870
Number of Iraqi artillery pieces destroyed: 2,600 of 3,110
Number of Iraqi Naval ships sunk/destroyed: 19/6
Number of Iraqi army divisions rendered ineffective: 42
Enemy Prisoners of War (EPWs.) by U.S. and released to Saudis First
reported capture, 15 Jan 91
Number of EPWs on 28 Feb 91: 45,302
Peak Number of EPWs: 71,204
Number of EPWs on 11 Apr 91: 67,006
Coalition Contributions/Cost Sharing (2 Aug 90–31 Dec 91

Total pledged contributions: 53,951,000,000 US Doll
Total amount outstanding: 1,454,000,000 US Doll

Germany:	6,572,000,000 (pledged)/0 US Doll outstanding
Japan:	10,072,000,000/30,000,000 outstanding
Korea:	355,000,000/112,000,000
Kuwait:	16,006,000,000/0
Saudi:	16,839,000,000/1,312,000,000
UAE:	4,088,000,000/0
Others:	30,000,000/0

Naval intercepts (August 90–16 January 92)

Total number ships challenged:	12,713
Total number boarded:	3,292
Diverted after boarding:	212
Allowed to proceed after boarding:	3,080
Allowed to proceed without boarding:	179
Diverted without boarding:	1
Boardings by U.S. Forces:	1,943
Boardings by allies:	1,349

Countries which assisted in intercepts/boardings:
Argentina, Australia, Belgium, Canada, Denmark, France, Greece, Italy,
Norway, the Netherlands, Spain, the United Kingdom and the U.S.

Countries still participating in intercepts/boardings:
Australia, France and the U.S.

Misc.

Total number of Iraqi Scuds launched:	88
Riyadh:	20
Dhahran:	14
Hafar Al Batin:	4
KKMC:	4
Bahrain:	3
Jubayl:	2
Qatar:	1
Tel Aviv:	33
Haifa:	6
Dimona:	1

Number of U.S. hospitals in theater: 64
Number of medical personnel in theater: over 41,000
Time Iraq invaded Kuwait: 1 a.m./2 Aug 90 (5 p.m./1 Aug 90)
Operation DESERT SHIELD: 12 Aug 90–16 Jan 91
Operation DESERT STORM: 17 Jan 91–
Operation DESERT SHIELD (and Operation DESERT STORM, if we went
to war) name was picked by General H. Norman Schwarzkopf on 24 Aug
90
Time General Schwarzkopf issued command to stop fighting:
5 p.m./27 Feb 91 (9 a.m./27 Feb 91) with command to go into effect at 8
a.m./28 Feb 91 (4 p.m./28 Feb 91 EST)

Time difference:
most of Southwest Asia is 8 hours ahead of EST

Press
Number of Press briefings in Riyadh:
98; 53 on the record and 45 on background, plus 13 educational briefings
on background

Number of journalists in Saudi Arabia

in Mid-December:	400
during Air War:	1,000
in Saudi Arabia/Kuwait during ground war:	1,200
in Saudi Arabia/Kuwait at war's end:	1,700

U.N. security council resolutions
Res. 660, 2 Aug 90, condemns Iraqi invasion of Kuwait
Res. 661, 6 Aug 90, Imposes economic sanctions against Iraq Res. 662, 9
Aug 90, declares Iraqi annexation of Kuwait null and void

Res. 664, 18 Aug 90, Calls for immediate release of foreigners from Iraq and Kuwait

Res. 665, 25 Aug 90, Authorizes use of force to halt maritime shipping to and from Iraq

Res. 666, 13 Sept 90, establishes guidelines for humanitarian aid to Iraq and Kuwait

Res. 667, 16 Sept 90, Condemns Iraq and demands protection of diplomatic personnel

Res. 669, 24 Sept 90, Authorizes examination of requirements for economic assistance under U.N. article 50

Res. 670, 25 Sept 90, Condemns Iraq and confirms economic embargo, including air

Res. 674, 29 Oct 90, Condemns Iraq and calls for release of third-country nationals and provisions of food

Res. 677, 28 Nov 90, Condemns Iraqi attempts to alter Kuwaiti demographics

Res. 678, 29 Nov 90, Authorizes the use of force to uphold resolutions unless Iraq with-draws by 15 Jan 91

Res. 686, 2 Mar 91, Demands Iraq cease all hostile actions and abide by resolutions

Res. 687, 3 Apr 91, Sets forth permanent cease-fire

Pentagon, 'Mediaw5:Desstorm.fct') 1992

APPENDIX

States	(1)	(2)	(3)	(4)	(5)	(6)	(7)	(8)	(9)	(10)	(11)	(12)	(13)	(14)
Oman						X								
Pakistan					X	X		X		X	X	X	s	
Palau										X				
Panama	X	X	X	X	X	X	s	X		X	X			
Papua New Guinea					X			X		X		X		
Paraguay	X	X	X					s		X	X	X		
Peru	X	X^a	X		X^b	X	X	X		X	X	X		
Philippines	X	X^a	X		X	X	X	X	X	X	X	X		X
Poland	X	X^a	X		X	X	X	X	X	X	X	X	X	X
Portugal	X	X	X	X	X					X	X		s	
Qatar					X	X	X			X				
Republic of Korea	X	X^a	X		X			X	X	X				
Republic of Moldova	X	X			X			X	X	X	X	X		
Romania	X	X	X	X	X			X		X	X	X	X	X
Russian Federation	X	X	X		X^b	X	X	X		X	X	X	X	
Rwanda	X	X			X	X	s	X	X	X	X			
Saint Kitts and Nevis								X		X	X			
Saint Lucia					X		s			X	X		X	
Saint Vincent & Grenadines	X	X	X		X	X		X	X	X				
Samoa										X	X			X
San Marino	X	X	X							X				
Sao Tome and Principe	s	s				X				X	s			
Saudi Arabia								X		X				
Senegal	X	X^a	X		X^b	X	X	X		X	X	X		
Seychelles	X	X	X		X	X		X		X	X			
Sierra Leone					X		s			X	X	X	X	
Singapore								X		X	X		X	
Slovakia	X	X	X		X^b	X		X	X	X	X	X		
Slovenia	X	X^a	X	X	X	X		X	X	X	X	X		
Solomon Islands	X				X					X		X		
Somalia	X	X	X		X	X	s			X				
South Africa	s	s			s					X	X	s	s	X
Spain	X	X^a	X	X	X			X		X	X	X		X
Sri Lanka	X	X^a			X	X		X		X	X		X	s
Sudan	X	X			X	X	X			X				
Suriname	X	X	X		X	X				X	X			
Swaziland					X					X		X	X	
Sweden	X	X^a	X	X	X^b			X		X	X	X	X	X
Switzerland	X	X^a		X	X					s	s			
Syrian Arab Rep.	X	X			X	X	X	X		X				
Tajikistan					X					X	X			
Thailand										X	X	X		

(15) Convention against Torture and other Cruel, Inhuman or Degrading Treatment or Punishment	(16) Slavery Convention of 1926	(17) 1953 Protocol amending the 1926 Convention	(18) Slavery Convention of 1926 as amended	(19) Supplementary Convention on the Abolition of Slavery, the Slave Trade, and Institutions and Practices Similar to Slavery	(20) Convention for the Suppression of the Traffic in Persons and of the Exploitation of the Prostitution of Others	(21) Convention on the Reduction of Statelessness	(22) Convention relating to the Status of Stateless Persons	(23) Convention relating to the Status of Refugees	(24) Protocol relating to the Status of Refugees	(25) Convention on the rights of migrant workers and the members of their families	(26)	(27)	(28)	States
														Oman
		X	X	X										Pakistan
														Palau
X	s							X	X					Panama
			X					X	X					Papua New Guinea
X								X	X					Paraguay
X				s				X	X					Peru
Xᶜ	X		X	X	X		s	X	X	X				Philippines
Xᶜ	X			X	X			X	X					Poland
Xᶜ	X			X	X			X	X					Portugal
X														Qatar
					X		X	X	X					Republic of Korea
X														Republic of Moldova
X	X	X	X	X	X			X	X					Romania
Xᶜ			X	X	X			X	X					Russian Federation
								X	X					Rwanda
														Saint Kitts and Nevis
	X	X	X	X										Saint Lucia
	X	X	X	X				X						Saint Vincent & Grenadines
								X	X					Samoa
				X										San Marino
								X	X					Sao Tome and Principe
			X	X										Saudi Arabia
X	X			X	X			X	X					Senegal
X	X			X	X			X	X	X				Seychelles
s			X	X				X	X					Sierra Leone
				X				X	X					Singapore
Xᶜ	X			X	X			X	X					Slovakia
Xᶜ				X	X			X	X					Slovenia
	X	X	X	X				X	X					Solomon Islands
X								X	X					Somalia
s	X	X	X		X			X	X					South Africa
Xᶜ	X	X	X	X	X			X	X					Spain
X			X	X	X					X				Sri Lanka
s			X	X				X	X					Sudan
	X			X				X	X					Suriname
									X					Swaziland
Xᶜ	X	X	X	X		X	X	X	X					Sweden
Xᶜ	X	X	X	X			X	X	X					Switzerland
	X	X	X	X	X									Syrian Arab Rep.
														Tajikistan
X								X	X					Thailand

CHRONOLOGY

1720 – Saud bin Mohammad reigns as a local sheikh in central Arab
Peninsular.

1745 – Mohammad, son of Saud, in alliance with preacher Abdul
Wahhab, campaigns for religious piety and control.

1818 – Ottoman forces put an end to Saudi control. Great-grandson of
Muhammad bin Saud killed.

1824 – Saud family takes back control of Riyadh.

1860s – Saud family divided over succession.

1891 – Saud ruler, Abdul Rahman flees to Kuwait.

1902 – Abdul Aziz campaigns for control of Riyadh.

1912 – The brotherhood 'Ikhwan' established. Provides combat troops
for Abdul Aziz.

1913 – Abdul Aziz takes control of Gulf Coast.

1925 – Abdul Aziz takes control of Mecca and Medina as well as all of
Hejaz.

1920s – Widespread rivalry and takeovers on the Arabian Peninsular.

1926 – Abdul Aziz ibn Saud becomes king of Hejaz and Najd.

1932 – Abdul Aziz ibn Saud establishes the Kingdom of Saudi Arabia
under his own name.

1933 – Abdul Aziz appoints eldest son, Saud, as crown prince.

1938 – Oil is found.

1955 – Abdul Aziz dies. Saud takes over.

1958 – Faisal, younger brother of Saud, takes over executive power
following family disagreements.

1960 – Saud retakes power.

1962 – Faisal promises to establish a consultative Shoura Council following
family feud over calls from princes Talal, Badr and Fawwaz for
greater liberality. Monarchy overthrown in neighbouring Yemen.

1964 – Following calls from members of royal family, the upper *Ulema*
calls for change of power. Saud is followed by Faisal.

1969 – Saud dies in exile.

1973 – Arab-Israeli October War. Saudi Arabia backs oil embargo of the
USA and others.

1975 – King Faisal assassinated by nephew. Followed by King Khaled. Prince Fahad becomes crown prince, sidestepping Saad and Nasir.

1979 – Shah deposed from Iran by popular revolution, led by ayatollah Khomeini. Sunni uprising in Grand Mosque in Mecca.

1980 – Iraq–Iran war.

1982 – King Khaled dies. His brother Fahad becomes king. Abdallah appointed crown prince.

1986 – Fahad decides to be 'the Custodian of the Two Holy Cities' instead of just 'Majesty'.

1987 – Riots in Mecca, instigated by pilgrims from Iran.

1988 – Saudi Arabia buys Chinese medium-range missiles able to reach Israel and Iranian capital Teheran; US protests; end of Gulf War.

1990 – Second Gulf War/ Iraq invades Kuwait 2 August.

1991 – US-led international forces liberates Kuwait. In Saudi Arabia King Fahad cancels old system of lifelong ministerial appointments and introduces four-year appointments.

1992 – King Fahad establishes a new consultative shoura by decree.

1993 – King Fahad appoints 60 members of new Shoura.

1994 – Widespread demonstration after arrest of religious radical Salman el-Ouda.

1995 – King Fahad acknowledges new emir of Qatar after his revolt against previous ruler, his father.

1995 – August; King Fahad replaces 16 ministers (finance, oil, information and others).

1995 – November; a car bomb in Riyadh kills seven people, among them five US advisers. Several movements claim responsibility.

1996 – April; four Saudi Arabian citizens are sentenced to death for the November 1995 bombing. US authorities refused permission to interview the group before public execution. In late June, another bomb kills 19 US servicemen in Dhahran. King Fahad seriously ill, Abdallah temporarily takes charge.

The Saud family: main line of succession

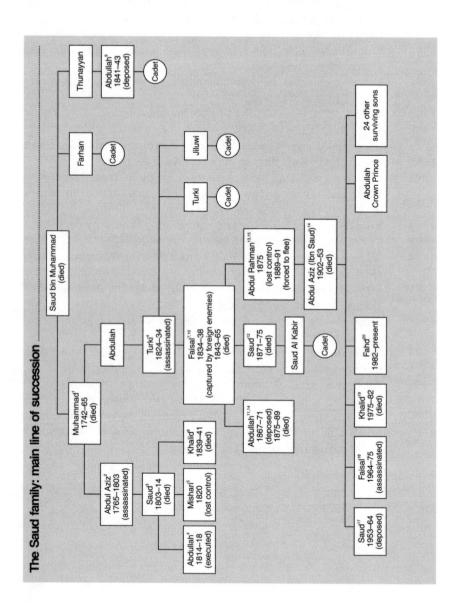

BIBLIOGRAPHY

Abir, Mordechai, *Saudi Arabia, Government, Society and the Gulf*, Routledge, London, 1993.

Amirahmadi, Hooshang, *Oil at the Turn of the Twenty First Century; Interplay of Market Fordes and Politics*, The Emirates Center for Strategic Studies and Research, Abu Dhabi, 1996.

Abureich, Saïd K., *The Rise, Corruption and Coming Fall of the House of Saud*, Bloomsbury, London, 1994.

Algosaibi, Ghazi A., *Arabian Essays*, KPI, London, 1982.

Almana, Mohammed, *Arabia Unified, a Portrait of Ibn Saud*, Hutchinson Benham, London, 1980.

American Community Services, *Welcome to Riyadh, Kingdom of Saudi Arabia*, Riyadh, 1993.

an-Naim, Abdullahi Ahmed, *Toward an Islamic Reformation, Civil Liberties, Human Rights and International Law*, Syracuse University Press, New York, 1990.

Article 19, *Country Report: Silent Kingdom: Freedom of Expression in Saudi Arabia*, London, 1991.

al-Azmi, Aziz, *Islam and Modernities*, Verso, London and New York, 1993,

Barber, Benjamin R., *Jihad vs. McWorld, How the Planet is Both Falling Apart and Coming Together and What this Means for Democracy*, Times Books, Random House, New York and Toronto, 1995.

de la Billiere, Sir Peter, *Looking for Trouble, SAS to Gulf Command*, Harper Collins, London, 1994.

Boulding, Elise, *Building Peace in the Middle East, Challenges for States and Civil Society*, Lynne Rienner Publishers, Boulder, Colorado and London, 1994.

Bulloch, John, and Darwish, Adel, *Coming Water Wars in The Middle East*, Victor Gollancz, London, 1993.

Canada Centre, International Pen, *Freedom of Expression in the Muslim World, A Comparative Legal Study of Blasphemy and Subversive Speech in International Human Rights Law and the Laws of the Muslim World*, University of Toronto, Toronto, 1992.

CDRL, *Saudi Arabia, Financial Crisis and the Price of Oil*, London, 1995.

CDLR, *Year Book 1994–95, A compilation of CDLR publications during its first year in exile*, The Committee for the Defence of Legitimate Rights, London, 1995.

Chubin, Chahram, and Tripp, Charles, *Iran-Saudi-Arabia Relations and Regional Order, Iran and Saudi Arabia in the balance of power in the Gulf*, Adelphi Paper, 304, IISS, Oxford University Press, London, 1997.

Crystal, Jill, *Oil and Politics in the Gulf, Rulers and Merchants in Kuwait and Qatar*, Cambridge University Press, Cambridge, 1995.

Dannreuther, Roland, *The Middle East in Transition*, IFS, Institut For Forsvars-studier, Oslo 1995.

Deegan, Heather, *The Middle East and Problems of Democracy*, Open University Press, Buckingham, 1993.

Dekmejian, R. Hrair, *Islam in Revolution, Fundamentalism in the Arab World*, Syracuse University Press, New York, 1995.

Dekmejian, R. Hrair, 'The Rise of Political Islamism in Saudi Arabia', *Middle East Journal*, vol. 48, no. 4, Autumn, 1994.

Economist Intelligence Unit, *Country Report: Saudi Arabia*, quarterly, London.

Field, Michael, *The Merchants, The Big Business Families of Saudi Arabia and the Gulf States*, Overlook Press, Woodstock New York, 1985.

Fried, Edward R., and Trezise, Philip H., *Oil Security, Reprospect and Prospect*, Brookings, Washington, DC, 1993.

Foreign and Commonwealth Office, Consular Department, *Living in Saudi Arabia, A Brief Guide*, London, 1994.

Fried, Edward R., and Trezise, Philip H., *Oil Security, Retrospect and Prospect*, The Brooking Institution, Washington, DC, 1993.

Fuller, Graham E. and Lesser, Ian O., *A Sense of Siege, The Geopolitics of Islam and the West*, Westview Press, Boulder Colorado and Oxford, 1995.

Goldberg, Ellis, Resat Kasaba and Joel S. Migdal, *Rules and Rights, Democracy, Law, and Society*, University of Washington Press, Washington, DC, 1993.

Goodwin, Jan, *The Price of Honor, Muslim Women Lift the Veil of Silence on the Islamic World*, Plume Penguin Books, New York, 1994.

Hallaba, Saadallah A.S., *Euro-Arab Dialogue*, Amana Books, Brattleboro, Vermont, 1984.

Henderson, Simon, '*After King Fahad, Succession in Saudi Arabia*', The Washington Institute Policy Papers, no. 37, Washington, DC, 1994.

Hippler, Jochen, and Lueg, Andrea, *The Next Threat, Western Perceptions of Islam*, Pluto Press, London, 1995.

Human Rights Watch, Middle East, *Empty Reforms, Saudi Arabias New Basic Laws*, New York, 1992.

International Institute for Strategic Studies, *Strategic Survey 1995/96*, IISS, Oxford, 1996.

Ismael, Tareq Y., and Ismael, Jacquline S., *The Gulf War and the New World Order, International Relations of the Middle East*, University Press of Florida, Gainesville Florida, 1994.

Kepel, Gilles, *Allah in the West, Islamic Movements in America and Europe*, Polity Press, Cambridge, 1997.

Khuri, Fuad I., *Imams and Emirs, State, Religion and Sects in Islam*, Saqi Books, London, 1990.

Lacey, Robert, *The Kingdom, Arabia amd The House of Saud*, Avon, New York, 1991.

Luciani, Giacomo (ed.), *The Arab State*, Routledge, London, 1990.

Macarthur, John R., *Second Front, Censorship and Propaganda ind the Gulf War*, University of California Press, Berkeley, California, 1993.

MacKey, Sandra, *Saudis, Inside the Desert Kingdom*, Penguin, New York, 1987.

Mernissi, Fatima, *Islam and Democracy, Fear of the Modern World*, Virago Press, London, 1993.

Middle East Watch, *Empty Reforms, Saudi Arabia's New Basic Laws*, New York, 1992.

Minnesota Lawyers International Human Rights Commitee, *Shame in the Haouse of Saud, Contempt for Human Rights in the Kingdom of Saudi Arabia*, Minneapolis Minnesota, 1992.

Mohaddessin, Mohammad, *Islamic Fundamentalism, The New Global Threat*, Sven Locks Press, Washington, DC, 1993.

Morris International Associates, *Voice of the Arab World, Intelligence Report: Saudi Arabia, its New Role in World Affairs*, London, 1993.

Munro, Alan, *An Arabian Affair, Politics and Diplomacy behind the Gulf War*, Brassey's, London and Washington, DC, 1996.

OPEC,: *Saudi Arabias oil industry – on course for 21st century*, OPEC Bulletin, Vienna 1992.

Royal Danish Embassy, *Vejledning for danske i Saudi Arabia ('Guide to Danes in SA')*, Riyadh, 1995.

Rugh, William A., *The Arab Press, News Media and Political Process in the Arab World*, Syracuse University Press, New York, 1987.

Said, Edward W., *Covering Islam, How the Media and the Experts Determine How We See the Rest of the World*, Pantheon Books, New York, 1981.

Salamé, Ghassan (ed.), *Democracy Without Democrats? The Renewal of Politics in the Muslim World*, I.B. Tauris, London, 1995.

Sclove, Richard E., *Democracy and Technology*, The Guildford Press, New York and London, 1995.

Siddiq, Mohammed H., *He does Not Play Fair*, Lincoln, Nebraska, 1990.

Siddiq, Mohammed H., *A Victim of Ignorant and Greedy Masters*, Lincoln, Nebraska, 1989.

Siddiq, Mohammed H., *Saudi Arabia, a Country Under Arrest*, Lincoln, Nebraska, 1991.

Siddiq, Mohammed H., *The Prince Ails My Country, He Does Not Play Fair*, Lincoln, Nebraska, 1989.

Siddiq, Mohammed H., *Why the Boom Went Bust: An Analysis of the Saudi Government*, Lincoln, Nebraska, 1995.

Tamimi, Azzam (ed.), *Power-Sharing Islam*, London, 1993.

Tawfik, Heidi, *Saudi Arabia, A Personal Experience*, Windmill, San Jose, California, 1991.

United Nations, *United Nations and Human Rights 1945–1995*, New York, 1995.

United Nations, *Human Rights, A Compilation of International Instruments*, New York and Geneva, 1994.

United Nations, *The United Nations and the Iraq–Kuwait Conflict, 1990–1996*, New York, 1996.

US Department of State, Bureau of Consular Affairs, *Consular Information Sheet: Saudi Arabia*, Washington, DC, 1994.

VO, Xuan Han, *Oil, the Persian Gulf States, and the United States*, Praeger, London, 1994.

Weisenborn, Ray E., *Media in the Midst of War, The Gulf War from Cairo to the Global Village*, Adham Center Press, Cairo, 1992.

World Bank, *From Scarcity to Security, Averting a Water Crisis in the Middle East and North Africa*, Washington, DC 1996.

Yergin, Daniel, *The Prize, The Epic Quest for Oil, Money and Power*, Simon & Schuster, London, 1991.

Journals and magazines

Aramco World, Houston Texas, USA.
Civil Society, Ibn Khaldoun Center, 17 Street 12, Mokkatam, Cairo.
Crescent International, Newsmagazine of the Islamic Movement, Ontario, Canada.
Index on Censorship, London, UK.
International Pen, Writers in Prison Committee, 33 Islington High Street, London.
Journal of Democracy, 1101 15th Street, NW, Suite 802, Washington DC, 20005, USA.
MEED, The Middle Easts Business Weekly, London UK.
Middle East International, London, UK.
OPEC Bulletin, Obere Donaustrasse 93, 1020 Vienna, Austria.
Saudi Arabia, Country Profile, The Economist Intelligence Unit, London, UK.

Organizations

American Islamic Group, PO Box 711660, San Diego, California 92171–1660, USA, Tel/Fax (619) 268–8189.
Amnesty International, 1 Easton Street, London WC1X 8DJ, United Kingdom, Tel (171) 413 5500, Fax (171) 956 1157.
Arab Organisation of Human Rights, Cairo.
Article 19, Lancaster House, 33 Islington High Street, London N1 9LH, United Kingdom, Tel (171) 278 9292, Fax (171) 713 1356.
The Committee for the Defense of Legitimate Rights, BM Box: CDLR, London WC1N 3XX, United Kingdom.
Egyptian Organisation for Human Rights, 8/10 Matahaf El-Manyal Street, 10th Floor, Manyal er-Rhoda, Cairo, Egypt, Tel (2) 363 6811, Fax (2) 362 1613.
Canadian Centre, International PEN, Suite 309, 24 Ryerson Avenue, Toronto, Ontario M5T 2P3, Tel (416) 860 1448.
Crescent International, 300 Steelcase Road West, Unit 8, Markham. Ontario Canada L3R 2W2, Tel (905) 474–9292, Fax (905) 474–9293.
Human Rights Watch, 1522 K Street NW, Washington DC 20005-1202 USA.
Index on Censorship, Lancaster House, 33 Islington High Street, London N1 9LH, United Kingdom, Tel (171) 278 2313, Fax (171) 278 1878.
International Pen, 9/10 Charterhouse Buildings, Goswell Road, London EC1M 7AT, United Kingdom, Tel (171) 253 3226, Fax (171) 253 5711.
Lawyers Committee for Human Rights, 330 Seventh Avenue, 10th Floor, New York, NY 10001, USA, Tel (212) 629 6170, Fax (212) 967 0916.
Minnesota Lawyers Human Rights Committee, now *The Minnesota Advocates for Human Rights*, 310 Fourth Ave. S, # 1000, Minneapolis, MN 55415-1012 USA, Tel (612) 341 3302, Fax (612) 341 2971.
Redress, 6 Queens Square, London WC1N 3AR, United Kingdom, Tel (171) 278 9502, Fax (171) 278 9410.
Royal United Services Institute for Defense Studies, Whitehall, London SW1A 2ET, United Kingdom, Tel (171) 930 5854, Fax (171) 321 0943.
United Nations High Commissioner for Human Rights, Palais des Nations, 1211 Geneve 10, Switzerland, Tel (22) 917 3134, Fax (22) 917 02 45.
The Washington Institute for Near East Policy, 1828 L Street, NW, Suite 1050, Washington, DC 20036, USA.

Electronic homepages

Amnesty International: http://www.amnesty.org
Arab Net: http://www/arab.net
Arab News: http://www.arab.net/arabnews/
CACSA (Committee Against Corruption in Saudi Arabia): http://www.saudhouse.-com
EOHR (Egyptian Organisation for Human Rights): http://www.eohr.org.eg
Index on Censorship: http://www.oneworld.org/index_oc/
Human Rights Watch/Middle East: http://www.saudhouse.com/hrights/watch.html
Lawyers Committee for Human Rights: http://www.lchr.org
Minnesota Advocates for Human Rights: http://www.umn.edu/humanrts/mnadvo-cates
Royal Embassy of Saudi Arabia, Washington DC: http://imedl.saudi.net/
State Department: http://www.state.gov
UN Human Rights: http://www.un.org/rights/
US House of Representatives/Internet Law Library: http//law.house.gov/184.html
Saudi Arabian Web Sites: http://www.liii.com/~hajeri/saudi.html

INDEX